Household Gods

The 'Dirty Shirt' series:

Dirty Shirt
A Green Bough
The World in a Sandbag
Household Gods

***

John Ware used to work in the construction industry until they made him stop. He now lectures in history in his home town of Cork.

Join John's mailing list for news, updates and **a free book**.

www.pagedor.co.uk/johnware

Household Gods

John Ware

PAGE D'OR
MMXXV

Page d'Or is an imprint of Prosperity Education Limited
Registered offices: 58 Sherlock Close, Cambridge CB3 0HP,
United Kingdom

© John Ware 2025

First published 2025

All rights reserved. No part of this book may be reprinted or reproduced or utilised in any form or by any electronic, mechanical, or other means, now known or hereafter invented, including photocopying and recording, or in any information storage or retrieval system, without permission in writing from the publisher.

The right of John Ware to be identified as the author has been asserted in accordance with sections 77 and 78 of the Copyright, Designs and Patents Act 1988.

A catalogue record for this book is available from the British Library

ISBN: 978-1-915654-53-3

Typeset in Times New Roman and Garamond by ORP Cambridge
Cover artwork: Siantura
Frontispiece: Royal Munster Fusilier cap badge. Image courtesy of the National Army Museum, London.

For further information visit: www.pagedor.co.uk

Ad infinitum et ultra.

Ireland! Ireland! That cloud in the west! That coming storm!

—William Gladstone, 1845

EXPLANATORY NOTE

The United Kingdom of Great Britain and Ireland had never functioned as intended. Bedevilling successive governments was the Irish Question, for which there was no equivalent Scots, Welsh or even English Question. By the beginning of the twentieth century the ancient wrongs concerning land and religion had for the most part been righted, but it was too late. Ireland's relationship with her government remained one of grievance. Independence, in one form or another, was the only remedy.

After years of wrangling, it had been accepted in 1914 that this independence would be granted in the form of Home Rule – self-government within the Union.

Then the war came and all such matters were shelved.

One place in which the Union appeared to work was the army. A disproportionate number of Irishmen from both sides of the religious and political divide wore the red coat. There were fifteen regiments of the king's army that were Irish. Some wore the crown on their badges. Some included the word 'royal' in their titles. All owed their allegiance to the king, yet all were proudly Irish.

The Royal Munster Fusiliers were one such regiment, and when the call came in 1914 they were not slow in answering, nor did they waver when put to the dreadful test.

A regiment of the day was composed of battalions which shared the same identity but otherwise followed their own paths. At the outbreak of war it was the 2nd Battalion of the Munsters that found itself in England and thus best placed to go and face the German onslaught in France. On its first day in combat it was annihilated at a place called Étreux. The battalion was reconstituted over the following months, in time to be destroyed at Festubert. Rebuilt around a core of survivors and reservists, it was smashed a third time at Aubers Ridge the next spring.

By then the 1st Battalion, brought home from the Far East, had met the Turks at Gallipoli. As with their brothers at Étreux, their first day in contact with the enemy had broken them down to something less than a viable infantry battalion.

By then four new battalions had been raised, although the Somme would reduce that number to two before the remnants of those two would be absorbed into what was left of the older battalions.

And what was it all for? To prove to the British that Ireland deserved Home Rule – deserved her place among the nations?

In the spring before the men marched to the Somme an Irish Republic had been declared in Dublin. It had lasted no longer than it took for the king's troops to storm rebel headquarters and tear down the green flag, but the spirit that had driven it was not dispelled so easily.

The rebellion had been organised by an unexpected coalition of nationalist splinters and factions that the public had trouble labelling. Because the rebels had been for a republic, blame was settled on the only Irish republicans who were readily identifiable: a minority party with nothing to do with the rebellion, named Sinn Féin.

Proving that there is no such thing as bad publicity, Sinn Féin got the credit as well as the blame. When public sympathy began to shift in favour of the rebels, the party grew in strength and became the face and the voice of radical nationalism. Home Rule had become a dead issue. The cause of Irish independence was now in the hands of the 'Shinners'.

Irishmen who had worn the king's uniform – Irishmen who had fought on Britain's side to prove Ireland's nationhood – would soon be coming home to face the sad realisation that perhaps they had been fighting the wrong war all along.

I

SMALL NATIONS

It is a war for the defence of the sacred rights and liberties of small nations, and the respect and enlargement of the great principle of nationality.

—Irish Parliamentary Party, 17 December 1914

1

The campaign in Burma was not one of the great battles, but it was one that called for the best qualities of the soldier – perseverance, endurance, and unremitting attention to duty.

—Capt. S. McCance, *History of the Royal Munster Fusiliers*

Fitzmullen-Brophy was dying.

He was sure of it. He was sure of it because of the way people acted around him. They peered in with an apprehensive look. They assessed him without addressing him. If they spoke to him they weren't expecting any answer. He was on the way out.

Even Tummy Belcher, who stopped by often, kept something of a distance. There he was now, leaning against the tent pole, hands in his pockets, looking a bit anxious, a bit embarrassed, rather gruff. He only cleared his throat to speak when he saw his friend's eyes open and looking right at him. Even then, Fitzmullen-Brophy had to speak first.

'Tummy.' His voice was pitifully weak.

'FitzEm. You awake? How're you feeling today, eh?'

'Beastly cold, Tummy.'

Lieutenant Belcher nodded in understanding. His moustache was sun-bleached to near invisibility, his hair plastered to his forehead, and his shirt open to the waist and translucent with sweat. Here on the middle reaches of the Sittang, a month at least before the monsoon, the mercury was already well on its way to forty degrees in the forenoon.

'There, there, old man. Why don't you close your eyes a while and you'll feel better presently, what?'

But Hugh Fitzmullen-Brophy, second-lieutenant, 1st Battalion, Royal Munster Fusiliers, feeble as he was, was not to be taken in. This fever had had him in its grip for days already and was only squeezing tighter. He'd already seen men die of it, and now it was his turn. He was sure of it.

There were things he should be saying to Belcher. Affairs to be put in order. An old hatchet, perhaps, that needed a proper burying. He tried to gather the strength. He tried to speak up. But Belcher wasn't listening. Belcher wasn't looking at him anymore. Instead the young man was standing respectfully, not quite to attention, for the officer who had just ducked into the tent, impatiently thrusting the canvas aside.

That was Captain Gorman all over. Nothing was allowed to get in his way. In this heat he was the only thing that moved with purpose. Even the flies were lethargic compared to him. The chinstrap of his sun helmet was worn so high under his tight mouth that it looked almost like a bridle, and a necessary restraint to the man. His tunic, made piebald by perspiration, was fastened all the way up to the throat. He looked Belcher up and down, did a precise quarter turn to inspect the patient, and spoke.

'Fitzmullen-Brophy. Still sick, I see. Not good enough.'

'Sir,' ventured Belcher in a low voice.

'Not good enough at all,' said Gorman, louder and sharper, keeping his eye on Fitzmullen-Brophy, clearly waiting for the subaltern to do something about this unsatisfactory condition.

'I beg your pardon, sir, but the doctor says...'

The captain swung back to Belcher.

'And *what* does the doctor say? Eh, Mister Belcher?'

Belcher coughed and lowered his voice further.

'What's that?' barked Gorman. 'Speak up, man!'

But Belcher wouldn't speak up. Not here. Not with his friend listening. Fitzmullen-Brophy couldn't make out the whispered words, but he didn't have to.

Captain Gorman heard Belcher out, scowling at such unsoldierly delicacy.

'Bloody nonsense!' he declared. He slapped the top of his boot with his whip, took two brisk and precisely measured paces to the edge of Fitzmullen-Brophy's cot, and glared down at the fever-stricken young man.

'You are to get better, Lieutenant,' he said. 'That's an order.'

Fitzmullen-Brophy could only stare, his jaws clenched against the shivering.

'You do not have permission to die, Lieutenant,' said Gorman. 'Is that clear? *A Dirty Shirt does not die in bed.*'

Susan Fitzmullen-Brophy felt she was approaching her wits' end. In the past twenty-five years she had endured hard climates, long separations; the often stifling and sometimes venomous social world of the army wife. Hers had been a life of temporary addresses in sun-baked or rain-lashed garrisons, with the penny-pinching and slow promotion of peacetime or the vexations and worries of active service. No matter how much there was to see to, there was always time for worrying.

In the past ten years alone she'd seen her husband laid low by the cholera and by gunshot wound. At least then it had been the army that had taken care of it, and the worst had been over by the time she had been told. But now it was the influenza, and it had struck right here under her roof and there was no one but herself to deal with it.

Just as before, there was so much to do but not enough to dispel the worry. She had a house to run as well as a gravely ill husband to look after. The girl Mary couldn't help because she had fallen ill herself. Molly couldn't do anything because she had the baby. If Molly caught sick then that really would be the end. Imagine! A husband, a daughter and the maid all down with the influenza, and a baby to look after on top of it all – that is if the baby didn't catch it too!

And Mrs. Fitzmullen-Brophy had to veer away from that line of thinking right quick. She concentrated her mind on the endless household chores and on the bothers of nursing. She didn't think about the illness, or how she had heard of people dying from this outbreak of influenza. The weak. The very young and the very old. She couldn't think about that. Anyway, babies withstood all sorts of things. And Hugh, grandfather or no, was only fifty-five this year and had seen off worse.

She wouldn't think about his soaring temperature or his laboured breathing. She put his delirious murmuring of Tummy Belcher's name from her mind – Tummy Belcher, dead in Flanders nearly four years now. She would concentrate instead on making some sort of lunch that wouldn't disgrace them all, before getting on with the multitude of other tasks that might just keep this draughty old house from falling down on all their heads.

She was in the kitchen, wrestling with that blasted stove, so she didn't hear the bell. It was Molly who heard it, and Molly who had to come downstairs, wrapped in shawls and carrying a grizzling baby, to tell her mother that Daddy was awake and in need of something.

With helpless gestures and inadequate instructions she left her daughter in charge of the stove, and upstairs she went, for what she reckoned was the tenth or twentieth or fiftieth time. The handbell tinkled plaintively from the bedroom all the while.

'Stop that, Hugh! You'll tire yourself out! Whatever's the matter?'

'Susan! I must get up!'

'Rubbish!'

She realised she was happy to be able to speak impatiently to him. He was alive enough to make trouble again. She took the bell away from him and pushed his flailing arms under the bedclothes. He protested and she ignored him. For all his vehemence he was too weak to argue. A colonel and holder of the Distinguished Service Order he might have been, but she was his wife.

In the end, Hugh Fitzmullen-Brophy compromised on a cup of beef tea, and found when it arrived that he barely had the strength to sip it. It didn't matter. He was over the worst of it, and in a few days or a week he'd be up and about again. Things to do. The war wasn't over yet.

'A Dirty Shirt doesn't die in bed,' he said to himself with a smile, and he drifted back into a less haunted sleep.

2

'Retreat, hell. We just got here.'

—Capt. Lloyd Williams USMC, Château Thierry, 1918

The men waited tensely.

They'd been told what to do – told over and over – but that didn't keep the uncertainty from rising within them. They watched the smoke drift across the field. They heard the uneven crackle of small-arms fire from somewhere ahead.

It was all feeling very real. Suddenly the differences that had defined them for so long were of little matter. The lifers who claimed to have eaten dust and sweated blood from Cuba to Mexico; the hicks fresh off the farm; the immigrant kids who barely knew English; the dudes and the Bowery toughs – they all felt the same now. They were all rookies.

They were wearing their new steel helmets – the ones that the British had supplied them with. They were wearing them tilted sharply because they liked the way it looked and because someone had advised them to angle their helmets towards the expected blast. For the same reason, they wore their chinstraps not under the chin but behind the head. They'd heard that blast could catch a man's helmet and snap his neck if he had his chinstrap under his chin. Nobody knew if that was true, but wearing their helmets this way made them look more like veterans – so they hoped.

There was only one veteran here, and when asked about it, he'd squinted through the smoke from his cigarette, nodded his head, and answered, 'Shells will kill you whichever way they kill you. I've seen men knocked stone dead without a mark on them and I've seen men shredded so there was nothing recognisable left besides their buttons. Made no difference if they had a tin hat or no.'

He was there with them now, the only man not wearing his steel helmet. He was their British liaison, and as some sort of compliment to the American Expeditionary Force he was wearing the American broad-brimmed campaign hat to which, out of abiding loyalty to his original corps, he had affixed his old British cap badge. At least it was supposed to be British. It was one of those old-timey heraldic affairs – a kind of fireball with a tiger of all things on it. Whatever it was, it was generally admitted that it beat hell out of the plain old brass US that was the only adornment everyone else here had.

The British liaison was only a lieutenant, but the American captain in charge of the company listened to him. The lieutenant had been in this from the start. He didn't have any medals, but he had a beat-up face and a big old German pistol that he wore stuck in his belt. It was too big for a holster. Right now he also had a hand grenade in his fist.

'Get them moving, Captain,' he said.

'We're supposed to wait until F Company goes forward on our right.' A moment ago the captain had been sure of the plan, and he was still trying to sound that way.

'Get them moving before the smoke clears! Get them moving while there's still cover!' The British lieutenant didn't usually sound this urgent.

'But we'll be advancing into our own barrage, damn it!'

'Listen to me!' said the lieutenant. 'The smoke clears and their machine guns can see you! You want to advance into that? A few casualties or a whole lot. You're choice, Captain.'

The captain didn't like being talked to that way and he didn't like to disregard the carefully worked-out plan, but a year ago he'd been running a small-town mercantile and doing part-time duty in the National Guard, while this fellow had been up to his neck in mud and blood at Ypres or wherever-the-hell.

Swallowing his misgivings, he raised his voice. '*Company!* Company will advance!'

Shoulders hunched, bayonets levelled, the men stepped off, the sergeants yelling at them to keep the pace. It wasn't enough for the lieutenant.

'Move it!' he shouted. 'Get into that smoke! Faster, damn you!'

But the sergeants had spent long enough marshalling these men, teaching them to keep their dressing and move as a unit. They knew that if they slipped the leash then Fourth Platoon was going to pile into the back of Third Platoon and make one godawful mess of things. But there was no use explaining that to the British lieutenant who was jogging along with them, shoving men from behind, regardless of the confusion he was sowing.

'Steady, men!' called out one of the sergeants. 'Keep it steady there!'

'Run!' yelled the lieutenant. The smoke, smelling of strange chemicals, was beginning to thin away. Beyond could be discerned the heaped earth and barbed wire stakes of the enemy entrenchments.

Fourth platoon, proud of their steadiness, and more scared of their sergeant than of the foreign lieutenant, slowed to allow for a more regulation spacing of ranks, and the lieutenant lost all composure.

'Come on, you sons of bitches!' he shrieked. 'Do you want to live forever?'

And in full view of them all, he yanked the pin out of the grenade and threw it – not towards the enemy line but *behind* the advancing Americans.

The men had done enough drills with grenades. They knew they had five seconds to make some distance. Or maybe it was only four. Fuses could be cut too short. Fourth Platoon ran.

A man can cover a lot of ground in five seconds – or even four – if he sets his mind to it. They were safely out of range and already halfway to their objective before the grenade went off behind them. Fourth Platoon did get mixed up with Third Platoon, and there was an unholy spat with F Company over who should have been where and when, but the objective was taken and the referees had grudgingly allowed that casualties suffered by machine-gun fire had been lighter than expected. For the casualties themselves, the only gripe was that they'd had to sit on the wet grass until the show was over.

The captain might have got chewed out by Battalion, but Battalion could still report to Regiment that the exercise had been a success. If there was any mention of a live grenade being used, nothing came of it. After all, a little added realism never hurt anybody.

3

Ship me somewheres east of Suez,
Where the best is like the worst,
Where there ain't no Ten Commandments,
And a man can raise a thirst.

—Rudyard Kipling, 'Mandalay'

Lieutenant Hoyt met Lieutenant Fitch in the mess later on. The mess was only another of those pine-board and corrugated tin huts that had sprung up like mould across England. This particular one had been standing for three years, which was far longer than anyone had intended. The years had bestowed leaks and draughts rather than history and tradition. Nevertheless, for the two young Americans it was a step farther from their old lives and a step nearer the war. It was a place where they could meet and measure themselves against the warriors they saw themselves becoming.

'Boy! – that Wyndham,' said Hoyt. 'Do you think he was drunk?'

'With that fellow, who knows?'

Fitch had been a college man when Uncle Sam had called, and Hoyt had been working in the family business. Neither of them was over twenty-one, and every day of this war was an experience for them. They had lived under canvas, they had travelled over the ocean, they had handled weapons. They still had a way to go before they saw any action, but who needed Germans when there were colourful characters like Lieutenant Wyndham? (Or *Leff-*

tenant Wyndham, according to the inexplicable Limey custom.)

'I heard they dragged him in front of the old man over that grenade stunt. Old man asks him what in hell's name he meant throwing grenades around during an exercise.'

'And?'

'Wyndham looks him square in the eye, says what's a few doughboys one way or the other? Get a few killed here or a lot killed over there. What's the difference?

'He said that?'

'That's what I hear.'

'And what did the colonel say?'

'Oh, I suppose the old man thundered a while and blew steam out of his ears and all, but nothing came of it. How do you put the scare on a man who's just not scared of you?'

Fitch gave it some thought. 'I guess if you've seen everything Wyndham's seen then a chewing out by the colonel won't mean so much.'

'I reckon so. Makes you wonder how long it'll be before *we* end up like that.' The way Hoyt said it, it appeared that being turned into a battle-scarred cynic wasn't anything that deterred him.

'Makes you wonder alright. But as a proper reward for all that grief, I hope I'd be something a little better than a lieutenant when it happens.'

'You will be. Promotion comes quick in wartime.'

'So how come Wyndham's a lieutenant?'

'Didn't you know? He started out as an enlisted man. Won a battlefield commission when all the officers in his outfit got killed.'

'You don't say! But I thought the British only had country squires and aristocrats for officers. You, know – true-blue lord of the manor types.'

'Maybe once. Not anymore.'

'The war. Right.'

'Besides – didn't you know? – he's not British. He's Irish.'

'*Irish?*'

'More or less. The guy's moved around a lot. Was living in Massachusetts before the war, I believe.'

'So on top of everything else he's some tough Boston Mick. No wonder he didn't back down in front of the old man. Say – how come you know all this? You haven't been talking to him, have you?'

'Talk to a guy who plays with live grenades? Me? Besides, I haven't had much of a chance. You don't see him much outside of training.'

'Well here's your chance now.'

'What? He's here?'

'Sure. That's him coming in now, isn't it? Why don't you and I go on over and introduce ourselves?'

'Well hell, I'm game if you are.'

From the sort of character he'd displayed at the exercise, it might have been expected for the British (or Irish) officer to be belly-up to the bar, shouting for whiskey, neat, and elbowing aside less hot-blooded men, but there he was instead, alone at a table, perfectly tranquil.

'Lieutenant Wyndham?'

'Call me Dan, old son. We're all friends in the mess.'

'Why thanks, uh, Dan. Mind if we have a seat?'

'Delighted, boys. It's ah—'

'I'm Fitch. He's Hoyt.'

They sat and called for drinks while Wyndham smiled at them like a simple soul who wasn't used to company but was glad to have it now. Their presence alone seemed to be enough for him. He made no attempt to open the conversation, but just nodded and sipped his drink. Fitch, because he'd started it, went to bat first, daring to get right to the heart of things.

'So – uh – Dan, that business with the grenade today. That was really something, eh?'

'You liked that?' Wyndham beamed. 'I *am* glad.'

'So is that the way the British train?'

Wyndham rolled his whiskey around his tongue, savouring the burning sensation, before he answered.

'Hmm. Hard to say, really. I'm afraid my own training was somewhat lacking. A little here, a little there. Picked up most of it on the job, as it were. One just does what's called for when the situation calls for it. Rulebook probably wouldn't approve, but what can a fellow do?'

'What? You're saying you weren't *trained* to be a soldier?'

'Truth to tell, boys, I'd barely begun my recruit training when the war started. Marched off to fight when I hardly knew the safe end of a rifle from the naughty end.'

Fitch put his elbows on the table and leaned in closer. Hoyt waved to the mess waiter to keep Wyndham's glass refreshed.

'My commanding officer at the time,' went on Wyndham. 'Terrible man. Almighty fire-eater. Major Fitzmullen-Brophy. Veteran of all kinds of mayhem. He marched us off without orders – slap-bang into the middle of the retreat from Mons. No more time for training or regulations or rulebooks. Next thing you know we're holding the Ypres Salient all by ourselves – or at least that's what it felt like. The line held, some of us got out alive, and once I got out of hospital I followed Fitzmullen-Brophy to his next command.'

'You *followed* him?'

'Naturally. I'm sure you'd have done the same.'

Wyndham stopped smiling and leaned in close himself, so their three heads made one conspiratorial cluster.

'Boys, it might sound – how might you put this? – "screwy", but it's the man who gets you out alive that's the man to stick to.

It doesn't matter what kind of mess he gets you into, so long as he gets you out again. You can't complain about nearly getting killed if you don't *actually* get killed.'

He leaned back again while they digested the lesson.

'So,' said Hoyt, slowly putting it together, 'You throw live grenades around on training exercises so we learn what it's like to nearly get killed?'

'I suppose so,' agreed Wyndham, thinking about it. 'Probably. Something like that anyway.'

He took another mouthful of whiskey and grimaced in pleasure. The two Americans waited for more. Wyndham squeezed his eyes shut and turned his face upwards for a little while.

'Might as well get used to the noise in any case,' he said at last, looking at them again.

'The noise?'

'Explosions. Very sudden. Very loud. Bad for the nerves.'

Hoyt started to say something bland about getting used to it, but Wyndham wasn't listening.

'Guillemont,' he said. 'Ginchy.'

'I beg your pardon?'

'On the Somme. Gillymong and Gintchy. The trenches weren't deep enough. Couldn't make them deeper. Couldn't raise our heads. No shelter from the Hun shrapnel. And then there was our own stuff going overhead. You could lie on your back and watch the shells going over. They were so thick in the air you could have reached up and struck a match on them.' He was looking at the ceiling again. 'Christ.'

Fitch ended the respectful silence by asking, 'You were at the Somme?'

'16th Division,' said Wyndham from his reverie. '16th Irish Division. All gone now.'

'So this Fitz—,' said Hoyt.

'Fitzmullen-Brophy.'

'He was Irish, right? In this Irish outfit you were with.'

'The Royal Munster Fusiliers,' said Wyndham, as if he were raising a toast. 'Irish indeed. Proudly Irish. Giant of a man. Finn MacCool come back to life!'

'Who? No, sorry – it doesn't matter. No, what I was wondering. Your old regiment. That badge. The tiger and all. Why does an Irish outfit have a tiger on its badge?'

Wyndham nodded his head for a while, even though no one had said anything he might be agreeing to.

'India,' he said at last. 'India. It's where we came from long ago. A hard country. Too hot for the red coat, you know. So we stripped off our coats and fought in our shirtsleeves. Because you do what's called for when the situation calls for it. Tigers. We fought like tigers.' He held his glass up to the light and squinted, no doubt seeing in the distorted paraffin flame the pitiless sun of Bengal.

'Fought like tigers,' he said again, and then blinked himself back into the present, and saw another situation that called for something to be done.

'I beg your pardon but my glass appears to be empty.'

'Please, allow me,' said Hoyt

'Why that's very decent of you.' Wyndham seemed genuinely surprised at the offer. When his drink came he politely raised it to his companions and then, instead of tasting it, looked at it with appreciation, acknowledging that it was a gift not to be taken for granted.

'India. A hard country,' he said. 'Whiskey. A man has to be his own doctor and sometimes whiskey is his only medicine.'

Fitch contributed his belief that it was much the same for the army in the Philippine Islands.

'You've served in the Philippines?' asked Wyndham.

'Well, no.'

'No. Didn't think so. In India, now...'

And he told them tales of rains that would drown you, of a sun that would beat you to death, of proud and warlike peoples testing themselves against the white man.

Fitch didn't want to say so, but it all sounded rather as though Lieutenant Wyndham's reminiscences had been cribbed from Kipling. He began to suspect himself gulled – just some greenhorn to be treated as a source of cheap whiskey.

'Sorry to interrupt,' he said, 'but – correct me if I'm wrong – wasn't the red coat done away with years ago? And didn't you say you were doing basic training in 1914 and went straight off to the war?'

'Why yes,' said Wyndham. His eyes were glittering with whiskey but his gaze and voice were perfectly steady. 'Yes I did. Why?'

'Oh,' said Fitch. 'Well – it's just that I was wondering when exactly you were in India.'

'What?' said Wyndham with happy astonishment. 'I was never in India! Of course not!'

'But you said—'

'The *regiment*, old man. The *regiment* was in India. Weren't you listening? Anyway, sorry to keep you so long. You young fellows will need your rest. Another busy day tomorrow. Thanks for the drink. My treat next time.'

And he rose, and took his extravagant hat, and bade them goodnight.

Hoyt and Fitch walked back to their quarters, feeling a little unsteady from trying to keep up with the hard-drinking veteran.

'Boy! That Wyndham,' said Hoyt.

'Boy!' said Fitch. 'I'll say.'

4

Macmorris: *Of my nation! What ish my nation? Ish a villain, and a bastard, and a knave, and a rascal. What ish my nation? Who talks of my nation?*

—Shakespeare, *Henry V,* Act iii, Scene 2

Moriarty felt he'd spent half his life in places like this. The Curragh, Deolali, Étaples – and now Limburg. The same geometric rows of huts. The same wire fences. The same bored guards. The difference here was that the pettifogging regulations were in German and the guards were under orders to shoot you if you tried to leave. Other than that, thought Moriarty, there wasn't much between them.

Oh – except the food. Food in army camps was notoriously bad. With multitudes coming and going, the cooks didn't have to win anyone's goodwill. But if what was slopped into your mess tin in a British camp was no more than boiled-to-death stew with all the good bits pilfered along the way, or even if it was no more than a dog biscuit slathered in cold bacon grease, at least there was food. The Germans might insist that there was food in Limburg too, but if they did, thought Moriarty, they were only codding themselves.

Maybe a bit of cabbage. A bit of watery soup. A bit of bread made with acorns. Sometimes nothing except turnips for weeks on end. A man couldn't expect to live on that class of a diet. Twelve thousand men – and that's how many there were in Limburg – were certainly feeling the pinch.

'I'll have that if you're not finishing it,' said Carney.

'Get away out of that,' Moriarty growled. 'I am finishing it.'

'So finish it so, and don't be flaunting it in front of a hungry man.'

'I will in a minute, only my fucking tooth is at me.'

Carney knew all about Moriarty's tooth, because with everyone cooped up together, and no diversions worth mentioning, everyone knew everything there was to know about everyone else. Moriarty's tooth had been broken for him when he'd got a belt in the face off a German rifle butt. That had been in March, when the Germans had swept over and through the British line along the Somme and had, by the look of things, taken half of Fifth Army prisoner.

However many men it was they'd captured, it was evidently more than they could feed. How could they, when the Germans could barely feed themselves? The British naval blockade combined with poor harvests ensured that prisoners of war weren't the only ones on short commons. When the *Landwehr* guards had first been rooted out of their comfortable civilian lives four years before, many of them had had to suck in their bellies before they did up their buttons. Now their uniforms hung looser. All across Germany, where once there had been meat, now there was turnip. For every good ingredient there was now some unpalatable substitute.

'You can't eat that bread with that tooth,' said Carney. 'It's all only sawdust and floor sweepings. Give us the bread and go and talk to the dentist.'

'The dentist is no bloody good,' said Moriarty and, to shut Carney up, he shoved his bread ration into his mouth, bad tooth be damned. He didn't owe Carney anything. Never even met the man until a couple of months ago. So they shared a hut. So what? There were fifty men in that hut. And Carney was Irish? The camp was teeming with Irishmen. And the dentist? Moriarty had no idea whether the dentist was any good or not, but he wasn't going to let any man go at his mouth with pliers. How big a fool did Carney take him for?

Wincing as he chewed, he stood up and brushed off the seat of his threadbare trousers.

'I'm going for a walk,' he said.

'I'll come with you,' said Carney, and Moriarty just couldn't be bothered telling him to go hump. If it wasn't Carney it would only be some other gobshite.

There was nowhere to go in the camp that was anywhere you hadn't been a hundred times already, and if there happened to be some new faces, they usually turned out to be no different to the old faces. They might be from somewhere different, or have something interesting to say, but then they'd ask, 'Is there anything to eat?' and after that they were much the same as everyone else.

But today there was something new. Today there was a new face distinct from the others, and a startling variation on the usual question.

'Are ye hungry, lads?'

Moriarty and Carney had been walking the perimeter fence, vainly eyeing up the odd vegetable patches that some prisoners kept. They were wretched things, already pillaged or not even worth the bother. Beyond was a gate, where a guard might – just might – have left a cigarette butt in the dust, and from force of habit the two men had their eyes on the ground when they were addressed by someone who'd just passed through the gate.

The speaker was undoubtedly Irish, but his uniform was German – or at least it looked German. It certainly wasn't the raggedy-arsed khaki worn by so many of the prisoners, or whatever bits and pieces the Red Cross might provide when the khaki wore out.

'Come on away out of this,' said Carney.

'Wait a second,' said Moriarty.

'Come on! You don't want to be caught talking to this fella.'

But Moriarty saw nothing to be wary of. The Irishman in the grey-green uniform was a novelty worth investigating, the question he had posed an obvious enticement.

'Am I hungry?' Moriarty didn't know if the man was mocking him or just plain thick. 'I might be. A bit. Why? Are you carrying sandwiches in your pocket or something?'

The man laughed.

'No, but I might know someone in the cookhouse. Do you want to come along with me and we'll ask him?'

'Moriarty!' hissed Carney. 'I'm fucking serious. Come on!'

Moriarty stood his ground, not even turning his head as Carney made himself scarce.

'The cookhouse?' he said, daring the uniformed to man to reveal himself as a fraud or a simpleton.

'No harm in taking a look anyway,' said the man. 'My name's O'Farrell. I heard your man call you Moriarty, is that right?'

'You might have heard him saying too that you're not someone I want to be talking to.'

O'Farrell laughed that one off.

'Here, go on, have a smoke,' he said. 'No one's watching. You can put it in your pocket until later. Go on.'

This O'Farrell might be a conman, thought Moriarty, but he was giving away a whole cigarette, fresh from the packet, and had got nothing out of Moriarty yet.

'Look,' said O'Farrell. 'You want to know who I am? I'm an Irishman, same as yourself. You want to know why there's many in the camp that don't like me? It's because they're soldiers of King George and I'm not. I'm a soldier of Ireland. I took Georgie-Boy's shilling back in Fourteen and you can bet he got his shilling's worth out of me.'

Moriarty was making a great show of stowing his cigarette

safely in a tunic pocket. There were things far more important than political talk. 'And what is it now?' he asked. 'Did the Kaiser offer you more? Is that it?'

O'Farrell laughed again. 'He offered me a whole lot more. He gave me the means to take my country back!'

Moriarty tried not to look impressed.

'An Irish Brigade!' said O'Farrell, as though that should have been enough to get Moriarty cheering. 'Irishmen together, armed by the Germans! Landed back in Ireland to fight for freedom! What do you think of that?'

Moriarty carefully smoothed out his pocket. 'And you say there's something to eat?' he asked.

'Come on,' said O'Farrell.

'I don't think so.'

'Come on. A bit of dinner while I tell you what I'm about. You can go straight back to your mates after.'

'I think I'm alright.'

'Come on. If you're worried about what the others might say, there's something I can do about that.'

'Is that right?'

O'Farrell winked. 'No names, no pack drill – isn't that the way of it?'

And he waved over two guards who'd been watching from the gate, and said something to them in German. His German couldn't have been up to scratch because he had to do a lot of pointing and gesturing, but the guards finally caught on. They grinned and nodded, and then they fell upon Moriarty.

He saw the rifle butts raised and was instantly on his knees, trying to cover his head, knowing that it was no good. He curled up tighter as boots kicked at him, but the boots, he realised, were just kicking *at* him. The kicks weren't connecting. Neither were the rifle butts. He vaguely heard O'Farrell telling him it was alright as he was grabbed under the arms, hauled upright, and bullied off toward one of the huts. Once they were all out of sight round a corner, the guards let go, and even went so far as to roughly dust Moriarty down and pat him on the shoulders. There were hearty words in German. All a bit of fun. No bones broken. Anything to liven up the day. And then they went back to their post, leaving the two Irishmen alone.

'For fuck's sake!' said Moriarty.

'Ah, you're grand.' said O'Farrell. 'Anyone who saw that will think you were giving me lip. You'll get credit for standing up to the Huns and all. Now come on – we'll get you something to eat.'

The hut O'Farrell led them to wasn't up to much, but it was clearly meant for guards and not prisoners. There was a steamy smell in the air that wasn't quite cooking, but certainly wasn't laundry either. It turned out to be coffee, or at least *kaffee ersatz* – two mugs of which were provided by a German orderly who acted like he had better things to be doing.

A beverage made from roasted acorns, with nothing to sweeten it, was small consolation for the momentary terror of the mock beating Moriarty had just endured.

'Sure it's hot anyway,' said O'Farrell. 'And it'll keep us going while he cooks us up something proper.

'Right. Cards on the table. I'm Tommy O'Farrell, lance-corporal, 2nd Irish Rifles.'

Moriarty knew his regiments. The Royal Irish Rifles. A Belfast mob. Black Protestants, all of them.

'Francis Moriarty, *corporal*, 1st Munster Fusiliers.' He wasn't so much putting cards on the table as throwing down a gauntlet. 'You don't sound like an Ulsterman.'

'I'm not, but I am a rifleman. Or at least I was.'

'Now you're a Hun, is it?'

'Now I'm a non-commissioned officer in the Irish Brigade.'

'Of the German army.'

'Alright – of the German army. But I'm Irish, and you're Irish, and tell me – which of us is doing anything for Ireland? You here behind the wire, or me getting ready to go home and fight the British?'

The question, *Who says I want to do anything for Ireland?* was at the back of Moriarty's mind, but he left it there. He might have been a British soldier, but in the presence of someone who'd seen fit to join an Ulster regiment, he was an Irish patriot.

So he just sipped his vile drink and listened to O'Farrell hold forth.

This Irish Brigade might not have been German but it certainly wasn't a brigade either. O'Farrell was cagey about the numbers of recruits gathered so far, but he admitted that it was far fewer than needed.

'If we'd had the numbers we'd have been there in Dublin in Easter Week, and it wouldn't just have been Dublin that would have risen.'

'Is that right? And if ye'd all arrived on a big German battleship, and kept the green flag flying, wouldn't there be a German flag flying above it?'

'Sure what do the Germans want with Ireland? They just want the British bate.'

'But why bother fighting at all? Isn't Home Rule on the way?'

'Asquith promised Home Rule four years ago and where are we? Asquith's out on his arse and Dublin's in ruins. You can't trust the British government.'

'But you're trusting the Germans.'

'I am. They've played straight with us so far. I joined to fight for Ireland – nothing more. No one's sending me to fight alongside the rest of the Germans. They're keeping us out of their war, no matter how much they could do with the manpower. I might be wearing German kit, but I'm an Irish soldier. Look.'

And O'Farrell stood up to give Moriarty a look at his belt buckle.

'There. Do you see that. do you?'

And all of a sudden Moriarty wasn't sitting at a bare table in a German hut, but standing at a bar in Tralee in all his Saturday-night finery, explaining just what his badges meant. By God, but it was so vivid he could taste the beer, and see the nervous curiosity in the face of that young Yank. Mister Daniel Wyndham. An awful eejit.

The eejit had only gone and been persuaded to join up and, being well-spoken, had ended up an officer. Had that been Moriarty's doing? Had it been Moriarty's beautifully shone buttons and badges, the glory of his walking-out uniform, and his stirring tales of service out east that did it?

O'Farrell had nothing to compete. Airy dreams instead of stories; *feldgrau* instead of scarlet and blue; and in the place of the snarling tiger on the bursting grenade, nothing but a shamrock on a shoddy belt buckle, and that cheap Irish symbol wreathed in the German motto: *Gott mit uns*.

'God is with us,' said O'Farrell. 'I don't want to come over all Holy Joe, but He is. And if God isn't with us, then justice is, and history is, and we can write *that* in Irish. You'll see. You don't trust the Germans? Fine. They're giving us rifles. Do you think we'll let them take them back? When the war's won, Ireland's ours. Do you want it to be yours too, or do you want to see if you can squeeze another shilling out of King George?'

Moriarty stayed silent. O'Farrell took that as a good sign.

'Tell you what: you think about it. What I'll do is talk to the man, and he'll come and talk to you. I'll just take down your name for him. First Munsters, am I right? And your Christian name is Francis.'

And he had taken out a little notebook and was licking a pencil.

'Prionsias Ó Muircheartaigh,' he said.

'What's that?'

'That's your name in Irish.'

'I thought my name was Irish enough as it was.'

'Not at all. That's only a West British name. That's what the man tells me. He's mad for that Gaelic League stuff. "Not merely free, but Gaelic as well," he says. My own name's Tomás Ó Fearghail, only I don't use it because the Germans can't pronounce it. To be honest, I used to have trouble myself.'

Moriarty was suddenly seeing the whole thing as inevitable. Questions about rights and wrongs and nations were too much for the moment. For now he just wanted to know: 'Would I still be a corporal?'

O'Farrell frowned. 'I don't know. I'd have to ask.'

Unteroffizier Ó Muircheartaigh. He wasn't the man he'd been when he'd woken up this morning.

And there was one more question, even larger than the rest.

'When's your man bringing the food?'

'I'll have a look,' said O'Farrell, and went to talk to the orderly.

Moriarty heard voices raised, and O'Farrell came back.

'Listen,' he said. 'I'm fierce sorry, only there's nothing right this minute. Your man says there's only spud peelings and he's keeping them for the pig. Don't worry. You can come back tomorrow and there's sure to be something.'

But Moriarty had seen the light. He stood up, took the notebook from O'Farrell's hand, and tore out the page on which his name was written.

'The Kaiser can keep his spud peelings,' he said, 'and you can keep your tatty old shamrock buckle. I'm a Munster Fusilier,' said Moriarty.

'Ah come on now.'

'Come on yourself. Irish Rifleman. Hah. You dirty Orange bastard.'

And knowing that he wouldn't be able to better that insult, Moriarty turned and left.

He wondered if O'Farrell was going to come after him, or call on the guards to shoot him, but he carried on, holding himself like a soldier. When he was back among the anonymous barrack huts he remembered his cigarette. It turned out that it had got broken in the pretend duffing-up the guards had given him. The cigarette was salvageable if he didn't mind smoking a makeshift roll-up of inferior tobacco mixed with pocket lint, but first he'd have to touch up Carney for a cigarette paper, and that meant he'd have to halve the smoke with him, the stingy hoor.

This, he reflected, was what you got for sticking up for your own.

5

...We shall fight for the things which we have always carried nearest to our hearts: for democracy... for the rights and liberties of small nations...

—Woodrow Wilson, 2 April 1917

AEF – American Expeditionary Force – 'After England Failed'. It was a jibe Wyndham heard often. Men who'd learned he wasn't English said it as joke. Men who thought he was said it too, and didn't care if he heard.

Sometimes it suited Wyndham to be English, sometimes Irish. It felt awkward posing as an American though, even though that was all he'd ever been. It was only four years since he'd left his own kind, but he was daily being reminded that his own kind were his family and immediate neighbours – gentlefolk of Lowell, Massachusetts. The wider United States and all the people therein were strangers to him. Having lived among the Irish, the English, the Scots and the Welsh – not to mention the French and the Flemings – he thought he'd have a decent grasp of accents by now. He'd even finagled his way into this posting on the grounds that he could speak American. But then he'd found himself trying to instruct a New York private and meeting nothing but incomprehension. He was saved by the intervention of Corporal Raffaelli.

'What, Lieutenant? You think this *Calabrese* bum understands good English like I talk?'

The Italians made Wyndham nervous. When they spoke in their

own language it always sounded to him like an argument or a conspiracy, either of which would shortly involve knives. It was Corporal Raffaelli who reassured him.

'Nah, Lieutenant. These guys is fine. It's the *Siciliano* bastards you have to watch out for. Those guys is worse than the fuckin Irish.'

A contingent of Midwesterners arrived. One of them got in the wrong chow line on his first day and his apologetic smile didn't cut it. Raffaelli, half the man's size, put the farm boy straight.

'Beat it, Polack.'

'I'm no Polack! I'm an American, darn it!'

'Well you can get your sorry American ass back to Muleshit, Tennessee or East Buttfuck, Kansas. This here ain't your chow line.'

Raffaelli watched the big blond boy go and shook his head.

'Fuckin hayseeds,' he said. 'Worse than the fuckin Irish.'

E pluribus unum, thought Wyndham.

There was a little more in the way of national unity and brotherly understanding when a lecture had to be delivered on the righteousness of the war. Taking the official pamphlet as his starting point, Wyndham had spoken of the cruelty of Kaiserism. He'd expounded at length on the Rape of Belgium. He'd urged his listeners to Remember the *Lusitania*. He had finished off with a solemn injunction from no less a person than an Anglican bishop that his audience must hate the Germans and kill the Germans without mercy or let-up.

He had been obliged to pause now and then so that Private Rosenblum could translate the finer points into German for the benefit of 'all the Squareheads, Yids and Bohunks in the outfit'. That was the term used by the kindly First-Sergeant Schwarz, who didn't want any of his guys to miss out on their education.

Sergeant Schwarz was right. The boys needed to be up to the

mark. The day was coming ever closer when the Yanks would take that last little boat trip and finally get to show the Limeys what they'd been getting wrong since 1914.

After England Failed.

The phrase recurred to Wyndham when he considered all the nations that were waiting to give it their own try. How would the great diasporas fare after England failed? He made some light remark to that effect to the chaplain, who didn't take it lightly at all. Rather he pondered long on it, and finally turned it into a sermon he delivered the following Sunday.

He spoke about the Mother Country, and the Pilgrim Fathers, and the faith and freedom they had nurtured in their New World. And now the sons of the men who had set their foot on Plymouth Rock were returning to aid their tired mother with that same faith and that same freedom, nurtured these centuries past in God's country. The troopship that brought them, he said, was the *Mayflower* coming home again, and all the Swedes, Norwegians, Dutch and Germans nodded in understanding.

The chaplain was so proud of his effort that he was only sorry he couldn't share it with all the Poles, Italians and Russians on the base. He was lucky in the end, however, to be directed to another properly Christian congregation, and by then he had expanded on his theme. He spoke of America's duty as a moral leader after England failed. He spoke of hard work and fighting the good fight. This audience understood, too. A labour battalion largely from Mississippi and Alabama, they had nothing more to learn about hard work. When it came to fighting, alas, they'd just have to take the chaplain's word for it, for their rifles had been taken away and replaced by picks and shovels.

But they certainly paid polite attention to the sermon. It wasn't as if they had anything better to do – not since they had all been confined to camp lest they mix with white folks.

6

Even if we are ruined by it, it will have been so beautiful.

—General Erich von Falkenhayn, Prussian Minister for War,
4 August 1914

The war ended on Monday morning, quite suddenly. It was still there at breakfast. It was gone by lunch. It wasn't a complete surprise. There had been few hours' warning, but it was such a huge thing to comprehend that the news was not wholly convincing. After all, the experts and the optimists had been predicting the end since the beginning of August, and that had been August 1914.

In August 1918 the German Army had taken a wicked beating, but if there had been any wavering in the German high command, it hadn't translated itself into capitulation at the front. The towel remained unthrown. The German army stayed in the fight that month, and the next, and the one after that. Even as November started, and the British and Commonwealth armies pushed eastward, and the French and Americans battled their way north, plans were being drawn up for 1919, and forecasts made for 1920.

And then it all stopped. The news filtered down in the early morning that it would all be over at eleven, but because the war had its own momentum, until eleven it was going to run on. Perhaps the pressure needed to be kept up to convince the Germans that it was they who'd run out of fight, and not the Allies. Perhaps it was just force of habit. But the guns kept firing and the calls for ammunition kept coming. The Americans even launched a full-on infantry assault that morning, sending men against machine-guns for the sake of a few yards of torn ground in the time-disgraced style. It was as if they had to make up for missing the splendid slaughters of the war's earlier years. In reality, though, they were merely conforming to a schedule. The war had its own momentum.

There were mixed feelings among the Americans still in training in England. The schedule had spared them. They would not have to die in France. On the other hand, they had come all this way to fight, and it seemed a shame to be denied that chance. How would they measure up to those who'd been Over There, who'd been in at the kill?

There was raucous celebration all the same. Bottles were opened, barrels were broached, the piano in the mess got a thorough battering. It would have been churlish to have had it any other way. All across the kingdom a normally staid people was surrendering to a frenzy of rejoicing.

Leland Fitch reeled out of the mess, red and sweating. Jimmy Hoyt was still in there somewhere, but that was his business. Fitch had lost track of his buddy a while back. He'd lost track of a lot of things. Fact was, he'd been overdoing it just a tad. He'd been sick, and he'd been hosed down with a soda siphon. Everyone had thought that was such a hoot that it had started off a general soda siphon fight until there was no more soda water. That meant they'd had to take their drinks neat, which only heightened the hilarity. Right now cocktails were being mixed in an ice bucket to be drunk as prize or forfeit – Fitch wasn't sure which – in the piggy-back duels being fought. Fitch needed to take a break before he got sick again.

He was astonished to see that it was still daylight outside. He supposed it made sense. The armistice had come into effect at – eleven? He wasn't so sure anymore, but the party had hushed for a moment to mark the time and then had exploded into wilder life.

So now it was only mid-afternoon. There was a whole lot more celebrating to get through before bedtime.

The sunlight and the fresh air made him light-headed, but he breathed deep and began to feel better. He just needed to sit down for a spell and then he'd be ready for anything this armistice could throw at him. He noticed someone lying out on the grass – an early casualty of the party. Then he saw the British uniform. It was Lieutenant Wyndham, flat on his back. Fitch went over to check that the man wasn't dead.

Wyndham's eyes were open, staring at the sky. They didn't flicker when Fitch approached.

'Say – Lieutenant Wyndham? Uh – Dan?'

Wyndham blinked, and blinked again, and sat up rapidly.

Fitch apologised for startling him.

'It's nothing,' said Wyndham, and it appeared he meant it. He wasn't acting like he'd been surprised, or disturbed, or imposed upon. 'It's Hoyt, isn't it? Have a seat, Hoyt. Tell me the news.'

'It's Fitch actually, but sure – I think I do need to sit down. The party's really swinging in there. Just came out for some air. You too?'

'Me? No,' said Wyndham. 'Might wander in later. Show my face. You know.'

And Fitch realised that Wyndham was perfectly sober.

'Are you OK?' he asked. 'I mean, lying out here and all?'

'Never better,' said Wyndham, wrapping his greatcoat around himself. 'A little cold, maybe, but very mild for the time of year.' He considered that Fitch probably hadn't been asking about the weather.

'Just having a rest. Taking a little time to think. You know. It's been a long few years. Cigarette?'

With his knees drawn up and the damp seeping through the seat of his pants, Fitch took the cigarette, and wondered about the years Wyndham had seen.

For want of anything better, he said, 'So – I guess you're glad it's all over.'

Wyndham drew on his cigarette, exhaled, and smiled almost bashfully, unable to come up with an adequate answer.

'You know something?' said Fitch. 'I envy you.'

Wyndham looked puzzled.

'I envy you,' said Fitch again. 'I sincerely do. You came all this way – all the way from the States – and you've seen the elephant, and you've lived to tell the tale. Me? The other boys? We won't have it so good. We wore the uniform but we never got to fight. We won't have any stories.'

And drunk or not, he instantly regretted saying it.

'Stories,' said Wyndham, and the word had set him thinking. He picked up his hat and turned it in his hands.

'Do you know why I wear this hat? I met a man in Ireland – oh, years ago now. A soldier. Real old seen-the-world type. Told me stories. Maybe I joined the army because of his stories. Know why *he* joined the army? He told me. He told me that the first soldiers *he* met had just come back from South Africa, and they were wearing big wide-brimmed slouch hats. Something like this, I suppose. Impressed the hell out of him anyway. Name of Moriarty. I haven't seen him since our front line caved in at St. Quertin last March. I made it out. He didn't. Poison gas so thick you couldn't see through it. German artillery blasting everything to smithereens. And I was there because of stories and he was there because of hats.'

Fitch wasn't sure what Wyndham was saying to him and had no idea what might be a proper answer. It was time to get away from all this maudlin stuff. There was a party going on.

'Come on,' he said. 'The boys will be upset if you don't have a drink.'

'I think I've already had enough.'

'Nonsense! Come and join the party! It's not every day you win a war!'

Wyndham shook his head. 'Really – I've had enough. No more drinking.'

Fitch, who'd been making an effort to stand up, sat down again heavily. 'I don't understand,' he said.

Wyndham, with the light of faith in his eyes, explained.

'If the war's over then I'm not going to get killed. I'm going to live. And I'm going to live cleanly. Properly. I'm going to live a good life. For her.'

'Her?'

Wyndham dew a photograph from his breast pocket and, not letting go of it, showed it to Fitch.

'Her. My Nora. We're going to be married.'

Fitch looked. It was a group snapshot, taken inexpertly in strong light. He looked closer.

'There,' said Wyndham, with affection bordering on reverence. 'Her.'

Fitch was just about clear-headed enough to keep himself from saying: 'That's a *her*?'

The tallest figure in the group, indicated by Wyndham's thumb, was dressed in overalls and driving coat. Given the harsh sunlight and the deep shadow of her hat it was hard to tell, but she appeared to be scowling.

'The tall one?' asked Fitch wanting to make sure, and aware that he was edging towards the brink of some *faux pas*.

'She's with the Voluntary Aid Detachment,' said Wyndham. 'She drives an ambulance. On the Salonika front.'

'Well, let me say that you're one lucky fellow,' said Fitch, hoping that he sounded sincere.

'I'll say,' said Wyndham dreamily. 'She's Irish. I'm going to wait for her in Ireland and then we can be married.'

Fitch made another stab at getting to his feet. He had to steady himself on Wyndham's shoulder but he made it look like a comradely gesture.

'So come on into the mess and let's celebrate your lucky lady and you. Come on – before the boys drink it all.'

'Thank you,' said Wyndham, 'But no. Those days are behind me. Nora deserves better.'

7

'It is little heed I give to yourself or your share of men,' said the Red Woman.

—Lady Gregory, *Gods and Fighting Men*

The war in Macedonia had ended some months before the armistice in France. For an embarrassingly long time the Allied Army of the Orient had been boxed in around its port of disembarkation. Instead of saving Serbia, knocking Bulgaria out of the war, and discomfiting the Central Powers, the French and British had, for the best part of two years, been able to do little beyond digging trenches, earning them the derisive nickname 'the gardeners of Salonika'.

But they'd broken out in the end. The new commander of the alliance, Louis Franchet d'Espèrey, took them in hand and demonstrated the same aggressive flair he'd first shown in August of 1914. Back then he'd said, 'I'm sick of this fucking retreating', and had turned and fought. Four years later 'Desperate Frankie' was no longer on horseback and waving a sword at the head of his troops, but he was still the same head-down, stop-at-nothing fighter. In a last brutal uphill offensive, Franchet d'Espèrey sent his men against the enemy wire and machine-guns, and they won through. The Bulgarians, driven from their strong position, sensibly declined to fight from a weaker one and sued for peace. That had been at the end of September. Now, two months later, all anyone wanted was to go back home, only it was discovered that a world war took a lot of cleaning up after.

Nora Maxfield, of the Voluntary Aid Detachment of the Red Cross, had not enlisted to do the cleaning up but that was what she was at. That was always the way of it: leave the women to sort out the mess.

The shooting might have ended, but that didn't mean that the men who'd been shot suddenly got better. And there was still the wide range of sicknesses that had beset the armies since first they had arrived here. Still the malaria and the dysentery, the frostbite and the sunstroke, and everything that a population of hundreds of thousands is prey to when living in the open on short commons. All of this needed attending to, and that was part of Nora Maxfield's job.

At least she wasn't washing the dishes.

It hadn't been the milk of human kindness that had called her to medical service. No angel of charity was she. She had volunteered because she'd wanted something different, because she'd needed to get away from everyone's nonsense.

Nora Maxfield's trouble was that all her life people had been giving her useless advice. They probably thought it was their job, but that was hardly an excuse.

All her life:

Pay attention. Stand up straight. Don't look so sulky. Think of what people will say.

And then, from the moment she was old enough to wear her hair up:

How do you expect to meet a nice boy acting like that?

She hadn't wanted to get married. That much she'd always been sure of. It wasn't that she rejected the institution of matrimony out of hand, it was just that she hadn't found anyone that she was prepared to be stuck with until one or other of them died.

And then, giving her no inclination to change her mind, there were the young men she'd meet. There were the ones who shyly held her with sweaty hands at dances and couldn't string two words together, and there were the ones who thought they were great wits altogether if they jocularly remarked on how tall she was. Useless, the lot of them.

Then there were those who took liberties because they thought that liberties were theirs to take. It was one of that sort who'd first sparked her interest in medicine. He'd had wandering hands and, in telling him so, she'd put her own hand against his face hard enough to crack a bone – in her hand, that was. She didn't know or care about his face. The doctor she'd been obliged to see had made light of the injury, and the means by which it had been acquired, but Nora had been impressed by the elderly nurse who'd bound up the hand – unsmiling, competent and with no ring on her finger. The woman hadn't inspired Nora to go all Florence Nightingale, but she'd planted a seed in Nora's mind, a shoot of which poked its head up when the war began and the posters for the Voluntary Aid Detachment appeared. She wasn't taken in by the pictured pretty girls with their chocolate-box faces and neat blue uniforms, but the posters promised something different at least: something far away.

And so she became a nurse in England – of sorts. Really all they wanted was a glorified housemaid, and she hadn't come for that. Because she was tall and forceful in regard to getting her own way, the medical staff took notice of her, and took her impatience for efficiency. The senior nurses were implacable, but the young army doctors could be bent to her bidding. She never flirted: just glared until they saw things her way.

But still there was all the stupid advice, only this time it was couched as instruction, and she got into trouble every time she ignored it. She refused to know her place. There came a colossal bust-up between her and a matron who strenuously objected to her girls smoking cigarettes, off duty or no.

It became a disciplinary matter, and it would have gone badly for her if the head of the hospital hadn't taken her side. He was a colonel in the Medical Corps, with a weakness for redheads and a long-standing ill feeling towards the matron, dating back to treatment he himself had once needed for haemorrhoids, and the lack of sympathy he'd received at her hands.

The troublesome Maxfield was not dismissed and sent home as was advocated. Instead she found herself happily transferred to France.

That had been more like it. For a while, anyway.

Discipline had been no less important in a base hospital in Rouen, but it was more sensible, and there were battlefield casualties to remind a woman why she was wearing the uniform. Even the importunate young officers weren't so much of a pest in France. There were more of them, and they were more insistent, but here they were so much closer to their own deaths, and thus it was easier to put up with them.

There was even one she'd taken a shine to. He was different insofar as he didn't make stupid jokes or think himself God's gift. Though at the same time he was as bad as the rest of them, trying to order her life for her. He wanted her to marry him, and he was in earnest. She thought him a really nice boy, and her thoughts of him had become thoroughly distracting, but it had been a relief when her transfer to an ambulance unit was approved.

Nothing like driving on bad roads in a war zone for keeping a girl's mind on what mattered.

And now it was all over, and soon she'd have to go home, and yet again people would be telling her what to do.

At this very moment, with the weather holding fine, the road empty, and no casualties in the back, she had time to think for the first time in a long time. There was much to look forward to. Civilian comforts. Freedom from military discipline. There was even the exciting prospect of the intensifying campaign for Irish independence. But a lifetime's experience told her that her own independence was the thing at stake. There was her boy, Dan

Wyndham, who expected her to marry him. But she'd spent her life not getting married and she'd be an awful fool to change that now.

What else was there, though?

Well whatever else there was, there were sure to be people who'd make it their business to tell her. Everyone was just itching to lay her future out for her. Same as always. She could hear the lifelong litany of stupid advice as she negotiated a bend in the road.

Try to be more agreeable, Nora.

Don't speak so sharply, Maxfield.

I shouldn't take that ambulance, miss – steering's been acting up.

She hit a bad pothole and it occurred to her that she really should have heeded what the mechanic had said to her earlier. But she liked this ambulance. She was used to it. It had always behaved itself for her. Until now.

She wrenched the wheel but it wouldn't answer. She hauled on the brake lever but it was too late. With heart-stopping inevitability the ambulance left the road, nose down.

And then it stopped.

She gripped the steering wheel and took a few deep breaths. Then she got out and had a look to see how bad it was. Bad enough. Nothing was damaged but only two wheels were still in contact with the ground, and the ambulance was half-on, half-off the road, backside in the air.

She knew this stretch well. From here it was a fairly easy road home. Her vehicle-maintenance skills didn't extend very far beyond topping up a radiator or changing a wheel, but she'd developed a forthright approach to anything more complex, and a few calculated wallops with a heavy spanner often served to make the machinery behave itself for just long enough. A year on the Salonika Front had posed worse problems than unresponsive steering. Now, if she could only get the bloody ambulance back on the road.

She was leaning against the rear mudguard, on her third cigarette, when the soldiers appeared.

There were five of them. Bulgarians by the look of them. Prisoners newly released and on their way home. They stared at her. And why not? There was nothing else on this road to look at. She stared right back, not moving. She could feel the weight of the small pistol in her coat pocket.

When they drew up to her, the one evidently in charge made a short speech involving hand gestures. There was nothing threatening about it but she put her hand in her pocket anyway.

The man was probably giving her advice, the same as everybody.

'I need a push,' she conceded.

She didn't speak any language besides English, but needing a push was something that could be explained with a few simple actions. The soldiers cottoned on. They had a little discussion. They smiled at her. She didn't smile back, but did deign to move off the mudguard and let them have their way with the ambulance.

It took no time at all, and the ambulance started on only the second attempt. Nora smiled then, but only to show that she was pleased with the work: not that she wanted to make friends. Then she handed out cigarettes – a whole one to each man – and set out carefully for home. The soldiers were going in the other direction and that was good. She was glad she hadn't had to give them a lift. Glad she hadn't had to shoot any of them either.

8

It was the appalling new silence of things that soothed and unsettled them in turn.

—Rudyard Kipling, *The Irish Guards*

To the general disgust, the end of the fighting didn't bring an end to duty or to army routine. Training continued as before. The pointlessness of it got everybody down. Lapses of discipline became more common. Men went over the hill, and when the MPs hauled them back after a wild weekend in London, they showed no contrition. They'd signed up for the war and the war was over. They should be allowed to go home or allowed to have some fun. Why the hell not? The guys in France were blowing off steam in Paris.

As one truculent absconder put it, 'Put me in the stockade or send me back Stateside, Captain. Either way is better than this horseshit.'

Wyndham was inclined to agree. He wasn't intending to go back to Massachusetts – not until Nora came back from Salonika and he'd won her hand – but a training camp in an English winter was far from the happiest place to wait for her. Draughty huts, poor food, worthless instruction doled out to mutinous men – what was the point?

His one-time commanding officer evidently thought as much. A letter arrived from Colonel Fitzmullen-Brophy, hard on the heels of a semi-official communication, both advising Wyndham to prepare for the colonel's visit. The duplication of effort was typical of the man. Neither message was very revealing, but Wyndham didn't mind. He was deeply fond of Fitzmullen-Brophy and the arrival of a friendly face was most welcome.

'Wyndham! Whatever are you doing in that hat?'
'United States Army campaign hat, sir. Don't you like it?'
'But you're not in the United States Army, Dan. You're a Munster. I should get rid of it.'
'It doesn't remind you of South Africa?'
'Not really. Get rid of it, there's a good fellow. It doesn't do to let standards slip – especially not in front of Americans.'
'I am rather American myself, sir.'
'That's neither here nor there, Dan. Now stop being so bally obstinate and see that you're properly dressed in future.'
'Very good, sir. And how have you been since last we saw one another?'

The last time they'd seen each other had been in the spring, when the Germans had made a last bold attempt to win the war. They'd failed in the end, but in the process they'd managed to break the deadlock on the Western Front, break British Fifth Army, and annihilate the 16th (Irish) Division. They'd pretty much annihilated Lieutenant Daniel Wyndham too, but Fitzmullen-Brophy was having none of it. He'd rescued a shivering Wyndham from the battlefield and then just got on with fighting the war as if defeat were something one should work through and eventually get over, rather like the common cold.

It had been a frenetic few weeks which Wyndham couldn't remember any too clearly. Of that he was somewhat grateful. Harried movement, fearful noise, sleeplessness, and through it all Fitzmullen-Brophy attempting to impose order. They'd been parted sometime in April, with a used-up Wyndham no good to anybody except perhaps the American Expeditionary Force, and

Fitzmullen-Brophy just carrying on one way or another.

'Of course I was rather hoping for a battalion,' he now explained. 'Irish for preference. The Munsters ideally. Thing was though, it was all up with the Irish Division. They'd done a damned fine job, but it had cost them heavily. The Sixteenth is just a number now. Used as a training cadre, I believe. Nothing Irish about them at all anymore. Doubt if they even still wear the shamrock. Damned shame. Tried to snaffle the command of one of the battalions that were being reconstituted. Nothing doing, I'm afraid.'

'What about the Cyclists, sir?' asked Wyndham.

The last time the two had *officially* served together had been in an English yeomanry battalion who'd been mounted on bicycles instead of horses.

'All up with the Cyclists too, I'm sorry to say. Converted to infantry, don't you know. Nothing at all wrong with that. Infantry was what was needed. I'd happily have led them as infantry.'

'But?'

'But they were just posted off in penny packets to fill the gaps in other units, which rather left me without a job. Ended up back in Ireland. Did my bit for recruiting. Poor show, Dan. Damned poor show.'

Wyndham could understand. He'd tried his hand at recruiting in Ireland himself. All the speeches, bands and banners they could rustle up hadn't been enough to net more than a handful of young volunteers. And that had been in 1915. He dreaded to think how things would have been a year later, after the rebellion in Dublin. Only a man with the heedless courage of Fitzmullen-Brophy, whose devotion to his regiment outweighed all doubt, would have voluntarily stood before a crowd of Irishmen and exhorted them to fight for the king.

'I did hear that there was some trouble over Irish recruitment, sir,' Wyndham ventured.

'Trouble? Shocking business! Those fools in Westminster tried to impose conscription. Conscription! In Ireland! I ask you!'

Wyndham wasn't sure what the colonel was asking him. Conscription had been a fact for the latter half of the war. Every man who'd joined these past two years had come because he'd been sent for, willing or not. But Ireland, suspended on the brink of Home Rule since 1914, had not been included in the scheme – not, that is, until the crisis of last spring had caused so much alarm. In the end, military servitude had not been imposed on Ireland's manhood, but the very prospect had caused loud protest, which played nicely into the hands of the nationalists, who'd been waiting nearly two years for some fresh evidence of British tyranny to rail against.

'There was some sort of demonstration in Tralee. Great big banner. "We Will Not Have Conscription." Some agitator or other speaking from a platform. A lot of ruffians standing around with hurling sticks, trying to look menacing. Police doing nothing at all to stop it. Well damn me, but I just wasn't having it.'

Oh dear, though Wyndham. 'So what did you do, sir?'

'Do? Why, I climbed right up onto their bally platform and I let them have it. Of course they tried to shout me down, but I just shouted louder until they saw I was talking sense.'

'They listened to you?'

'That they did, Dan. And why not? At bottom, we were in perfect agreement. Conscription for Ireland? Ridiculous! And I told them so. "Ridiculous," I said to them. That rather took the wind out the Sinn Feiner's sails, let me tell you.'

'I can imagine, sir.'

'Told them all that an Irishman shouldn't be told to fight. Given a good reason, he should *want* to fight. Any Irishman of spirit, any Irishman with blood in his veins, would have the common decency to throw his cap on the green, roll up his sleeves, and give Fritz what for. We don't stand for bullies, I told them. Not our own government, and certainly not the Germans. So none of this conscription nonsense, I said. Come volunteer!'

'And?'

'Rather a mixed reception. Given a little more time I'm sure I'd have got more of them on my side, but the rowdies set to shouting again. Couldn't make myself heard. Had to chuck it.'

'Oh well, sir. At least you gave it a good try.'

'Well that's what I said when I was called to account.'

'Account?'

'Hmm, yes. The various authorities in Tralee took a dim view of my aggravating an already fraught situation, as they put it. Then it made the paper, do you see. Naturally, the blasted journalists got the wrong end of the stick.'

'Oh dear.'

'So anyway, I had to go to Dublin to explain why I, a serving officer in uniform, had spoken at an anti-conscription rally. Silly really. Perfect storm in a teacup. Then, just to put the jolly old tin hat on things, I came down with the blasted influenza.'

'Oh dear.'

'By the time I was myself again things had moved on. Opportunities missed.'

'It can't have been too much of a setback, sir – I see they promoted you.'

Fitzmullen-Brophy smiled in spite of himself.

'Oh yes – but it's of no matter really. Not a reward for anything in particular. I imagine I just got to the top of some list.'

'Well-deserved nonetheless. My hearty congratulations.'

'Thank you, Dan, thank you. If I thought the higher-ups capable of anything so calculating I'd suspect that they were kicking me upstairs.'

'Sir?'

'Full colonels don't really command anything, Dan. Too high for a battalion, too low for a brigade.'

'Oh well.'

'But all that's by the bye.'

Wyndham found himself nodding, because he knew where this was going. The colonel was going to outline some foolhardy scheme and Wyndham was going to take it on trust. It had been thus ever since August of 1914 when Major Fitzmullen-Brophy had halted some raw recruits on a route march through Kerry and told them that their ultimate destination was not Castletownbere but Maubeuge. A few years later Wyndham had stood in front of a map and watched Fitzmullen-Brophy sketch out an assault on the Passchendaele Ridge by bicycle. He'd been nodding along then too.

'This job of yours – this American job. There's really not much point to it, is there, Dan?'

'One goes where one's sent, sir.'

'Precisely. But it's time you were sent somewhere else. Back to the regiment, Dan. Back to the Munsters. I've had a word with the commanding officer here and he has no objection. Pack your kit and we can be on the next train to Dover.'

Nodding was one thing. Being uprooted at Fitzmullen-Brophy's whim was just one of the periodic wartime disturbances he'd got used to. But Dover?

'Dover, sir? What about Ireland? Everyone will be coming home, sir. Shouldn't the regiment be coming to us, rather than we to them?'

Fitzmullen-Brophy looked exasperated. He'd been putting up with this sort of attitude from too many people already, and had a right to expect better from young Wyndham of all people.

'Don't say you think the war's over, damn it all, man!'

'Well, sir, wasn't there that business on the eleventh?'

'An armistice! Merely a ceasefire! And Lloyd George was a fool not to see through it. Haig too, I'm sad to say.'

'I'm not sure I follow, sir.'

'All it's good for is giving Fritz a breathing space. Give Kaiser Bill a few months to recover and he'll be up to his old tricks again.'

'I thought the Kaiser had abdicated, sir.'

'Oh, you know what I mean.'

'I'm—not absolutely sure I do, sir.'

Fitzmullen-Brophy sighed. 'The war isn't over yet, Dan.'

'I see, sir.'

'Until the Germans sign a formal surrender we must be prepared for hostilities to resume.'

There it was: *be prepared.* A motto that had been ringing in Wyndham's ears since first he'd been seduced into the army. Robert Baden-Powell and Hugh Fitzmullen-Brophy were brothers under the skin.

'So this demobilisation nonsense is just nonsense, do you see, Dan? I for one mean to have nothing to do with it. The Munsters are still in France. We must ensure that they are standing ready.'

Fitzmullen-Brophy went on the same vein, speaking of how the British army had been denied its final victory, but how that victory might be won yet, and how the Royal Munster Fusiliers would add further honours to their name, and how Wyndham should hurry if they wanted to catch their train, and how he should be sure to bring warm clothing, particularly socks, because accommodation on the Continent was likely to be quite primitive still and the influenza was about.

And Wyndham nodded.

It wasn't as bad as he'd feared.

Molly Fitzmullen-Brophy had once charged him with her father's welfare, so for her sake if nothing else he was going to go with the old man to France. If the colonel asked him to steal two bicycles so they could attack across the Rhine, just the two of them, he could see himself going along with that too. But it wouldn't come to that. The war was truly over. Fitzmullen-

Brophy would cause a fuss, and get into some scrape with the military bureaucracy, and that was as perilous as it would get.

And who knew? Once on the Continent he'd be just that little bit closer to Nora. Perhaps he could meet her on her way home. Perhaps in Paris. Perhaps in that very same hotel.

He was dreaming and he knew it.

Still, he was going to go with the colonel.

After all, anything was better than this horseshit.

9

When this lousy war is over,
Oh, how happy I will be!

—traditional

It all come to nothing, of course.

Wyndham found that travelling in the company of a full colonel was a smoother and more comfortable ride than he was used to, but he also found that Fitzmullen-Brophy's authority had its limitations – not least in how much longer the man himself would be able to exercise it.

The promotion would be his last, and it wasn't a reward so much as a reminder that he was to be retired. Fitzmullen-Brophy had entered this war as a major in the reserve, and he was leaving it only two ranks further up and no particular command to his name. This, when there were brigadier-generals still in their twenties. The old warhorse had his DSO and could now have an ex-colonel's honours, and that should be enough for him.

Wyndham slowly realised all of this as they made their cold and dreary way across northern France. Fitzmullen-Brophy was treated with all the courtesy a full colonel deserved, but France was filled with senior officers, and there was nothing that could be done about a transport system that had been under strain for four years and, with the urgency of war suddenly gone, was exhibiting the weariness that everyone was feeling. There were long waits and inconvenient detours that the colonel's rank could do nothing about, and it was during one such, when the two fusiliers waited in the rain for a lorry driver to change a tyre, that Fitzmullen-Brophy hinted that the good times were coming to an end.

'I expect there'll be rather more standing about in future,' he said. 'After all, who's likely to hurry himself for another poor old soldier?'

And there was more in this vein as their journey went on. The final frank admission came when they found the regiment, and were welcomed most civilly, and pretty much sent on their way as soon as they'd been given something to eat.

Fitzmullen-Brophy was allowed to inspect the camp and greet old acquaintances, but it was made quite clear that there was nothing for him to do here. Everything was being scaled back. Men were being demobilised. A colonel had no business arriving as all the other ranks were in the business of leaving. The depot at Tralee, Fitzmullen-Brophy was advised, would doubtless be a more fruitful place for him.

Wyndham, on the other hand, was invited to stay.

'Battalion sports coming up, old man. Didn't I hear you used to box? No? Care to start? Are you sure?'

But Wyndham explained that, his loyalty to the regiment not withstanding, his duties kept him at Fitzmullen-Brophy's side, and back to Tralee he must go. Sorry.

It wasn't the first time he'd had to use such a dodge to escape the ring. It was one of the difficulties in fellows thinking that he had a pugnacious nature. That nose he'd had broken for him by a couple of careless stretcher bearers one Christmas would be the death of him yet.

So after a dinner among near-strangers and a night in a cold hut, the two adventurers were turned around and sent to retrace their journey across the broken roads and blasted land.

It had all been for nothing – except that Wyndham found Moriarty again.

In the course of their visit they'd met few faces they recognised. The cataclysm in March and the reorganisations that came after had left little that was recognisable of the battalion that had seen 1918 in. Even that battalion had been an amalgam of other formations, ground down and played out by the years of war. There was still a handful who knew Wyndham – there were even one or two who remembered Fitzmullen-Brophy – but beyond the polite smiles and good words there was little in the way of comradely reunion. There had been too many comrades. Too much had happened. For a few years the regiment and the war had been these men's life, but now they were putting it all behind them. So after the, *I'm glad to see you well, sir*, there came the inevitable, *Do you know when they'll be leaving us go home, sir?*

Happily, the answer for many of them turned out to be, *As soon as the army can be decently rid of you*. On his departure, Fitzmullen-Brophy was asked to take charge of more than fifty men bound for home and demobilisation.

They were a well-behaved lot for the most part, wanting nothing more than a speedy transit. When lorries halted or a train was late they didn't wander off to get drunk, but grumbled and stayed put, lest they miss a vital connection and have their war service lengthened by a few more hours.

It was at Arras where everyone was ordered off their train and told to wait for another one. Travelling by themselves, the two officers could have ignored that or found a quick way round it, but with all these men to look after, Wyndham was obliged to find a Railway Transport Officer and argue with him. When that was insufficient, Fitzmullen-Brophy went to apply the full weight of his rank. Wyndham was left waiting on a platform, keeping half an eye on his homebound charges, but not caring too much. There was a lot to see in the station. There was even a brawl in the making.

Out of all the parties of soldiers crowding the place, a battalion of US troops held the majority. Maybe it wasn't a battalion. Maybe it was only an American-sized company. Whichever, there were a lot of them, burdened with all their kit, trying to make room for themselves. Someone was not obliging them. Even above the train noises, Wyndham could hear the voices raised.

'That's my train! You're not putting me off my own train, you Yank bastard!'

'You don't own this train, fella, and you better watch your mouth. I'm no Yank, boy. I'm from Texas and I'm a goddamn sergeant.'

'I don't give a shite what you are, you big gobshite! I want to go *home*!'

The last word was drawn out into two passionate syllables.

It was none of his business, but Wyndham was drawn in anyway. Men were jostling each other to make some room or to get a better look. He heaved his way through them. And there was Corporal Francis Moriarty.

Moriarty dressed like a charity case. Moriarty thin and pale. Moriarty, spokesman for a party of prisoners of war, roaring defiance at the American Expeditionary Force.

In the summer of 1914 it had been Moriarty who'd introduced the innocent Wyndham to the army – that strange and proud tribe that lived not so much for king and country as for the regiment. They were men who barely earned a living wage but had their scarlet and blue uniforms tailored to perfect fit at their own expense. With boots like lacquer and buttons like gold, they'd drink themselves senseless in mean pubs.

And here was a last of that dying breed, dressed in ill-fitting surplus khaki, his hair prison-cropped and his belongings in a brown paper parcel, spitting obscenities and waving his fists. Wyndham wanted to run over and hug him. The dizzying impulse passed, thank God, but all the same, Moriarty was an old comrade and a man with whom Wyndham had literally fought shoulder to shoulder. That had been in March, against Ludendorff's shock troops. Wyndham had made it out. He'd never heard what had happened to Moriarty.

A survivor of the Salient in '14, badly shell-shocked at Festubert, invalided out from the Somme with a self-inflicted wound, and back in the trenches in time to fall victim to Operation *Kaiserschlacht*. And here he was now, barely coherent in the face of the Texan sergeant whose men had priority.

It was none of Wyndham's business, but that wasn't stopping him.

The sergeant was a square-built, corn-fed type from one of those big square-built, corn-fed regiments that had been flooding into France since the autumn and were now being turned around to be shipped home with not a shot fired. He was taller than Moriarty and outweighed him by some margin. By his stance it was easy to tell that he saw Moriarty as an annoyance rather than any sort of threat. There was a look of contemptuous amusement on his face that wasn't doing anything to calm the Irishman down. He had gone so far as to plant his hands on his hips and lean forward, daring Moriarty to try and plant one on him.

'Right here, you little sonofabitch. Go on.'

Wyndham never cared to confront big confident men, and like many a junior officer, he was diffident in the face of senior NCOs – especially hefty rough-hewn sergeants like this one. Nevertheless, he'd been pretending to be a soldier for more than four years now, and was willing to try it on one more time.

Listening to the language being used, and remembering the attitudes of the American soldiers he'd known in England, he judged it wise to forsake the high-handed tone. For some men, the well-bred voice, the whipcord breeches, and the air of feudal privilege were enough to command respect. Not these men. This outfit didn't look like they'd give the time of day to any fancy-pants Limey who came at them all high and mighty, no matter what kind of officer he was.

Wyndham wished he'd kept his broad-brimmed campaign hat. He wished he still had his big German pistol in his belt. He even wished that he was chewing tobacco. Was his emphatically broken nose enough to suggest a two-fisted, hairy-chested roughneck? It would have to.

'Just what in hell's name is going on here, Sergeant?' he demanded.

The big sergeant stopped his goading of Moriarty and considered the interruption. He did not snap to attention. Not for Wyndham, and not for the US captain who shouldered himself to the fore an instant after Wyndham's arrival.

'What *is* going on here, Sergeant?' said the captain.

The sergeant ignored Wyndham and explained to his officer that the Limey with the moustache was causing a ruckus about whose train it was. Moriarty, restrained by his mates, and thunderstruck at the dawning realisation that he was looking at Mr. Daniel Wyndham of all people, was holding his peace for the minute.

The captain looked at Wyndham and, indicating the late POWs with distaste, asked, 'Are these your men, Lieutenant?'

The implication was obvious to Wyndham's ears. These shabby and indisciplined louts were bad soldiers, and thus Wyndham was a bad officer, and so it was no damn wonder the war had lasted as long as it had. Wyndham, in short, did not care for the American captain's tone. He drew himself up to his full height. It was nothing special, but he felt his indignation added to his stature.

'Captain, the last time I saw that man he was being a one-man rearguard for the whole damn Fifth Army. And he's no Limey. He's Irish, from the fightingest goddamn regiment there is. He's a Munster. A by-God Royal Munster Fusilier. And so am I. We've been out here since nineteen and fourteen, Captain, and now we want to go home.'

The captain blinked. He had expected better of the Anglo-American alliance. Unable to go toe-to-toe in a bragging contest with a veteran of 1914, he fell back on military punctilio.

'*Lieutenant*,' he said. 'My outfit has priority on this train. What you or your men have been doing in this war has nothing to do with it. My men have priority and that's flat. We have to get to Le Havre. You're not the only one who wants to get home.'

Wyndham saw that he couldn't fight a whole US regiment or the French railways either.

'Well if you're so hell-fired fixed on getting back to Asshole Bluffs, Missouri so soon, Captain, then maybe you shouldn't have left in the first place.'

And quite proud of that parting shot, he gathered up Moriarty and dragged him somewhere quiet.

Moriarty was trembling and his nose was running.

'Dirty Yank bastard,' he said, and it was practically a sob.

'Shhh. Calm down. *I'm* a dirty Yank bastard, remember? Here, have a smoke. You'll feel better in a minute.'

Moriarty took the cigarette like a sick man being fed with a spoon. He slouched against a steel column and let himself slide down until his backside was on the ground. Unbecoming the deportment of an officer and a gentleman though it might have been, Wyndham got down there beside him.

'I'm tired,' said Moriarty.

'That's alright,' said Wyndham. 'I thought you were dead.'

'No,' said Moriarty and then, as though he had to pause to think hard about it, 'No.'

Wyndham couldn't think of how to reply to that. Moriarty, his confrontation with the Texan sergeant having emptied him, had nothing more to say either.

They sat for as long as it took to smoke a cigarette until, in coal smoke and steam, the war's backwash pulled them apart again.

10

'Give them rifles and rum, a flag to follow and a master to drive, and they would start another war tomorrow!'

—R.H. Mottram, *The Spanish Farm Trilogy*

The journey to Boulogne was typically uncomfortable. Broken windows, rickety carriages, unexplained halts and delays – the war was over but these remained. Maybe when all the soldiers had finally gone home things could get better. Maybe civilians would carry on the soldiers' practice of sticking their backsides out the doors and relieving themselves while their mates helpfully kept hold of them, but it was hard to imagine that the railway authorities would put up with fires being lit inside compartments. Military authorities, on the other hand, could be more indulgent, such as when Fitzmullen-Brophy went to investigate the smoke that was filling the corridor.

'Is it bothering you at all, sir? We're very sorry, but the draught in here is only terrible.'

Thus spoke a clump of cheerful old sweats huddled around a makeshift brazier. Seeing that the fire was contained in a bucket, and that the only people complaining about the smoke were French, the colonel merely smiled and bade them carry on.

'Only do be careful, men.'

A while later, near the end of their journey, one of the men sought out the colonel in the officer's own compartment. He knocked and stuck his head in without waiting for a reply, an ingratiating smile on his face

'I beg your pardon, sir. Might I trouble you for a minute at all?' Fitzmullen-Brophy nodded that he might.

'It is Colonel Fitzmullen-Brophy, isn't it? I'm right, amn't I?'

The colonel nodded again. The man smiled even wider and squeezed himself through the door, somewhat encumbered with a sack.

'You wouldn't know me, sir. I was in the 8th Battalion,' he said. 'But I'd know you well enough, Colonel – to see anyway. Many's the time you've been pointed out to me. "That's the bold Colonel FitzEm with the DSO," they'd tell me.'

There was nothing Fitzmullen-Brophy liked better than a simple Irish soldier who could be respectful and familiar all at once.

'And your name?' he asked.

'Kelly,' said the man. 'Kelly from the 8th Battalion as was. And from Skibbereen before that.'

But to Wyndham's eye there was something off about Kelly. Even after four and a half years he was still finding new varieties of Irishry, but if he'd been told that this Kelly from Skibbereen was in fact a man called something like Bellamy and came from somewhere like Birmingham, and that he earned his living in the music halls, Wyndham could have well believed it.

Has Anybody Here Seen Kelly?
Kelly From The 8th Battalion?

'And what can I do for you, Kelly?' asked Fitzmullen-Brophy.

'Bless us, but I hate to be troubling you, Colonel. It's only that when I saw you turning the blind eye to our little bit of a fire back there I knew you weren't just a gentleman, but a true soldier – and a man who knows soldiers and their little wants.'

Fitzmullen-Brophy gave a gruff chuckle at that, as if he could see right through Kelly's game. But Wyndham could see too that it was a game the old colonel was eager to play one more time, notwithstanding that Kelly might be a far better player.

'Go on, man.'

Kelly held up his sack. 'I'd be imposing on you, sir, I know, but it's just the matter of a few oul' souvenirs, so it is.'

'Souvenirs?'

'A matter of souvenirs and customs officers, Colonel,' said Kelly. 'These are just a few things that me and the lads picked up in France, and I hear that the customs men in Dover mightn't be too happy with me bringing them in. They might be what they'd be calling *contraband*, do you see?'

And he actually pronounced it '*conthra-band*', and he even winked.

Fitzmullen-Brophy, wily old soldier, narrowed his eyes and smiled.

'Now what have you got in that bag, Kelly?'

'Ah well, Colonel, it's just a few keepsakes. Trophies, you might say. Bits and pieces. And there's this wee bit of a pistol I took off a German officer at Wipers. I don't think I'm allowed to bring that back to Blighty.'

'You took this pistol from a German officer?'

'At the point of me bayonet, Colonel, and I can tell you that he wasn't too pleased at all about it.'

Fitzmullen-Brophy guffawed at that. 'I should say not!'

'And well, Colonel, I wouldn't want to think of a customs man *confiscating* it, or taking my other few souvenirs and end up decorating his own mantelpiece with them maybe.'

'Of course not,' said Fitzmullen-Brophy. 'Of course not.'

'It's not like he earned them, sir, is it? A customs man might be wearing a uniform, but it's not the uniform that yourself and myself have been wearing.'

'Nor is it, man.'

'So myself and the lads were hoping, sir, that a good fusilier like yourself might just mind our few things until we're safe out the other side. Only I wouldn't want to impose on you at all, at all.'

Fitzmullen-Brophy laughed, and then delivered a wink of his own.

'You have more brass in your neck than you do in your buttons, Kelly, but seeing as you've done your bit and we're all going home, I'll let you get away with it. Give your things to the lieutenant here and he'll look after them for you.'

And with much grateful beaming and nodding, and a touch of the finger to the side of the nose instead of a salute, Kelly handed the heavy sandbag to Wyndham, and backed out into the corridor again.

Dover was as hectic and officious as feared, with packs and kitbags turned out, and soldiers trying to explain away bottles of brandy and unauthorised weapons under disapproving stares. But officers were spared the worst of it.

Outside, Kelly didn't keep Wyndham waiting long at all, but retrieved his bag of souvenirs before the officers even had to consider the possibility of missing their train. As before, Kelly was all smiles and blessings, but Wyndham was glad to hand over the man's goods and see the back of him. On the cross-channel boat he'd taken time to root through the sandbag that Fitzmullen-Brophy had so innocently passed into his charge.

If Wyndham had thought he'd have got useful answers he might have asked Kelly some questions.

Such as: just how many pistols had this German officer been carrying anyway? And why was one of them a British Webley? And, when all's said and done, how much ammunition does a souvenir really need?

II

HEARTH AND HOME

Let us make this a land fit for such men to live in.

—David Lloyd George, November 1918

11

Out of this world-chaos nations with new ideals and great aspirations are being born. It is for you to see that Ireland alone of the small Subject Nations is not left alone in her bondage.... This election is a momentous election...

—Constance Markievicz, Holloway Prison, 6 December 1918

Posters for the general election were everywhere in Dublin. Fitzmullen-Brophy shook his head.

'It's all changing, Dan,' he said. 'The old order is on its way out, I dare say. When I was your age it was either Tory or Liberal and that was that. Then suddenly it was Home Rule. Nothing at all against Home Rule, mind. Some of Redmond's lot aren't quite the thing, but that's politicians for you. So long as they're loyal to the king and leave the army alone, I believe an independent Ireland would be a perfectly good idea. Take some of the wind out of the sails of the damn Shinners anyway, what? Blasted nonsense. And look at this!'

He rapped his blackthorn against a poster.

'*Vote Labour!* Well really. I mean to say. Damn it all.'

Wyndham said something anodyne about creeping socialism and admitted that he was glad it wasn't his concern.

'What do you mean? None of your concern! You're a young man! You have a duty to make your vote count.'

'Well yes, sir, but I'm still not a British subject. Ineligible to vote, you see.'

'Oh, not that again. A fellow wears the uniform for four years. Ridiculous.'

To Fitzmullen-Brophy that was the problem in a nutshell. If only people could look past all these silly rules and see reason, dammit. A foreigner, if proven a gentleman, that is, shouldn't be cut out. Not after he'd done his bit. Not if he was a good sort who could be trusted to vote the right way. And then Ireland could be a free and independent part of the United Kingdom and everything could get back to the way it had always been. Why even have elections anyway? They only stirred things up. Proud parliamentary tradition would uphold the will of Britons and Irishmen alike, the same as always. Green flags, red flags – if only people would be reasonable.

Fitzmullen-Brophy was glad he was a soldier, and not have to trouble himself with political thinking.

'But that's all by the way, Dan. The question is what are you going to do now, eh? Now that it's all over, I mean? I mean are you going back to America?'

'Not just yet, sir. I intend to stay in Ireland a while longer.'

'Well good for you, my lad. I don't know if I pull much weight anymore, but I imagine I could wangle you a permanent commission if I set my mind to it. In the Reserve, of course. Regulars are out I'm afraid. But now that I think of it—'

Wyndham headed him off before the colonel suggested petitioning the king or something.

'I won't be staying in the army.'

'No? No – I don't suppose so. Can't see why you should really.'

Fitzmullen-Brophy poked at the ground with his stick, trying not to look too crestfallen. The world, as he'd just pointed out, was changing.

'So what will you do, Dan?'

'I'm not quite sure yet, sir. I could continue my literary studies. After all, that's what brought me here in the first place. And it would give me a rest. And I need a rest.'

'Not a bad idea at all, my boy. We could all do with a rest. Not sure if books would do me, though.'

'Well I was thinking I could find work, sir.'

'Work? What sort of work?'

'I really don't know. Something in an office perhaps. Just to keep me occupied.'

Officers seeking office work. It would never have done at all in Fitzmullen-Brophy's young day. Still – modern times and all that.

'But that doesn't sound anything like a career, Dan.'

'No – no, not at all. I'm not looking for a career. Not right now. Just something to keep me occupied until, well—'

'Until?'

'There's a young lady, sir.'

'Ho ho!'

'I intend to marry her.'

'Do you indeed? Splendid! Absolutely splendid! And who is this young lady?'

'Her name is Nora Maxfield, sir. She's a VAD.'

'A girl in uniform, eh? Wonderful!'

'And she's Irish, sir. Her people are from somewhere in West Cork, I gather.'

Fitzmullen-Brophy's mood was improving in bounds.

'Good Church of Ireland people, I believe, sir.'

The colonel fumbled with his stick so that he could clap Wyndham's shoulder and shake his hand at the same time. The world wasn't going as badly as he'd thought – not if young people were falling in love. He laughed all the more heartily to see Wyndham blush.

'No date set?'

'Well nothing's quite settled.' And that was the truth – up to a point. Wyndham had asked her to marry him a year ago and she'd turned him down flat.

'I'll tell you what, Dan,' said Fitzmullen-Brophy. 'You're

coming back to Tralee with me of course, and you're staying as long as you jolly well like.'

'That's most kind of you, sir,' Wyndham stammered.

'Not a bit of it! The memsahib always had a soft spot for you, and now that Molly's married we have acres of room.'

He was still shaking Wyndham's hand.

'*I* know! With your books and everything you can help me write a history of the regiment! A memoir even!'

And Wyndham just had to join in the laughter.

'The proud old 11th Battalion!' he said.

'Haha! There you are! Give you something to do while this girl of yours makes up her mind.'

They went on their way, no longer dismayed by the hectoring posters or the sorry damage left over from the Easter Rising. The disappointing trip to France was behind them and the prospect of the long journey to Tralee didn't seem so depressing.

'So tell me again about this girl of yours,' said Fitzmullen-Brophy, and Wyndham did so happily.

Fitzmullen-Brophy, already seeing the arch of swords at the church door, was thoroughly approving.

'And she's serving in an ambulance unit, is she? That shows pluck. She'll be the making of you, Dan, just as Susan was of me.'

'I hope so, sir.'

'And I'm glad she's one of us – I mean I'm glad she's not Roman Catholic. Nothing at all against the RCs of course. Some of my dearest friends are RC. But mixed marriages? That's just creating a muddle right at the start.'

'Exactly, sir.'

'And in Ireland there's that dashed sectarian question too. Dashed nonsense, of course. But still. Those blasted Shinners with their green tricolour – all rather RC at bottom. Rosaries and what have you. Be glad that your young lady isn't likely to be mixed up in of that.'

'Indeed, sir.'

'So when do you think she'll be coming home?'

'I wish I knew, sir. I hate to say it, but she isn't the best for writing letters.'

Salonika
3 December 1918

To the Secretary of Sinn Fein, Dublin.

Dear Sir,
I am at present serving with the Red Cross in Macedonia and am not able to vote anyway (yet), but I earnestly wish to aid the Irish Republic in her struggle.
I enclose a money order for five pounds (£5) to show that I am in earnest.
I hope to be returning to Ireland soon and I hope to find work that will aid the cause of the Irish Republic I would be grateful if you might forward particulars of the Women's Branch of the Volunteers where I think my talents would be best employed.
I can drive a motor vehicle and am proficient in small arms.

Yours faithfully,

N. Maxfield (Miss)

PS. Éirinn go Brág

She read it back again.

She really wasn't one for writing letters, but this one said what she wanted to say. She was in earnest, and she'd spelled it correctly (not like the boy's name). And she was sure of the spelling of the postscript too because she had copied it from a souvenir ashtray. But spelling didn't matter. Her heart was strong, and five pounds said so.

12

'But what good came of it at last?'
Quoth little Peterkin.
'Why that I cannot tell,' said he,
'But 'twas a famous victory.'

—Robert Southey, 'The Battle of Blenheim'

'A Dirty Shirt doesn't die in bed. That's what old Gorman said to me.' Fitzmullen-Brophy jabbed the stem of his pipe in Wyndham's direction to show that this was something that should be noted down.

'Nor does he,' he went on. 'I certainly didn't. Weak as a kitten I might have been, but I hauled myself off that charpoy as soon as I was able. How I did it is beyond me.'

'Charpoy, sir?'

'Charpoy. A bed. A native bed. Made primarily of ropes. But you're missing the point, Dan,'

'I do beg your pardon. Please.'

'Fighting fit – hah! Nothing of the sort. If they'd had a grave already dug for me I wouldn't have been the least bit surprised. Might have even lain down in it, don't you know. But it wasn't on. Gorman was right. There was work to be done. A company had to be sent to deal with those dacoits.'

'And this was at Meiktila.'

'No, no, no. We'd advanced *from* Meiktila. What the name of the dacoit village was I could no longer say, I'm afraid, but it was hardly Meiktila. I mean, how could it have been? *Really*. Do pay attention, Dan.'

'Forgive me, sir. You were saying. A company had to be dispatched.'

'And this wasn't a company that you'd be used to. A company before the war was only half the size, you know. And let me tell you that after an outbreak of fever such as the one we'd had, it was barely half the size again. And I tell you that a company was being dispatched because that was all that could be spared. If the job needed two companies or half the battalion, that was just our jolly old bad luck.'

Wyndham had crossed out the name 'Meiktila' in his notebook, changed his mind and written 'stet', and then added 'north' and a question mark. Now the historical record was clarified with '½ coys' scribbled into the margin.

They were back in Kerry, in the Fitzmullen-Brophy house, with Wyndham sitting as close to the fire as he decently could and the colonel sitting opposite him, or pacing about the room as the mood took him.

They had gone back to the Third Burma War because the short-lived 11th Battalion of the Munster Fusiliers, no matter how intimately both men remembered it, was never going to make a good story. The old 11th had been raised on the dying swell of the recruitment wave, with never enough men to put on a decent show. They'd all done their best, spending 1915 in a remote camp in North Cork before being poached out of business by larger and hungrier units. Not only had the battalion never fired a shot in anger: long-standing deficiencies in equipment meant that for most of its existence it had never fired any sort of shot at all. For instance, the machine-gun platoon, of which Wyndham had been in command, had been armed with a machine-gun they'd made themselves. Asking for that wonderful improvisation of scrap metal to fire actual bullets would have shown a mean-spirited lack of appreciation for the men's initiative and skill.

The only excitement the battalion had lived through had come when real weapons had been finally issued and the Irish Volunteers had attempted to steal them. Because that hadn't done Fitzmullen-Brophy's career any good, and because Wyndham happened to know more about it than he would ever tell, the subject was a non-starter as far as a commemorative history went. So they broadened the scope, drawing in adventures of the greater regiment in the wider empire as Fitzmullen-Brophy remembered them.

'Beastly march,' he said. 'Perfectly hellish. Air like soup. Bad enough for a fit man, but pity poor old me! Lord! I was soon wishing that I'd died in bed, and the Devil take Gorman's orders.'

'But you soldiered on, sir?'

'Of course I did. Well – I did my best.'

Fitzmullen-Brophy poked at the fire, sat down in his armchair, and abruptly stood up again, stung into action by memory.

'It was no use, I'm afraid. Just didn't have it in me. Had to fall out. Missed all the fun.'

'The fun?'

'Well, not much fun to be honest with you. Rather a damp squib as it happened. The dacoits must have known we were coming. Didn't think much of their chances. Got while the going was good. Can't blame them really. Cheated our fellows of a fight. Wasn't the first time either.'

Fitzmullen-Brophy frowned deeply at the mantelpiece, the sense of anti-climax troubling him still after all these years. Wyndham tried to be encouraging.

'But you did drive the dacoits off though, didn't you? I mean that was the point, wasn't it? To establish peace and order?'

'Well, yes.'

Wyndham looked at his notes again. They weren't as wholly coherent as he'd have wanted.

'Just one thing, Colonel,' he said. 'Dacoits – these were the Burmese irregulars, right?'

'Well, yes. It's something of a catch-all term, you know. Not so much irregulars as bandits and miscreants.'

'But they had organised to resist the British?'

'Exactly.'

'And forgive me – and I know this sounds foolish – but what was it the war was about?'

Fitzmullen-Brophy looked at Wyndham with exasperation.

'What was it *about*? We were at war with Burma, man! The Burmese king – whatsisname – had – well he'd done something at any rate. But it couldn't be allowed stand. Action had to be taken. In the interests of the empire, you see. And for the Burmese people's own good, naturally. You can look up the details if you must.'

As it happened, Wyndham went to do just that. The barracks didn't have a library. The officers' mess never ran to anything more literary than *The Field*, but there had to be old ledgers and unit diaries stored away somewhere. The army had obliged him to fill out enough paperwork during the war, so it stood to reason that there were hoards of the stuff stacked up wherever the army called home.

And a trip to the barracks got him out of the house and moving, which on these winter days did him good. He could buy the paper at least.

He didn't feel wholly comfortable about returning to the barracks. This would be his first time out of uniform. He didn't believe he'd be condemned as a fraud and an interloper or – worse yet – that they'd drag him back into the army. Those who knew who he was knew him for a Dirty Shirt, and those who didn't at least knew him as FitzEm's protégé. But he had no friends there, and it held no pleasant associations.

Also, there was an uncertain mood about the place. They had fought the greatest war in history, and what now? Too many men would not be coming back, and where were the fruits of victory? Was their reward merely to lapse back into their conservative languor and their armchairs in the mess? Were they to revert to being a drowsy county militia after their terrible adventure? Hang a *pickelhaube* on the wall; embroider a new name on the colours; consign this war to memory along with Burma and everywhere else?

Things were too unsettled. Things didn't match the idea of peace.

The last time he'd visited he'd been button-holed by a young subaltern of a type he hadn't encountered before – an educated young man who read the papers and held political views. The old army would never have stood the like, but that had been the old army. Either because Wyndham had a reputation as a bookish sort or, more likely, because he was rumoured to be an American, the lad had tried to entangle him in an argument about the Fourteen Points, and what should be decided at the Peace Conference, and whither the world was going now. Wyndham had been in no mood to debate What The War Had Been For then and he had no desire to do so now. He particularly feared that the importunate youth would start up on the Irish Question, and could easily imagine the boy propounding his sophomoric views, oblivious to the outraged stares of his seniors even as Wyndham withered under them.

Today the barrack gate was a scene of unusual liveliness. Instead of just the sentry there was a small group of various ranks, looking up and gesticulating.

'Bloody outrageous!' said an over-age captain.

'They must have done it in the night time,' said a sergeant. 'I'm surprised no one heard it.'

It was a tree that was holding their attention, but Wyndham couldn't tell what it was about the tree that was causing the trouble.

'I don't bloody care when it was done. Get it down! Now!'

'Easier said than done,' said another officer. 'Look at that. Clever buggers lopped off all the lower branches.'

'I don't give a damn how many branches they've lopped off. Get someone up that tree this instant, Sergeant!'

'Hanrahan, get up that tree.'

'Ah Jesus, Sergeant – you know me. I've no head for heights at all.'

'*I'll* do it, Sergeant.'

'Good man, O'Dowd. Hanrahan, give him a leg up.'

Wyndham joined them, and saw he wasn't the first passer-by to stop and gawk. There were amused murmurings from the onlookers that grew into laughter when the bold Private O'Dowd attempted to shin his way up the tree.

'Ah for the love of Christ!'

'What's wrong with you?'

'The dirty hoors have only painted axle grease all over the trunk! My trousers are only destroyed!'

'Never mind your bloody trousers, lad! Get up that tree!'

'I can't, Sergeant. It's all slippery!'

Wyndham backed off to see what it was they were trying to get at. He squinted upwards and wasn't sure until a helpful flurry of wind buffeted the tree, and from a high branch there unfurled an Irish tricolour. A couple of the onlookers raised a cheer – patriotic or derisive, he couldn't tell. He decided against going into the barracks. Not today. He didn't care to visit with everyone in bad temper. And with the tricolour in the tree defying the Union Jack on the barracks flagstaff, he could certainly do without a debate on Why We Fought and the Freedom of Small Nations.

13

How ya gonna keep 'em down on the farm (After they've seen Paree?)

—Joe Young & Sam Lewis, 1919

Wyndham was the best-dressed man in Tralee that winter.

In truth, there wasn't much competition, but you'd have had to go a long way to match the cut of his suit – possibly even all the way to Paris, which was the very place the suit had been cut. He'd had it made in defiance of wartime privation, dreaming of the day he could stride forth a new man, Nora on his arm, sharply dressed in a world that he'd fought for. It wasn't that he didn't like wearing uniform. He would have hesitated to admit it, but the uniform was the one thing he unreservedly liked about the army. Not the rough serge that had first been issued to him, but the officer's service dress in all its subtle varieties. During his long stay in Paris the year before, he'd had his uniforms supplemented and elaborated during indulgent sessions at a tailor's and, with his pocket full of back-pay and his head spinning with romance and vanity, he'd had this suit cut too.

It hadn't been an altogether unreasonable indulgence. He had found, during his very first leave, that the army had altered his shape so that his coats didn't quite fit anymore. Also, his civilian clothes had been made in the distant pre-war days, in a suburban life lived according to the approval of his family, when he had not yet drunk with the gentry, or fought alongside men or fallen in love with a woman.

So the suit was made, hang the expense, and there it was waiting for him when he came back to Tralee. The Fitzmullen-Brophy house wasn't the stage he'd envisaged for so fine a wardrobe, but choice was limited. It was either this or something that didn't fit. Uniform, alas, was no longer an option. He'd had himself photographed in his military finery, posted the picture to Nora, and then with some regret packed away tunics, breeches and all. The Parisian suit was his consolation.

Given the tenor of Ireland that winter, exemplified in the tricolour outside the barracks, he was happier not to be so readily identifiable as an officer of the crown forces. So here he was now: ex-officer, ex-gentleman, but damnably stylish. The Fitzmullen-Brophy ladies were complimentary, but the colonel looked askance, and made some rueful remark about a world changing too fast for an old chap like him.

That had been before. Today, the colonel had worse things than contemporary fashion to offend him.

'Outside the barracks?' said Fitzmullen-Brophy. 'A rebel flag? Outrageous! I've never heard of such a thing!'

'Hugh, calm down! I'm sure they have the matter in hand.'

Susan Fitzmullen-Brophy had seen her husband walk out the door in 1914 and not come back for six months, and then with a gunshot wound. She had good cause to be alarmed every time he made for the hall.

'Mrs. Fitzmullen-Brophy is quite right, sir. They were fetching a ladder by the time I left.'

'That's not going to do much to catch the blasted culprits!' the colonel raged. 'They should be going door to door. Where's my stick?'

As her husband stormed about, his wife had presence of mind enough to invent a distraction.

'Hugh! Hugh! I believe the dogs have got out! For heaven's sake don't let them dig up my delphiniums!'

'Never mind your blasted delphiniums, woman!'

'Hugh! How dare you speak to me that way!'

'Oh I am sorry, old thing. Really. My temper ran away with me. I'll see to the dogs directly. Who on earth left that door open? It was closed a moment ago.'

And the colonel, all fire gone, hurried apologetically out to round up his unmannered dogs and save his wife's flower beds.

Mrs. Fitzmullen-Brophy, who didn't even know if the dogs had taken advantage of the door she'd left open for them, considered the weather.

'Daniel, be a dear and take Hugh's scarf out to him.'

But Wyndham was forestalled.

'*I'll* go, Mummy.'

Molly Bryant, only daughter of the house, had come to stay for Christmas and an unspecified number of weeks either side of it. With her husband not yet free of the Army Service Corps, and using the last of his time there to make useful business contacts, Molly saw no reason to return to their home in Dublin just yet. In Kerry there was less risk of catching the influenza. In Kerry things were cheaper and there were people to help her in her motherhood.

'Daniel – take Baby.'

The baby's name was Mae, after a paternal grandmother and after the queen, but she was usually referred to simply as 'the baby' or less impersonally as 'Baby'. Only a few months old, she was an unhandy bundle of pudgy dissatisfaction. The sad look she fixed on Wyndham was unable to articulate her grievances, but it was clear that he was the answer to none of them.

At their first encounter they had done nothing beyond stare at each other warily. Since then they had established some sort of rapport. Wyndham didn't expect that the baby smile for him or express her delight to be on his lap, and the baby largely refrained from discharging noxious fluids onto his suit. All in all, minding the baby was less demanding and no more unhygienic than minding an infantry platoon. The baby still made him a little nervous, but he admired her forthright approach to life. He imagined they shared some sympathetic bond. All either of them wanted was comfort and feeding and sleep. With the baby on his lap, inspecting his finger, he found himself almost at peace. Certainly he was unable to fidget, and fidgeting had become his besetting sin since he'd come back from the war.

Maybe it was the whiskey, or maybe the deprivation of whiskey. On the colonel's advice he was trying to switch from cigarettes to a pipe, but a pipe merely gave him an excuse and a focus for fidgeting, and he would still smoke his way through half a packet of cigarettes when he was out of the house.

Chain-smoking aside, long walks did him good, even if the weather so often prevented them. And then there was his suit. It was far too good for rambles in the Kerry countryside, and for looking after a baby, and for a cold house with too many dogs. As soon as he was able, he intended to acquire clothes like the colonel wore: stout weaves that could stand up to rain and dogs and brambles. But that would cost money, and Wyndham was broke.

For much of the war the fiction had been maintained that His Majesty's officers were gentlemen of private means. There was a long-standing belief that paying officers a living wage encouraged the wrong sort. Wyndham did have private means, or rather he'd had private means once, in the form of traveller's cheques to the value of several hundred dollars. Tailored whipcord and barathea, whiskey at eight shillings a bottle, and wartime inflation had seen to that little fortune. The army had provided eight and a half shillings daily, but a junior officer on the Western Front did not practise thrift nor, with a life expectancy measured in weeks, did he save for the future.

There was money coming to him, he knew, but his position in the army had been so irregular that it would likely be a while. Until then he was an underqualified secretary and occasional nanny to the Fitzmullen-Brophys. And then?

A ring. Two tickets to America. A future.

14

In the verdict of history, weakness today would be even more criminal than the indifference of the past few months. Sedition must be rooted out of Ireland, once and for all.

—The Irish Times, 28 April 1916

There was nothing out of the ordinary in Fitzmullen-Brophy rummaging around upstairs, or in announcing that he and Wyndham were going for a walk. He was a man who could never sit still for very long. He was also a man to whom distance meant nothing. When the war began he had marched a scratch company of fusiliers from Kerry to Belgium. Four years, a bullet to the pelvis, and grandfatherhood had done little to slow the man down. They covered the miles into town at a rapid pace, with Wyndham naturally if self-consciously keeping in step.

'I didn't want to say it in front of my good wife, but I'm damned well not going to let that business of the flag lie. We're going to look into it, Dan.'

Beyond an inward *Oh dear*, Wyndham could think of nothing to say. No good would come of this. On the other hand, he'd been faithfully following Fitzmullen-Brophy since he'd first set foot in Ireland, and he was hardly going to stop now.

Their first stop was the tree itself, followed by the door of the house by which the tree stood. It was opened by a woman who was glad of the interruption.

If Mrs. Donoghue, as she introduced herself, was an agent of Sinn Féin she was a clever one. Rather than take the expected line of clamming up in the face of interrogation, she deluged this representative of the crown with talk.

'It's Colonel Fitzmullen-Brophy, isn't it? From out beyond Caherleheen, isn't that right? Sure, I'd often see you passing, Colonel. You have great energy altogether, striding along like that. And did I hear that your daughter, God bless her, is after having a child? A little girl, is it? Ah sure, isn't that lovely?'

Fitzmullen-Brophy beamed and blushed and tried to get a word in. Finally, after the baby, and the health of the mother, and the well-being of Mrs. Fitzmullen-Brophy, and the weather, God love us, it was Mrs. Donoghue herself who brought things around to the flag.

The flag! She had to laugh. Oh, but weren't they the bold lads! And the branches cut away! And they not hearing a thing at all, although the wind was bad that night and her hearing wasn't the best now, and Mr. Donoghue wouldn't hear the last trump if you blew it in his ear – not once his head had hit the pillow – he'd sleep as sound as sound. And right across from the barracks! And the grease painted all over the trunk! And the poor young soldier nearly losing his life having to climb up there! You had to laugh.

It took a while to disengage.

'I don't believe she did it, sir,' said Wyndham.

'Well of course not, dammit.'

'And you're really not planning on going door to door, are you? I mean, there aren't too many hours left before dark, and if everyone is as voluble as that lady...'

'No one is going to tell us anything, Dan.'

'Well, then. Shall we just pick up those bits and pieces for Mrs. Fitzmullen-Brophy and head back?'

'Of course not.'

'Oh.' *Oh dear*.

'Say what you like about this Sinn Féin nonsense, but at least it's served to draw these Fenian rascals out into the open. Can't keep in the shadows while you're speaking from a platform, what? Come on.'

After all this time Wyndham hardly needed reminding that everyone in Ireland knew everyone else, or if they didn't they knew someone who did. It took no time at all to track down a certain house on the outskirts of town that, to Fitzmullen-Brophy's delight, had a tree growing in front of it.

'Where are we, sir?' asked Wyndham.

'This, my boy, is the house of none other than that anti-conscription chap who was causing all that anti-conscription rot. Sinn Féin, Dan. A Fenian by another name. Shooting our chaps in the back in Dublin while we were in the trenches – if he had any courage, that is. I know his sort. I'll warrant the bravest thing he ever did was slip three votes into the ballot box at once.'

'Sir, you're not going to cause trouble.'

'It was he who started it, Dan. He, or one of his accomplices.'

'Sir, please.'

'Oh stop worrying, Dan. I don't know what's got into you. You used to be game for anything.'

Wyndham couldn't remember any such time.

'All we're going to do,' said Fitzmullen-Brophy, 'is give him a dose of his own medicine. Here – take this.'

And he was pulling from his pocket a yard or so of coloured material that revealed itself as bunting – all red, white and blue, with a couple of triangular little union jacks attached.

'Molly made it. For the coronation, you know. Don't suppose she'll mind me making use of it. Come on, Dan – up you get.'

'The tree, sir? No, sir. I'm afraid not. Not with the shoulder I broke at Messines.' *Not with the trousers I bought in Paris.*

Fitzmullen-Brophy didn't protest too much. He didn't even try to scale the tree himself. Instead his eyes lit upon a troupe of small boys, idly kicking something about the road. The colonel called to them.

'I say! I bet there's none of you can climb a tree!'

They looked at him puzzled, suspicious.

'Bet you can't climb *that* tree,' said Fitzmullen-Brophy, rounding on the tallest one, perhaps ten years old and evidently a leader type.

'I can so, sir,' said the boy, but not committing himself beyond that.

'Prove it,' said Fitzmullen-Brophy. 'Show me and I'll give you a penny.'

'That tree?'

'Here,' said the colonel, putting his money where his mouth was and reaching into his pocket. 'Well, well,' he said, seeing what he'd come out with. 'It seems I don't have a penny after all. Thruppence it'll have to be.' And he held up the silver coin, no bigger than a thumbnail, and the boys clamoured.

'Me! Sir! Sir! Me!'

But their leader wasn't leader for nothing, and he pushed them back.

Fitzmullen-Brophy laughed. 'That's the stuff! Tell you what – my eyes aren't up to much. Hang this bunting when you make it up there and I'll then know you did it.'

The boy could climb. Barefoot and determined, he made short work of it. To his friends' and Fitzmullen-Brophy's admiration, and Wyndham's alarm, he took considerable risks. Even though it was too late to do anything, Wyndham had to voice his concern, but Fitzmullen-Brophy was having none of it.

'Look at him go! Just look at him! Bless my soul but I used to be able to do that! A few more years and the regiment'll be lucky to have such a lad.'

And Wyndham considered every mad thing he himself had done just because Fitzmullen-Brophy had asked. He remembered the long march to Mons when he was the rawest of recruits. He remembered the screaming terror on the Aisne, where he'd first come under fire. And then there'd been the trenches in front of Armentières. And all for no more than a shilling a day. His life risked over and over again for a shilling and some cold bully beef.

He craned his neck to watch the boy edging along an upper branch, the bunting in his teeth.

'But don't you think three pence is a bit too generous, sir?'

15

Even though you may yourself escape, you will return in bad plight after losing all your men, in another man's ship, and you will find trouble in your house, which will be overrun by high-handed people.

—*Odyssey*, Book XI

Whichever way you were going in Cork was usually uphill, and as often as not into the rain. It wasn't raining today, which was something. The air stank of cow dung all the same. It always did up around here. The farmers came in from the country driving their stock before them, and the farmers made money, and cattle dealers made money, and the slaughterhouses made money, and everyone else had to live with the stink.

Of course, there were also those who made money off the people making money. The pubs made most of it, with the cattle deals being concluded over a jar. And there were the shopkeepers who sold whatever it was you couldn't buy up the country, or whatever you wanted when you were in town and were after a few jars and had money in your pocket. Some establishments dealt in quality merchandise and some were just huxter's shops. On a sloping side street, where the effluent had run downhill and crusted between the cobbles, never quite washed away by the rain, there was a shop that wasn't catering to the wealthier trade. From the window it was hard to tell even what was sold inside. That it was even a shop was only evident from the sign over the front.

Jerh. Moriarty.

Francis Moriarty stopped in the street and looked at the sign. He put down his kitbag and lit a cigarette. He wasn't up to coming home just yet.

Corporal Francis Moriarty, Royal Munster Fusiliers. He didn't look the part. No tall fur cap, no scarlet tunic, no brass shining like gold. Not even a badge to his cap or stripes to his sleeve. The uniform he wore had no distinctions. It was clean, more or less. It fitted, more or less. It was certainly good enough for a man just out after months behind the wire of a German prison camp. He'd been given two extra pairs of grand warm socks – did he think they'd have regimental badges to dole out too?

This wasn't how he'd wanted to come back.

With his fag nearly finished and neighbours beginning to notice him, he hefted his kitbag again just as two children ran out into the street, stopped, and stared at him. He stared back. The boy, slightly older than the girl, spoke.

'Are you my uncle Francie?'

The boy's name was either Finbarr or Anthony. Moriarty couldn't be sure which. The girl was Mary. Most girls were. He scowled at them and gave a grudging nod.

'Uncle Francie's back! Uncle Francie's back!' they screeched, and ran back inside. He reluctantly followed them. There was another boy inside, a little older again – maybe ten or eleven – and this was most certainly Finbarr. He was happy to abandon the school exercise book open on the table in front of him.

'Whatcha bring us back from Germany, Uncle Francie?'

'The Kaiser's bollocks on a string. Is there anything to eat?'

And the cry rang through the house, heralding the return of the warrior.

'Mam! Mam! Uncle Francie is using soldiers' language!'

16

Ireland to-day reasserts her historic nationhood the more confidently before the new world emerging from the war, because she believes in freedom and justice as the fundamental principles of international law; because she believes in a frank co-operation between the peoples for equal rights against the vested privileges of ancient tyrannies; because the permanent peace of Europe can never be secured by perpetuating military dominion for the profit of empire but only by establishing the control of government in every land upon the basis of the free will of a free people, and the existing state of war, between Ireland and England, can never be ended until Ireland is definitely evacuated by the armed forces of England.

—Message to the Free Nations of the World, Dáil Éireann, 21 January 1919

On the 14th of December, 1918, the United Kingdom had gone to the polls. In Ireland, once the Labour Party withdrew from the contest, it was a straightforward matter of nationhood. The choice was between embattled Unionism, increasingly irrelevant Home Rule, or surging Republicanism. Sinn Féin won the Irish constituencies by a landslide.

True to their election pledges, the winners declined to take their seats in the parliament of the United Kingdom. Instead, on the 21st of January 1919, they met in Dublin and declared that the Irish Republic, first proclaimed at Easter 1916, was established. Its democratic mandate notwithstanding, the assembly – called

Dáil Éireann – was, like the republic it represented, unrecognised by His Majesty's government. Many of the delegates were unable to attend the first meeting because they were in prison. In due course the body as a whole would be condemned as illegal.

Coincidentally, on the day the representatives of the new republic first sat in session, a detachment of the Irish Volunteers ambushed a shipment of explosives in Tipperary. The Volunteers – once the militia safeguarding Home Rule, but since converted to militant republicanism – got away with 160 pounds of gelignite. They left behind the bodies of the two constables who had made up the police escort.

Two days later the region was designated a Special Military Area. A week after that the Irish Volunteers published a justification for their action and any future actions of that nature. It was, in effect, a declaration of war against all forces of the Crown.

It was on that day that Wyndham was arrested.

He'd got into the habit of walking away from the roads, going by narrow paths and across fields, staying, as much as was possible, away from people. The solitude was a necessary respite from the genteel chaos of the Fitzmullen-Brophy house. He dressed in his army breeches and boots, an old hacking jacket and leather gaiters borrowed from the colonel, and – his one purchase – a soft felt hat resistant to the Irish weather. There was an adventurous tilt to the brim that appealed to him and served to demilitarise the ensemble of boots and trench coat.

In an earlier life he'd have wandered these wild acres in the hope of finding a host of golden daffodils, but not only was it the wrong time of year, he no longer believed that sublime nature would calm the restlessness in his soul.

For a start, he found himself uncomfortable with open spaces, no matter how bewitching they might be, and he didn't care to linger in any one spot. He avoided ridge lines. He took the lower path. He paused and listened at turns in the road. Boggy places and barbed wire fences made him shudder and change direction abruptly. Wherever he did stop, he unconsciously chose a place with stout cover, and when he smoked he held his cigarette cupped in his hand.

On that last afternoon in January he came out of a gap in the hedge onto the main road and was seen not by a German sniper but by two members of the Royal Irish Constabulary. They apprehended him without hesitation. Given that one held a carbine on him and the other a revolver, Wyndham guessed that he was suspected of more than trespassing.

In the vain hope that he wouldn't be recognised to the disgrace of the Fitzmullen-Brophys, he turned down the brim of his hat and turned up the collar of his coat, and let himself be marched off to the police barracks.

'I can tell by your accent, Mr. "Wyndham", that you're not from these parts.'

'I'm from Massachusetts. And it's Lieutenant Wyndham, actually.'

'Lieutenant in what, I wonder? And what brings you to Kerry? Would it be politics by any chance?'

The questioning was repetitive but not intense.

When an inspector came on the scene the case against this 'Wyndham' character was laid out. The questioning became more pointed.

'So you're an army officer.'

'Correct'

'And you were just taking a walk.'

'As I said to the other officers, yes.'

'But you have no identity papers on you.'

'No,'

'What you do have, on the other hand – besides articles of military clothing – is this notebook.'

'The contents of which are personal.'

'A personal code, do you mean? Because I can't seem to make much sense of it at all.'

Wyndham frowned, turned red, took a deep breath, and confessed that he'd been trying his hand at poetry. The inspector reconsidered the evidence in light of this revelation. He flicked through a few more pages, smiling and nodding.

'Roses are red, violets are blue. I think I understand.'

'Good. Might I have my notebook back?'

'Of course you can, sir. In a minute. Now that I see the whole picture, I must say that it's all in keeping with that elegant green tie you're wearing.'

During the war it had been the fashion among racier junior officers to push the definitions of uniform to their limit. Regulations specified khaki, but it was a colour of many shades. Thus breeches grew paler and shirts grew darker. Privately purchased items deviated quite widely from the prescribed norm. For some, the hunting stock or patterned scarf was the preferred neckwear. The proudly Irish Wyndham had in a wild moment bought himself a tie in green silk. A cigarette burn had ended its decorative days but Wyndham reckoned it was still good enough for a country gentleman to wear on his ramblings.

'But of course as an American you'd have no idea that the wearin' of the green might single you out as a man of Fenian sympathies, now would you?'

'It's just a tie, Inspector. Until specific laws are passed against clothing, I intend to wear whatever style and colour I like. Now I've explained often enough who I am, and I believe you now must either charge me or let me go.'

'You'd think it would be that simple, wouldn't you? And before the war you might well have been right. Why, even last month you might have been right. But DORA casts her net ever wider these days. That'd be the Defence Of the Realm Act to you. It gives us all sorts of powers I'm barely getting the measure of yet. And with certain types coming travelling around the country – on the run from Dublin and organising Volunteers in Limerick, say, or wanted in Belfast and gathering intelligence in Kerry – we have to be on our guard.'

'For the last time: I am an officer in the Royal Munster Fusiliers.'

The inspector smiled and pushed the notebook across the table to him.

'I know well who you are, Mr. Wyndham. You're staying with the Fitzmullen-Brophys out Caherleheen way. I'll not keep you any longer.'

Deflated and angry, Wyndham went on his way. His time in the army had somewhat eroded his middle-class respect for the police. The books he'd been reading had also caused to evolve in him a romantic sympathy for the cause of Irish freedom. These past wasted hours – nervous and humiliating – had heightened that sympathy and stripped all the romance from it. At least for the time it took him to walk home, he counted the RIC his enemy, and the enemy of Ireland alike. The words 'Royal' and 'Irish' had no business together.

His anger was refuelled every time he remembered the inspector's parting remark about that stupid notebook. After explaining the act of government that was binding the realm in ever tighter bonds, he'd at least, he said, given Wyndham something that would rhyme with Nora.

17

The people of Ireland ought not to fraternise, as they often do, with the forces which are the main instruments in keeping them in subjection.

—Éamon de Valera, 10 April 1919

A letter came, notifying Wyndham that the day was close at hand when he would cease to be a soldier. This was rather disconcerting because he'd thought that day had already been and gone, but it transpired that Fitzmullen-Brophy, full colonel or not, could not merely wave his hand and discharge a man from the army. There was, as Wyndham was informed by official letter, a dreary bureaucratic process to be gone through before His Majesty would fully dispense with the services of Daniel P. Wyndham, Lieutenant (temporary).

At least his final settling of accounts with the crown might see some money come Wyndham's way at last. His wardrobe needed a middle ground between cosmopolitan dandy and Fenian desperado. Some gifts for the Fitzmullen-Brophys would make him feel less like the poor relation. He fancied getting a bicycle of his own. And then, never far from the forefront of his mind, there was a ring for Nora.

If he ever saw Nora again, that was. Her communications, always desultory, had gone completely silent of late. His lovesick yearning was periodically turning to dejection, veering sometimes into downright resentment.

So – an engagement ring or a single ticket back to America. A little money would come in handy for either. For this present moment, having learned never to presume on the army's bounty, he would be satisfied with some pipe tobacco.

By coincidence, the customer in front of him in the tobacconist was a soldier too, evidently with something to vex him besides being kept in uniform months after the Kaiser had packed it in.

The uniform belonged to the Duke of Lancaster's Own Yeomanry which had been occupying part of the Munsters' barracks since the previous spring.

The girl behind the counter – and she could have been no more than fourteen – did not appear too concerned with serving her customer. Indeed, she was making quite a point of it, her arms folded, her gaze directed resolutely to a corner of the ceiling, while the soldier stood and fumed.

Wyndham's arrival broke the impasse.

'Yes, sir,' she said. 'How can I help you, sir?'

'I believe this man was before me,' said Wyndham.

'How can I help you, sir?' repeated the girl testily.

'Oi! I was here first!' said the soldier.

'He was actually here first,' confirmed Wyndham.

The girl took a deep breath and tried again.

'*How* can I help *you*,' she said. '*Sir.*'

Wyndham had no idea how long this drama had been going on, but it was plain to see that the soldier had had enough of it.

'Never bloody mind him! You bloody look at me when I'm talking to you!'

The girl's face was bright red and she was trembling, but she didn't take her eyes off Wyndham.

'We don't serve that class of person, sir,' she explained through tight lips.

'That class—?'

'Soldiers, sir. Nor policemen neither. Forces of the crown, sir.'

It was too much for the soldier.

'I want twenty Woodbines, you little Shinner bitch!'

Well that was it. And again that nice Mr. Wyndham had to pretend to be Dangerous Dan, the by-God tough guy again – or at least a version that an Englishman would appreciate. He squared his shoulders and conjured up his haughtiest demeanour.

'You will not speak to the young lady that way, Private,' he said.

The soldier didn't need this, and he wasn't going to be pushed around by a civilian in an Irish shop.

'You bloody well stay of it, you.'

Wyndham had faced down worse in his time. This fellow might have been loud and angry, but he had no medal ribbons on his breast nor service chevrons on his sleeve. If he'd spent his war anywhere livelier than this, it hadn't been at the front. And of course Wyndham had one more thing over the man.

'I should warn you, Private, that you are speaking to an officer. Now damn well stand to attention.'

'Sir.'

'Apologise to the young lady.'

'Yes, sir. Sorry, miss.'

'Now get out.'

'Sir.'

And then Wyndham had to spoil his heroic moment by wondering if the young lady could furnish him with an ounce of Evening Flake – he being a just-confessed officer of the crown, after all. The young lady was at a loss until a man who'd entered unseen behind Wyndham gave her the nod.

'It's alright, Kitty,' said the newcomer with a wink. 'Sure isn't he out of uniform?'

Wyndham acknowledged all concerned with a smile, paid up and left. He thankfully noticed that the soldier wasn't waiting for him outside. It would have been unlikely, he had to admit, but he wasn't feeling sure of himself. As some great strategist had no doubt said, victory can unbalance as much as defeat.

He did notice, however, that the man from the shop followed him out. There was something familiar about him. Wyndham was sure he'd seen the man before. Of course, he'd probably seen half the people in the street before but that was different. Had he seen the man earlier on the road into town? The same intelligent idler, with sharp eyes and easy gait? A fish in water if ever Wyndham had seen one.

Wyndham changed direction abruptly, heading up a street where he had no business. After fifty yards he stopped just as abruptly and looked in a shop window, seeing not the goods on display but the passers-by reflected in the glass. Then he quickly headed back the way he'd come, switched down a lane, and spent a good five minutes in zig-zags and dog-legs before he turned his nose for home. He was a mile on his way, alone on the road, when he thought he heard rapid footsteps some distance behind. He didn't look over his shoulder but waited until he rounded a bend in the road and then he slipped through a gate and ducked down behind a low wall.

He waited. There was no doubt about the footsteps. They came closer. A man's footfall – hurrying, hesitating and hurrying again. Just as whoever it was went past, Wyndham stood up and stepped back into the road. It was the man from the shop. Wyndham was genuinely surprised to have his suspicions vindicated.

'You there!' he called out. 'Have you been following me?'

The man turned and grinned. 'There you are!'

'I said have you been following me?'

'I have, seeing as you ask.'

'Why?'

'Orders, Mr. Wyndham – or should that be Lieutenant Wyndham?'

'Who the hell are you?'

But of course Wyndham knew the answer to that. Still a British officer, it was only natural that he should be a target of the Irish

Volunteers' attention.

He'd had a run-in with them before – shadowy figures stealing army rifles, conducting covert meetings in derelict houses, spreading low tendrils of dissent across the soil of Ireland. They were the latest iteration of the oath-bound secret societies that had been plotting revolution in the shadows for a hundred years and more.

'Gearóid Ó Tuama,' said the secret revolutionary without being asked.

From the O in the middle, Wyndham recognised it as a name, but would have hesitated to pronounce it unaided.

'I suppose I really should be putting a bit more menace into this, but what you did in the shop made me think better of you. You don't deserve having me as your threatening shadow all the hours of the day – and sure haven't I better things to be doing myself?'

And his smile was so open that Wyndham was compelled to half-return it.

'Menace?' he asked. 'Threats?'

To one who'd lived for endless months with only a few hundred yards and some barbed wire between him and men who would willingly creep up in the dark and kill him with a sharpened entrenching tool, this Ó Tuama looked positively friendly. Provincial middle class would be how Wyndham would have categorised him. The son of a moderate small-town businessman, perhaps studying for one of the professions. Not in the least threatening. No menace about him at all.

'Look,' said Ó Tuama, 'I'll just come right out and say it. We want to know everything there is to know about officers of the crown and we don't mind if they know that we know. We don't want you lot getting comfortable.'

'I think you'll find, sir, that I barely qualify as an officer of the crown anymore. I'm resigning my commission as soon as I work out how. You can take the credit for that if it helps any.'

Ó Tuama laughed at that.

'You're very generous. No, I don't imagine you'll be any trouble to us. But Colonel Fitzmullen-Brophy on the other hand...'

And now Wyndham was on his guard. Up until now he'd had nothing to lose in this fight.

'What about the colonel?' he asked, mentally squaring off and setting his fists.

'Well I'm sure he's a grand man altogether, but a dim view was taken over that little bit of bunting he hung outside Peadar Hegarty's house. He keeps up with that kind of carry-on and it's not going to go well for him. That's a warning, by the way: not a threat.'

'The colonel's retired.'

'So he should keep out of things. Look, I'd hate to see any harm come to the fellow. Would you ever do me a favour and warn him yourself? He doesn't deserve the likes of me sending him intimidating letters or – God help us – turning up at his door some dark night. So would you do that for me? Just have a talk with him?'

Maybe Wyndham should have stood defiant, but all he said was, 'Colonel Fitzmullen-Brophy is a rather independent man, you know. He doesn't really heed a talking-to.'

'Sure try anyway. At least keep him from doing anything more. Start him on crossword puzzles or something. Just for the love of God keep him away from speech-making and flag-waving and all that codology. Please.'

Wyndham stammered out something along the lines of giving it a try, and earned a broad smile from Ó Tuama.

'I'm most grateful to you, Lieutenant Wyndham – or Mr. Wyndham as it should be,' he laughed. 'I knew you were a gentleman even before I saw you in the shop. The Irish Republic is grateful to you!' And he doffed his cap. 'I'll leave you go so.'

'You're not going to follow me anymore?'

'Sure why should I? I know where you're going and it's a bit out of my way.'

The way Wyndham understood it, Irish independence was an inevitability. Before the war independence had meant Home Rule, and it had been almost but not quite fact. Now independence meant the Republic, which happened to be illegal, but to Wyndham that seemed only a technicality. The Irish people had voted for Home Rule and it had (almost) become law. Now they had voted for a republic, and if the government in Westminster was behindhand in recognising it, then that was surely something that could be worked out in due course. At present this working out entailed occasional shootings. That bothered Wyndham much less than it would have done before his time on the Western Front, where even a quiet day might bring casualties from casual sniping and impersonal shelling. And the upset in Ireland now? Well it wasn't like the Easter Rising – a full-dress bid to seize the country and overthrow the government.

If he wanted to take the high ground, then he could declare that he'd fought for the freedom of small nations, and nations didn't come much smaller than this one, where everyone seemed to know everyone else's business. Instinctively though, he just liked the idea of Irish freedom. Leaving high-flown argument aside, it boiled down to this:

Nora believed in the Republic.

This Ó Tuama fellow seemed like a reasonable sort.

The Easter Rising had been ages ago.

Oh yes – and the police had been rude to him.

So he didn't go all out and start subscribing to seditious broadsheets, but when he read the newspapers he tried to see things from the other side. Republican activities were not sedition. This was not a revolution. Sinn Féin was merely the voice of the Irish people speaking to a British government that would not listen. If the odd shooting was the only way to answer British intransigence, then so be it.

Wyndham had been brought up to revere the first shots fired at Lexington and Concord. Seeing things that way, he could find no reason to condemn the shots fired in the Tipperary ambush.

So the next time he saw Ó Tuama in the street he smiled and tipped his hat to him, and was happy to have the gesture returned. He never did sit down with the colonel, knowing it would be useless to expect the man to rethink the certainties of a lifetime, but he ran the colonel's errands for him and hinted to Mrs. Fitzmullen-Brophy that it would be better that her husband stay away from the barracks, and from political gestures, and from Tralee as a whole, and she was in agreement.

No one ever did trouble the Fitzmullen-Brophys. No slogans were chalked on their walls. No one refused to serve them in the shops. If forthright and gentlemanly types like Gearóid Ó Tuama were making the Irish Republic, then Wyndham was all for it.

When he was tidying away the vestiges of his career as a soldier of King George, he found himself wondering what to do with the various manuals and army books he'd acquired during his officer training. It didn't seem too rebellious an act to donate them discreetly to the local Volunteer Hall.

18

I went to the war for no other reason than I wanted to see what war was like, to get a gun, to see new countries and to feel a grown man.

—Tom Barry, *Guerrilla Days In Ireland*

Wyndham's formal demobilisation was to be done in Dublin. Perhaps it could have been done in Cork or even in Tralee if he'd cared to look into it, or practise some army wiles, but he was glad of an opportunity to go to Dublin. And he wanted to wear uniform one last time.

He was proud of his uniform – not because it marked him as an officer, but because it was the manliest outfit he could imagine. He'd paid enough down the years to make it show him off to his best advantage. He wasn't even sure if he'd be expected to appear in uniform for this tying-up of business, but he was damned if he wasn't going to give his military persona a final outing.

It was a thoughtful journey – sombre in its way. It was the end of Daniel Wyndham, Munster Fusilier.

After all his long talks with Fitzmullen-Brophy he knew what he was leaving behind: the regiment – his regiment – that had first guarded England's trading post in the Bay of Bengal; the regiment that had matched itself against all the nations of the East.

In the early months of 1805 the men of the regiment had thrown themselves against the Maratha stronghold of Bhurtpore. They had dug their trenches, laid their guns and

then, in the final desperate moment, had launched themselves against the walls deemed to be impregnable. To cross flooded ditches, to fight uphill through a narrow breach, through the galling fire of a determined enemy, was so terrible a feat that no man could be expected to undertake it more than once. Four times the regiment assaulted the walls of Bhurtpore, scaling bastions with their bare hands – their faces so blackened with powder that European and Indian couldn't be told apart – and four times they fell back, leaving their dead, shot-torn, sabred and bayoneted, behind them.
In the end the commander, General Lord Lake, had inspected the remnant, too few now even to labour in the siege lines.
'Only fit for fighting,' said Lord Lake with regret.
And the regiment? They apologised to His Lordship for not having changed their shirts in weeks.

This was the regiment that had gradually absorbed so many footloose Irishmen as to gain an Irish character and an Irish identity to entwine with its Indian one: this was the regiment that had, for a few years, enfolded within itself a wandering New Englander who'd known no better.

He'd been without a clean shirt in the flooded trenches south of the Ypres Salient, and in the shallow ditches between Guillemont and Ginchy. He'd led men like the men of Bhurtpore. They'd followed him on a hot day across the fire-swept ground, where many of them no doubt still lay.

Staying in the regiment, wearing the tiger badge, wouldn't do those men any good at all: not the men of the Somme and not the men of Bhurtpore either. They'd stay as dead as ever whether Wyndham honoured them or not.

But it made him sad all the same.

In Dublin there was another old Dirty Shirt that Wyndham had been wanting to see for a long time. This was one of the fallen of the Somme, who'd been lucky enough to make it out on a stretcher.

Bartholomew Curran was an old comrade. An almost-member of parliament in the Home Rule cause, he had learned to be an officer alongside Wyndham when Fitzmullen-Brophy had commanded his short-lived battalion in Cork when the war was young and optimistic. Curran had been wounded on the Somme and that had been enough war for him. He had beaten Wyndham by a couple of years in the relinquishing of the king's commission.

It was not the reunion Wyndham had hoped for. Curran was not the same man who'd braved the German shrapnel north of Guillemont. It wasn't just that he'd grown fat and had aged visibly. Unlike Wyndham who was still wearing his Munster badges even though he'd been out of the army for hours, Curran had disassociated himself as much as possible from his brief stint as a British officer. It had been a career misstep not in keeping with his vocal nationalism. He didn't hide his irritation that Wyndham was in uniform. It meant that they couldn't dine at Curran's club lest Curran's patriotic credentials be besmirched.

Wyndham was sad to realise that Curran had fallen behind the times. A few years earlier his opinions had been shrewd and radical. Now he sounded pompous and out of date. The wild romantic who had cast aside everything to serve in the Great War for Freedom was now put out by Wyndham not possessing evening clothes.

They stayed up late talking, but it was a reunion that Wyndham could have done without – and not just because he was left the next morning with his first hangover since before the armistice. His spirits were still depressed when he found a jewellers, but could not bring himself to go in. Seeing him staring at the window display, a passing idler said: 'If it's the price of the joolery that's stopping you, Lieutenant, you should have been here three years back. You could have filled your pockets with rings and watches! Sure that's what they was all doing – rebels and throops alike!'

And he passed on his way laughing, leaving Wyndham even less inclined to buy anything.

In the end it was neither the joke nor his new-found habit of frugality, but a superstitious impulse that decided him. Empty-handed, he went to catch his train. Of all the imponderables in this uncertain world, Nora Maxfield ranked high. He had once carried around a gold cigarette case for more than a year before she'd deigned to receive it. Presuming that she'd accept an engagement ring was just asking for trouble.

He had a compartment to himself until Newbridge, where two army officers came aboard. They were both senior to Wyndham and they invaded his space with the dismissive Old Army rudeness that the war had not managed to kill. They had both been drinking. Despite their being engaged in a conversation that had endured for several whiskies, Wyndham gathered that the two men were strangers to one another. Indeed one of them – a major in the Warwicks – already appeared unhappy to have made the acquaintance of the other – a major in the Army Service Corps, and was contributing to the conversation in grudging monosyllables only.

Unsurprisingly, the subject under discussion was the lamentable state of Irish affairs at the moment.

'Bloody disgraceful!'

No response.

'I said it's bloody disgraceful. A policy of shoot-on-sight is the only answer.'

A desultory grunt.

'What they should do is send in the Air Corps, or the Air Force, or whatever they're calling themselves now. Make themselves ruddy useful. Bomb these blasted Sinn Feiners. Machine-gun them from the air.'

That elicited a reluctant reply. 'Bit indiscriminate, don't you think?'

'Not a bit of it. They're all blasted Shinners. Look at the election results. And if they're sheltering bandits who shoot policemen in the back then they're just as guilty. They're all the same. Bomb the bloody lot of them.'

Getting no argument one way or another, the ASC major turned narrow eyes on Wyndham. 'You're not Irish, are you?'

Wyndham shook his head. It was the licence the ASC man needed to carry on. His companion wasn't interested. He'd taken a pull from a hip flask and lain his head against the window. The ASC man wasn't going to let him get away with that.

'We're in a damned war zone! The Irish are as bad as the Germans! Worse! At least you knew where Fritz was. Knew he wasn't going to sneak up and shoot you in the back when you thought you were safe. Well, you're not bloody safe! Cowardly bastards are all around us. Could strike at any time. And you're not even wearing your holster.'

It was true. The major in the Warwicks didn't have a holster. He did, on the other hand, have more wound stripes than Wyndham had ever seen on one sleeve before. How had the man even found time to be wounded if he was always being treated for wounds? Perhaps it was only fair that he be given a little peace and quiet now.

The ASC major was in no mood to permit a withdrawal. He raised the stakes by unbuttoning his own holster and drawing out the big Webley revolver.

'*That's* the stuff to give 'em! *That's* all they understand!'

'Oh put that away, man! You'll have someone's eye out!'

Annoyed that his call to arms hadn't been met with any enthusiasm, the ASC major holstered his pistol and the Warwick determinedly folded his arms and closed his eyes.

Having lost his audience, and with it the righteousness of his stance, the ASC man turned on Wyndham again.

'Here's another one. You don't have a blasted gun either, do you?'

No. Wyndham didn't have a revolver. The one he'd owned had been taken from him by some German storm troops in March of 1918 and he'd never replaced it. He did have a Mauser automatic that had been acquired in a dubious transaction a long time before, but he'd never found any ammunition for it.

'Waltzing around, blithe as you please. What are you going to do when you run afoul of a horde of Fenian gunmen?'

Wyndham was actually a preternaturally good pistol shot, by fluke of nature rather than by practice. It was his only military skill and – typically – one with no practical application. The war on the Western Front had not been fought by gentlemen exchanging pistol shots at close range.

The counter-questions crowded in on him.

How many in a horde? Will they give me fair warning?

But he hadn't even opened his mouth when the angry major said, 'Typical!' and decisively folded his arms and withdrew into a sulk, which shortly became sleep.

The train stopped at Limerick Junction and the two majors stayed sleeping. The ASC major was drooling from the corner of his mouth. Wyndham looked him over properly.

No ribbons of imperial service. No decorations of any kind. Not even a wound stripe. There were Army Service Corps men who had shared the danger, who had delivered ammunition under fire. This wasn't one of them. This was a man who'd earned his promotion behind a desk. This was a man who'd never held anything more dangerous than a clipboard, now advocating that civilians be shot to keep him safe.

His holster was still unbuttoned. Wyndham shook him by the

shoulder but elicited nothing beyond a mumble. Then he took the man's revolver and shoved it into his own pocket. It wasn't that he was joining the revolution, but if anyone deserved to have the weapon, it most surely should not be its original owner.

Perhaps when the major woke up and raised a fuss he'd remember a quiet fusilier lieutenant who'd been sitting opposite, but they'd never find him. That officer of the Royal Munster Fusiliers had ceased to exist.

19

I find that it is the pleasant part, the good comradeship, the recollection of gallant deeds, the humorous incidents, that remain most in one's memory and that one most frequently recalls. The horrors, mercifully, are, comparatively speaking, relegated to oblivion.

—Life of an Irish Soldier: reminiscences of General Sir Alexander Godley

The army was surprising in its bounty. Lieutenant Wyndham, on formal demobilisation, received a gratuity of more than two hundred pounds – which wasn't much for four years' service and too many moments of mortal peril, but was still more than two hundred buckshee quid. On top of that there was a modest weekly allowance to tide him over until he found employment, and that meant he didn't have to find employment any time soon.

Instead he bought a bicycle.

He bought gifts for the Fitzmullen-Brophys, and clothes that would withstand the Irish weather, and a bicycle. He was going to do what he'd first come to Ireland to do. He was going to see the place.

Of course, he had already seen it. He had lived in North Cork for the best part of a year, marching on its roads, navigating across its fields with map and compass, assessing every eminence and declivity of its ground. But he'd had enough of tactical appreciations and military precision. He wanted to idle his way down the byroads, and let time pass unmeasured, and hear old tales and live in a world where nothing happened.

He still had his books of poetry and heroic legend, even if they didn't mean so much to him any more. The actuality of love had put the wild romances into perspective, and he'd had more than his fill of war stories. It was less easy now to thrill to an account of Cuchulain slaying right and left when you'd seen an infantry attack broken by concentrated machine-gun fire. Nevertheless, the books were Wyndham's talismans these years past, and they didn't take up much room.

The war had taught him to travel light. A few things wrapped in his old waterproof cape strapped to the back, his old blackthorn across the handlebars, and the open road was his.

On the first bright day in April he set out, not knowing or caring where. If he was feeling energetic he took the wilder path. Otherwise he followed the contours of the land, meandering with the road. Rain and wind rarely stopped him for long. He found the passing discomfort preferable to being stuck indoors under a strange roof. He was happy to talk to people, but found he liked being alone better. If he couldn't have Nora then he'd rather not have anybody.

He didn't know where she was. Her last letter had been as vague and noncommittal as always. Someday her unit would come back from Macedonia, or Bulgaria, or wherever it was now, and she would adjust herself to civilian life, and then – whenever that might be – she would decide what to do with herself, and Wyndham would be on hand to steer her decision by might and main. But until that uncertain time came, he might as well have the cold wind and the bright sun; his muscles working and his mind as empty as he could make it.

He was away for more than ten days. Twice he was stopped by police, but he nowadays made sure to carry papers identifying him as a citizen of the United States and as one of His Majesty's lately commissioned officers – take your pick. The RIC didn't keep him in either case.

The only other trouble he met was from the odd farm dog, but that was what the blackthorn was for. A man did not live long in the company of Colonel Hugh Fitzmullen-Brophy without knowing how to handle unruly dogs.

He came back to Tralee leaner, fitter and sunburned. After a couple of days' rest he went off again, and this time he wasn't back for the best part of a month.

He wended his way northwards and then, obeying a long-ignored impulse, he found himself in the valley of the Boyne, tracing the footsteps of bygone heroes. It was for this that he had first come to Ireland, five years ago now. Then, wars had been noble affairs fought with spears and chariots, and the woman of his dreams had been Niamh Golden-haired or Deirdre of the Sorrows.

He trespassed across fields to look at old things. He climbed ancient mounds and tried to see the land as it once had been. With his fingers he traced the spirals cut in dead stones. But something had happened to his imagination, and the legends that had once enraptured – the stories that he still read in his hotel of an evening – no longer lived for him as they once had.

He stood on the Hill of Tara. He went all the way north to Navan Fort. He couldn't see Cuchulain, with the flames of the hero light about his head, like a red-thorn bush in a gap.

It was only when he found himself at a little bridge in the town of Ardee that the ghosts appeared to him, but they were not the ghosts he'd sought.

Once, so very long ago, this had been a ford, where Ferdia had fought against Cuchulain, his dearest comrade, and had been slain by him after three days of battle. Wyndham knew the story so well he could recite it in parts, and though there was nothing to see of the old combat, Wyndham saw it.

A ford the ravens will be croaking over. A fight that will be heard of till the end of life and time.

The wheel of a passing cart or somesuch had scraped moss from the low wall and scored the stone.

...And at the ford where Calatin and his sons got their death, there is a stone with the marks of their sword-hilts, and the butt-ends of their spears on it to this day.

Cuchulain had stood on the north bank, there where the town was now, and his enemies had come against him from the south, day upon day. The river crossing had been a ford because the engineers had demolished the bridge. The men of Connacht, in helmets of steel, not of bronze, had infiltrated their way forward, spreading out along the bank, always more of them. Faces masked, snout-like, with blank glazed eyes, against the drifting chlorine, laced with the invisible phosgene.

...Every man of them had poison in himself and in his weapons; and there was not one of them ever made a cast of a spear or a stone that missed, and there was no one that would be wounded by them but he would die, either on the spot or within the week.

And the mustard gas so thick that it condensed in the air and dripped from the gutters.

Always more of them, with those stripped-down machine-guns they always had so many of, and if you held them off long enough you only gave them time to bring up their light mortars.

...So they began with their casting weapons, and they took their protecting shields, and their round-handled spears, and their little quill spears, and their ivory-hilted knives, and their ivory-hafted spears, eight of each of them they had.

Lewis Gun and *Null-acht-fünfzehn*, with 'Spandau' stamped on the cover plate. Seven point nine-two millimetre and point three-o-three inch, *flying from them and to them like bees on the wing on a fine summer day.*

> *...And the witches of the valley screamed from the rims of their shields and from the hilts of their swords, and from the handles of their spears.*

Eighteen-pounder shrapnel answering seven-seven whizz-bangs. A man could usually tell to a nicety the calibre of the shell that screamed towards him, but with both sides firing thick and fast on the same target there was nothing to distinguish in the noise and in the sudden bruising changes in air pressure that could make the nose and ears bleed.

Last March – or was it April by then? – the men of Ireland, the 16th Division, picked up and thrown about like rag dolls.

> *...Till there was nothing left of them but limbs and little pieces eastward and westward over the whole face of the ford.*

Cuchulain had to hold the crossing or the army of Queen Maeve would push through to Amiens and cut the railway line that held the whole Western Front together.

'Sir? Are you alright there at all?'

Wyndham wondered how long he'd been standing at this little bridge by this little town. Long enough to invite the concern of one of the locals anyway. He pulled himself together. He was just a harmless tourist, taking in the sights.

Nothing to worry about.

He offered a smile to the man who had stopped.

'*I have fought with heroes, with chiefs of armies, with troops, with hundreds before now,*' he said, and remounted his bicycle.

On his return to Tralee he found a letter waiting for him from Nora. It had arrived the day after he'd left. She was in Cork and hoping that maybe they could meet.

20

Do not blame me; I often lie awake
Thinking that all things trouble your bright head.
How beautiful it is—your broad pale forehead
Under a cloudy blossoming of hair!

—W.B. Yeats, *The Land Of Heart's Desire*

Wyndham was wearing his Parisian suit, sponged and pressed. His tie was expensive. His shirt collar was as white as could be. He'd brushed his hair to a glossy sheen and applied just enough oil to keep it from being disarrayed by his hat. He had shaved so close it was dangerous. His fingernails and his socks were without blemish. His shoe leather could not have been faulted by the sergeant of the guard. He hadn't been this well prepared for the Battle of Messines.

The house to which he'd been directed was in a quietly prosperous street, sufficiently respectable to have a maid to open the door for him. All he knew was that this was the McInerney house and that Nora was staying here.

He was conducted through a polished hall to an over-furnished sitting room where two women were standing, waiting for him. One was middle-aged and smiling in welcome. The other was Nora.

Nora Maxfield was a perfect case of beauty being in the eye of the beholder. If you'd long held dreamy fantasies of the queens and heroines of Irish legend, then her striking height and magnificent colouring were without a doubt beautiful. If not, all you might see would be an awkwardly tall woman with violently red hair, whose expression ranged from guarded to hostile and back again. Wyndham was in the first camp. His first sight of her was a physical sensation running from throat to groin, with the point of impact dead centre in his chest.

They'd parted a year and a half before in a fever of kisses and entreaties and cigarette smoke. If it hadn't been for the great German offensive to take his mind off it, Wyndham might well have found their separation unbearable.

And now here she was: so immediate and real and yet so unlike his memories or dreams.

She was in civilian clothes – the first time he'd ever seen her so. They had lived within a war. Everything they'd done together had been bounded by the war, and now that world of theirs was gone, and they had to make their own decisions and dress in their own clothes.

And she was smiling nervously, uncomfortable with the nuances of polite company, and because having a young man was an admission of weakness.

And she had cut her hair.

Wyndham was not up to date with ladies' fashions. He did not go to the cinema or peruse the illustrated papers. The women of Tralee were not especially *à la mode*. He wasn't used to women's hair cut short. Maybe on the Parisian coquettes it looked chic. Maybe on the Hollywood glamour girls it looked cute. On an ambulance driver in the dust and mosquitoes of the Struma Valley it looked neither, but it was practical.

Even though it had been months since her hair had been freed of the weight of everything below the jawline, it hadn't yet calmed down. Rather than behave itself and lie straight, or even curl endearingly below the cheekbone, Nora's hair stood out from the sides of her head in a way that the uncharitable eye might liken to ill-laid thatch.

In all the long months and miles that had kept them apart, he'd dreamed of what he'd say at this moment. 'You've cut your hair,' hadn't been it.

And Nora, because effortless social grace was still not her strong suit, held out her hand, but then used it to indicate their hostess.

'This is Mrs. Julia McInerney.'

'Delighted,' said Mrs. McInerney. 'Now sit down. Sit down, both of you, and we'll have some tea. Mary, you can bring in the tea.'

The ensuing conversation reminded Wyndham of the Chinese labour companies he'd seen when he'd accompanied Fitzmullen-Brophy to France after the armistice. All along the old front line these gangs had been engaged in clearing away the barbed wire – tackling great tangles of the stuff, all uprooted and balled-up by shellfire. It all somehow had to be untangled at least enough to allow it to be bundled into the back of a lorry before being carted off. It was thankless work, made all the more trying by the possibility of finding unexploded munitions or undiscovered corpses in the midst of it all.

What Wyndham untangled over a cup of tea and a too-dry scone was that Nora had been back in Ireland since March but had been 'getting herself settled'. The settlement consisted of taking a room in Mrs. McInerney's house and a job in Mrs. McInerney's business.

It was a draper's shop, left to Mrs. McInerney by her late husband (God be good to him), and Nora would be working behind the counter. Wyndham would never have thought Nora to have the temperament suitable to shop girl, and hadn't known her to have any experience or interest in the drapery business, but then he knew hardly anything about her at all.

'I'm teaching her a little book-keeping,' said Mrs. McInerney, who was carrying most of the weight of this conversation.

'Julia's teaching me a little book-keeping,' confirmed Nora.

And that was a thing that Wyndham noticed: that Mrs. McInerney was 'Julia' even though she was an employer, and much older, and no relation at all. Indeed, the connection between the two women was most recent – a mutual acquaintance having put them in touch with one another only a little while before. The employment and the accommodation, it seemed, were largely secondary to what had brought them together. The main thing had been an enthusiasm for some sort of social or political club, which sounded to Wyndham something like nationalist suffragettes.

'*Cumann na mBan*,' explained Nora with some small pride.

'I beg your pardon? Come on *who*?'

She clarified, and with greater ease and more animation than she'd shown so far, she began to tell him of meetings and organisation. But Mrs. McInerney headed her off, and took charge again.

'So Nora tells me you're from Massachusetts, is it? My Barty, God rest him, had a brother in Boston. Do you know any McInerneys in Boston? I suppose you wouldn't. I imagine it's an awfully big place. Will you have another scone, Mr. Wyndham?

'But we had plenty of Americans over here ourselves. Sailors. Nora and I went down one Sunday to have a look at them. Down to the harbour where they had all their ships anchored. They weren't allowed to come up to town themselves, you know. The sailors. A bit wild. I suppose you would be too if you were cooped up on one of those little submarine chasers. Are you sure you won't have another scone?'

And thus she drove things along until she tactfully looked at the clock.

'I'm sure the two of you have plenty to be talking about. I've things to be doing around the house so I'll leave you to catch up.'

And then the Nora that Wyndham remembered was sitting across from him, wary and disapproving, waiting for him to say the wrong thing.

He put down his teacup deliberately, looked her square in the eye, and took a deep breath. She got in before him.

'Are you going to propose?' she demanded.

'Nora, I—'

'Are you? Because you tried that once already and I said no then as well.'

He attempted to marshal some sort of answer to that, but it was difficult under her hard gaze, with her toe drumming nervously on the carpet.

'Nora—'

'I don't want you thinking you have some sort of hold on me just because we…' She lowered her voice. '…Because we got into a bit of mischief once.'

'Rather more than once,' he corrected her. He couldn't help himself, and he marvelled at the look of utter outrage she hit him with. She leaned in close so as not to scandalise the whole house.

'I never heard the like!' she said. 'And it was one night so that only counts as once! And I thought better of you!'

'I apologise, Nora. That was just downright unmannerly of me. I am sorry.'

She straightened up, still scowling.

'We're not in France now,' she said.

'Of course.'

After that it was difficult to get the conversation started again. They both made hesitant tries, with Wyndham making a tentative start before tripping up over something Nora seemed to be about to say, and with Nora opening her mouth and then clamming up again before a word came out. Wyndham got a grip and went back to where he'd begun.

'You've cut your hair,' he said.

She touched it self-consciously. 'Do you like it?'

It was not a flirtatious question. This was a straightforward, *is the accused guilty or not guilty?*

Her hair. It was a mutilation. A disfigurement.

'I think it's very nice.'

She didn't contest the verdict, but patted the back of her neck again for reassurance.

'Sure it's too late to change my mind anyhow,' she said. 'And it saves washing like you wouldn't believe.'

'I'm sure.'

'What would *you* know? Honestly. Long hair is like having to do extra laundry.'

'It's very nice.'

'Really?'

'Very nice.'

'Liar.'

It was not a kind word, nor was it delivered kindly, but Wyndham could feel conciliation in the air. He was smiling at her, unstrained for once, and she smiled back.

'Don't you have a train to catch?' she said. 'You wouldn't want to miss it.'

This is what being stabbed must feel like, thought Wyndham. But perhaps Nora's time in a military hospital hadn't been wasted, because she was quick to apply treatment to the hurt.

'We might have time for a cigarette before you go,' she said. 'Julia doesn't like me smoking so much and I think she's right, but she'd hardly object if I joined you in one.'

Cigarettes had been the salvation of their earlier cautious encounters, and Wyndham knew there'd been a good reason not to switch to a pipe. Like Nora's haircut, it was too late now. He explained that he had no cigarettes to offer. One could hardly offer a lady a draw on a pipe.

Nora took the news with composure, but it was suddenly clear to Wyndham why her fingers had been twitching and her foot tapping all this while.

'I could get some,' he said. 'It wouldn't take a minute. I saw a shop.'

But Nora shook her head. Too late.

The last time they'd parted it had been outside a Parisian hotel where they had spent the night together. They had both been returning to the war – a war that snuffed out futures and made mock of all hopes. This time Nora told him that McInerney's shop was on Washington Street and that Tuesdays were her afternoons off. This time was sadder.

III

HITHER AND YON

...Later would come organisation and cool-headed reason. Now was the lyrical stage, blood sang and pulsed, a strange love was born that for some was never to die till they lay stiff on the hillside or in quicklime near a barrack wall.

—Ernie O'Malley, *On Another Man's Wound*

21

And have we done with War at last?
Well we've been lucky devils, both,
And there's no need of pledge or oath
To bind our lovely friendship fast.
By firmer stuff,
Close bound enough.

—Robert Graves, 'Two Fusiliers'

It was unfair that he'd have to go through all this again. He'd endured all the heartsickness once already. He'd been as lovelorn as had been expected of him. He'd won Nora. Now he was supposed to start all over?

Cork.

Wyndham was going to have to move to Cork. There was nothing else for it. A year and a half ago he had set himself up in Paris as he courted Nora who was stationed in Rouen. It had worked, because it had only been for a short while, because they were both used to wartime exigencies, and because fortune had for once chosen to smile upon Daniel Wyndham and the affairs of his heart.

But this was not then and Tralee was not Paris. For the time being, as he tested the situation, he could just get used to a long-range love affair – provided that the country didn't descend into anarchy. And provided that Nora actually wanted to carry on with him. Every time he considered that this might not be the case his blood ran cold. After all, it had been a year and a half. Anything could have happened. Her regard for him might have cooled over time. Worse. Had there been someone else? He could see a handsome surgeon, sleeves rolled back from strong forearms, a lock of dark hair falling over his brow, and her at his elbow, joined to him in saving a quivering life.

He would most certainly have to move to Cork.

That meant he would most likely have to find a job in Cork. He bought the paper to see if this post-war employment slump he'd heard about had much basis in fact. The Situations Vacant column wasn't exactly disheartening, but reading it he felt a sinking of the spirits. He could, in clear conscience, answer one of those advertisements for a young man to take on clerical work, yet an office job was something he'd had once back in Lowell, Massachusetts, and was, if he had to be honest with himself, part of the reason he'd left Lowell in the first place.

He'd left home for the sake of romance and adventure. He'd found far too much of the latter and not quite enough of the former to satisfy him. Now, in going back to a desk, he would be admitting that the adventure was over and the romance was about to congeal into mere domesticity.

It could wait a little while. With his officer-like initiative he sketched out a plan. First, gauge and assess Nora and all obstacles and opportunities relating to Nora. Next, establish himself in Cork. Then he could think about a job.

And there was one other thing, which might as well be faced sooner rather than later.

It took some finding, but as the flies revelled in the warm afternoon air about the nearby cattle market, Wyndham found himself at a shop bearing the sign 'Moriarty'.

'He's out.'

Well at least that established that he lived here.

'He'll be down the pub, devil a doubt.'

For someone so tight-lipped and unwelcoming, the woman of the house was proving hugely informative. Wyndham had barely to open his mouth in inquiry before she said, 'Phelan's'.

'Ah, thank you. And—?'

'It's on Dominick Street.'

'Thank you, ma'am. You're most kind.'

'You're not the police, are you?'

Interesting to note that she had no hesitation in telling her brother-in-law's whereabouts to a suspected police detective.

'Army actually. We served in the same regiment.'

That explanation earned no more than a pursed mouth and a little 'hmph', making it clear that for all his new suit and good manners, here was one of those soldiers who'd be coming back after closing time, arm in arm with Francie, and the pair of them roaring drunk and using filthy language.

Moriarty was where Wyndham expected to find him – in the corner with the paper. He didn't look up as Wyndham came in. Once, a long time ago, Moriarty would have stood facing the room, chest out and elbows on the bar, but that was before Festubert. Since then he'd looked at the world as if through a steel loophole in a sandbag parapet, keeping his head well down.

Wyndham ordered himself a whiskey. He didn't want a whiskey, but he felt enough out of place as it was. No – he *did* want a whiskey. Very much. Only he didn't want one here. He'd enjoyed drinks in establishments where the roof had been torn off. He'd drunk in dark holes in the ground, dressed in dead men's waterproofs and passing a tin mug around. He'd found such places more welcoming than this one. Irish pubs he'd known tended to be like front parlours or grocer's shops – which they frequently were. This public house was more public and less house, and the public element wasn't here to make friends.

Moriarty still didn't look up until Wyndham planted his glass down in front of him.

'Holy Mother of Jesus,' said Moriarty.

'I believe you have me mistaken,' said Wyndham, and took a seat.

Neither man said anything more for a little while as they measured the situation.

Would Moriarty drag up some old grievance? Would Wyndham try and sell another of Fitzmullen-Brophy's mad schemes? Wyndham folded his arms and left his drink resolutely untouched. Unusually, it was Moriarty who weakened first.

'I suppose they told you in the shop where to find me?'

'That's right.'

'Jesus. A man can't get a bit of privacy.'

'That's just family for you.'

'Family,' said Moriarty and sniffed.

Was it that compulsive sniff he'd brought back from Festubert, along with a fear of the dark and an occasional tendency to hug the ground and cry? Wyndham couldn't tell. *You wanted to go home: you got home. Stop complaining.* Instead he said: 'It's been a long time. It'll take some getting used to on both sides, I imagine.'

Moriarty answered that with another sniff.

'They're always at me. Saying I'm rowdy. Saying I'm always making noise. That's just not true. And the bloody children. They wouldn't leave a fella alone. Always at him like little bloody shitehawks.'

Wyndham's army lexicon interpreted. Shitehawks – what old India hands called kitehawks – the birds that swooped down on a man's mess tin even as he was eating from it.

'It's just family,' said Wyndham, even though no one in his

family could ever have been reasonably accused of rowdiness, and they could never have held their heads up in Lowell society if they deserved the name of shitehawks.

They didn't talk about the last time they'd met, or about the time before that either. The closest Moriarty came to mentioning a certain trench in the St. Quentin sector was a complaint about his tooth – yet another thing that was 'at' him.

Wyndham was sorry for Moriarty – up to a point – but he wasn't here to listen to the man's complaints. Rather than do that he started on his own complaints. He didn't intend to, but an account of his doings since he'd left the regiment placed an undue emphasis on the negative.

The profitless time with the Americans; the pointless journey with Fitzmullen-Brophy; the directionless life in Tralee; and now, after the war, after the peace, some strange dissatisfaction that Wyndham couldn't quite put his finger on.

'Is this about your foxy-headed one?' asked Moriarty.

'She's cut her hair.'

Moriarty didn't know what to make of that so he said nothing.

'I don't suppose it should make any difference,' said Wyndham. But it did. It marked a change. Nora's hair, which he had once (once!) seen unbound, had been cut off and swept out of the way. The old world of risk and passion was gone.

'When did I ever tell you about her anyway?'

Moriarty thought about it.

'Nineteen-seventeen,' he said. 'Probably more like November or December of nineteen-sixteen, but definitely all the way through to the following summer. You'd still have been going on about her until the Messines Ridge. I didn't see you for a good while after that.'

He noticed the way Wyndham was looking at him.

'What? You think I'm having you on? Do you not remember Hazy Brook? You never shut up about your one. All the blessed time. Two drinks and you'd be getting all wistful and spouting poetry and that. Two drinks? One drink was more like it.'

Wan drink.

And now Wyndham recognised a moment of decision. The first time he'd ever had a drink with Moriarty he'd woken up in the cells of Ballymullen Barracks with mild concussion. The next time had ended with the pair of them agreeing that a return to the Western Front in time for the Battle of the Somme was something they should just get on with.

Drinking with Moriarty was just plain unlucky.

Where might it lead now? Would he wake up in a shared bed above that mean shop, with his good suit ruined and Moriarty's sister-in-law giving him the evil eye over an unwanted breakfast grudgingly furnished?

Or would the two of them just go the whole hog and find themselves another war to join? One drink and the next thing he knew he'd be facing Russian hordes in Poland or the Mad Mullah in Somaliland. He pushed his glass towards Moriarty.

'You'd better have this. I really must be going. If I hurry I should be able to catch an earlier train.'

Moriarty made no attempt to hide that he was being slighted.

'Well Jesus – don't let me keep you.'

Wyndham was surprised that he was allowed to get away so easily. Maybe Moriarty had just given up on him. It was easy to see things Moriarty's way. There was something about Moriarty's voice that had managed by some evil trick to insinuate itself into Wyndham's conscience a long time ago.

Mister Wyndham was too good to be drinking with the lower orders now. Mister Wyndham in his fancy suit, who'd forgotten that he ever wore the scratchy bulls-wool straight out of the stores. The sort that would let a fella down when they're facing off against all the Huns in France was the sort who'd let the regiment down without a second thought. Wouldn't even raise a glass to the old Dirty Shirts.

But Wyndham, for all that, was free and sober and walking downhill with a clear head and a firm resolution. He would leave his dissolute ways back in the war where he'd found them. He would live decently, and court Nora all over again. He would move to Cork in due course and until then he would do what he'd done in France, and accept that long train journeys were part of his life again. He had surmounted the distance between Paris and Rouen, and in wartime. The journey from Tralee to Cork should be no great obstacle.

He was in good time for his train because it was running several hours late. A railway strike of some sort, a guard explained to him.

'Any minute now, sir. You'll be grand.'

As the long summer dusk darkened slowly into night he was several times on the brink of giving up and finding a hotel. And then, just has his patience came to an end, there was the sound of a steam whistle and the guard smiled and said, 'There you are, sir. What did I tell you at all?'

The train stopped somewhere beyond Mallow, and would neither go forwards nor backwards, because of those bloody Bolsheviks up in Limerick, according to the man with whom Wyndham shared a compartment.

Irish rebels and invasive police were factors that Wyndham had taken into account. Now he must reckon with Bolsheviks too? The sooner he closed the distance between himself and Nora the better.

22

The bells are ringing for me and my gal.
The birds are singing for me and my gal.
Everybody's been knowing
To a wedding they're going...

—George W. Meyer, Edgar Leslie, E. Ray Goetz, 1917

Molly was the only one there to welcome him back.

'Hush, Daniel! I've only just got Baby to sleep!'

She was wearing two cardigans, sitting at the piano that hadn't been tuned since before her marriage.

'I've brought you some Turkish Delight,' said Wyndham, crossing the room as softly as he could manage.

'Daniel! You remembered!'

Because her moments of indulgence were brief these days, Molly wasted no time in opening the little tin of coloured lumps dusted all over with sugar. She chose a pond-green irregular block and put it in her mouth. Her face contorted with pleasure and her cheek with the size of the thing. On the whole Molly was content with life in Kerry, but there were some metropolitan sophistications that she missed.

Even after his long journey and missed meals, Wyndham was not tempted to try one.

'No, no,' he said. 'They're for you.'

'So tell me about Cork,' said Molly as soon as she was able. 'Tell me about Nora.'

Nora Maxfield was a figure of avid curiosity for Molly. She understood her to be a wild romantic who had adventures in far-off places, smoked cigarettes and drove an ambulance. A sort of Irish Boadicea and Edith Cavell combined.

She sucked sugar off her fingers and leaned forward. 'Go on,' she said.

Wyndham gathered his thoughts. Where to begin?

'She's cut her hair,' he said.

Molly thought the short hair wonderfully daring, and waved away Wyndham's further doubts and misgivings.

'Oh, of course she's going to marry you,' she said at the end. 'You're tying yourself in knots over nothing.'

Wyndham was tired and hungry, and he sensed in Molly's attitude an overoptimistic disregard for the facts. It reminded him of her father's annual assurances, dating back to 1914, that this would be the year of victory.

'Everything will turn out right in the end,' she said. 'You'll see. Look, I'll prove it to you.' And she got up, and after a brief search presented Wyndham with the London *Times*, a few days old.

'Daddy said you'd want to see this. There. Look.'

She was pointing at the Betrothals column.

Captain Edward Fleming MC, Royal Munster Fusiliers, to Miss Daisy Watkins.

'There. See?' said Molly, as if that did indeed prove it.

And why not? An old comrade had married. She herself had married. Therefore Wyndham would marry. It stood to reason. And that, Wyndham supposed, was how the world worked for army officers and their daughters from Tralee to Mandalay: privileged but penurious, rootless and ill-educated, but muddling through somehow and ruling the world while they were at it. If you stopped believing, it all disappeared.

Wyndham was glad that good old Bog Fleming – last seen

attempting to hold an inadequate trench against the best that Ludendorff could throw at him – was alive and well and had found love. It did nothing to reassure him though. If anything, the marriage announcement made him feel more hopeless: as if he'd missed his chance; as if Bog and Daisy had gaily hopped on the back of the last marriage bus just as it was pulling away.

He acknowledged that this was a mean way of thinking. He was out of sorts. Something to eat would put him right.

'Cook's away, I'm afraid,' said Molly. 'She left some cold mutton but the dogs got at it somehow. I'm sure we can manage until she gets back. Have some Turkish Delight, do.'

23

Forever henceforth, the owners of our soil must be Irish.

—James Fintan Lalor, 1847

'No, no, Daniel. You *must* stay a while longer at least.'

Wyndham was gratified that his plan to move out of the Fitzmullen-Brophy house was met with such emphatic opposition from Mrs. Fitzmullen-Brophy.

'If the girl is all you say she is I'm sure she'll wait for you a little longer. You can visit on weekends. A little time to think will do you both good. No – you *must* stay a little longer. Hugh depends on you.'

Which was a way of saying that the Fitzmullen-Brophy women depended on Wyndham to keep the colonel happy, or at least occupied.

'I worry about him, Daniel. I really do. He's always had the army before this. Even before the war he had the reserve battalion and poor old Tummy Belcher. Do be a dear and keep him company until – well, until he finds *something* anyway.'

Put like that, Wyndham could hardly relinquish his position as saviour of the family's well-being.

'Just for the summer at least,' said Mrs. Fitzmullen-Brophy. 'He's showing an interest in fishing. You never know, it might be the very thing for him. I can't abide the smell of fish in the house, but it's better than Hugh pining.'

Fishing wasn't a sport for which Fitzmullen-Brophy had ever had any appetite. It required that a man stay still for too long. But now, with summer upon them and his wife shooing him from the house, it did no harm to take a new neighbour up on an invitation to cast for trout in his stream.

The neighbour's name was Ogilvie, lately arrived from England with the intention of spending his years in retirement from industry as a country gentleman. He had met Fitzmullen-Brophy while trying to establish himself in Tralee society. Fitzmullen-Brophy may not have had money, but he was a colonel and a holder of the Distinguished Service Order, respected in the county. He had also shown an immediate interest in Ogilvie, as he did with everyone, and had thus filled the post of Ogilvie's friend, which had been vacant so far.

Ogilvie's house was better than six miles off but such a distance was nothing to a couple of infantry veterans with bicycles under them on a summer day. Fitzmullen-Brophy had never been there before, but map, compass and thorough planning ensured that it was easily found. Whether for the byroads of Kerry or the passes of the Northwest Frontier, Hugh Fitzmullen-Brophy was a man prepared.

The house was built on land granted to one of Dutch William's supporters more than two hundred years earlier, and Ogilvie was the first person since then to put any money into it. Ogilvie had a lot of money, but spending so much of it on renovations was galling.

'It's not the money, of course,' he was saying. 'It's the damned *slowness*. If I'd known how damn slow Irish workmen are I'd have brought men from England. May well have been dearer, but it wouldn't have been so damn *slow*.'

'Quite, quite,' said Fitzmullen-Brophy, thinking about the leaks and draughts in his own house that would likely never be fixed. He had never had money, and never would, and didn't quite understand it. It was the same with trade and industry and commerce. There had to be textile mills so that the army could be clothed. There had to be shipyards so that the army could go off to fight for the Empire. There had to be finance to make sure it all got paid for, but Fitzmullen-Brophy was damned if it had anything to do with him. He didn't particularly share the old army's snobbery regarding trade, but he and Ogilvie, though much the same in age, were of different breeds. That much was glaringly clear to Wyndham.

Ogilvie greeted them dressed as a townsman should dress in the country – if he had a decent tailor, that is. His guests were attired more or less identically in durable hairy suits that, in Wyndham's case, had just taken him on a long cycling tour of Ireland in all weathers and, in Fitzmullen-Brophy's case, had been cut for him sometime after the colonel had come home from the Mohmand Expedition, back in the olden days.

Wyndham also couldn't help noticing the rather splendid motor car and the humble contrast their bicycles made with it. The house itself, even if still a work in progress, was teetering between modern comfort and baronial affectation – ranks of antlers on bright new wallpaper.

There was a Mrs. Ogilvie who offered a limp greeting before returning to invisibility. There were photographs of Ogilvie children, grown up and living expensively in England. None of it drew more than a polite smile and the expected words from Fitzmullen-Brophy. He didn't express any heartfelt warmth or enthusiasm until they encountered Boru.

Boru was something acquired to go with the antlers and the adopted role of Irish squire. It was a wolfhound, and when it padded into the room Wyndham's instinct was to back behind some furniture and prepare to sell his life dearly. His moment of cowardice went unnoticed because Fitzmullen-Brophy took centre stage.

'I say!' he said. 'I *say*! What a thoroughly magnificent animal! How absolutely wonderful!'

And it was lucky that the hound was of placid temperament, because nothing would keep Fitzmullen-Brophy from pulling its ears, ruffling its fur and looking at its teeth.

'I say!'

'Like him, do you?' said Ogilvie, happy to have impressed his guest at last, and bemused at what it had taken.

'The Irish Guards have one as their mascot, you know,' said Fitzmullen-Brophy.

'I did, as a matter of fact. That's where I took the name from.'

'Superb.'

'*I have a great fierce hound,*' said Wyndham, '*and he has in him the strength of a hundred.*'

'What's that, Dan?'

'Something I read once, Colonel. The Hound of Culain. Irish legend.'

'Is it now? Well, well, well.'

But you could have told Fitzmullen-Brophy that a fortune of diamonds had just fallen out of his back pocket and he'd have shown no more interest.

'Shall we?' said Ogilvie. 'The trout, I mean.'

'What?' said Fitzmullen-Brophy. 'Oh, yes. Yes, certainly.'

'The dog can come along.'

'Oh, *jolly* good.'

Wyndham decided to take the dog's docility on trust, even though it was perfectly reasonable to be apprehensive about this woolly cheetah that had been specially bred to run down and rend apart wolves. Maybe the hound was harmless because, having hunted the wolves to extinction, its species was now, like its master, enjoying a quiet retirement.

Ogilvie's purchase was small for a country estate but lavish for a garden. The steady impoverishment of the landlord class in the previous century and the government purchases of recent years had stripped the manor of all its farms and tenantry, but Ogilvy was well pleased with what was left: wide lawns and old trees, and of course the trout stream.

All Wyndham knew about fishing was what Fitzmullen-Brophy had told him on the journey over. Fitzmullen-Brophy was no fisherman either, but being a gentleman he was acquainted with the rudiments and had excavated an antique but well-made rod from his attic, along with various pieces of tackle. Fitzmullen-Brophy, as a man prepared, never threw away anything that might yet come in useful. By way of waders, he had a pair of those army waterproofs so jealously guarded by quartermasters and so highly prized by the soldiery: Boots, gum, thigh, pairs one, flooded trenches for the uses of.

There was much fiddling and fussing preparatory to the first cast, and Wyndham left the other two at it while he made tentative friends with the dog. If Boru turned out to be anything like the Hound of Culain, it was best to get on his good side early on.

Later, when Fitzmullen-Brophy had done with his tangling and untangling, Wyndham took his turn with the rod, and once he got the hang of it he could see how men could enjoy such a pastime. Just to stand on a sunny riverbank, untroubled, and lose oneself in the rhythm of wrist and rod and line and fly was dreamily pleasant. Of course there was Fitzmullen-Brophy to tell him he was doing it all wrong and Ogilvie to offer advice, so Wyndham thought it preferable in the end to hand the colonel back his rod. With his rolled-up jacket for a pillow and his hat over his face, he dozed alongside the huge dog while the older men talked fishing in outdoor voices.

A valuable skill the army had taught him: a soldier can sleep anywhere.

Nobody caught anything, or so much as saw a fish, but no one was too put out about it. Wyndham had had a nice day out,

Fitzmullen-Brophy had found someone new with whom he could share his views, and Ogilvie had set a firm foot on the lower rung of North Kerry's social ladder. The two gentlemen had nothing at all in common. Fitzmullen-Brophy's politics were naive and his understanding of business was nil, while Ogilvie's military experience was limited to making an inordinate amount of money from the war and naming his dog after a regimental mascot. Still, the day could be counted as a success. In his role of expansive host, Ogilvie offered an open invitation to come and fish anytime Fitzmullen-Brophy might feel like it.

'I might not always be home, but just let them know up at the house.'

For Ogilvie, listening to the likes of Fitzmullen-Brophy through a hot afternoon was asking rather a lot of a fellow, but having the old soldier about the place was appropriately decorative. The invitation included Wyndham, even though he was a nobody.

There was only one thing to cloud the day and they came upon it as they were returning to the house. There were hoof prints marring the newly-laid turf of the tennis court, and a pat of cow dung attracting flies on the baseline.

'Damned cattle!' said Ogilvie.

'Hmm. I dare say,' said Fitzmullen-Brophy. 'They do that, you'll find. Stray, I mean. And graze and whatnot.'

'*Stray?*' Ogilvie thundered. 'Not a bit of it! This was deliberate! And not the first time! If they've had my fence down I'll have the law on them!'

Ogilvie thundered for a bit but gave in to Fitzmullen-Brophy's soothing and to his duties as host. The neighbours – former tenants, he explained – had taken it into their heads that his gardens somehow constituted common grazing land.

'Sinn Feiners behind it, you know. Did much the same to Lord Listowel last year, so I'm told. Turned up, proud as you please, and started ploughing. *Ploughing!* His lawns!'

Wyndham had heard something about that, but in the spring of 1918 he'd had more to concern him than Lord Listowel and his lawn. Fitzmullen-Brophy, who'd also been in the midst of the destruction of British Fifth Army, couldn't quite summon up the necessary conviction to match Ogilvie's outrage.

'Ploughing, eh? Disgraceful. Tell you what – let's have that tea and forget all about it. Then we really must be on our way. It's been a perfectly splendid afternoon. Superb sport. Most grateful.'

24

If the nationalists want me to believe in and labour for independence, they must first show themselves willing and strong enough to stand between me and the power which a single Englishman, a landlord, wields over me.

—Michael Davitt, 1878

Every week or so Wyndham and Fitzmullen-Brophy spent an afternoon fishing in Ogilvie's stream. If there was a rod going spare, Wyndham was happy to learn how to fish. Otherwise he was happy to read or doze in the shade. His contentment was only superficial because he felt how time was pressing and how far he was from Nora. He had made the long trip back to Cork, and they had met in a pleasant café, and at the merest hint of physical affection on his part she'd reminded him that they weren't in France now. She had lightened when she'd told him of the life she was living. Evidently her political pursuits involved fundraising dances. Wyndham could too easily imagine Nora dancing with a fine, strapping young nationalist, and reckoned that he had pressing work to do on the Nora front.

Fitzmullen-Brophy, for his part, seemed to enjoy the fishing too but, like Wyndham, it was largely a distraction from weightier concerns and how helpless he was regarding them. Back in Tralee Barracks the regiment was being rebuilt without him.

More than thirty years he had given to the Munster Fusiliers. Their traditions were his commandments. Their history was his heritage. Their blood was his blood. And now in this deceptive peace they were attempting to restore the old pre-war regiment without one of the few officers who knew how it had been before the war. Fishing was all well and good on such a sunny afternoon, but it was a sad occupation for a man who could share the experience won in Burma and South Africa. A Dirty Shirt should not die in bed, nor by a trout stream for that matter.

And it wasn't as if he ever caught anything.

Susan Fitzmullen-Brophy was the only one perfectly pleased with the situation – especially with the lack of fish, and not having their smell permeating the house. Hugh was away tiring himself out in the fresh air, with Daniel to keep an eye on him, and a new friend of sorts in that Mr. Ogilvie.

As for Ogilvie, retirement in the Irish countryside was proving less than he'd hoped for. His fine house was perpetually damp and draughty even in summer, and workmen were slow in addressing his complaints. And worse than idle workers were the trespassers. Fitzmullen-Brophy suggested barbed-wire entanglements, and even went to the trouble of reproducing a sketch from a tactical manual, but otherwise his attitude was that this was Kerry, and one might try arguing with a Kerry farmer if one cared to, but hoping for satisfaction, order or even mutual understanding was rather too much to wish for.

'Let it alone and you'll get used to it,' was Fitzmullen-Brophy's advice. 'Nothing at all personal about it. Certainly nothing shady or political.'

But on that he was proved wrong.

It had been an afternoon of ill omen – an afternoon of sudden downpour on the road and tangled line on the riverbank. An afternoon of horseflies.

Wyndham and Fitzmullen-Brophy had been fishing on their own and were giving it up as a bad lot. There was an understated conflict over whether they should drop by the house for civility and refreshment or just skip it along with Ogilvie's conversation – which could be tiresome, particularly when it expounded on politics – and head for home on empty stomachs. Circumstances, however, decided that they must put up with Ogilvie's views and Ogilvie's politics, and much else that they hadn't reckoned on.

There was a disturbance on the lawn: men, and cattle, and Ogilvie.

'I say,' said Fitzmullen-Brophy.

'Oh dear,' said Wyndham.

Ogilvie was red-faced and loud-voiced. He was a man used to getting his own way. Confrontations usually didn't go this far. The men he was confronting didn't look much like dairy farmers. Certainly, they had the air of outdoor men who could turn their hand to anything and not be found wanting when it came to driving cattle. On the other hand, they carried themselves with assurance. Herding cows wasn't why they were here. This was a demonstration. Ogilvie could stamp and bellow: they were right where they wanted to be. If they were farming men at all, that wasn't why they were here. They were here as representatives of the Irish Republic.

'And the Irish Republic, Mr. Ogilvie, lays rightful claim to all the land of Ireland.'

'Preposterous! Get off my land, damn you!'

'And how did you come by this land? Bought it, didn't you? From a man whose forefathers confiscated it from its true owners. Well now the dispossessed are retaking possession.'

The man doing the talking didn't look like one of history's dispossessed. He was a strongly-reared, devil-may-care, handsome young man, standing four-square, hands on hips, in decent clothes. His cap was pushed back, and across the front of his waistcoat was stretched the strap of a holster. A rogue, but a capable rogue.

Wyndham scanned the group looking for Ó Tuama, and to be

sure, there he was. That confirmed that these drovers were the Irish Volunteers or, to use the more impressive name that he'd been hearing lately, the Irish Republican Army.

'Now look here,' said Fitzmullen-Brophy, stepping forward. 'Would someone be so good as to explain what the matter is?'

The matter took little enough explaining. To prevent cattle from grazing on Ogilvie's land was to deny Ireland her national destiny, or words to that effect – quite a lot of words, clearly rehearsed and delivered grandiloquently.

Fitzmullen-Brophy knew that what was needed here was calm and common sense. He himself, as he saw it, was a living argument for how Ireland could live and prosper under the British crown. There was a case to be made for a *United* Kingdom, and by Heaven this was the time to make it.

'Yes, well,' he said. 'But a chap's lawn, what?'

This appeal to reason failed to cool any passions

'I'll call the police!; said Ogilvie.

'You've already called the police,' said the Volunteer. 'We know all about it. There was nothing they were willing to do. They won't be coming again.'

'I'll have the bloody law on you!'

'Good luck with that. I'm the Sinn Féin magistrate for this district.'

'You're a damned blackguard!'

'I'm the law,' said the Volunteer, and he was clearly enjoying his status as such.

'You just damn well wait!' said Ogilvie, and strode off toward the house.

Left in charge, Fitzmullen-Brophy tried again.

'Look here,' he said, in the voice that always worked on raw recruits, junior officers, and the small and bewildered. 'It's just not on, you know. Driving cattle onto a fellow's lawn and his tennis court and so forth. Must be heaps of other places with good grass. Politics aside, I mean. No point making a point of it. All good neighbours, what?'

'There's no need for you to be getting yourself mixed up in this now, Colonel,' said the Volunteer. 'Best if you and Mr. Wyndham take yourselves home.'

Because of course the Volunteers knew exactly who they were talking to.

Wyndham was all for following this advice, but he wasn't going to abandon the colonel and he was most curious to see how it would all play out. Ogilvie presently returned to provide some sort of answer, with a rather fine shotgun in his hands.

'Oh I say, Ogilvie! You can't just shoot a fellow!'

Ogilvie fumbled a cartridge into the second barrel and snapped the gun closed. 'I'm damn well going to shoot *something*,' he said.

The cattlemen behaved as men always behave when finding themselves at the wrong end of a loaded firearm. Wyndham had seen it often enough. No one wanted to make any sudden moves, or stay as they were for that matter. Men sidled outwards, at once trying to keep the threat in plain sight and look for something to hide behind. Fitzmullen-Brophy raised his hands in calming gestures.

Any of the Volunteers who had come armed could have drawn down and shot Ogilvie there and then if their lives were in danger, but Ogilvie wasn't aiming at any of them. He had his sights fixed on one of the cows. Committing homicide over a cow wasn't anything anyone here had been prepared to do. On the other hand, the threat of a cow being killed put everything into a new perspective. It was one thing to offer your life in the republican cause, but a cow was pounds and shillings and another matter entirely.

Ogilvie sensed his advantage.

'Don't think I won't do it!' he said. 'Now clear off, the lot of you!'

And that seemed to work. The Volunteers stood their ground a little longer just to save face and then, at a gesture from their leader, they began to withdraw. The farmer who owned the cattle was already in retreat, beating his little herd before him. The leader took the setback in his stride. The last to leave, he tipped his cap before he turned his back on Ogilvie's gun.

Ogilvie, still breathing hard, watched them all go, and couldn't be persuaded to come indoors until the intruders were well gone. The guests poured a couple of large whiskies into him but his temper did not cool. He fulminated still against damned upstarts and their blasted cattle, and even spoke sharply to his wife when she upbraided him for his immoderate language. That was the moment when Fitzmullen-Brophy and Wyndham thought it best to be gone.

'A rum business,' was Fitzmullen-Brophy's verdict.

It was Saturday, the 28th of June, and in Versailles the war had finally been brought to an end. International harmony, though, was too much to ask for just yet.

The Poles were unwilling to keep out of Silesia and there were plenty of Germans reluctant to surrender the Rhineland. The newly-drawn borders along the Baltic were already becoming battle lines. It remained to be seen how inviolate Ogilvie's land would remain.

A rum business, without a doubt.

25

There has been an organised attempt to boycott and intimidate the police, their wives and relations. The hon. Member will realise that I cannot publish the steps that are being taken to cope with the campaign of murder, outrage and intimidation, but I can assure him that the means available to the Government for protecting all servants of the Crown in the discharge of their duties, and for bringing to justice those who commit or connive at outrages, are steadily improving.

—Lieut.-Colonel Sir H. Greenwood, Chief Secretary for Ireland,
19 October 1920

It was one of those mornings when the garden was far warmer and more pleasant than the house, and Colonel Fitzmullen-Brophy had even gone so far as to wonder where his shorts – last worn in India ten years before – might have got to. While his wife mounted a delaying action, and spoke about a cold spell forecast and the lingering influenza, the old soldier was content for the moment to amuse himself on the lawn with his grandchild.

He was down on his hands and knees, slapping the ground, saying, 'Here now, Mae! Here! There's a good girl!'

'Oh Daddy, she'll crawl in her own good time, I'm sure,' said Molly. 'She's not a dog you can teach to do tricks, you know.'

Wyndham, for his part, just sat and watched. The glare of the astonishing sun and the familial bustle made it impossible to concentrate on his book. He was watching the baby. She, in turn, was ignoring the big man with his big moustache under his big nose. Instead she suspiciously assessed this strange green environment, and looked up only at the sound of a car's engine. So did they all. A motor car wasn't something often heard on this road – still less a motor car of this assertive confidence.

It was Ogilvie.

The Fitzmullen-Brophy women were so very glad that the colonel was not after all wearing shorts. Ogilvie had the manner of a serious man, out to do business with other serious men over serious matters. He was through the garden gate almost before Fitzmullen-Brophy had time to rise to his feet.

'Ogilvie! This is a surprise. My dear wife. Our daughter Molly – Mrs. Bryant, I mean.'

Ogilvie lost some of his head of steam in the pleasantries but he did a poor job of hiding that he hadn't come to pay his compliments. Susan Fitzmullen-Brophy recognised as much and was determined to rob him of his momentum. The man was clearly here to drag her husband off into something troublesome, and any delay she could impose would be worth the effort.

'Charmed, Mr. Ogilvie. Hugh was telling us all about you. Do come inside and have some tea. It doesn't do to be rushing around in this heat. If India taught me anything it taught me that much.'

'Too kind, Mrs. Fitzmullen-Brophy, too kind. But I'm afraid I can't stay. Urgent matters, I'm afraid. Urgent matters, Colonel. I'll need your help.'

'Help, Ogilvie?'

'It's those blasted Sinn Feiners, Fitzmullen-Brophy – I do beg your pardon, ma'am, ladies – those confounded Sinn Feiners, I mean. Again! They won't get away with it, Fitzmullen-Brophy. I'll not let them get away with it.'

Despite having journeyed here in the back of a well-appointed car, Ogilvie was breathing heavily.

'You're a military man and you know the people round here. I'd be obliged, Fitzmullen-Brophy. I would be very much obliged.'

'Of course, yes. Well, I mean of course. But what is it, Ogilvie?'

'Come with me. I'll explain on the way. There's no time for chit-chatting.'

Mrs. Fitzmullen-Brophy did not care to have her chit-chatting so dismissed, nor did she want her husband spirited away. It was clear, though, that Ogilvie would have his way.

'Well if that's the case then Daniel should go too,' she said. 'You'll go with the colonel, won't you, Daniel?' And the look she gave Wyndham made it clear that he would – that he must. Just because the war on the Continent had finished didn't mean that it was safe to leave Hugh to rush into a crisis on his own.

'Certainly,' said Wyndham. 'If there's room in the car, that is.'

It was an unnecessary concern. Ogilvie's car could comfortably seat all three of them as they ran smoothly down the road. Ogilvie irritably explained on the way.

'My house, Fitzmullen-Brophy! They broke into my *house*!'

The story was easily told. A window broken. The shotgun missing.

'And they had the blasted cheek to leave money for the window! A little pile of change left behind with a note! The impudent—'

Any soldier would have found the appropriate obscenity in an instant, but Ogilvie had spent the war in a safe occupation and words failed him. He looked, for a moment, that he would burst, but got a grip and concentrated on what he could do.

'That note,' he said. 'It's as good as a confession. We're taking it to the police. You can tell them who was there that day they brought the cattle. I'll see they get two years' hard labour apiece for this. See if I won't, God blast them.'

The small rural police barracks was not the safeguard of Ogilvie's property nor the bastion of good order he had presumed. For a start, Ogilvie was denied his grand entrance. On the way in, his self-righteous outrage collided with that of someone on the way out. The someone, from the rifle-green colour of his trousers, appeared to be a police constable. That he was not wearing his regulation tunic and cap was down to the fact that he was not a police constable anymore. Forced to halt by the arriving visitors, he made the best of things by turning his head back towards the door and shouting, 'And you can keep your bloody pension too!'

The man's uniform, along with his career, was still on top of the counter when Ogilvie, Fitzmullen-Brophy, and Wyndham went in. The other police officers were standing around, the uncomfortable audience to an unhappy drama just ended.

'Who's in charge here?' demanded Ogilvie.

A sergeant stepped forward and asked what might be the trouble. His tone hinted that he had trouble enough already but was willing to have a look at this new variety in case it offered some relief or diversion from his present cares. In fairness to Ogilvie, his frustration didn't keep him from making a clear case, with all stages of the complaint presented in chronological order and the damning physical evidence – the note – flourished at the end as a crowning conclusion.

The sergeant studied it without surprise and handed it back.

'It's politer than some I've been seeing,' he said.

'House-breaking?' said Ogilvie? 'Burglary? Polite? What the devil do you mean – *polite*?'

'I mean, Mr. Ogilvie, that Sinn Féin has been clear about who they think is in charge here lately. Sometimes they post warnings, sometimes they make threats. To be honest with you, sir, this is the first time I've seen a nice wee note of apology or explanation – unless you want to construe it as a kind of a threat, mind.'

'And you know who these villains are? You suspect at least?'

'We have more than a good idea.'

Ogilvie was wondering what his taxes were good for.

'Well?' he said – a lather of impatience and disbelief.

'To be frank, Mr. Ogilvie, we might know who they are but they certainly know who we are, and the big difference there is that if we choose to call on them they may choose to be elsewhere, but if they want to come looking for us they know right where we'll be. They know where we live and where we work. I'm not going to tell you that a broken window and a stolen gun aren't important, sir, but they're not worth my men going haring off, endangering themselves. I have few enough men as it is. You ran into one of them on your way in? Well that's one man less.'

For a sudden strange moment Wyndham was back in a cellar in Guillemont where a tired officer of the Dublin Fusiliers had explained to the newly arrived Munsters how things were. Ideals and training and strategy were of no matter here to the north of the River Somme. Here there were German machine-guns. And here, and here. The enemy artillery had the whole area blanketed with shrapnel. Just keep your heads down. That's all you could do.

'Constable Tracey isn't the first man I've lost this month,' the sergeant was saying. 'Minehane walked out the door before him – three weeks last Friday. Menacing letters, he said he was getting. Tracey said he was getting threats too, but that wasn't what made him leave, he said. He wasn't afraid of any man, he said, but he was damned if he was going to oppress his own people at the government's behest, was how he put it. Blessed eejit – begging your pardon, gentlemen.'

Fitzmullen-Brophy was intrigued. Also, his butting in might give time for Ogilvie's temper to cool a little.

'Do you mean to say, Sergeant, that the police are being intimidated? By just a few agitators?'

For all that Fitzmullen-Brophy was something of a known agitator himself, albeit in a different cause, the sergeant was happier to turn away from Ogilvie for a moment.

'I think you'll find, Colonel, that it's more than just a few.

Have you not seen the numbers drilling?'

'Yes, well. I mean, but surely. Idealistic lads, don't you know,' said Fitzmullen-Brophy. 'A little marching, a little drilling, some cheerful songs. No real harm. Quite healthy if it's not actually seditious. They were at it before the war, you know. Fine young chaps. I had any number of them in my regiment.'

'They're a bit of a different breed now, begging your pardon, Colonel. It's the Republic or nothing for them now. And it's the characters behind all the marching and parading that're the fellas we need to be worried about. They're out there day and night, building up their own government and their own army and police in the shadows. And they're doing it by flouting us everywhere they can, and getting everyone in the district to do the same.'

The sergeant was giving the impression that no one had been paying much heed to his problems lately, so an army colonel, even if retired, was a suitable recipient of his unburdening.

'And you're not the only one having to worry about people breaking in and stealing guns. You may have noticed as you came in that we're having the windows measured for steel shutters. You didn't? I'm not surprised. Finding anyone to do any work for the police these days isn't an easy matter. They're all either Shinners or they're afraid of the Shinners.'

Ogilvie brought things back to the matter at hand.

'Are you telling me, Sergeant, that you intend to do nothing?'

'I intend to take note of the incident and inform my superiors, Mr. Ogilvie, but until they see fit to furnish me with more men—'

'I knew it! Bloody useless from start to finish! Come on, Fitzmullen-Brophy! I've had enough of my time wasted!'

Fitzmullen-Brophy could have stayed a while longer, and given much sound advice to the sergeant on all points – up to and including, Wyndham suspected, the care of the men's feet and the most beneficial breakfast for them – but it was time to go. Wyndham didn't care to be in an RIC barracks and he was curious as to where Ogilvie's self-important wrath was leading. He pulled the colonel along with him and they bundled back into Ogilvie's car.

'Right!' said Ogilvie, decisive and undaunted. 'This is where you come in, Fitzmullen-Brophy. Which way is it to the barracks?'

'Do you mean the army barracks?'

'Of course I mean the army. It's not as if the police are going to do me any good.'

'But it's really not a military matter, Ogilvie. I mean, that's not what the army's for.'

'Rubbish, man! I see them out assisting the police all the time.'

'That's as may be, but the army's still not the police, you know. One can't just summon them over a broken window. I believe the lord lieutenant of the county has to order them out or something. Rather hazy on the details. Never really happened in my day.'

Ogilvie took a deep breath, mopped his forehead and tried a softer approach.

'Look here, Fitzmullen-Brophy. You're their colonel. You may be retired, but you know them. You'll know your way around them. A word in the right ear, surely. That's all I'm asking.'

'It's not on, I'm afraid. It's one thing to drop by the mess for a chin-wag, but calling out troops just as a favour to a chap is really out of the question. Nothing I can do, old man.'

'Rebels and ruffians have invaded my property and broken into my house! They've armed themselves with *my* blasted gun! How is that not the business of the army?'

Even in such a spacious car, the long-limbed colonel's shrug took up quite a bit of room.

'It just isn't, I'm afraid.'

Ogilvie lost his temper.

'Then what's the point of your blasted regiment anyway?' he demanded.

Fitzmullen-Brophy met the question in silence. He'd never

had the wit for sharp ripostes. He waited for just as long as it took to make Ogilvie uncomfortable and then he leaned forward to tap the chauffeur on the shoulder.

'Driver, you can drop myself and Mr. Wyndham home now, there's a good fellow.'

'All the same,' the colonel was saying over dinner, 'Ogilvie has something of a point. Law and order going to wrack and ruin and all that sort of thing.'

Susan Fitzmullen-Brophy had been watching her husband come around to this all day. He'd started off with Ogilvie's attitude and how he simply couldn't understand how a fellow like Ogilvie could be so insulting to the regiment and so purblind about the army's place in the great scheme of things. I mean, dammit, how could Ogilvie not appreciate what the war had been about? But then, that out of the way, the defeatist spirit of the police had been the focus of complaint, and the unaccountable way they could just sit back and let a man be robbed, and let themselves be barricaded in behind steel shutters. And now, over a heavy and uninspiring dinner, she was listening to Hugh come around to Ogilvie's way of thinking, which meant that once he'd had his after-dinner whiskey, he'd be moving onto what he himself could do about the whole bally trouble.

'I mean the whole bally trouble is so much more than Ogilvie and his window and his gun. His attitude to the army may be frankly disgraceful, but he has a point. I don't wonder if I shouldn't do something about it.'

And there it was already, with no whiskey needed.

She hoped that he and Daniel could return to Hugh's memoirs or to the regimental history or whatever it was, and she hoped that he might follow Daniel's example and forego whiskey altogether, but even then she knew for a certainty that it would be no more than a postponement. She would have to take Daniel aside and impress on him the absolute importance of keeping Hugh distracted. But of course that wouldn't work for very long either, because Daniel had his heart set on going to Cork so he could court this sweetheart of his.

Oh dear.

'Of course you know you always have a home here, Daniel. We look on you as one of the family, you know.'

'You really are most kind, ma'am, but I think I've imposed on you quite long enough.'

'Nonsense. But I suppose if this Nora Maxfield won't come to you then of course you must go to her. If the girl as any sense she'll know what a catch she has in you. You must bring her back here. We'd all simply love to meet her.'

'I will most certainly do that. And look – Mrs. Fitzmullen-Brophy – it's not as if I'll be very far away. If there's any trouble – if the colonel – well, I mean, you know where to find me.'

'Don't fret about us, Daniel. I've been managing with Hugh for nearly thirty years, and managing without him too. The men go away. Hugh was off to the wars and now you're off following your heart. Don't blush, Daniel. The men go away and the women manage.'

'I suppose so, yes.'

'It's something an army wife learns quickly. Hugh had the regiment before he had me. I was never fool enough to challenge his first love. Now I'm without a rival and we're all at something of a loss.'

'I'm sure everything will be alright.'

'I'm sure too. I just hope that there won't be any repercussions from that business with Mr. Ogilvie.'

'As a matter of fact, I'm meeting someone about that before I go.'

26

I turned it in my hands; the stains
Of war were on it...

—W.B. Yeats, *The Wanderings of Usheen*

'Gearóid, I'm glad I ran into you.'

'Sure, you know me, Dan. I'm always around. What is it I can do for you?'

'It's the Colonel – Colonel Fitzmullen-Brophy.'

'The Colonel Fitzmullen-Brophy who's been talking to the police? The same Fitzmullen-Brophy that's been consorting with a certain Mr. Bertram Ogilvie, land-grabber and war-profiteer?'

'Oh damn it, Gearóid – I was consorting with the man too, you know, if that's what you call fishing in his stream and playing with his dog.'

'I'll allow him the dog, but that's not Ogilvie's stream. An Englishman can't just come here and claim title to Irish water and all the fish in it. Ireland isn't for sale.'

'Yes, well – could we just leave the colonel out of it?'

'Maybe the colonel could just leave himself out of it and not be helping Ogilvie in organising some class of an Anti-Sinn Féin League, or whatever they want to call it.'

'I believe I've talked the colonel out of that. He's going to be busy with the Munster Fusiliers Veterans Officers' Association for a while.'

'That's one I haven't heard of.'

'We just thought it up. He'll be writing letters and calling on old comrades for the foreseeable future. Nothing at all political about it.'

'A coven of unionist army officers and there's nothing political about it? I'll believe that when I see it.'

'Really, Gearóid – it'll be about India and the war and that sort of thing.'

'If you say so, Dan.'

'So just turn a blind eye, is all I'm asking. He might make some ill-judged noise but he's perfectly harmless.'

'If it's anything like the noise he made over that anti-conscription meeting last year then it's no small favour you're asking me, Dan.'

'Please, Gearóid.'

'I really don't know. Doing favours for ex-army officers for the benefit of other army officers is a bit much.'

'I know. But here, look – I brought you something. I really don't know what to do with this, but I thought you might like to have it.'

Ó Tuama instantly knew from the weight of the little parcel that he wasn't being given another book. He made sure there was no one looking in their direction as he partly unwrapped it. He looked at Wyndham in wonderment.

'It was just lying around,' said Wyndham, unwilling to clarify that it hadn't been so much as lying around as secured in the holster of a sleeping officer in a second-class compartment at Limerick Junction.

'I'm afraid there's no ammunition for it,' he said, 'but I don't suppose you'd have much trouble finding some.'

'Point four-five-five inch?' said Ó Tuama, still astonished. 'No – I don't suppose so. Listen, Dan – do you know what you're up to at all?'

'Of course I do, Gearóid. I'm bribing you. This is a bribe.'

'Right, right. That's what I thought.' He stuffed the pistol under his coat and buttoned up despite the warmth of the day. 'So you're off to Cork, is it?' he said, trying to sound conversational again.

'I am. Day after tomorrow. You once told me that you knew the place? I wonder if you know of somewhere I could stay.'

'I've always found Cork to be quite disagreeable in the summer,' said Molly. 'It can get rather warm and close.'

'A Munster Fusilier never minded the heat, Molly. We marched from Dagshai to Delhi in the hot season in 1857, remember?'

'Oh, you. You've been spending too much time talking to Daddy. You really do need a change. Just make sure you don't talk regimental history to Nora. Some girls don't find it the least bit alluring.'

'I'll remember.'

She was holding the baby who, of all the Fitzmullen-Brophy women, was not showing any strong feeling over Wyndham's departure. As usual the infant looked at him with a mixture of bewilderment and disappointment.

'Give Daniel a kiss now,' said Molly. 'There's a good girl.'

The child offered no more than a podgy frown, but let herself be kissed all the same.

'Chin up, kid,' said Wyndham.

And then, as all men of that household had been doing for generations, he went away.

27

Never had I such fun and pleasure as in the Fenian times.

—W.B. Yeats, *The Celtic Twilight*

It was a small private hotel within easy reach of the university, and there was a vacancy.

'Mr. Ó Tuama's room? Of course it's still free,' the landlady was saying. 'Only I'm delighted to let it to a friend of his before the term starts. It might well have been taken by then. It is a friend of Mr. Ó Tuama's you are?'

'Yes indeed,' said Wyndham.

'I was sorry to hear he wouldn't be coming back to finish his degree, but I wasn't very surprised either. He told me that the politics were causing him to neglect his studies, which was an awful shame. And then there were the police after him, of course.'

Behind every counter in Ireland, at every door and in every kitchen, there were women who would tell you everything unasked. On the one hand, it should have made intelligence gathering so easy. All you had to do was walk into a shop, ask for a half pound of tea, and wait to be told all the gossip of the neighbourhood. But that wasn't the way it was at all. In broadcasting the news to every stranger, these women weren't giving anything away. They were showing that nothing escaped them. They saw. They heard. They knew. And when they retailed any of it they were telling any listener that here – behind every counter and in every kitchen – was an intelligence network that could neither be evaded nor defeated.

He faced the Nora situation directly and firmly by calling on her place of work as soon as he'd unpacked.

'I never told you to move to Cork,' she said blankly.

'I am my own man and I come and go as I please,' he told her. 'Right now it pleases me to invite you to dinner.'

'Lunch,' she said. 'I'll get my hat. And take that glint out of your eye.'

And that was how their courtship began a second time. On her days off he took her to lunch. On Sundays she invited him to tea.

'Julia's taking a liking to you,' she explained, in a manner suggesting that there was no accounting for some people's odd fancies.

They took chaste walks together. They argued incessantly.

'I did not "just run off" to Salonika! My unit was posted there.'

'You volunteered! And you didn't even write very often.'

'You were doing more than enough writing for the pair of us. It was embarrassing.'

'I wrote because I truly love you, Nora.'

'Stop that. You only think you do. You just want to – you know.'

'Well that too. If only we could—'

'Ask me to marry you one more time and I'll hit you.'

'You wouldn't dare. I'd howl and make a scene.'

'I don't even know what I'm doing with you. I have better things to be doing than carrying on with boys.'

'And I have nothing I'd rather be doing than trying to win you.'

'Like I'm some sort of prize in a raffle, I suppose? That reminds me – there's a fundraising thing I want money for.'

'For Sinn Féin?'

'Of course. You can't have a government without money.'

'Are you sure they're spending your money on governing? I ask because I have reservations about buying arms.'

'Says a man who spent four years fighting the Germans.'

'The Germans were not amenable to a democratic solution.'

'Neither are the British. I need ten shillings.'

'It's not about the money, Nora. Everything I have is yours for the asking.'

'I won't be asking, and I'll not be a kept woman. Now let me have ten shillings.'

'Look, I admire your principled stance, but don't you think you're diving head-first into all this political stuff? Shouldn't you – I don't know – be asking more questions?'

'What do you mean?'

'Well, in your eyes everything the Republicans do is right, but back in Kerry I was hearing stories of intimidation, and there were robberies and such. I get the feeling that not everything Sinn Féin or the Volunteers do is strictly above board, but it seems to me that all anyone has to do is wave a tricolour and you're following along without hesitation.'

'There's a dance they're having on Saturday. You can take me.'

'What time?'

Somewhere, in some Dublin back room no doubt, there was a body calling itself the Ministry for Finance of the Irish Republic, and with harried staff and rented furniture this ministry was raising money and moving money and hiding money before the next police raid. No doubt it was all very thrilling. For the plain people who had voted Sinn Féin and who were willing to pledge their faith with actual money, fundraising had become a fact of life. Sometimes they might be rewarded with promissory notes crudely printed with inadequate Irish type. More often, all they got was pride that they had staked five or ten pounds in the cause. Sometimes though, they would get a grand evening's entertainment out of it. Sinn Féin was having modest success in subverting British rule through dancing.

'I don't have evening clothes,' Wyndham had said.

'It's not that kind of dance,' Nora had told him.

Nor was it. It was a wild swirling, gallumphing square dance, or set dance as such affairs were called here.

'A céilidh,' said Nora, having to raise her voice above the solid murmur of the crowd even before the music began.

'A what?'

'A céilidh.'

'Spell it.'

'I can't.'

Wyndham was a fair dancer, but this sort of thing was beyond him. It occurred to him that these were the evolutions of the parade ground in quick time. Drill without arms to accordion and fiddle. Square bashing for both sexes. What saved him was that Nora was worse at it than he was, and out of all the throng there were indeed precious few who really knew what they were doing.

But everyone was trying hard. In forsaking their gramophone records and cinema shows for this adopted tradition, Young Ireland was learning to be Old Ireland.

And it was enormous fun.

As at every such gathering, there were young men not dancing. Here though, they weren't standing at the side in surly little clumps. Instead they were moving about the edges of the hall, keeping an eye on everything, rather like sheepdogs or society hostesses. They didn't detract from the party atmosphere in any way. Rather, they worked hard to encourage it, with greetings and welcomes, chaffing and cajoling. Wyndham could tell that at least two of them had guns in their pockets.

The few hours passed noisily and sweatily. The dancing was graceless and enthusiastic. The intervals were taken up with fundraising. There was no drinking.

When they were leaving, Nora unexpectedly tried to drag Wyndham behind a pillar for an impulsive clinch. Alas, the shadowy seclusion was already occupied, and by a plain-clothes policeman taking notes. They exchanged embarrassed scowls and, to Wyndham's great disgust, Nora took it as sign to regain her propriety. It was another black mark against the Royal Irish Constabulary.

The Irish could lament the ancient wrongs piled on them for seven and a half centuries. Wyndham could sympathise. He'd only been here a few months and already the grudges against the crown were piling up.

28

There existed a camaraderie extending through all ranks, a cheery good-fellowship, with, perhaps, little thought for the morrow.

—Captain S. McCance, *History of the Royal Munster Fusiliers*

In mid-August Nora had to go home to have a row with her family. It was a row that had been going on for as long as Nora had known her own mind, had reached screaming pitch in 1915 when she'd gone off to join the Red Cross, and had been periodically refuelled every time she chose to return on a visit.

The occasion of this visit wasn't the row for its own sake. Rather it was her sister's wedding.

'But there'll be an awful row all the same,' she told Wyndham. 'There always is. No, of course you can't come.'

So Wyndham decided to make the best of their separation by going back to Tralee. His plan was to go by bicycle, because he felt the want of the open air again. Staying in Cork, waiting on Nora, was like a spell in the line. You might be in a quiet sector, but the routine of vigilance could not be relaxed. *Be prepared,* as General Robert Baden-Powell and his disciple Colonel Hugh Fitzmullen-Brophy commanded. Be prepared for Nora to make a date, or cancel a date, or run off to Macedonia again, or show up at his door and throw herself at him. And just as there had been in the line, there was the lurking shadow of Moriarty to make him feel vaguely guilty of poor comradeship.

It was nice to get away from all that. That was what his excursions were always about. Not going anywhere, but going *away*. More than a year out of the trenches and he wasn't comfortable with staying still. Stay in the same place and you suffer the attentions of disapproving superiors, needy subordinates, German snipers. So off, northward and westward, fifty, sixty, seventy miles in a day, and the weather better than a Flemish spring, and the way not as potholed as the Menin Road.

He made it to Tralee in time for the regimental sports, a day out for one and all that Fitzmullen-Brophy had written to tell him about.

'Like the old days, Dan!' he said when they met. 'The regiment getting back to the way it was! Splendid! You really should have put yourself down for one of the veterans' events.'

'If only I'd known in time, sir.'

'And if only *I* didn't have this blasted hip – and if I were a dozen years younger, eh?'

'You joke, sir.'

It was strange to watch the regiment and to be outside it: to hear orders barked and be able to ignore them, to see senior officers and not salute them. And to see the barrack square, where Wyndham had undergone his recruit drill, become a place of recreation for the day was strangest of all. Where was Lance-Corporal Sheehan, screaming at him to keep the fucking time?

As if to tempt the ghosts, he put his hands in his pockets and strolled where once he'd had to march stiffly. No window opened, and no sergeant stuck his head out to roar the traditional rebuke, '*Hey, you! Only dogs and officers walk across that parade ground!*'

Lance-Corporal Sheehan was dead at Festubert. The terrible sergeants? There couldn't be too many of them left. They'd been men too ramrod-stiff to duck their heads and too proud to flinch before the enemy.

Wyndham had heard that the regiment had suffered three

thousand dead during the war. He worked it out in his head. If you added up the two regular and three reserve battalions as they'd been in the summer of 1914, three thousand was round about what you'd get. So that meant everyone had been killed once. That seemed about right. Wyndham certainly felt that he'd been killed at least once. Private Wyndham had been carted out of St. Yvon on a stretcher. Lieutenant Wyndham had been killed at a place called Rosières, only it had taken nearly a year before he'd stopped moving. This character walking around here in civilian clothes, invisible to all, was someone else.

Fitzmullen-Brophy was feeling a little out of place himself. He was coming back to the family home after new people lived there. The wallpaper was different, and you couldn't go upstairs for a lie-down if you felt like it.

One old comrade had slapped him on the shoulder. 'Good old FitzEm back with us! All's right with the world! Part of the furniture for so long that they named the barracks after you, what? Place hasn't been the same without a Fitzmullen in Ballymullen!' And he'd gone off laughing in search of another drink, leaving Fitzmullen-Brophy suddenly very sad. His spirits were only mended, as was so often the case, by a dog.

The regiment had acquired a wolfhound of its own a few years earlier, and after the winds of war had stopped their blowing it had fetched up here in the regiment's home. Fitzmullen-Brophy was delighted to make the dog's acquaintance, even though it reminded him of everything he'd missed, and would miss forever.

He'd nearly wrecked his career in 1914 in his enthusiasm to get to the war and he'd still missed out on Mons and Étreux. When the 1st Battalion was going ashore at Gallipoli and the 2nd was advancing on Aubers Ridge, Fitzmullen-Brophy had been in the obscure townland of Knocknahanna, a barely acknowledged training camp in Cork. The battalion he'd nurtured there had been taken away from him before he'd had a chance to lead it in battle. The Munsters had fought on the Somme and in the Salient, and he'd been somewhere else, doing his damnedest to get back with them, but somewhere else all the same. They'd won for themselves three Victoria Crosses and a wolfhound, and he hadn't been there for any of it.

The dog's name was Garryowen, and as a full colonel and an old fusilier Fitzmullen-Brophy was permitted to make much of it. Ordinarily, a regimental mascot on a regimental day was too holy a thing for affectionate manhandling. Ruffling its ears would have been almost akin to laying profane hands on the colours, but rank had one or two of its privileges yet.

When Wyndham found him, the colonel was parting from the dog as a pauper child might turn away from a toyshop window in the week before Christmas.

'There you are, Dan. Where did you get to?'

'Just wandering, sir.'

'Well let's go and join the ladies. I believe there are sandwiches, and we can all watch the sack race together.'

'That will be fun, sir.'

It was such a pleasant day, yet a strange mood pervaded. It was as if they all knew that the old days were dead and gone, and that this day – with the band playing, and the men running and jumping, and the regiment at its most hospitable – was but a shadow of those older days, and that shadow too would fade.

In the tug of war the Munster Fusiliers lost to the Royal Irish Constabulary. After all his musings on the past, Wyndham took this as a bad omen for the future.

29

And all because of some one
Perverse creature of chance,
And live like Solomon
That Sheba led a dance.

—W.B. Yeats, 'On Woman'

Nora was in better humour than expected when they met up again after her trip home.

'It all went well then? With your family, I mean?'

'Oh the wedding?' she said, clearly thinking of something else. 'No, that was awful. Well, stupid anyway. You know weddings.'

I wish I did, thought Wyndham. 'But your family's well, I hope.'

'I suppose. There was a blazing row like I knew there would be, but it was bound to happen and it makes no difference.'

'So you're cheerful because it's done with and out of the way?'

'No, no. If you don't count the wedding then I had a very useful couple of days. I met people.'

People? Men? Handsome men with brawny forearms and locks of dark hair falling into their eyes?

'People? What people?' he asked, more sharply than he intended.

'People in the organisation. Cumann na mBan people. Up till now I think I was on some sort of probation – being vetted, you might say. But now I think they're happy with me.'

'Well that's nice.'

'I was being introduced to people from all sorts of different branches: Clonakilty, Bandon – even Skibbereen.'

'You have contacts in Skibbereen now? I shouldn't be taking you for granted anymore, then.'

'*You*,' she said, as though that summed him up completely. In a way, he supposed, it did.

He had deduced that this organisation was like an Irish continuation of her role with the Voluntary Aid Detachment. There were probably no ambulances to drive, but he understood there was the possibility of first aid work, and there was certainly a host of organisational tasks that were beneath the men. He imagined that if it were anyone else but Nora, she'd be knitting socks for the IRA.

'There's to be another dance,' she said. 'If you ask me very politely I might let you take me.'

'Miss Maxfield, would you do me the inestimable honour of partnering me to the ball?'

'Delighted, Mr. Wyndham, I'm sure.' She took a deep draw on her cigarette. 'It's Saturday week. I might be helping to organise the next one after that.'

'Wonderful! Does that mean I can get out of being squeezed for five bob at every interval?'

'It means nothing of the sort.'

But if filling Sinn Féin's coffers was the price of Nora's goodwill, well – he'd spent his money on worse in his time.

'Will we be seeing each other this Sunday?' he said as they got up to leave.

'Why wouldn't we?' she asked.

He had hopes. For every invitation or suggestion he offered, a wary look was returned, with the assumption that every motive he had was carnal and improper, but she hadn't pushed him away – except, of course, for those times she physically shoved him for the taking of what she judged liberties. He had the distinct feeling though, that her chief inhibition was the lack of privacy. 'We're not in Paris,' she would say primly. And still there were the suburban walks and the Sunday teas and the Tuesday lunches.

At the end of one such lunch they were having a lazy cigarette before he walked her back to the shop.

'Correct me if I'm wrong, Nora, but I'm sure you once owned a particularly handsome cigarette case.'

She said nothing, but put her cigarettes quickly back in her handbag, as if he might think that he'd been mistaken about the common cardboard cigarette packet.

'Gold,' he said, pressing the point. 'Engraved with your initials. You still have it, don't you?'

'I don't, as a matter of fact,' she said, as if it were any of his business.

'You lost it?' Now he was genuinely hurt.

'No – no.' She didn't meet his eye. 'Not lost it. It's on loan. I lent it. Sort of.'

'Who on earth would borrow a cigarette case with your initials on it?'

She fiddled impatiently with the clasp on her handbag.

'Nora?'

'Oh all right then! I pawned it!'

'You did *what*?'

'It's only temporary. I still have the ticket. I just needed money, that's all.'

'But you have a job – a paying job.'

'It was for the cause. They were passing round the hat. It was for the Republic.'

'It was a gift! My gift to you!'

She frowned, annoyed at having been caught out yet knowing

she was in the right at the same time.

Wyndham at least knew now that he stood in second place to the Irish Republic. That didn't mean he was going to let the matter drop just yet.

'So how much did you get for it?'

She dropped her evasion.

'Two pounds, but I beat him up from thirty shillings.'

'I paid seven guineas for it!'

'It's bad manners to tell someone how much you paid for her present,' she said.

30

And when the war is over,
What will the soldiers do?

—'Salonika' (traditional)

He needed a job. He needed something to fill up the hours and days he wasn't with Nora. He needed money if things were to go on as they were. Redeeming the cigarette case had put him back more than he'd reckoned.

He sought out Moriarty. He harboured the suspicion of a debt unpaid with Moriarty: a feeling that he'd run out on the man. Then there was the fact that Cork was Moriarty's town, and a little local knowledge could only benefit Wyndham.

'Sure I don't know the place at all anymore,' said the old fusilier. 'It's only been donkey's years since I went away. It's changed altogether since I was a young fella. A job? You're looking for a job? You're not the only one, boy.'

The army's bounty wasn't looking so generous anymore. The prices that had gone up during the war hadn't come down again. With the training camps closed there weren't the homesick soldiers idling around town, looking for a place to spend their pay. The American fleet had upped anchor. A number of local women had upped stakes and followed them, but that didn't make things much better for the many who stayed behind, wondering who'd be spending money on them on all the Saturday nights to come. With the demobilised men coming home there were no more remittances or separation allowances. And the government was no longer buying all the beef and butter the farmers had to sell, at whatever price came into the farmers' heads.

No, the army's bounty just wasn't the invitation to idleness it had been at the start.

Moriarty's trouble was that he wasn't suited to civilian employment. As an experienced soldier, he knew work as something to be dodged. As a corporal, he had found the ultimate dodge of getting lower ranks to do the work for him. A soldier's life was a labourer's life but, relevant experience aside, a man like Moriarty, who had worn the king's uniform with stripes on his sleeve, was not going to settle for common labouring.

He and Wyndham sat in the sun, scanning the paper, the warmth radiating off the stone wall at their backs. Moriarty liked to have a good stout wall behind him. Wyndham found that he did too.

'Wanted: dairymaid,' said Wyndham.

'What are you talking about? You can hardly be wanting to be a dairymaid.'

'It's not that I'm interested in the vocation – I just think it's remarkable that dairymaid is an actual position worth advertising in the paper. Are you expected to bring your own three-legged stool and rosy complexion, I wonder?'

'What's so funny? Don't you have milk in America?' Moriarty sniffed. 'I often wonder how you ever came to be an officer with your head wandering all over.'

Wyndham ignored that, as he'd been ignoring remarks of similar intent ever since His Majesty had granted him a commission. Instead he pointed to another ad in the paper.

'Here's a wine merchant's that needs someone.'

'Show us. Oh, them. I know those bastards. I wouldn't go next, nigh or near them. But you'd be alright, I suppose.'

'How so?'

'No Catholics Need Apply.'

'It doesn't say that.'

'It doesn't need to. Everybody knows. Those high-and-mighty so-and-sos think dirty Catholics know nothing about wine, and they think that if they're let near the stuff they'd drink the place dry. Wine?' He spat. 'They can keep their fucking wine. I had enough of it in France and I can't see what's so special about it. God between me and any more *van plonk ordinaire*.' he spat again, as if to rid himself of the taste.

'Please don't do that.'

'Ah Christ – don't you start. I get enough of that from your one.'

Yer wan. Wyndham quickly translated in his head. A woman – not necessarily anyone's. 'Your sister-in-law?' he ventured.

'The sister-in-law. Jesus. All airs and graces. All, "you're not in the army now". All going to Mass and chewing the altar rail and not be using bad language. And would the brother stick up for me? My own brother? Would he, my arse.'

He paused long enough to cadge one of Wyndham's cigarettes.

'It's the shop. The shop has given her notions. When the brother was dealing out of a yard it was different. There was a job there for me if I wanted. She never said anything against having a brother-in-law in the army back then. But now they've got a shop she's got above herself, and he's not letting a peep out him in disagreement.'

He squinted up at the sky, wondering if it too was going to start having a go at him now.

'Eleven years in the army. Four years in the war. The last seven months of that behind the wire. All I wanted was a rest. A little bit of peace and quiet, you know? And my own family is begrudging me that. Here, go on with those advertise-ments. The sooner I can get a job the sooner I can be rid of the lot of them.'

As luck would have it, they both were taken on at a warehouse down by the docks. Wyndham successfully applied for a job as clerk, which he knew to pronounce 'clark'. Maybe that was what impressed them. That, or the fact that they were getting an American gentleman and ex-army officer who didn't turn up his nose at two pounds ten a week. So taken were his employers by the cheapness of their new acquisition, that when a position as storeman shortly after fell vacant, they accepted Wyndham's recommendation of Moriarty for the job. To him they had to pay union rate, but you can't have everything.

31

So let us rejoice,
While we are young.

—'*Gaudeamus Igi*tur' (traditional)

The college term began and Wyndham's lodgings began to fill up. His housemates weren't slow in welcoming him. They were almost all students of one thing or another: young men not quite used to manhood, making up in heartiness what they might lack in self-assurance.

It reminded him of the officers' mess in Knocknahanna back in 1915. That had been a small hotel too, with them all learning how to accommodate themselves and each other, establishing the inexact boundaries of civility and familiarity. So guests tended to knock, but not wait for an answer before entering.

'So you've got Gerry's old digs, have you?'

'I beg your pardon?'

'Gerry Twomey – this was his room.'

'I'm not sure.'

'Ah, I think he's calling himself by his Irish name now. Gearóid Ó Tuama. I don't know. Sure, I knew him when he was Gerry Twomey.'

'I see.'

'You're the American, they were telling me.'

'That's right.'

'And you're not studying – you're working?'

'That's right.'

'A rich Yank. You should keep that to yourself or they'll all be touching you for money before they're halfway through the term.'

'I'll remember, thank you.'

'Not a bother. Do you think I could trouble you for a smoke?'

Another caller was more respectful of Ó Tuama's choices and appeared to share his national sympathies.

'You're a friend of Gearóid?'

'Of sorts, I suppose.'

'He said he wasn't likely to be back. Listen, do you mind if I have a look for something he might have left behind?'

'Please. Go right ahead. I don't think there's anything, though.'

'You never know. I won't take a minute.'

And then, to Wyndham's surprise, the visitor was on his knees and pulling back the carpet. With a penknife he levered up a floorboard.

'What,' asked Wyndham, 'are you hoping to find there?'

'Lecture notes,' said the man.

'Lecture notes,' said Wyndham, as he watched the man reach into floor and sweep his hand around inside the cavity.

'Well he didn't leave them here anyway,' said the man, rising to his feet and dusting off his knees. 'That's a relief. Gearóid's a careful lad, but you can't be too careful.'

'Not with lecture notes. Evidently not.'

And that was the autumn of 1919.

Wyndham settled into his dull but undemanding job and waited for his reward to come due. A man toiled, a man proved himself, a man waited, and in due course it all came right. It was the way of things ever since Jacob was promised Rachel. It was life in peacetime. It was perfectly normal.

Except that there were occasions to make him think that things were askew. There was Nora herself, of course – that squarest of pegs, whose odd humours and unpredictable motives would keep any suitor wrong-footed – but he was used to her, more or less. It was other things that reminded him that the world in which his parents had met and married was very far away.

Mrs. Julia McInerney, for example, was capable of steering a conversation in the oddest directions.

'Nora was telling me that you were a signals officer when you were in the war. That must have been very interesting altogether, Dan. Military telephones – I wonder what that would entail now.'

'Oh – well an army telephone is much like any telephone, you know.'

'Yes I'm sure – but the switchboards and the networks and that. That must be very interesting.'

And he was prompted to tell what he remembered from an unsuccessful training course; trying to sound like neither a bore nor a show-off (and certainly not the unsatisfactory signals wallah he'd so briefly been). And he was doing his best to entertain, skimming over the tedious intricacies, only for Mrs. McInerney to pull him up and get him to clarify on some technicality. And, oddest thing of all, there was Nora with an attentive smile to match Mrs. McInerney's, as Wyndham sketched out the chain of communication from company to battalion to brigade and back again.

And there were his neighbours, crass and boisterous at times as was only to be expected. Less expected were the secretive activities. Galvin, the friend of Ó Tuama's – the man who'd dug under Wyndham's floorboards – was obviously in cahoots with another man called O'Hare. Wyndham could only guess what it was all about, but whenever he came across them in one of their furtive conversations, Galvin would just give him the nod as if Wyndham was somehow part of their conspiracy.

Then one evening after Wyndham had come back from another

weekend in Tralee, Galvin dropped by his room again.

'Ah – tis yourself,' he said, when Wyndham answered his knock. 'I thought you might still be away.'

'What can I do for you?'

'Could I just check one little thing there?'

'What do you mean?'

'I think I might have missed something when I was last here. Honest to God, it'll hardly be a minute. Do you mind?'

And as he had already edged in, it was all one whether Wyndham minded or not.

Galvin was at the loose floorboard again and this time he drew out a wad of papers bound in a rubber band. Wyndham was thinking up something suitably dry and sarcastic to say when Galvin reached into the floor again and came out with a pistol-shaped object wrapped in an oily rag. Galvin smiled apologetically as he shoved his trove into various pockets and saw himself out.

'Thanks very much,' he said. 'I'll not bother you again, thanks.'

Nor did he. A week passed without Wyndham bumping into Galvin in the hall or meeting him over breakfast. The man had just disappeared without a trace. He told as much to the policemen who came asking for him, only he thought it wiser not to mention the secret compartment in the floor of his room.

32

And when he came he was received with honour and attendance, and he was served with pleasant drinks, so that he grew merry, and his mind was confused.

—Lady Gregory, *Cuchulain of Muirthemne*

That happened in late October. A Saturday shortly after, with the weather uncannily fine and Nora working, Wyndham decided to go on a last outing by bicycle. It was just for the day. He was going to take a train out to a point thirty or so miles distant and ride all the way home before it got dark. He'd been sitting in a miserable little office for too long.

His plan struck an obstacle early on. It was fair day in the little town where he got off, and he was obliged to thread his way through crowds of people and livestock before he could reach the open road. He cursed himself when he realised that, it being a Saturday, he'd be likewise hindered in the next town. Rather than face that he resolved on a detour.

When he'd cleared out so much of his army papers, he'd kept the maps he'd trained on. Good Ordnance Survey maps, and a good army compass to go with them. A detour would add maybe an hour but he reckoned he had the time. He was no more than a half a mile on his way when he was stopped by a signpost unhelpfully knocked sideways and pointing exactly midway in the fork of the road.

He looked up from checking his bearings against his map to see a couple of men approaching, no doubt on their way to the fair.

'I beg your pardon,' he said, squinting into the autumn sun, 'but am I headed the right way for Bally—?' he checked the map again. The name was spelled strangely and was obscured by a worn fold besides. Bally-something. Nearest identifiable feature, a police barracks.

'Bally—?' he tried again, hoping that someone would rescue him from his ignorance by finishing the word for him. As he took a proper look at the two men he felt even less sure of himself. One of them was fearsome. Broad-shouldered, deep-chested, swag-bellied, of overbearing height and disfigured face, he hailed Wyndham in a booming voice.

'You there! Yourself, sir! I know you!'

I smell the blood of an Englishman.

A mutilated hand stretched out at him. The alarm bells in Wyndham's mind were silenced in an instant of recognition.

'Sergeant Duffy?'

Cornelius Duffy, cook-sergeant, 3rd Battalion, Royal Munster Fusiliers.

Also, acting company sergeant-major in a detachment with no official designation except in the mind of its commander: the Fitzmullen-Brophy Commando, which had marched out of Tralee without authorisation in August of 1914 and wasn't seen again until it was well on the road to Mons. Across all those miles Sergeant Duffy had been the man calling the step and making the porridge. In the trenches near Armentières he'd taken Wyndham the raw recruit as an assistant, back when Wyndham was too useless for a soldier and innocent enough to be trusted with the rum ration.

Sergeant Duffy who'd fought hand to hand like a hero; who'd led a desperate charge against an enemy machine-gun; who'd run into two German bullets but hadn't let that stop him.

Sergeant Duffy, with the most obscene tattoos you could hope to find this side of Suez.

'He remembers!' said Duffy. 'Of course he does!'

This was partly addressed to his understated companion, dressed much the same way as Duffy – just another countryman on his way to the fair – but barely registering beside the florid old soldier.

'Young Wyndham, begod! The bold American!' And Wydham's hand was clasped and his shoulder clapped. The couple of fingers Duffy had lost at Armentières didn't lessen the strength of his grip one bit, nor had the bullet wound to the face done anything to keep this great man from showing his good humour. The two old fusiliers expressed amazement at their chance encounter and gladness that the other was still alive.

'Ah, sure I was grand. There was no way on God's earth they were going to allow me back in the line with my hand all bollocksed up like that. I hung on in 3rd Battalion, doing my usual bit in the cookhouse. They had us down in Aghada. It was a grand cushy number. And they made you an officer? Of course they did. Young Wyndham was always too much the gentlemen to be kept down among the louts and the bowsies like the rest of us.'

He was not interested in directing Wyndham on his way. He would stand for nothing but bringing Wyndham along to where they could both drink the health of the old battalion, and the Dirty Shirts, and each other – the lucky pair that they were. Wyndham protested that he didn't want to put Duffy out of his way, and that he himself had a long road ahead of him, and he didn't really partake these days, but Duffy's arm was about him and Duffy was almost capable of pulling a whole tug-of-war team off its feet, so back to the town they went, with Duffy pushing cows out of their way with ease, and the last push being on the door of a pub.

Despite his straight and narrow living since the armistice, Wyndham had always had an uncommonly good head for drink so, once at the bar, he wasn't going to balk at raising a glass with an old comrade. But it wasn't going to be that simple. Duffy called for a pint of plain and a ball of malt, and Wyndham was wondering which one was for him until Duffy called for the same for himself. Duffy's companion, whose name Wyndham never caught, didn't join them, but vanished after a few quiet words that Wyndham couldn't catch either.

'The Munster Fusiliers,' said Duffy, with appropriate solemnity, and Wyndham followed suit and they drank.

Duffy had heard what cook-sergeants hear about what the regiment had been getting up to – and that was a sight more than subalterns in the front line ever knew – but he plied Wyndham with questions nevertheless: about Fitzmullen-Brophy; about Knocknahanna and the 11th Battalion; about Ginchy and Guillemont and Messines.

'Here's to them,' he said. 'Here's to the brave lads who won't be coming home from France.' And he drank and called for another round.

Wyndham drank up and said he must be going, but Duffy wouldn't hear of it.

'No, really,' said Wyndham. 'The days are so short and it's quite a distance back to Cork. Just point me on my way.'

'Ah sure it's no good the way you were going. It'd take you miles out of your way and you'd only get lost. Stay here a while longer. Have another and the streets will be clear by the time we're finished.'

A man who wasn't introduced had just come in to confer briefly with Duffy, and he confirmed in the brief moment he was there that the road was very bad.

'Colonel Fitzmullen-Brophy,' said Duffy. 'And his DSO.'

'Here's to the colonel,' said Wyndham.

'And Major Belcher, God rest him.'

'And Major Belcher. Here's to him.'

'The same again there, Frank.'

Frank the barman was also of the opinion, when pressed, that

Wyndham was better off where he was for the time being.

'That bit of road is fierce stony,' he said. 'Twould cut the tyres off your bike.'

Later, when another unnamed man dropped by (or maybe it was one of the same men from earlier on), the information was volunteered that Wyndham would be an awful fool if tried to cycle the proposed road, which had been washed out by a flood and still hadn't been repaired.

Duffy asked about America and spoke about India, and around the world they went, only to return to the trenches south of the southern shoulder of the Ypres Salient as they had known them five years before.

'Five years,' said Duffy. 'Five years since poor old Charlie Robinson got killed. You remember Robinson of course? And his mate Dwyer? Ah, by God but they were real old soldiers. More rum than blood in their veins. Left a trail of broken hearts and broken glass all the way from Jullundur to Rangoon, I'll be bound. Here's to them.'

'Here's to them,' said Wyndham, remembering. 'And here's to Moyle. You remember Moyle?'

'A quare lanky fells from up the west somewhere? Marksman first class? I do indeed. And what was the name of that young fella who was killed at the same time?'

'Whelan,' said Wyndham, his eyes beginning to swim and his chin was closer to the bar than he realised. 'Timothy Whelan.' He wiped his nose. 'Frank, you'll be so good as to pour us a drink for Private Timothy Whelan.'

And they drank to the dead of the old battalion: to the men with the tigers on their cap badges, who had gone to join those men who had marched from Dagshai to die under the walls of Delhi, and those more distant men who had followed Clive out of Calcutta to cut their way through an army ten times their number. The dust of India and the cold mud of Flanders had received them, and the gods of the regiment, honoured here in balls of malt and pints of plain, cherished them yet.

Wyndham drank until he didn't care about the time anymore, or the road. By the time he finally unstuck himself from the bar he was in no fit state to cycle anywhere, and Duffy had to put him on the train home. He was still drunk and melancholy when he arrived in Cork and he'd have forgotten his bicycle in the guard's van if the guard hadn't reminded him.

Sore and ashamed the next morning, he concentrated on putting himself in trim for his tea with Nora. On Monday for some reason or other he missed getting the paper, so he never saw the report of a certain police barracks being attacked and burned, somewhere between a certain market town and a village called Bally-something. Arms had been seized before the building had been fired, and it may well have been those same arms that were then used to ambush the police reinforcements on the road.

Of all this Wyndham learned nothing. If he had, he might have been reminded that ex-Sergeant Duffy, who'd served the crown for more than twenty years, had, more flamboyant even than the fornicating Indian figures, an Irish harp tattooed upon his body and, misspelled below it, the legend: *I Am New Strung And I Will Be Heard.*

There were gods other than the gods of the regiment.

IV

LAW AND ORDER

The only way of starting a war was to kill someone, and we wanted to start a war.

—Dan Breen, 3rd Tipperary Brigade, IRA

33

But what is liberty without wisdom and without virtue? It is the greatest of all possible evils; for it is folly, vice, and madness, without tuition or restraint.

—Edmund Burke, 'Reflections On The Revolution In France'

1920 made no sense. There had been some strange goings-on through the previous year, but Wyndham saw them as anomalies or as ill-understood parts of a process that was working itself out. It didn't. Not in 1920, at any rate.

If 1918 had been the Year of Victory, and 1919 the Year of Peace, then 1920 fast became the Year That Made No Damn Sense At All.

Wyndham was wrong-footed from the get-go. Naturally, it was Nora who began it. Nora Maxfield, from whom all unreasonable things sprang. With typical perversity she began it a month before New Year.

They were in what they'd settled on as their favourite café, she looking at the streetlights through the rain-speckled window and he looking at her.

Let's do something special for Christmas. Just the two of us. We could go away somewhere.

He left the words unsaid. There was too much to lose. Instead, in a spirit of light devilment, he said, 'I'm going to get you something nice for Christmas.'

'I should only hope so,' she said, playing along while still looking out at the passing traffic.

'A cigarette case,' he said. 'Gold. Monogrammed.'

She turned a face on him. 'You're not going to let that go, are you? Either give it back to me or keep it, but don't be taunting me about it.'

'You can have it back if you promise not to hock it this time.'

She stuck her nose in the air. 'I make no promises under duress,' she said.

'*Are* you going to pawn it again?'

'A lady is free to do as she pleases with her own property,' she said loftily, but then gave up on the game. 'No, probably not. I have enough money to be getting along with. Besides, I'll be starting a new job soon.'

'Really? What sort of a job.'

'I'll be working in the post office. A friend of Julia's fixed it for me.'

'Well I think that's pretty good. I'm not sure you were perfectly suited to being a shop girl. Not servile enough. Which post office?'

'I can't quite remember the exact place but it's just outside Listowel.'

'*Listowel?* In Kerry?'

'That's right – in Kerry. Will we pay now? I'm not going for a walk in this rain. Let's go to the pictures instead.'

Wyndham did not enjoy the show. Nora had a perfect excuse for shushing him any time he tried to speak. On top of that, they'd missed the first half of the main feature.

His temper had not improved by the time they were outside again.

'You're moving to Kerry?'

'You're fuming at me, Dan. No one likes being fumed at.'

'You waited until I moved all the way from Kerry to Cork, and found a place to live, and a job and everything, and then you up and go to Kerry?'

'It was the only place I could get a post office job.'

'Why in hell's name is that important?'

'I always wanted to work in a post office.'

'Nora, you are telling me lies. You never wanted any such thing.'

'Alright, so I didn't. But it will be good for me. I'll be learning things.'

A penny dropped. 'Is this a part of this organisation you're a part of?' he asked.

'*Shh!*'

They walked on in silence: Nora worrying that they were being spied on and Wyndham morose.

'I think I might as well go back home to the States,' he said at last.

'Ah, Dan, don't,' she said, and it sounded so much like she meant it.

'I might as well.'

She was going to say something but stopped. He watched her try and formulate some sort of argument. In the end she gave up. 'Ah don't,' she said again.

And that, in the three and a half years since they'd first met, was the first time that she'd ever given Wyndham the impression that her picture of the future included him. It would have to do.

He seriously considered going back to America – just for a month or two – but he didn't really have the money. And he didn't like to think of an ocean separating him from Nora, with nothing to stop her from being seduced by the heady passions of revolution and swept into the arms of some revolutionary type. He was familiar with rural post offices and they honestly didn't seem like the sort of places where such things went on, but he didn't want to take any chances.

The Fitzmullen-Brophys, with whom he stayed for Christmas,

insisted that he was one of the family and would always have a home under their roof, and they sounded perfectly sincere in saying it. Wyndham said he wouldn't dream of imposing on them any further, and he was sincere himself – up to a point. Where his pursuit of Nora was concerned, promises meant little.

For the time being, he resigned himself to long rail journeys. Nora would not be given the opportunity to cast him loose.

'So your girl's given you the elbow,' said Moriarty.

'No!'

'Only bit of her she has been giving you, I'd bet.'

'You watch your mouth.'

Moriarty was a problem, and not just because of off-colour remarks. He was proving to be less than the perfect employee.

'They think you're skrimshanking,' said Wyndham.

'That's a bloody lie.'

'They say you're never there when you're needed.'

'Ah well – y'know.'

And Wyndham did. He knew that Moriarty had never really recovered from the shell shock that had put him in hospital after Festubert. The man had been left with all manner of ticks and foibles which had been largely overlooked during the war, when everyone with more than a few months' service to his name had bad nerves. By the spring of 1918 you'd have been lucky if you so much as saw Corporal Moriarty above ground, but seeing as he'd been out since '14 he was given quite a bit of tacit leeway. No such latitude was afforded in peacetime to a man who took to lurking in corners of the warehouse. The world that the soldiers had fought for – the world fit for heroes – did not know the term 'neurasthenic'. It said 'work-shy' instead.

'They're blaming me,' said Wyndham. 'I was the one who recommended you for the job, so they see it as my fault.'

Moriarty contemplated this, considering what he owed his

employers and what he owed his old comrade in arms who'd stuck his neck out for him.

'Tell them to go on away and fuck themselves,' he said.

Over the following weeks Wyndham gave serious consideration to doing that very thing.

Galvin, the student of Wyndham's floorboard, never did reappear, but one evening another scholar, professing to be a friend of Galvin's and of Ó Tuama's, dropped by with an 1888-pattern German rifle under his coat.

'No,' said Wyndham. 'Absolutely not.'

'But it'd just be for a few days. The lads said it'd be alright.'

'But I didn't. Please – just go.'

'They said you'd need to saw through one of the floor joists to make it fit, but only the one.'

'*I'd* have to saw?'

'I don't think it'd take too long.'

'Get out.'

After that, certain of his neighbours regarded him with coldness.

34

I knew that I would continue to shoot their officers... If we shot enough of them it would make the others think a little.

—Ernie O'Malley, 2nd Southern Division, IRA

On a bright January day he set out early, heading west, intending to think out his situation in the hypnotic turning of the wheels, and to burn away his troubles in the rhythmic pumping of the pedals. No trains this time. Just push on until the day was half done and then turn around and head back. On a poor stretch of byroad that caused him to worry about a puncture he was surprised by two men stepping into his path with guns in their hands. Or, looking at it another way, he was hardly surprised at all. It was all of a piece with his life in Ireland.

The men were not police. Remembering his encounter with the constabulary in Kerry a year earlier, Wyndham noticed the similarity between his dress then and the way this pair presented themselves now. Belted trenchcoats on both of them. Soft hat with a turned-down brim on one and military-style gaiters on the other.

His heart was beating fast as he came to a stop and raised his hands, but there was a sense of detachment too. For a young man who'd left home with the intent to immerse himself in Irish literature, and who since then had formed no greater wish than to marry the girl of his dreams and settle down, it was surprising how often he found himself held up at gunpoint. Indeed, it had been an annual event for some years now: German storm troops, the Royal Irish Constabulary, and now, presumably, these bold men of the Irish Republican Army.

'Can I help you fellows?' he asked.

'Well you're a cool one anyhow,' said one of the gunmen. 'Who are you and where are you headed?'

'My name is Wyndham, if you must know. I'm on my way to Macroom.'

'You have business in Macroom, Mr. Wyndham?'

'None at all.'

'I can't quite place your accent.'

'I don't suppose you can.'

'Oh, but you're a cool one alright. You'll be so good as to empty your pockets.'

You'll be so good as to get stuffed, thought Wyndham, but knew that such merry banter was unlikely to get him far.

'What's this?' said the other man, uncommonly observant. 'A fine bit of blackthorn.'

'It is, isn't it?' said Wyndham, suffering to have his walking stick detached from his crossbar.

'2/Lt. D.P. Wyndham 11/RMF,' said the gunman, reading the little brass name plate near the handle.

'Hmm,' said Wyndham, not committing himself.

'Empty your pockets now, Lieutenant.' The pistol was unwavering.

Because it was an encounter with the police that Wyndham had feared, his wallet still contained papers identifying him as an army officer.

'Retired,' he clarified. 'Discharged. Whichever you prefer.'

And now it was the IRA man's turn to *hmm*.

'I no longer work for the crown,' Wyndham went on. *Some of my best friends are Sinn Feiners. I'm going to marry one of them.* 'I'm an American citizen.'

'And what was an American doing in the British army?'

'It's a long story. May I have my wallet back?'

But no. They kept his wallet, even if they were decent enough to give him back the two pound notes therein. He knew better than to argue. He knew they could have taken him to some out-of-the-way place for more thorough questioning. They could even have shot him and left his body there in the road as a warning to any other servants of the crown who might have thought they were safe to ride through Ireland as if it still were theirs. But he turned back for Cork with his heart somewhat hardened against over-zealous revolutionaries.

A few miles from home he ran over something jagged in the dark and had to wheel his bike the rest of the way.

That was Sunday, and the last fine day. The following morning he woke, his limbs stiff from his day out, to hear the rain slapping at his window. Why couldn't it snow in winter like it did in civilised countries? He arrived at work in squelching shoes and sat through a morning with wet socks. Had he survived the war only to die of bronchitis or pneumonia in a miserable little office? Shells and bullets had been replaced by professional pettiness and the cheapest brands of ink and pen nib. By the time the working day ended the rain had eased off, leaving the cold streets deep-puddled, with coal smoke pervading the dank riverine smell. It matched Wyndham's mood.

'Wyndham, a word before you go.'

That was Creevy, his employer.

It was never 'Mister' Wyndham with Creevy, and it was never at a convenient time: never when Wyndham was at his desk. No – always, like now, when Wyndham was tired and not being paid for his time.

It was about Moriarty. Creevy was dissatisfied with Moriarty and that was somehow Wyndham's fault.

'It was your recommendation that we took into consideration

when taking him on,' said Creevy, suggesting that it was only his inherent generosity of spirit that had made him to quell his doubts.

Wyndham was running through his standard excuses and blandishments when something said, *to hell with it.*

What came out was, 'Moriarty isn't my responsibility, Mr. Creevy – not before and certainly not now.

'What do you mean by that, Wyndham?'

'I'm leaving, Mr. Creevy.'

He'd had no notion he was going to say such a thing, but he was glad he did. It was only when he was outside that Creevy's disappointed words sank in, along with Creevy's mention of the extra five shillings a week that would have been his if he'd stayed on, and of course Creevy's solemn outline of a man's sorry prospects in this present slump, and what a man could expect if he threw off jobs so carelessly. Wyndham had two pounds and some change on his person and an inadequate sum in the bank, and try as he might he could not shake off the respectability of his upbringing and its reverence for thrift and financial probity. And he'd probably left Moriarty in the lurch again. And it was still only Monday.

It was surprising how quickly the street could empty. Ten minutes ago, when the various businesses had let out, there would have been a small crowd of hurrying men. Now, in the course of Creevy's little talk, they had all put their hurrying to good use. Everyone was gone. The silence was unnerving, the dark more noticeable, as was the louring aspect of these warehouses.

And then Wyndham saw that there was someone. A suspect character peeled himself out from the shadows as Wyndham approached.

Well hoo-ray, thought Wyndham. *And on top of everything I'm going to get beaten and robbed by some dockside thug.*

And then for a second he believed it, because the stranger was making straight for him, shoulders bunched and a hand concealed in his jacket.

Wyndham had his umbrella. He'd never fought with an umbrella and didn't know how. He was damned if he was going to run. Where could he run? And what if the man only wanted a light or some change? All this was rushing through his mind when the stranger handed him his wallet back and disappeared into the January night.

35

This house
You are to leave with some old trusty man,
And bid him shelter all that starve or wander
While there is food and house room.

—W.B. Yeats, *The Countess Cathleen*

He returned to Tralee, feeling like the prodigal son. Every misfortune these past six years had sent him back to the arms of the Fitzmullen-Brophys.

Get bushwhacked by a couple of merrymaking fusiliers on a Saturday night? Fitzmullen-Brophys to the rescue. Invalided out of the Western Front? Back to the Fitzmullen-Brophys. Can't keep your girl and can't hold down a job? Where else but the Fitzmullen-Brophys?

Colonel, I and am no more worthy to be called thy son: make me as one of thy hired servants.

But of course they professed nothing but gladness at his return, and if there wasn't fatted calf, there was certainly some flabby ham served up for lunch.

'A job, my boy? I'm sure I can help you find something. Don't you worry.' That was the colonel.

'Your young lady will come around once she knows her own mind, Daniel. Of that I have no doubt.' That was Mrs. Fitzmullen-Brophy.

'When she sees you chasing after her she'll know you mean business.' That was Molly. 'I think it's awfully romantic in its way. Jolly inconvenient for you, of course. Here, hold Baby a moment. No, no, darling – don't put that in your mouth. Not when the dog's been at it.'

The colonel was only too happy to be sent out to find a job for Wyndham. It was a mission. It busied him. It gave him licence to meet fellows and buttonhole chaps, and generally pry in a good cause. The sole drawback was that the only job he himself had ever had was army officer, and his ideas of suitable employment were somewhat limited and outdated. Nevertheless, he was justifiably pleased when he found Wyndham a position in under a week.

'Right up your street, my boy. Exactly in your line of country. Books and that sort of thing. Old books, I mean. Not your cheap paperbacks at any rate – at least I don't think so.'

Fitzmullen-Brophy's inquiries around Tralee had led him to an antiquary named Sefton, who admitted, when pressed, that he could probably do with an amanuensis,

'Whatever that is,' the colonel told Wyndham. 'Never quite sure myself. Something like a sort of literary adjutant, I always thought.'

'Something like,' said Wyndham.

'Anyway,' said Fitzmullen-Brophy, 'It'll all be dry as dust, no doubt – old books and such – but what matter? I reckon you've done enough man's service out in the world that it won't do you much harm to go back to your books.'

'Thank you, Colonel. I'm most terribly grateful for your efforts.'

And he was. Truly. It was just that, within a few days, he was wishing that the colonel had a wider notion of the sort of work that befitted a gentleman.

The antiquarian was everything Wyndham imagined, only crankier.

He sneered at Lady Gregory, inveighed against someone called Crofton Croker and habitually berated Wyndham for being unable to spell or even pronounce names in Old Irish. Their arrangement came to an end when Wyndham raised the question of money. Sefton parried with a request for the loan of two pounds ten. They subsequently parted company with little regret on either side.

'Never mind,' said Mrs. Fitzmullen-Brophy. 'Something better is bound to turn up. In the meantime you can be company for Hugh. He needs something to do.'

And he did. The colonel was like a schoolboy, bored with the summer holidays but unwilling to admit it, picking at one thing or another, making his dissatisfaction felt.

'He tried the Boy Scouts,' Mrs. Fitzmullen-Brophy told Wyndham, 'but it just wasn't on. Captain Baxter-d'Arcy's the scout master, you know, and he's most jealous of his charges. He was perfectly happy to have Hugh come and give a talk, but he absolutely wasn't going to surrender command. Hugh might have outranked him in the army, but Paddy Baxter-d'Arcy has seniority in the Boy Scouts and won't let Hugh forget it. To be honest, I'm relieved. The Scouts might have been the very thing for Hugh, but the Tralee troop is pitifully small and they're always being set upon by those boys from Fianna Éireann these days. There have been desertions and even defections, I gather. Fianna Éireann have more fun – spying on troop movements and shadowing police agents and so forth.'

Life in Kerry seemed to agree with Nora.

When she found that Wyndham had followed her all the way from Cork she called him an awful fool and then kissed him properly.

He gathered that whatever suspicion she'd been under as a

Protestant, and one who'd served in the war, had dissipated.

'I kept on telling them I worked for the Red Cross and that's international. It wasn't like I was in the army auxiliary or anything. No crown on *my* badge. Besides, I wouldn't have been caught dead in that uniform – it was even worse than our own. And no one could accuse me of being a hireling of the British government seeing as they never paid me. The VAD took "voluntary" literally. Bed and board and that was it. I even had to pay for my own aprons when I was a nurse, and you wouldn't believe how many aprons we used to get through.'

'So you're enjoying your new job?'

'Well enough. I could do without the remarks I get from some of the customers. The men, I mean.'

'They've never seen such exotic and sophisticated beauty.'

'Shut up, you. You're worse than any of them.'

'I couldn't be – not when I'm so exotic and sophisticated myself.'

'Are you now?'

'Of course I am. I'm a mysterious foreigner with a romantic past.'

'Is that a fact?'

'I even sojourned a while in Paris.'

'Don't you dare mention Paris!'

'But—'

'I think I might like you better, Dan Wyndham, if you kept your innuendoes to yourself. "Sojourning" indeed!'

'Have a cigarette.'

'I will, thank you. Only stop smiling.'

'I'm not!'

'You're thinking, then. Stop it.'

'Alright then. You can tell me how you're building a new Ireland out of a rural post office, and I'll listen with pure thoughts like I'm in church. I can't do any better than that.'

36

If you have the Physique – if you have a Good Character
And especially – If you are an Ex-Service Man
You can join the RIC to-day.

—Recruiting poster, 1920

The steel shutters never did go up on the little police barracks where Ogilvie had lodged a complaint. Instead the place was shut, along with so many others. The rural police stations were too isolated and too vulnerable.

The Sinn Féin government in Dublin was a government in name only – outlawed, fugitive, and penniless if not for the faith and generosity of patriots. It was in the rest of the country that the Republic was becoming a reality. Every RIC barracks that closed was another district where law and order were decided by the Irish Republican Army. Every RIC constable removed from his post was a measurable reduction in the crown's administrative power.

And it was oh-so easy to reduce that power. No matter how stout a barracks' walls, a policeman was just a man, and a local man. His whole life lay open to his neighbours, who might just as often be his enemies. Sometimes a strong hint was enough for him to seek other employment. Sometimes a shot from the dark, the report of other shootings – of a constable wounded or even killed – would make a man think. And if he were resolute to the end, that end could be quickly brought about.

The RIC withdrew from the countryside, and in the towns they took care. As the country slipped from its grasp, the crown needed more policing, and steadily there was less.

The solution made its appearance in the early spring. Fitzmullen-Brophy was the first to notice.

It was the colonel's custom to drop by the Munsters' barracks once every so often, which was to say once a fortnight, regular as clockwork. Having no business there at all was no impediment. No one was going to bar a full colonel, retired or not. So the sentries at the gate knew to recognise and salute him, and the mess president was always at hand to invite him in and offer him a drink. After that, someone would be found and detailed off to keep the old man happy for half an hour or so. There weren't many left from the pre-war days, and there were never many men in Ballymullen Barracks in the first place. Yes, it was the home of the regiment, but it was really home only to the depot company, which maintained an administrative presence and no more. The two battalions of the regiment proper were never in Tralee, and indeed hardly ever in Ireland for that matter. Tralee was a way station and a forwarding address – little more. For most of the year the main activity was processing the new recruits.

And despite everything, there were new recruits – quite a steady number of them. It did Fitzmullen-Brophy's heart glad to see them sweating on the square whenever he dropped by, and the regiment indulged him by letting him give impromptu little speeches of welcome. The new recruits, sweat chilling and limbs cramping, would be called to attention in the raw air to listen to the glories of the regiment and the splendid opportunity of which they should make the most.

'And in short, men,' he rounded off after one of these addresses, 'I have not the faintest doubt that you will live up to – and even add to, what? – the regiment's proud traditions. Jolly well done, all of you. That will be all, Sergeant.'

'Yes, sir. Thank you, sir.' And as Fitzmullen-Brophy moved away, 'Right, you shower! You heard the colonel! Fucking sort yourselves out!'

And it was then that a small convoy of motor lorries came rumbling and growling through the gate. The men who piled out over the tailboards were armed and equipped as soldiers, and by their packs and kitbags were evidently here to stay, but Fitzmullen-Brophy couldn't place their uniforms. It was an inconsistent mixture of service khaki and the darkest green of the rifle regiments, abandoned since the war's beginning along with infantry scarlet and artillery blue, and only seen nowadays in police uniforms.

These men were too far away for Fitzmullen-Brophy to discern their badges, but their caps had something of a highland cast to them. He buttonholed the adjutant as soon as he could find him.

'Highlanders, Colonel? No,' the adjutant told him. 'They're police, believe it or not. Special reinforcement for the RIC. They've been recruiting them since the new year. Seems we have to put them up, given that we've got the space. I only hope they don't expect to use our mess.'

'I must say they don't look much like police,' said Fitzmullen-Brophy, who had standards about this sort of thing. 'Can't say I like the look of them at all.'

'Neither do I, if I'm honest. Not enough police uniforms to go around, I gather. Hence the khaki. Rough looking mob. Might be just the ticket for dealing with the Shinners though. Not sure what they call themselves.'

Black and Tans. The name appeared in some waggish newspaper report or somewhere and soon outran and overwrote any official name this new constabulary might have had. The nickname had already belonged to a well-known pack of foxhounds, and the hunting analogy seemed appropriate.

The new policemen were nearly all old soldiers, and almost all English. They were here in Ireland for the same reason there were fresh recruits on the barrack square. The post-war slump was making itself felt, and a job was a job. The policemen were getting the better deal than the lads in the Munsters. Their term of enlistment was shorter, and their pay was better.

Ten shillings a day. Three pounds ten a week. A job was a job, and jobs that paid so much were few and far between. Most of the men who answered were English because it was in England the advertisements had first been posted. It wasn't long, however, for the news to spread across the United Kingdom.

Ten shillings a day. Three pounds ten a week. And allowances on top of that. For an Irishman who'd worn the king's uniform once already, it was an offer that merited serious consideration.

37

Left,

Left,

I had a good job

and I left,

Right?

—traditional

The Barracks.

It had been properly named after the old queen a long time before, but to everyone, military and civilian, it was just the Barracks. There were barracks all over Ireland – all over Cork, even – but this one was big enough not to need a name.

Moriarty had done his best with himself this morning. He'd brushed his clothes and put a shine on his boots. He'd even pinned on his medals. He didn't have a uniform to wear anymore, but anyone who looked at him would know him as a veteran: not just of the war, but of 1914 and of the wider empire before that. Moriarty had served his time, and he wanted the young gawm at the gate to see that.

By Christ but he remembered well the first time he'd come through these gates. The slant-wise look the sentry had given him. The up-and-down look of the corporal. The sergeant.

The sergeant in his sash and his shiny boots, his legs moving like scissors as he crossed the square. The sergeant grinning under his waxed moustaches.

'What is it you want, lad? Tradesmen round the back, don't you know.'

'I want to join up.'

'Join up? And you need joining up, no doubt. Look at you, boy – no two pieces of you holding together. Stand up straight now.'

'I want to enlist.'

'Enlist! There's a notion! Well you've come to the right place then, haven't you? What do you want to enlist in? Eh, boy? That's the question!'

'I want to be a Munster Fusilier.'

'No you don't!'

'I do so.'

'They wouldn't have you – not if your father's married to your mother, they wouldn't.'

'Well I'll go on away so.'

'Haha! Don't be in such a rush, my lad. I was only having my little joke. The Munsters are a fine lot I'm sure. But you know what they call themselves, don't you?'

'The Dirty Shirts.'

'The Dirty Shirts! And why's that, eh?'

'Cause of India. Cause of fighting in the heat and that, without their coats. Getting their shirts all dirty with blood and gunpowder and that.'

'Well that's what they say, right enough, but there's some will tell you that it's because they never saw a wash house in all their born days. Come join a smart regiment, boy. There might just be a couple of vacancies in my own corps – the Durham Light Infantry.'

'I'm not from Durham.'

'Why, neither am I, and you don't hear me complaining! Become a Durham, lad. It's a fine regiment and a fine life. You'll find any number of Irishmen here to keep you from being lonely.'

'I want to be a Munster.'

'Well don't look so surly about it. The doctor hasn't had a look at you yet, and until he does you're not anything, are you? How old are you?'

'Nineteen.'

'My eye, you are.'

'I'm nineteen.'

'Maybe I'll believe you better once we've fed you up a bit and taught you how to stand up straight. And given you a bath. Maybe the Dirty Shirts are the lot for you after all.'

'I had a bath on Saturday.'

'I'll take your word for it, son, even if thousands wouldn't. Come along – smartly now – and see what the doctor makes of you.'

And then came Moriarty's first real taste of the army – the army that told him to strip off, stand still, shut up, bend down, straighten up again, get dressed, get out.

'So he passed you fit, did he? The poor old man's wits aren't what they used to be, I'm sorry to say. Still sure you want to be a soldier?'

'I am.'

'Say, "Yes, Sergeant".'

'Yes, Sergeant.'

'Seven years, boy. It's no little undertaking.'

'I know that, Sergeant.'

'But you'll be a man when you come out the other end, won't you?'

'Yes, Sergeant.'

'Maybe even a man like me, but I doubt it. Do you shave yet?'

'Of course I do.'

'Of course he does, he says. With what? A pumice stone?'

'A what, Sergeant?'

'Never mind. Just from now on you don't shave your upper lip. Not in the army. Not even in the Munster Fusiliers. Come to the *end of your seven years and you'll want your knees brown and you'll want moustaches like mine. Then you'll be fit for another seven, eh?'*

'Yes, Sergeant.'

'Still have your heart set on the Munsters?'

'Yes, Sergeant.'

'Well, until they swear you in you're not a soldier yet. They give you any money?'

'Not yet, Sergeant.'

'Well, you'll be entitled to one and sixpence for today, even though you've done nothing to earn it. One and six! And nothing to pay in income tax either! Now ain't the army grand?'

'Yes, Sergeant.'

'So because I'm a soft-hearted soul I'll lend you a shilling until tomorrow – but I'll need fourteen pence back, mind. And because you're not a soldier quite yet, I can still talk to you one man to another, and not a sergeant to a recruit. So what I'll do is let you take me to the public house across the way and we can talk, one man to another, and I'll try to change your mind about what regiment you're set on.'

'Alright, Sergeant.'

'Right, come along. Did you know the Durhams won two Victoria Crosses in the Crimea? Two! Step smartly, now. The Munsters were never even in the Crimea. In here. Lounge bar for commercial travellers and tarts: saloon bar for soldiers of the King. It was a Private John Byrne won the first of them. There's an Irish name for you, lad. John Byrne VC. Here's your shilling then. Mine's a pint.'

And there was the pub, same as before. Seven years, that the war turned into more than eleven, and Francis Moriarty had come a long, long way, but it was the same pub. Pubs always stayed. They might get a lick of paint every so often, but that was it. They didn't get sunstroke or malaria or bullet wounds or shell shock.

He eyed the barrack gate, and thought about what was waiting for him there, and how, three pound ten a week or not, he'd not be a free man again for a long while, and he thought a last drink would be in order. Not that he could well afford to be drinking, but he could get in out of the weather at least.

He had known the pub well of course, long before the Durham sergeant had taken him in and drunk his money, and lectured him on regimental history. He'd hung around there, and places like it, for years. He'd always liked to be around the soldiers and hear them talk. And amid the big men in red tunics and the gawping youngsters like Moriarty, there had always been some older man, a bit down at heel, a bit shabby, cadging smokes and drinks on the strength of his own stories of his own service. Some broken-down fellow, old before his time, who'd done his years out east or wherever and was now indulged by the soldiers but no more than that. Moriarty suddenly saw himself that way. A man on the wrong side of thirty. A man looking for work, in a suit he'd borrowed from his brother.

He dredged up a sufficiency of pride, unpinned his medals and put them in his pocket. With shoulders squared he walked inside and called for a glass of stout as if the sixpence he put in the bar wasn't his last in all the world.

He hadn't so much as wiped the cream from his moustache when some new customers came in, pushing open the door like they owned the place. Typically enough, they were wearing khaki, but they were wearing it with rifle green. Police tunics with army trousers. And they were all armed. Moriarty had never had so close a look at these Black and Tans before. He made the most of it. He didn't need any beer to give him courage. He was a Munster Fusilier and he'd stare down any man anywhere.

One on the Tans saw him staring.

'Alright, mate?' he asked, neither friendly nor hostile.

'Right enough,' said Moriarty. 'You'd be some of those new policemen, I suppose. Special constables.'

The Tan was new to Ireland and was just here with his mates for a drink. He took Moriarty at face value. 'That's us,' he said.

Moriarty nodded. He could have left it there, or carried on in a conversational way, but it was as though a devil had got into him – that old regimental devil that had sent the Dirty Shirts out, badges bright of a Saturday night, to line any bar in any pub they liked and defy anyone to ask them to keep the noise down, or suggest that the Munsters were not the finest men to ever wear the red coat.

It might well have been the case that, had Moriarty presented himself to a medical board in this present frame of mind, they would have concurred that the balance of his mind had still not recovered from his war experiences.

'So what's that thing on your head, at all?' he asked.

This new breed of policeman did not wear the peaked cap or spiked helmet of the regular RIC, sporting instead an affair like a tam-o'-shanter. This was evidently the army's latest manifestation of its love of outrageous headgear and its careless reinterpretation of what constituted national dress.

The man took the question in good spirit, and pulled at the side of his cap to accentuate its rakish tilt.

'It's Irish, isn't it?' he said.

'Is it now? I'll take your word for it, even if thousands wouldn't.'

The Tan frowned. He'd been here a week and was finding the famous Irish good humour rather thin on the ground. It was one thing to get dirty looks from guttersnipes and rebel sympathisers in the street, but he wasn't expecting the cold shoulder from some bloke in the pub – nor any lip either.

'So you don't like my cap?' he said, giving notice to his mates of the way things were headed.

'I'm sure it'd look just grand on the Shetland and Orkney Militia,' said Moriarty. 'Is that where you were in the war – up minding sheep?'

The Tan's fists clenched.

'No, mate. Nottinghamshire and Derbyshire Regiment. In France. Giving the Hun a pasting.'

'Is that a fact? I heard it was your mob that was sent to Dublin at Easter, and it was the rebels who were giving the pasting.'

And then Moriarty turned his back on the Tan, took a last swallow of his pint, and recited a little piece of doggerel to the barman.

The Notts and Jocks are a lousy lot,
They lost their colours in Aldershot.

He saw the first punch coming in the mirror but it did him no good. There were three of them after all.

The publican, torn between his fear of the Black and Tans and his regard for his furniture, could do nothing except shout, again and again, 'Not in here!' Out of surprising regard for him, they took it outside and continued their beating of Moriarty in the street. They had more room to move out there anyway.

They released him the next day without charge. Maybe the Tans shouldn't have been in the pub in the first place. Maybe they just needed the cell for a real Shinner.

When the swelling on his face went down he noticed that the tooth that had been troubling him since 1918 no longer hurt. It had been kicked free, along with the one beside it.

The loss was strangely liberating. Moriarty felt clearer in his mind for it.

38

Those blackguards should never have been let loose in this country; they are not gentlemen.

—Major-General Sir Oliver Nugent, 1920

The new police were a far cry from the bobby on the beat. That was exactly how Fitzmullen-Brophy put it.

'No bicycles for them, I see,' he added, as he and Wyndham watched a lorryload of Black and Tans roaring down Nelson Street. The lorry was of that type that the armed forces called a tender. Wyndham didn't know what precisely the vehicle was supposed to tend. In his own military career he'd always treated any motor lorry as either a luggage van or a bus. These special constables passing by didn't look like passengers on a bus. They were all armed and on the alert. For them the lorry was a vantage point and, if necessary, a fighting platform. From the back of that lorry they looked ready and able to bring fire down on anyone in sight.

No – not bobbies on the beat at all.

The colonel was in town because his wife had sent him, and Wyndham was there for the same reason.

'The house needs doing to it,' Mrs. Fitzmullen-Brophy had said. 'Baby will catch a chill or the croup or somesuch. Hugh, you should see to it.'

And that was how Fitzmullen-Brophy was to be kept occupied. He wasn't expected to do any of the actual work, whatever that might entail, but he could see what might be done and talk to tradesmen and so forth. His wife was necessarily vague as to the details, implying that it was the sort of task that only a man – and an intelligent man – could do.

'Daniel, you'll be so good as to help the colonel. Of course you will. You should take your time about it. I'm sure I don't know what sort of things need to be done.'

And thus she got the men out of the house, and her husband a purpose for a while at least. In the pre-war days he had help with organising the reservists' annual training season. Now, in the colonel's mind, '*when Molly next comes to stay...*' took on the same gravity as, '*when the brigade forms...*'.

Now, passing the court house, they were given a glimpse of the post-war world.

'I wonder where they're off to,' said Wyndham, looking at the Tans and thinking of Ó Tuama.

'Out after rogues, no doubt, said Fitzmullen-Brophy. 'That's no way to catch them, of course. If they'd ever known the Northwest Frontier they'd know that much. Can't let your enemy hear you coming. Have to creep up on 'em. If the Shinners have a grain of sense they'll be miles away the moment they hear a motor.'

'Remind me, sir, but how does a battalion of infantry creep up on tribesmen in the Northwest Frontier?'

'Well it doesn't, as a whole. Leave that sort of thing to frontier scouts and the like. No – what the battalion does is march in to show everyone that the Empire is at hand and they should jolly well behave themselves. Then you fire a few villages and tear down a few forts or what have you. Distasteful business, really, but it shows the natives that we won't put up with any nonsense. Of course these Black and Tan fellows won't be able to do that. I mean, what about the decent people? The law-abiding people? You can't go around terrorising the taxpayers in the hope of catching a brigand or two. Impossible. Just not British.'

'Of course not, sir. I have been hearing disquieting reports, though.'

'Hmm, yes well – so have I if it comes to that. Coloured by nationalist hysteria, I expect. But a new force. Poor training. Inexperienced officers. No doubt it will be set right in due course. Here – before I forget – I need some tobacco.'

They rounded the corner, making for their usual shop, and got a closer look at the new constabulary. It was the same shop where Wyndham had first run into Ó Tuama – the shop where the girl had refused to serve a serviceman. The establishment had grown more strident in its political affiliation in the past year, with a green flag in the window alongside signs in Irish. If the signs were anything like the ones Wyndham had been seeing all over lately, they were urging customers to support Irish industry and commerce. It was a little odd, perhaps, for a place selling mostly Turkish and Virginian products but, as the local idiom had it, what harm?

But now the window was broken and the signs and the flag were lying in the shards of glass on the pavement. Two Black and Tans were leaving, and hard on their heels was the girl from the shop, tears on her face and her hair disarrayed. For all that violence had been done to her and her home, it was as if her only concern was for the business in her charge.

'You didn't pay for those cigarettes!' she was screaming. 'Come back!' And it showed remarkable fortitude to insist that the men who'd slapped her and pulled her by the hair and broken her window and robbed her should come back.

The rearmost Tan turned and gave her a shove, but that didn't stop her.

'They didn't pay for those cigarettes!' she wailed to the street at large, clawing at the Tan's sleeve.

He shoved her again, harder, and she bounced against the door jamb and ended up sitting on the step, momentarily shocked into silence. The Tan, finally shook of her, turned to follow his mate, but was stopped again – only this time by Colonel Hugh Fitzmullen-Brophy.

Wyndham had known the colonel for six years. He had served under him in camp and in battle, had eaten at his table and lived in his house. And yet he'd never seen him truly enraged before.

When, in the course of his past duties, anything offended Fitzmullen-Brophy's military eye, he would admonish the offender, no more. Colonels don't bawl men out. It is unseemly and unnecessary. The simple command, 'Take that man's name, Sergeant,' should suffice in most cases.

There was no sergeant now, and sometimes an officer has to get his own hands dirty.

'You!' he barked at the Tan. 'What's your name?'

'Colonel—,' said Wyndham, partly to restrain him from a dangerous confrontation with armed men, but also to warn the Tans what manner of man they were facing. He might as well have kept his mouth shut. Nothing would keep Fitzmullen-Brophy from facing down indiscipline in his own town, and on the other hand nothing could make any ex-serviceman take the angry gentleman for other than a senior officer. The hairy suit of outdated cut; the vigorous moustache; the complexion that years in Kerry could not fully bleach of its imperial bronze: thus was the colonel known.

The colonel was taller than the Tan. The colonel was angrier than the Tan.

The Tan had a revolver on his hip and a rifle in his hand. They were nothing to the colonel.

'I asked you your name, man!'

The man squared his shoulders, squared his jaw, and answered. 'Gibson,' he said.

'You're a disgrace, Gibson! A blasted disgrace!'

'See here now,' said the other Tan.

'Be quiet!' snapped Fitzmullen-Brophy in a parade-ground voice. 'I'll deal with you directly!'

'Colonel—,' said Wyndham again.

'Wyndham, see if the young lady's been hurt.' And it sounded as if Wyndham were a near stranger to the colonel: a minor functionary on his staff.

The shop girl had picked herself up, and she and Wyndham listened to Fitzmullen-Brophy in awe.

'Constable Gibson, I have never seen such filthy behaviour from any man wearing the King's uniform! What is the name of your commanding officer? *Answer me!* Stand up straight!'

And the Tan stood up straight, and through gritted teeth he answered as he was bid.

'He will be hearing from me,' snarled the colonel. 'You are disgusting, Gibson! I am appalled at the sight of you! At the pair of you!'

And it was clear he meant it, every word. His knuckles were white on his walking stick.

'Empty your pockets! Now!'

And like truculent schoolboys, they did. A dozen cigarette packets fell on the pavement.

'You will return to barracks this instant! If there's any justice you'll be spending the next twenty-eight days in cells! Now get out of my sight! Get out! *Now!*'

Fitzmullen-Brophy was afraid – afraid that he would lay about these two men with his stick. He cared not one whit for their rifles and their pistols and the grenades, no doubt, in their pockets. An officer must not strike a man – no matter how much of a lout the man is.

The Tans went. A lesser man might have drawn breath then, and gathered himself after such an outburst, but not Hugh Fitzmullen-Brophy.

After a *There, there, my dear* to the shop girl he said, 'Come along, Dan,' and was off in the wake of the disgraceful policemen – off to the barracks.

The inspector who received them heard the colonel out, and nodded sternly and even noted down a few details, but his heart didn't appear to be in it. He promised Fitzmullen-Brophy that he'd look into the matter. He gave the name of his own superior. He did not, however, seem to appreciate the importance of the complainant nor his complaint.

'That shop *was* displaying seditious signs,' he said, as if that excused the outrage. From the colonel's expression it clearly didn't, so the inspector offered some hurried platitude about discipline and politely showed his visitors the door.

There was no suggestion of unburdening oneself on the Munsters' adjutant or wangling a drink in the Munsters' mess.

'I need a walk,' said Fitzmullen-Brophy. And he turned his back on the barracks as if it were a house sullied by its new occupants – the happy home of the regiment disgraced by brutish guests.

He strode in silence for a mile. His only show of emotion was to whip the head off the odd roadside nettle with his stick. They were well clear of town and all its corruption when he at last spoke.

'Let us hope that this has been an isolated incident,' was all he said.

39

Times have changed, and the pikes which your forefathers used in the battle of Oulart and in the streets of Enniscorthy and on the stricken fields of Tubberneering and Ballyellis would now be of little avail in your hands.

—John Dillon MP, November 1898

On a fine day it was absurd to think that one was living in a country at war.

'Good morning, Gearóid,'

'Morning, Dan. I was hoping I'd run into you.'

Well if you hang around at my gate waiting to waylay me, you'll certainly improve your chances of that.

But of course that wasn't what Wyndham said out loud. Instead he said, 'What can I do for you this lovely morning?'

'If you're on your way to town I'll walk with you. You're doing some work at Keenan's, I hear?

Of course you hear.

'Something in the clerical line, yes. Short-term only. Barely enough to keep me from idleness, and next week I'll have to look for something new.'

'Ah, I'm sure you'll find something,' said Ó Tuama. 'But it's good news for me, maybe – you being at a bit of loose end and that. You might be able to give me some help.'

'How so?'

'Weren't you telling me this funny story the one time about how you made a machine-gun – back in Cork?'

'Well it wasn't really me: it was a couple of my men. And it wasn't really a machine-gun: it was a mock-up just so we could get used to the heft of a real gun. Why do you ask?'

'But it had a carriage, like?'

'If you can call a piece of repurposed bicycle frame a machine-gun carriage, then I suppose so.'

'Did it have any sort of a recoil mechanism by any chance?'

'Not as such, Gearóid, no. Perhaps you can tell by the tone of my voice that I am treating your line of inquiry with due caution.'

'Ah don't mind me, Dan – but before I forget – weren't you in trench mortars too?'

'For about an hour. About three years ago.'

'Oh right. So you and your lads didn't make a trench mortar then?'

'No. I just watched one being demonstrated before deciding against a career in short-range artillery. It attracted the wrong sort of attention. The Germans were inclined to take offence.'

'But would you know about the recoil mechanisms at all?'

'Gearóid, answer me truthfully: are you and your colleagues attempting to build a trench mortar from scratch?'

'What? God, no! Whatever gave you that idea?'

'Well seeing as you ask, you've reminded me of the theft of a pair of antique cannon from in front of Sir Gavin Whatisname's house. It was in yesterday's paper. The colonel commented on it. The guns were trophies Sir Gavin's ancestor brought back from the Battle of Salamanca, I believe.'

'Talavera.'

'Really?'

'And they're only little things. Four-pounders.'

'For a man who swears he has no part in homemade ordnance, you know a lot about it, Gearóid.'

'I said I wasn't making anything from scratch. We've got one of those guns and all we need is something to handle the recoil. We're looking at something worked up from car springs. You know, the leaf springs off a Model T.'

'I don't know anything about cars either. And may I suggest that before you go to all that effort, please consider: I may not know as much as you'd like, but I feel strongly that any gun that's been sitting out in Irish weather for a hundred years is unlikely to be warranted as safe – most particularly if you use a quart of gelignite as a propellant.'

'Ah, now. We're not fools, Dan. We were thinking a half pint would be nearer the mark.'

'Nevertheless, Gearóid. You are an educated man and are no doubt familiar with the phrase, "Hoist by your own petard"?'

'It's a four-pounder, Dan, not a petard, and we have to show the police that they're not safe.'

'They already know. Hence the steel shutters.'

'I'm not talking about the regular peelers, Dan. It's the Tans. The Tans are the lads who need the telling.'

So this is where we are now, thought Wyndham. Not so long ago the police might be addressed with a strongly worded letter to the editor. Now they were to be answered with vintage field artillery. The road to freedom was leading through rough country.

40

They stand for the honour of Ireland,
As their sisters in days that are gone,
And they'll march with their brothers to freedom —
The soldiers of Cumann na mBan!

—Briar O'Higgins, 1916

Even in the midst of the uncertainties the farmers tended their herds, shopkeepers looked after their customers and lovers courted in the byways.

Were they lovers? Wyndham believed they were. The actual loving was tentative in the extreme, but he reckoned that he was Nora's only boy if only through virtue of habit. She wasn't rejecting him and, after all these persistent months, she was more often affectionate than otherwise. The affection tended to be tight-lipped and sharp-tongued, but not always.

'Dan?'

'Nora?'

She looked at her feet as they walked, and moved in a little closer to him, as if unsteady on the road, and she slipped her hand into his.

'I was wondering.'

And now he was wondering too. Her tone of voice was off. Anyone else but Nora and he might have said she was flirting with him.

There was sometimes something to be said for being foreign. As aliens from West Cork and America, they could live free of the morality that commonly constrained people in these parts. Also, it was known that they were both Protestants, so would be going to Hell whatever they did, God love them. Not that they did much that might have brought censure, but it was nice at least to be able to go for walks together and not have to face disapproving questions.

On a stretch of road where there was no one to see her, and in a stretch of country where no one knew her, Nora was more inclined to show any fondness, which she sometimes did in short unexpected sallies.

So far these hadn't amounted to much more than a quick squeeze of the hand or a peck on the cheek. Only once, when she'd been *absolutely* sure that there was nobody looking, had they engaged in a brief tussle. The approach of a cow had brought a sudden end to their moment of passion.

'That could have been someone,' Nora had said, red-faced as she straightened her coat.

Wyndham, feeling himself unable to stand decently upright, knew that argument would be useless and felt that chaste courtship was preferable to this sort of frustration.

So that was the pattern for those months. Wyndham made no advances. He stood ready, watching for the changes in her temper. She, for her part, negotiated her life as a single woman in a troubled times, threading her narrow way between the kitchen sink on one side and the prison cell on the other.

She did as she thought necessary. She did as she wanted. Her boy's feelings didn't come into it.

Wyndham thought he understood. He believed he was getting the measure of her. That was why this coyness surprised him so much.

'What were you wondering, Nora?'

I was wondering that maybe we've waited long enough now

and we should get married at last and get into a big bed together and stay there for weeks and weeks.

'Listowel.'

'Yes?'

'I'm not sure it's altogether safe there.'

He hoped the firmness of his manly hand in hers conveyed how he would keep her safe.

'There's noises at night,' she went on. 'I don't like to be on my own.'

Well that's easily fixed, my love. Just say the word and I'll—

'I think I should have a gun. Didn't you tell me once you had a pistol, Dan?'

'Well, I—'

'I'm sure you did. A German pistol you got on the Somme. A Mauser automatic. You still have it, don't you?'

'Yes, but—'

'You'd never let me have it, would you, Dan?'

'Well I don't know. I'm not sure that—'

'I could keep it under my pillow at night.'

Wyndham could think of nothing useful to say. He suspected her motive. He knew he was being manipulated. But at the same time he couldn't stop thinking about Nora in bed, about Nora taking comfort from having something of his in bed with her.

She was looking at him now, smiling with childish expectation.

'I suppose,' he said.

And she took his arm in both of hers and pulled herself close in one of those bursts of tenderness that always unbalanced him. In this case, it almost sent them both toppling into the ditch. They recovered; she laughed and kissed him on the ear, having been aiming at his cheek.

'I should warn you there's no ammunition,' he said.

'That's no trouble,' she said. 'I think I know where I can get some.'

'In Listowel? Really?'

'Seven point six three millimetre? I think so.' And she hugged his arm, smiling delightedly.

Lovers quarrelled, Wyndham knew that. Everyone knew that. They quarrelled passionately because their passions for each other were heightened to the stars, and they argued bitterly because, bound in union as they were, neither could accept that a part of themselves could be so wayward.

That wasn't how things were here.

Wyndham was well used to Nora's irritability and he thought he knew how to skirt around her touchiness. So they argued and they disagreed with each other over anything and everything, but they'd never had a quarrel – at least nothing that could be classed as bitter or passionate – until one day they did.

What do lovers fight over?

Misunderstandings? Jealousies? German automatic pistols?

In all his imaginings, Wyndham would never have dreamt that his first real quarrel with his true love should be about an 1896-pattern Mauser.

A machine-gunner's weapon of last resort. A cavalry officer's preferred side-arm in a war not suited to sabres. A prize souvenir for anyone who had a fancy for such things. That's what one might think on seeing such a pistol.

The grounds for an almighty bust-up with your girlfriend? Who'd have guessed?

'But you said I could have it! You said so!'

'I didn't. Not really. I just didn't say "No" straight off.'

'Oh is that the way of it then?'

'I just don't think you should be going around with a great big gun.'

'Because I'm a woman, is it? Because I'm just a silly little thing who'd do something silly?'

'Nora, that's not it at all.'

'Did you know I was driving an ambulance around Macedonia in the middle of a war? Did you know that?'

'Of course I knew that,'

'Bad roads and armed men and Lord knows what else! Just me and a little Browning in my pocket.'

'Nora, please. This is different.'

'How? Because now the country's running wild with uniformed hooligans? The sweepings of England's gutters acting like a law unto themselves? They have no respect for anyone, leastways women! The Bulgarians were better-behaved. Is it that you want me to be attacked?'

'If you go marching around the streets of Listowel with a Peter the Painter in your handbag you're only going to attract trouble!'

'Well you just keep your stupid gun, Dan Wyndham!'

'Nora, please.'

'Isn't it a good thing I kept my little Browning then?' And then her eyes widened and her mouth snapped shut.

'You did *what?*' he said.

'Never mind,' she said.

Wyndham saw the moral high ground emerge out of the mist. He climbed towards it.

'You already had a pistol and you wanted mine?'

She glowered.

'Just how many intruders were you expecting to face down?' he asked.

She glowered all the harder.

'I know!' he said. 'How about I get you a dog? I'm sure the colonel could find a dog for you in no time. It could bark at Black and Tans and scare them away.'

He said it because he was tired of being the mild-mannered young man, and because he wanted to see if blue sparks really would start out of her eyes. They didn't, but if Nora Maxfield ran on steam pressure then inside her there was a needle pushing into the red.

He watched her with perverse curiosity, genuinely wondering what she would do next. He felt detached because his mind was made up now. Nothing she could do would make him give her the gun. He knew it as a certainty. His worrying and his dithering had been dispelled by a single clear memory of a German soldier framed in the foresight guard of his rifle. Five years ago. The German hadn't seen him – didn't know he was there – was no threat to him. And Wyndham had pulled the trigger.

In all the time that had come after there had been frantic moments when he'd pulled other triggers at other Germans, and maybe he'd even hit some of them. The first one, though... He'd never even found out if the bullet had struck home, but five years on and it could still wake him up in the night.

He didn't want Nora to shoot anyone. She could blow up at him here and now, and afterwards walk into a police barracks and kill every man in the place, but she'd have to use that little Browning of hers, because Wyndham would have nothing to do with it.

She must have seen that resolve in him, because she deflated slightly.

'A dog,' she said. 'You're very funny, aren't you?'

'It's the best I can offer you at present,' he said, all businesslike, without a shadow of a smile.

'*Very* funny.'

It was grim silence after that but she didn't storm off, spitting vitriol as she went, so Wyndham counted his stand a victory.

Why was it mere things that came between them? Love should transcend material concerns. Proper romantic upheavals were based on jealousies or misapprehensions – not an automatic pistol or a cigarette case. That wasn't an argument that was going to score him any more points, but he had to break the silence.

'But you're still coming to the Fitzmullen-Brophys next week?'

'I am,' she allowed. 'But if you go around telling them that I'm your intended than I'm going to find that pistol of yours and I'm going to shoot you with it.'

'Can't say fairer than that,' he said.

He did, through Molly, let the Fitzmullen-Brophys know that Nora wouldn't care to have her matrimonial plans made common currency. Then, through Ó Tuama, he let Sinn Féin and the IRA know that his fiancée, Miss Maxfield, presently engaged in he knew not what manner of clandestine service to the cause of independence, was a dear friend of the Fitzmullen-Brophys.

That, he felt, should cover everything.

It was a pity the Paris Peace Conference was over. With his skill for back-channel negotiation he could have landed himself a nice job there.

41

...And all through the length of the feast he was not content unless he could be looking at her.

—Lady Gregory, *Gods and Fighting Men*

The time had come for Nora to meet Wyndham's surrogate family. It was at their insistence, which was to say at Mrs. Fitzmullen-Brophy's insistence. Army wife to the core, hers was the planning and the organising too. If she could relocate with every one of her husband's postings, or transplant from the plains to the hills every hot season, she could arrange the transport of one healthy young woman the twenty or so miles across northern Kerry. It was mostly by rail, so Nora had no excuse, try as she might to find one.

'Tell them I'd be delighted,' she'd told Wyndham with resignation. He'd accepted her surrender with dignity.

'You'll love them,' he'd said. 'You honestly will.'

And now here she was, conveyed from the station by an obliging neighbour, with Wyndham riding along as escort, and all bundled up against the weather. For all her bull-headed approach to life, Nora could suffer bouts of acute social discomfort when she feared that her best behaviour might not be good enough. To Wyndham's eye she was looking pale and tragic, as if this cheery little horse-drawn car were a tumbril, and she having exhausted all appeals to clemency. He'd seen the like before when she'd finally showed up for their tea date in Rouen. It was the look of one who knows not quite what she's in for, but will not turn back now.

The house was as warm as unstinting consumption of coal could make it. The dogs were corralled somewhere out of the way. Wyndham took her coat, and they were off.

The baby, now a sturdy toddler, was introduced. Nora was ill at ease, knowing that she was being assessed for maternal instinct. The baby didn't know anything at all. The two measured each other with nervous frowns.

There was the expected interrogation – gentle, polite and relentless – by which the Fitzmullen-Brophys weighed and measured their guest, and all her connections and antecedents, and it went well. They recognised her and she them.

These were Nora's people. She wasn't from an army family but these were her people all the same: the people who'd been born here, reared here, had roots going back generations, had no intention of ever leaving, and yet didn't quite belong. They thought they belonged. They made a point of belonging. They maintained that their contribution to the country far outweighed the distant centuries they had no claim on because their forebears had been elsewhere. And yet it made no difference. They were a people apart, outnumbered, and forever identified with a mistrusted ruling class.

Nora looked at the ornaments.

There were no stands of arms mounted on the old warrior's walls: nothing to tempt a nationalist with a taste for firearms, at least. At most there was a small spear, with a piece of wire holding it to a hook.

'A Burmese threw that at me,' said Fitzmullen-Brophy with satisfaction. 'In '86. At least I think it was at me. Can't be sure. Either way, I didn't take it personally. Molly carried it in a play once. Do you remember, Molly? *Robin Hood*, I believe it was. You played one of the sheriff's men and you got into trouble for stabbing that boy.'

'Jeremy Hartigan, Daddy, and he deserved it, and I was only

ten, and it was *The Idylls of the King.*'

There was nothing Nora could contribute to someone else's family story. She politely inspected the spear and the rest of the decoration.

The trophies were all small things – pieces of Benares brass, a small silver cup, photographs of people dressed in white on parched lawns – little shrines of imperial service.

'I expect you were wondering about heads, Miss Maxfield.'

Nora whipped around as if someone had stuck her with a pin.

'Heads, Colonel?' she managed.

'On the walls. Susan wouldn't have them, you know.'

'I absolutely would not,' confirmed Mrs. Fitzmullen-Brophy. 'It's the eyes, you know. I just couldn't stand all those eyes staring at me. And the way they gather dust is simply ridiculous.'

Nora managed a tight smile, not knowing where this conversation had turned.

'Mabel Heffernan gave me a stuffed ibex once in Cawnpore. I'm sure she just wanted to be rid of the wretched thing, but I couldn't refuse. I was only a captain's wife at the time and her husband was a major, so she outranked me. I always felt it took up half the bungalow – and the eyes! I could always feel its eyes on me every time I turned my back.'

She laughed. 'Imagine if it had been a tiger!'

Nora's smile was more genuine now that she'd caught on.

'I did come close to bagging a tiger once,' said Fitzmullen-Brophy. 'You remember, my dear? We were staying with the Horgans. That time near Fatehpur? Bunny Horgan laid on a shoot.

'So there I was, me and my syce, a lance-naik in the Ludhiana Sikhs. and it's an hour at most past noon. Absolutely blinding sun. Beastly insects. Might have blundered right into the blessed thing if the syce hadn't alerted me. Even then it took me a moment to make it out in all that brush. Tiger. Magnificent brute.

'Funny thing, you know, but I didn't have the heart to shoot it. Well, I mean it was a *tiger* wasn't it? I'd been a Munster for years. Worn the tiger on my buttons. It's there on our colours, dash it. I *couldn't* shoot it. I'd have been killing the guardian spirit of the regiment or something, what? It was just a fancy of mine, but I absolutely would not pull the trigger. Call me foolish. The syce certainly did. Said it was a poor thing for the sahib to be dragging a chap all around the bush in the heat of the day if he wouldn't shoot anything in the end – or words to that effect. Rank insubordination, if you like. I suppose he reckoned on my Urdu not being up to snuff. Not that I minded. I've always found that it's the privilege of the really loyal retainer to speak his mind. You'd hear worse from an Irish soldier. Thoroughly splendid fellow. Six foot four if he was an inch and a beard like W.G. Grace. Took twenty-six runs off us in the match the next day too. A pleasure to lose to a man like that. A few more men like that and the Empire will last forever.'

The dinner itself was pretty execrable. The Fitzmullen-Brophys' cook was either no good or she held a bitter grudge against her employers.

'But we daren't get rid of the woman,' Molly had once admitted. 'I mean, what would we ever do without her?'

Despite that the evening itself was a success. Everyone knew not to talk politics. The hostess practised the resolute sociability she'd learned in a dozen garrisons. By his second glass, her husband was all sentimental geniality. Molly, though, was the clear winner with her invitation that Nora teach her how to smoke cigarettes. This happened after the ladies had withdrawn and there was only her mother to scandalise.

'Oh don't make such a fuss, Mummy! I'm a grown-up, and I'm not going to let Nora smoke all by herself.'

Nora had in fact relinquished the prospect of smoking for the duration of her visit, and was supremely grateful to Molly. By the time the men joined them the young ladies were wreathed in pale blue smoke – Molly looking triumphant at her new accomplishment and Nora as close to relaxed as could be hoped for.

The prohibition on such words as 'fiancée' was observed, no matter how sentimental the colonel became. Molly played the piano. There were songs and reminiscences and time for a card game before bed.

Wyndham supposed that if you force good humour hard enough you'll get there in the end.

Nora was staying the night. Of course she was. How could she be expected to get back to Listowel at this hour? All evening Wyndham tried to push from his mind the thoughts of the last night they'd spent under the same roof. He guessed she was being just as unsuccessful in the same effort.

When the older generation retired to bed, and Molly made some unconvincing pretext to leave the two of them alone together for a little while, Wyndham wasn't sure what to do. Nora had a better notion of it, and pushed him onto the couch. They had half a minute of passionate fumbling before the noise of dogs and Molly somewhere kitchenwards made them separate like repelling magnets.

They wished each other goodnight as though they could only just remember each other's names.

There was a suggestion of tears in Wyndham's eyes, but that was only because of the unintended blow he'd taken on the nose. He was deeply happy to know how ardently his feelings were reciprocated, but he got damn-all sleep that night.

V

LUCAS AND SMYTH

You may make mistakes occasionally and innocent persons may be shot, but that cannot be helped and you are bound to get the right persons sometimes.

—Lieutenant-Colonel Gerald Bryce Ferguson Smyth DSO, Listowel,
19 June 1920 (attributed)

42

Mr. Swan *asked the Secretary of State for War: How many generals are missing from Irish commands?*

Mr. Churchill: *One*

—House of Commons, 5 July 1920

The IRA grew bolder. Burning police stations was nothing to them now, and they counted their victories in the hundreds. Even the increasing deployment of troops failed to cow them. The country was theirs, and an ambush here and a killing there served to remind the authorities that this was so. In June they even went so far as to kidnap a senior British officer. Wyndham didn't care. So long as the Fitzmullen-Brophys were left alone, Wyndham refused to be bothered by any of it. The weather had grown warmer. So had Nora.

The armed police at the station with their English accents and brusque demands for identification were an imposition that he could shrug off. So long as the train ran and the weather held he wasn't complaining.

And then he saw Ó Tuama, who was obviously looking for him. Like the Tan by the ticket office, he was going to ask Wyndham his business and then, in that friendly and innocent way of his, was going to draw Wyndham into his disorienting and troublesome world.

'Dan! 'Tis yourself! Where would you be off to at all?'

Wyndham closed his eyes and took a calming breath.

I am going to Listowel to meet my girl. We intend to stroll about and take in the sights, such as they are, and perhaps the fine weather will find her in the mood to go somewhere secluded where she may make free with my person and permit me to make free with hers. It is her day off. The cause of Ireland's freedom may take the day off too.

That out of the way, he turned a bright face on Ó Tuama.

'Morning, Gearóid. I'm off to Listowel as a matter of fact.'

'I thought you might be. Paying a visit to your Miss Nora Maxfield, is it? A lovely young lady. Everyone speaks very highly of her.'

Nora was new in the district. She was not a secret. She and Ó Tuama were, to some degree or other, in the same line of work. But damn it, that didn't give Ó Tuama licence to know about her, or speak of her – highly or not.

'Do they now?'

'Between you and me, the high command have their eye on her.'

Then I may have to have words with the IRA high command and tell them to keep their filthy eye elsewhere.

'But lookit,' said Ó Tuama, 'I wanted to ask you – do you play bridge by any chance?'

This wasn't at all what Wyndham was expecting.

'Do I play bridge?' he asked. 'A little – I mean, whist is more my game – but bridge, yes, a little – I mean, why?'

'I hoped you might. Officers' mess and that.'

'Are you saying that you need someone to help make up a bridge party?'

'That's it exactly. Could you manage this evening?'

And because the invitation was so genuine, and had nothing to do with shady revolutionary activities, and was not going to spoil his day with Nora after all, Wyndham found himself grinning.

'This evening? Sure – why not? I should be back in Tralee before six.'

'Well that's grand so. I'll see you later, Dan.'

He saw him much earlier than Wyndham had supposed. Wyndham was hurrying back into Listowel in the state of frustrated elation that always came in the wake of happier hours with Nora, and there was Ó Tuama waiting for him, leaning against the side of a lorry.

'I thought I'd give you a lift,' he said. 'Save you the train fare.'

'Actually, I bought a return ticket.'

'What harm? Hop in anyway. Michael here had business and he's happy to give us a lift.'

Seeing no sense in arguing, Wyndham hoisted himself into the cab of this Michael's lorry, which had no sign painted on the side and no load to be seen under the tarpaulin in the back. Ó Tuama got in beside him, which made everything a little uncomfortable for Wyndham, stuck in the middle, astride the gear stick.

'This is Michael,' said Ó Tuama. 'Where we're going is on his way.'

The driver gave a nod and a grunt. He didn't look like a bridge player.

Wyndham had cycled these roads often enough to realise after not too many miles that they were not going in the direction of Tralee. Ó Tuama had the decency to look shitty when this was pointed out.

'We're headed towards Limerick,' he confirmed, as if that made everything clear. 'And I sent word to the Fitzmullen-Brophys that you wouldn't be home for your dinner,' he said, as though that made it all better.

Wyndham thought that it had been such a *good* day up until then.

'Where are you taking me, Gearóid?' he said, with an edge to his voice.

'I told you, Dan – out Limerick way. Well, a bit beyond Limerick maybe. I'm not altogether sure. Michael knows, though.'

'*Mm-hmm.*' Wyndham nodded, prying back the layers of falsehood.

'And you're taking me to a card game.'

'I swear to God, Dan.'

'A card game.'

'A game of bridge, Dan. Honest to God.'

Wyndham said nothing, but nodded again, folded his arms, and shut his eyes against the world and all its lies.

He dozed intermittently. When he finally chose to re-engage with his surroundings it was late. They had stopped somewhere.

'Where are we?' he asked.

'Clare,' said Ó Tuama. 'I think.'

Wyndham said nothing. He knew that Ó Tuama might have every intention of getting them back to Tralee safe and sound, but intentions would only ever go so far. Wyndham should consider himself lucky to be only in Clare. The way things were turning out, he could likely expect to find himself in Petrograd in the middle of an arms deal, with Bolsheviks fingering their knives and Ó Tuama saying, 'Sure it'll be grand, Dan – but you'd never have five pounds I could borrow, would you?'

Michael the taciturn driver dropped them at the entrance to a lane and drove off without a word, leaving them to the gathering darkness.

'It's up this way,' said Ó Tuama. 'I don't think it's very far.'

'But you don't know,' said Wyndham, shoving his hands in his pockets and kicking at a stone.

'Not for certain.'

'You don't know and I don't know, but we might be in Clare unless it's Limerick. Have I got that much right?'

'Look, I'm fierce sorry about this, Dan, but you're doing everyone a great big favour by coming.'

'Everyone?'

Ó Tuama thought for a moment. 'Everyone,' he confirmed.

Calling to mind all the times he himself had ordered men from pillar to post, and kept them standing about in ignorance in the rain, Wyndham heard again the tunes of protest that always started up in such moments – the '*Oh Why Are We Waiting?*' sung to the tune of '*Oh Come All Ye Faithful*'. Now, in that same mutinous sprit he pursed his lips to whistle '*What Did I Join The Army For?*' when it occurred to him that there was every chance he could be shot dead right there and then. This was not country where it was safe to advertise yourself with British army songs.

They carried on in silence, Ó Tuama speaking only to say that it shouldn't be much farther. And then a voice from the hedge told them they'd gone far enough.

'That's far enough, gentlemen. Put your hands up.' The voice was quiet. The accent was Irish.

'Ó Tuama,' said Ó Tuama, keeping his voice low as well. 'From Tralee. This is the man.'

'What man?' said the voice, and a figure became half visible – the soft hat and service rifle the only things discernible, but enough to mark him as IRA.

'To see the general,' said Ó Tuama.

The IRA sentry chuckled. 'Which general? If it's brigade commanders you want, you're spoiled for choice. We have the boss man stopping by at the minute. He'll want to see your fella, I suppose. Hundred yards on, through the gate on your left.'

Was it for this that Wyndham been lifted off the street and carried halfway across the country? A general wanted to speak to him? A general of the Irish Republican Army? For the first time since this stupid escapade had begun he was more scared than angry. Nothing good could come of this meeting.

It was an ordinary house. Even in broad daylight Wyndham would have been hard pressed to distinguish or remember it. That was probably the point. He certainly wasn't expecting a headquarters with a flag flying and guards mounted at the door. The generals he'd seen during the war hadn't been showy types. Superior, yes – but not showy. So what to expect here in guerrilla Ireland? Expensive boots and deferential staff, or bandoliers of cartridges and buccaneer swagger? Was he about to meet Douglas Haig or Pancho Villa?

Of course it was neither. The man sitting at the kitchen table – the only man seated – was no more martial than a country schoolmaster or a village curate. Serious, bespectacled, younger than expected, he had the look of one whose life moves at a higher tempo, whose thoughts are on a higher plane, but who must deal all the same with the dragging concerns of less able men, because they just can't do everything by themselves.

Ó Tuama stood up straight before him.

'Ó Tuama. Kerry Number One Brigade.'

The bespectacled man answered with no more than a curt nod and addressed his words to another man – an adjutant, possibly.

'We're going a long way if we're going all the way to North Kerry.'

'We'll take whatever we get, won't we? The word went out, and it was Shanahan or one of Shanahan's people who gave us this fella's name. If he's here now I don't mind where we got him from.'

And the IRA commander's eyes were turned on 'this fella'.

'Your name is Wyndham, is that right?'

Wyndham was no longer angry. He was not intrigued. In truth, he was feeling sick. It took him two attempts to admit his name.

'You wouldn't be related at all to George Wyndham who was Chief Secretary for Ireland a few years back?'

Wyndham stammered that he was no such thing.

'Not related to anyone in the British government?' The questions were clear and sharp: not so much an interrogator as an official with a form to fill. Wyndham still wasn't reassured.

'No – not related to anyone,' he said. 'Except my family, I mean. Obviously. No. And they're all in America.'

'You're American?'

'From Massachusetts, yes.'

'But you're an officer in the British army?'

'*No!* Well, yes. Well, not anymore. Royal Munster Fusiliers. Wartime service only. All finished now.'

'And you can play bridge?'

'I beg your pardon?'

'Bridge. The card game. You can play it, yes?'

'A little, yes. I mean I'm not very good.'

'Not very good is good enough for our purposes. I'm sorry to have put you to all this trouble. We're very grateful for your time, Mr. Wyndham. These men will take you where you need to go. Thank you again.'

And that was that. Wyndham was escorted from the house by another armed man. He turned one last helpless look back at Ó Tuama who was being given a seat and a cup of tea.

'He'll be grand,' said the escort, pushing Wyndham along. 'And don't worry – you'll be getting your own tea in a little bit.'

'Where are you taking me?'

'Weren't you listening? We're taking you to see the general.'

'I thought that was the general.'

'You're going to meet the other general. Come on – he's been waiting long enough.'

It was another unmemorable house, and this general wasn't wearing uniform either, but he looked much more the part. Indeed, if Wyndham had been told he'd already encountered the man in France he would readily have believed it. The war had created a multitude of brigade and divisional commanders who looked just like this one. Firm-jawed, forty-ish, forthright. Off duty they all tended to look alike too, even though this one's tweeds were rather rumpled – in consequence, no doubt, of being kidnapped by republican gunmen and held prisoner this past week.

'Lucas,' said the general, rising with a smile.

'Wyndham,' said Wyndham, shaking his hand.

'Shall we?' said Brigadier-General Cuthbert Lucas, indicating a table set up for cards. 'I don't mean to rush you, but they've kept us waiting rather a long time and it is quite late already.'

'Of course,' said Wyndham, all at a loss.

'There'll be sandwiches later, I gather, or – I say – you *have* eaten, haven't you? I do hope they didn't make you miss dinner.'

'To be honest, I think I could do with something,' said Wyndham.

The first something to be supplied happened to be a large whiskey. He drank it without hesitation.

The other players were introduced. One was a local IRA company commander and the other was his brother-in-law, a solicitor.

'I really shouldn't be here at all,' said the solicitor, and it was evident from his brother-in-law's look that this wasn't the first or second time he'd raised this complaint.

'My name's Malone,' said the IRA man. 'I'd sooner not tell you that and I'll thank you not to remember it for long after tonight, but it'd only be awkward if we couldn't call each other by name. You'd better go partners with your man here so you can just call him "partner" and not have to worry about names.'

'My name is O'Keeffe,' said the solicitor. 'And in spite of what my brother-in-law says, and my professional standing aside, I wouldn't want to appear in any way rude. We can draw for partners.'

It was much like any other card game, and a sight more civilised than some that Wyndham had known. He was pretty sure that Malone was armed, but that was nothing. Wyndham had spent pleasant card sessions where the players not only all carried pistols, but left them on the table if there was room, and used them to shoot at rats in between deals. The table here was an actual table and the whiskey was served in glasses rather than army-issue tin mugs. The IRA men might, at a stretch, be considered outlaws, but no one here was playing with the recklessness of men who expected this day to be their last. This was an evening of bridge that had no prospect of being obliterated by a five-point-nine-inch shell. All perfectly tame, really.

Lucas sorted his hand. 'I take it from your accent that you're not Irish, Mr. Wyndham,' he said. 'You're not an American by any chance, are you? I hate to be so inquisitive, but what brings an American into – well, into all this?'

Wyndham wondered if there was a real answer and if so, if it would make any sense. He shrugged.

'The war,' he said.

Lucas nodded in understanding. 'American Expeditionary Force?' he said.

'Royal Munster Fusiliers,' said Wyndham.

That opened Lucas's eyes.

'Really? Good heavens. I say, but you're not a prisoner too, are you?'

Well actually—

'Just doing a favour for a friend, General.'

Some friend.

'One thing,' said Malone. 'If I hear you talking Arabic to the man you'll never see the light of day again.'

'Arabic?'

'Arabic, Hindustani – anything other than English, understand?'

'Um, I'm not quite sure I do.'

Lucas interjected with a smile. 'I'm afraid that I tried to get away by plotting in Arabic with my companions when we were first taken. Turned out rather badly, I'm sorry to say. Won't happen again. Word of honour and all that.'

'Word of honour's all very well, General. I just want this gentleman to know that if there's to be any nonsense it's to be in English, and it's to be so's I can hear it.'

There was an interlude when Wyndham found himself alone with the general.

'They're really most thoughtful, you know. I really can't imagine the Hun being so very accommodating if this were the war and I were in Germany. No interrogation. Certainly no violence – well, I mean except for when we tried to escape and they shot Danford and nearly throttled me – but of course any reasonable fellow would have done as much. I mean it was a kidnapping after all.'

'Of course,' said Wyndham, because anyone would agree that throttling and shooting chaps was well within the accepted rules of kidnapping.

'No, I mean they're decent in other ways,' said Lucas. 'Thoroughly gentlemanly. I'm fearfully concerned for my wife, for instance. She's expecting a child at the moment. Our first, you know. So naturally I'm fearfully concerned.

'Well I said as much to them and they said they'd send word that I wasn't hurt. And do you know? That's what they did. I confess I suspected that that they were merely telling a story to mollify me, but no. They even went to the trouble of giving Poppy – my wife, that is – an address to which she could write back.'

'And she's well? Your wife?'

'Oh, thriving!' said Lucas. 'Baby hasn't arrived yet, but any day now. Most good of you to ask.'

'But naturally you're worried, General. And not just about your wife.'

'Precisely. I mean it's all well and good to be held captive by decent fellows, but one's still a captive. And I mean they are the enemy after all. One worries what they have in store.'

'I know only what they print in the papers, General.'

'Really? Look, Wyndham, I don't want to put you in a bind, and I certainly don't want you to betray whatever side you're on, but I must ask you all the same.'

'Go on.'

'As one soldier to another, I ask you frankly: are there any negotiations for my release and if not, how likely is it that these fellows are going to shoot me?'

'I know only what I read in the papers, General.'

'Of course, of course.' It was clear to Lucas that Wyndham was not the type to be shaken in his loyalties by any trite emotional appeal.

But this Wyndham wasn't altogether heartless.

'But if it's any consolation, I believe you'll be safe,' he said. 'These men see themselves as soldiers too. They're not murderers.'

43

The country around Fermoy is still being scoured and searched by military and police for tidings of Gen. Lucas, but so far without success.

—*The Kerryman*, 3 July 1920

They drove him by dark roads and left him in the early light by a small rural railway station.

'Do you know where you are at all?' asked Malone.

'No.'

'Good. That's as it should be. If you find out, mind, it won't matter a damn. We'll be long gone. If you want to know more you can read the papers – they're full of it. But come here to me—'

He leaned in close so that Wyndham would know he was serious.

'Say whatever you like. But whatever you say, say nothing.'

'Understood.'

His sole consolation was that he'd be able to tell Nora if no one else. She set great store by her work in Republican intelligence, although as far as Wyndham could see it, she was no more than a post office girl. And here was he: briefly at the heart of sensational events through no effort of his own.

He could at least tell her the story, and make it a good story at that.

'Dan Wyndham, you are such a big liar!'

'Nora!'

'An unholy great liar!' she laughed.

'I'm no such thing!'

'You are so! You and your stories!'

At least she was taking it in good humour.

'Now what,' he asked, 'leads you to such an unmerited accusation?'

'*I* don't know,' she said. 'You're bored, you read about General Lucas in the paper, and your imagination runs away with you. Your head's always in the clouds and you've got a desperate appetite for making things up.'

They were walking back from lunch at the Fitzmullen-Brophys'. The weather was delightful, Nora was happy, and it was only Wyndham who was out of sorts, now that the news he'd been waiting to impress her with all week was being so light-heartedly rubbished. He had nothing to give credence to his claim – not a shred of substance to hold against her ridicule.

'Nora, you are too grown-up to skip, and you're swinging your handbag in an unseemly fashion. I'm telling you the God's honest truth.'

'I blame the books,' she said, brightening with every degree of downturn of his mouth. 'I tried reading the one you gave me. Honestly! If that's the sort of thing you've been filling your head with, it's no wonder you're inventing wild romances.'

He let go of General Lucas and his own reputation for truth. There was something more important at stake.

'You didn't like Lady Gregory?' he asked.

She heard the earnestness in his question. 'It was alright, I suppose,' she admitted not very convincingly. 'It just wasn't for me.'

She could see that this wouldn't be enough for him, and tried harder. She squinted into the middle distance and searched for the language of literary criticism. 'It's all very makey-uppy,' she said.

'It's Ireland's heroic past! It's ancient legend! She made nothing up!'

'Well somebody made it up, and this Lady Gregory of yours

just put it into fancy new words.'

'Those fancy words are preserving Ireland's heritage.'

'Well I'd rather not be having the gentry deciding for me what's my heritage and what's not. "Lady" Gregory indeed. I'd bet she wouldn't be too happy to see a real Irish hero up close. It was against her sort that we've been fighting since the olden days.'

Mighty big talk for somebody with a name like Maxfield, he thought, and was wise enough to leave it unsaid. Instead he made another bid for credibility.

'General Lucas is worried about his wife and the child they're expecting.'

'Of course he is. And that's in the paper.'

'He has a tendency to overbid at bridge.'

'And that can't be proven one way or another.'

'He has a mole on his left cheek that can't be seen in newspaper photographs.'

'Well unless he shows up right here in front of us, I won't know if you're making that up.'

'Actually, I am making that up.'

She laughed at him and took his arm and hugged it, and only let go when she saw they were coming to the edge of town.

Wyndham was feeling his usual sadness as they neared the station. Despite all the civil and military disruptions the train to Listowel was always still there to take his love away.

'Well I'm sorry my attempt to impress you fell so flat,' he said.

'Never mind,' she said. 'You can make up a better one for next time.' And she was leaning in for the most daring kiss she could decently get away with in public when a car pulled up beside them. A motor car arriving outside the station was nothing remarkable, but what grabbed the attention was a man with a gun under his arm leaning out the passenger door and saying, 'Mr. Wyndham? Get in.'

Wyndham didn't need to ask how these men knew him. Of course not. They knew everyone. The man in the car proved as much by touching his hat to Nora.

'Miss Maxfield,' he said. 'Sorry about this. You can make your own way home from here, I think?'

Wyndham's last glimpse of her before the car carried him off was her face, a picture of consternation but her eyes alive with excitement.

44

The question is not whether General Lucas's life will be jeopardised by the drive taking place, but whether Government policy should be influenced by such a consideration. On this point, however painful, no alternative course is possible.

—Winston Churchill, Secretary of State for War, July 1920

'I'm beginning to feel rather like the Tsar of Russia.'

Wyndham had seen men crack under pressure before, but it had usually involved more in the way of trembling and gibbering. In as sympathetic a tone as he could manage, he requested clarification.

'What? Sorry,' said Lucas. 'What I mean is I'm being held captive somewhere comfortably out of the way while my fate is being decided by God knows whom. Everything's very comfortable, but one can't shake the fact that the chap who asks you how you like your egg done happens to be your sworn enemy. Someone higher up might decide I was no use alive anymore and that would be that. Everyone's jolly civil here but I can tell they wouldn't hesitate to obey an order. Dedicated men, Wyndham. Admirable fellows. Wouldn't let a passing friendship stand in the way of cutting a man's throat and burying him by the garden wall.'

'It won't come to that, General. I don't know anything about negotiations, but I know that the army and police are scouring the country for you.'

'Well that's the thing, isn't it? What if the Shinners feel the noose tightening? What if they feel they won't be safe in moving me one more time? I must confess, I was rather apprehensive when they brought me here. The last place they held me was pretty remote, but this place is even more isolated. And there's quite a large garden behind. Big enough for a tennis court. High walls. Made me think of a prison yard. Firing squads and so forth. They took me out there on my first morning. I half feared that someone somewhere had decided that my time was up and I'd be leaving my bones under that old tennis court.'

'But what happened then?'

'Oh – we played a game of tennis. The grass badly needs mowing but the ground is good and dry.'

'I see.'

'And now they're talking of taking me fishing near here. I'm rather uneasy about that too.'

'You suspect they're just trying to lull you before shooting you and dumping your body in the river?'

'Not really. It's the bailiffs I'm worried about. It wouldn't do if I were caught poaching.'

The senior man at this new location was called Brennan. Brennan had a guerrilla company to command, a high-ranking hostage to keep hidden, and now an American with petty complaints.

'Look, you can't keep lifting me off the streets every time your captive needs a fourth for bridge,' the American was saying. 'I do have to earn a living, you know.'

'At present, Mr. Wyndham, we understand you to be a gentleman of leisure.'

'Which doesn't mean I'm rolling in money. Would it be too much to ask that the Irish Republic pay me for my time?'

'You took eight and a half bob off the commandant last time you played. That'll have to do you.'

45

I desire to repeat a question which at the request of the Chief Secretary I postponed on Monday, namely, what information he can give the House in regard to certain incidents in the Listowel police force and the speech attributed to Commissioner Smyth?

—T.P. O'Connor MP to Sir Hamar Greenwood, House of Commons, 14 July 1920

'Dan?'

Nora had no talent for subterfuge, and when she used that innocent-seeming voice it was a clear warning that she was going to propose something disruptive to the stability of Wyndham's world. That being the case, he thought he might as well make the best advantage of her wanting something from him. They weren't anywhere suitable for amorous adventure, but at least he could lean in close and croon those endearments she hated.

'What is it, Nora, macushla?'

'Stop that,' she said. 'I wanted to ask you something.'

'Ask me anything, my little love.'

'I will if you stop making that stupid face.'

He composed himself and waited for her probably impractical and possibly ruinous request.

Dan, you'd never happen to have half a ton or so of blasting powder that you could lend me?

Dan, I was wondering if you'd ever wander into Dublin Castle for me and see what military intelligence has in the safe?

'Dan, you wouldn't have a typewriter at all?'

'A *typewriter*?'

'Did I say something funny or something? Yes – a typewriter. I need one.'

'Well, no. I mean, I suppose I could borrow one if I asked around. But doesn't the post office—?'

'No – and this isn't for post office work,' she cut him off, giving him that look that suggested she'd said too much already.

'I wouldn't need it for long,' she added. 'You can use one can't you? You can show me how it works and everything?'

'Well no, I'm afraid not.'

'You don't know how to use a *typewriter*?' It was if he didn't know how to butter bread.

'No, but neither do you.'

'That's not the point. I'm not American.'

And that, thought Wyndham, was that argument fought and lost in short order. 'I'll see if I know anyone,' he conceded.

'A small one if you can manage it,' she said. 'One that doesn't make any noise, if they make them that way.'

'I'll ask around. Failing that, my love, I'll get you a Sears Roebuck catalogue for you to peruse at your leisure.'

'You and your jokes. This is serious, and I don't have any leisure. I have all sorts of communications to copy and pass along.'

'Would it be too much to ask what this is all about?'

'It would, but seeing as you're doing what you're doing I can give you a hint.'

She looked left and right to make sure they weren't overheard. 'You're not the only one keeping an eye on army bigwigs.'

'Oh Lord, Nora! Don't tell me they're roping you into this affair with General Lucas too?'

She gave a haughty little smile, as if Lucas were old hat.

'No,' she said. 'My fellow's called Smyth – Smyth with a Y.'

Fitzmullen-Brophy had had enough.

'Have you heard, Dan? Outrageous!'

'Sir?'

'Hugh wants to go to Cork, Daniel,' said Mrs. Fitzmullen-Brophy, 'I do think it would be best if you were to go with him.'

It was clear from the colonel's manner that this would not be a shopping trip.

'It's high time I did something. I'm going to damn well talk to somebody.'

'Hugh, language!'

'Awfully sorry, my dear, but really.'

It was, of course, about law and order. Ever since the business of Ogilvie's lawn the colonel had been saying that something should be done. The behaviour of the Black and Tans had hardened his views. Now, finally, something had happened that forced him to act.

'But what is it, sir?'

'You didn't hear, Dan? In Listowel?' And he forgot his anger long enough to smile. 'No, I suppose you and your young lady are hardly going to spend your time talking politics, what? No – the fellow they put in charge of police in Listowel has overstepped the mark – and overstepped it by a fatal degree unless I'm very much mistaken. It absolutely can't go on. It will lead the country into anarchy. I have a plan. I'm going to Cork to talk to whomever will listen. I'm certainly going to talk to that fellow.'

'That fellow, sir?'

'That commissioner in charge of the police in Listowel, Dan. Do pay attention. I'm told he's gone to Cork. Fellow name of Smyth.'

'Smyth with a Y, sir?'

46

'Shoot, and shoot with effect... The more you shoot the better I will like you.'

—Lieutenant-Colonel Gerald Bryce Ferguson Smyth DSO, Listowel, 19 June 1920 (attributed)

The story was told in summary, in detail and in instalments while they packed, while on the way to the station, and during the journey to Cork. Fitzmullen-Brophy was not letting it go.

'He told his men to shoot on sight! Shoot without warning! Policemen! Authorised to shoot any man who's slow to take his hands out of his pockets! What utter poppycock. What appalling balderdash! His superiors will hear of this!'

'But won't they have already?'

'Well yes – but now they're going to damn well hear it from me!'

Wyndham was uneasy throughout the journey, and it was a long journey. The railway workers had declared that they would have nothing to do with any train carrying soldiers or war material, and the way things were now, that meant a lot of trains being halted while railwaymen argued with officials. At one unscheduled halt Wyndham had to do his utmost to restrain the colonel from sticking his oar in. There was no problem on this earth that could not be made worse by the interference of Colonel Hugh Fitzmullen-Brophy. Wyndham was ashamed to harbour such a view, but there it was. The colonel might have right on his side, but Wyndham was coming to believe that much of what was right was pretty damn inconvenient just now and should decently make way for less troublesome expediency.

As the train lurched on towards Cork, later than ever, he listened with only half an ear as the colonel again outlined his schemes for police reform in North Kerry – how the disgraceful Black and Tans would be properly disciplined and how order and trust would be maintained by volunteer officers of the community.

'Men who know the district, Dan. Men who are known in the district. Fellows of standing. Fellows of military experience.'

'Yes, sir. Of course, sir.' But although Wyndham knew that it was rather too late, and far too dangerous for any such scheme, and knew moreover that he would be roped into it, it was all in some dreamy future. For the present there was Smyth. Lieutenant-Colonel Gerald Smyth, who had allegedly ordered his men to kill nationalist suspects on sight; Smyth, to whom Fitzmullen-Brophy was going to voice his objections, and before whom he would lay is plans; Smyth who was firmly in the sights of the Irish Republican Army.

Wyndham wished he'd had time to talk to Nora again, even though he suspected it would have been useless. For all her *I-know-something-you-don't-know* smile she was close-mouthed when she needed to be. As a liar she was transparent, but she could obstinately hide the truth until the cows came home.

On the one hand, he could imagine British officers on the telephone hearing her sighing impatiently in the background or even drumming her fingers against the switchboard every time they exchanged sporting pleasantries rather than military secrets. On the other hand he could see her turning her nose up at the most brutal interrogator and saying, 'As if I'd tell *you*.'

And Nora couldn't change anything even if she wanted to. The plans were already in train. Wyndham could see it with perfect clarity. Colonel Smyth was going to be kidnapped and Wyndham was going to have to play bridge with him. Because of Nora, because of Lucas, he would be dragged into yet another secret and perilous affair. Of course he would. Didn't he have excellent references? Fraught and sleepless nights. Social niceties among desperate men. Whist in one hideout, tennis in another, and the threat of a bullet in either.

Fitzmullen-Brophy yanked him out of his imaginings. 'We're here,' he said, and in his tone there was something to remind Wyndham of sterner times long ago.

Stand up, Dirty Shirts.

Smoke and steam; summer glare through smeared glass. It was an odd place to be reminded of the trenches in front of Armentières. Yet there on the station concourse was another man who'd followed Fitzmullen-Brophy over the top.

'Moriarty!' barked the colonel, as though hailing family – distant and wayward family as it might be, but blood nonetheless. No passer-by would mark a resemblance between the undoubted gentleman and the seedy character on the concourse, but a Munster was still a Munster, even if selling newspapers, and like called to like.

Moriarty didn't snap to attention or even touch his cap, but he stood with his back straighter and his head higher than Wyndham was used to seeing. The paper seller and the retired gentleman were still both of the tribe that had strode this ground like redcoated gods in olden days, and if the lesser people milling about in the station did not recognise them for heroes then that was of no matter.

'Colonel,' he said, and it was enough. The bale of tuppenny newspapers under his arm and all the conquests of the earth were there for the colonel's inspection, should he care to look at them. And the two fusiliers looked each other in the eye, seeing how much fusilier was still there and how much civilian softness might have seeped in.

'Keeping up to the mark, Moriarty. Jolly good.'

'Looking grand and healthy yourself, sir.'

'Selling newspapers, I see. Well done.'

'It's a job, sir. Suits me well enough. And sure isn't any job a good one in these times?'

'Quite so, quite so. Mind you—' and here a wily look came over Fitzmullen-Brophy.

'Sir?'

'Mr. Wyndham and I are in Cork on business, Moriarty. That business just might include you.'

'Sir?'

And Wyndham's heart fell. It was one thing for the old man to have a scheme. He was always having schemes. But once he started dragging others in then the chance of the scheme getting blown away by a stiff breeze or the judgement of his wife grew less.

'Fancy putting on uniform again, Moriarty?' said Fitzmullen-Brophy.

Wyndham could see them: a three-man constabulary (for surely they'd never find any more than three unless Ogilvie would be fool enough to get roped in), with no more uniform than a self-important brassard, and no more authority than Fitzmullen-Brophy's voice and a half-hearted warrant from a half-hearted magistrate. It would be the old 11th Battalion but with the silliness magnified in inverse proportion to the numbers engaged: a feeble force without the excuse of innocence. They would look foolish, and then the IRA would shoot them and that would be the end of it.

But thank heaven that Moriarty was there to burst the balloon.

'I'm grand, Colonel,' he said, and both the former officers knew enough to recognise in that seemingly non-committal phrase a resolution that couldn't be shifted with block and tackle. Wyndham felt a superstitious fear lift from his heart. After all, this was a railway station of ill omen. It had been from this very station that one Private Wyndham, D., had blindly followed Major Fitzmullen-Brophy and his dyspeptic old comrade, Major Tummy Belcher, when they had illegally embarked a body of deluded men for the Continent. This had been back in the summer of 1914 when the war was something a man of spirit might fear missing.

But no. None of that this time. This time Fitzmullen-Brophy's scheme was thwarted. So a few meaningless pleasantries were uttered and no more. Fitzmullen-Brophy bought a paper he didn't want with a shilling he couldn't quite spare, and insisted that Moriarty keep the change and drink the health of the Dirty Shirts, and then the two former officers left the former corporal and went to see about a hotel.

Ever since Fitzmullen-Brophy had put a shilling into his own hand – a very particular shilling, the *King's* shilling – Wyndham had been following him. As a recruit he's just been doing what he was told. As a commissioned officer he'd tried to pretend he was something of a dutiful adjutant – a second-in-command, even. But really it was because Fitzmullen-Brophy was a leader and Wyndham a follower, and the habit of following was six years old now, and Wyndham accompanied his old leader up the hill to Cork Barracks with no more independence or decision than one of the colonel's dogs might have exercised. The hill was steep and Fitzmullen-Brophy declined to take a taxi. Wyndham marvelled how the old man took it in his stride and still had enough energy to tackle the army's bureaucracy head-on.

It took more time and persuasion than it would have in Tralee. Cork was bigger, and the Royal Munster Fusiliers held no sway here. A retired colonel up from the country could be made to wait, and wait again. Fitzmullen-Brophy waited, and husbanded his restlessness, his fingers dancing distractedly on the crook of his walking stick. Forty years a soldier and he still never could sit quite still. It was late in the day before he was allowed to see anyone of any consequence. This turned out to be a colonel by name of Wallace, whose greeting was cordial but distracted. He was another of those officers with service chevrons up to his elbow and a mind still half-rooted in the urgencies of Flanders or Mesopotamia – as yet unsettled in the safe emptiness of this post-war world.

Fitzmullen-Brophy took a seat and laid out his concerns with clarity. The fussy, sometimes bumbling old man under whose roof Wyndham had been living had fallen away. It was as if Fitzmullen-Brophy were reading from prepared notes. It was soldierly and direct, with just the right amount of emotion injected to hold the attention.

It failed to have its desired effect.

As Fitzmullen-Brophy spoke, Wallace took a paperclip and folded it, and refolded it, and put the resultant little wire sculpture on the desk in front of him and looked at it. It clearly did not meet his satisfaction, because he put it to one side along with the litter of previous disappointments and took a fresh paperclip from the box. While his fingers worked he nodded along to what Fitzmullen-Brophy was saying. Only when his visitor's voice rose in anger did Wallace look up. He gave Fitzmullen-Brophy a look of placid sympathy, but Wyndham believed his mind was elsewhere, pursuing the platonic ideal of the crumpled paperclip.

'Drunkenness,' said Wallace, repeating Fitzmullen-Brophy's last word to prove he'd been listening.

'Drunkenness, Colonel! Damage to property! Rough hands laid on women! Seen it with my own eyes! Heaven knows what else! This is the sort of beastliness one would have expected from the Hun in Belgium. It's frightful, and the country'll not stand for it – mark my words.'

'Hmm,' said Wallace, his eyes not quite focused. 'Disgraceful.'

Seeing that he had failed to communicate sufficient outrage,

Fitzmullen-Brophy grasped the initiative. If a man like Wallace couldn't see his way to mending the situation, it was up to Fitzmullen-Brophy to tell him how.

'Good policemen are resigning in protest over this sort of thing, Colonel. Honest Irishmen forgoing their pensions and leaving the way clear for these guttersnipes and blackguards. So what I propose, Colonel – what I mean to do—' he began.

Wallace saw his way out clearly. He smiled and raised his hand to forestall this angry old Munster.

'Oh but you're not going to do anything, Colonel,' he said. '*We're* not going to do anything. Police business, you see. Not army. Not our pigeon.'

'I can't accept that. I wish to see General Strickland.'

'The general is at present unavailable,' said Wallace, and then he smiled more brightly as the idea dawned. 'You might write to him, I suppose.'

Fitzmullen-Brophy, who'd been angry all the way from Tralee that morning, lost his temper.

'Don't be so bloody stupid, man! When the hell is Strickland likely to read a letter? The country is going to rack and ruin *now*. Something must be done *now*. Who the devil can I speak to *now* who can rein in the likes of Smyth?'

Wallace didn't seem the least put out by the suggestion that he might be bloody stupid.

'Well you could talk to Smyth himself, I suppose.'

Fitzmullen-Brophy drew a deep breath. 'And what in the thundering blazes have I been asking to do all this time?'

'Sorry. Mustn't have been listening too closely. Hearing's been off the mark since I was blown up at Neuve Chapelle. No need to get hot under the collar, old boy.'

'Colonel, I have been *waiting* and *waiting*—'

'Well wait another minute or two and one of my chaps ought to be able to dig out Smyth's address.'

While they waited, Wallace arranged his little wire bundles in a neat line, happy that things had worked out and it was the weekend.

Smyth was supposedly staying at the County Club, but did not respond to the note Fitzmullen-Brophy sent round. Wyndham would have thought it too late to do anything more, but Fitzmullen-Brophy was not of the same mind.

'Nothing for it but to go and see the man,' he said.

'Now, sir?'

'*Forthwith.*'

47

I have been told the new policy and plan and I am satisfied, though I doubt its ultimate success in the main particular—the stamping out of terrorism by secret murder. I still am of opinion that instant retaliation is the only course for this, and until it is stamped for good and all, the same situation is only likely to recur.

—Brigadier-General Cyril Prescott-Decie, RIC, June 1920

The club was one of those handsome buildings that fitted in well with the various banks and superior premises on the street. Wyndham didn't know if Fitzmullen-Brophy happened to be a member or was merely able to talk his way past the porter on the strength of his rank and bearing. Wyndham missed all that. His attention was on the street, and on the early-evening traffic. He was looking for men who weren't out with their girls; men who loitered too watchfully; men with bulges under their coats.

'Do come along, Wyndham,' said the colonel. No first-name familiarity there. It was all business and duty now, and the colonel had grown snappish with a day's pent-up impatience.

Neither of them had evening clothes, so they were politely shunted to a corner of the smoking room and left there, isolated, without so much as the offer of a drink. To Wyndham, who'd never set foot in a gentlemen's club in his life, it was all quite familiar. He was back in the officer's mess, where the studied silence might be broken only to speak of horses or other sporting matters of great import. No one hailed Fitzmullen-Brophy. No one seemed even to know him, even though every man here looked as if he'd handled a billiard cue in Quetta, quaffed whisky and soda in Heliopolis or risked his neck pursuing a fox across any field from Galway to Suffolk. Not so much as a nod was directed at the colonel. Just as any of them could have been anyone of their set, so could he. There was nothing to distinguish him, so he could be ignored.

Because it was the smoking room Wyndham smoked. After a brief interval, to still his hands, Fitzmullen-Brophy filled his pipe and did the same. Having been all day in each other's company they had nothing to say. It was a small consolation that Smyth was not dodging them. He just happened not to be there.

Twice the colonel sent word to remind the porter of his mission. Once he made to stand up and see to matters himself, but sat down again in frustration. Wyndham stayed quietly wrapped in his sorrows and his fears. They would be kept waiting for Smyth because Smyth was already kidnapped or already killed, and it was so because a certain telephone operator in Kerry had listened to a conversation she shouldn't have, and told certain dangerous men what she had heard. That was why Smyth would not come.

And that was why it was such a surprise when Smyth finally arrived.

Lieutenant-Colonel Gerald Bryce Ferguson Smyth DSO was young to have been a brigadier-general during the war, but so were most men holding that qualification. He was missing an arm, and that wasn't so unusual either. He was in day clothes too, befitting a man of action and a man who could keep visitors waiting until ten. More than that: if Wyndham had been asked to bet money, he'd have bet that this man of action had a gun in his pocket. When Fitzmullen-Brophy was pointed out to him he crossed the room quickly because it was late and he still had much to attend to. He had no embarrassment in telling Fitzmullen-Brophy so.

'What's this about, Colonel?' he said, cutting short introduction and preamble.

Taking the measure of the man and situation, Fitzmullen-Brophy adopted a similarly brisk tone.

'Listowel, Colonel. It's what you said at the police barracks in Listowel.'

'Rot,' cut in Smyth. 'All of it rot. Misquoted and blown out of proportion by the Shinner papers.'

Fitzmullen-Brophy took this in, and pushed on regardless.

'But constables resigned over what you said to them – resigned in protest. Good Irish policemen who refuse to behave like these dreadful Black and Tans. That being the case, you can't deny that your words were inflammatory.'

'My words, Colonel, were intended to put some spirit into my men. Buck them up. Show them that their superiors are on their side. All in all, I'd rather have confident and aggressive men under my command than fellows too afraid of the courts and the press to do their duty. If that happens to cost the lives of one or two suspect characters, I rather think that's a price worth paying. Don't you, Colonel?'

'No, sir, I most certainly do not! It's no way to police a country! What you fail to understand about the Irish—'

'I'm Irish myself, Colonel,' said Smyth, 'And if you don't mind, I must speak to the commissioner here. Good evening to you.' And then he was on the other side of the room with a man he greeted as Craig who clearly warranted more attention. Smyth took possession of an armchair to hear what Commissioner Craig had to say. Fitzmullen-Brophy, the superannuated colonel from Kerry? Already forgotten.

Wyndham felt sorry for the colonel, but he wasn't surprised that their errand had come to nothing. Nor was he disappointed that Fitzmullen-Brophy's ideas for a reformed police force were being smothered so early.

'Come along, sir,' he said softly. 'It's late.'

Fitzmullen-Brophy cast a look back at the last two men in the smoking room – the men who were deciding between them the governance of Ireland. Well God help Ireland, that look said. Fitzmullen-Brophy might be yesterday's man, the look said, but better to have yesterday, when fellows had standards. Because if tomorrow were to be determined by Smyth and his ilk, then a decent man would want nothing to do with it.

'Come along, sir. We can have a drink back at the hotel before bed.' Wyndham laid a persuading hand on the colonel's shoulder, and Fitzmullen-Brophy allowed himself to be steered towards the door.

It was a good thing that they weren't attempting a dramatic exit, because just as they were leaving someone else was trying to get in.

The door to the smoking room was opening as Wyndham had his hand on the doorknob. He stepped back. There was some hesitation on the other side, as if the men coming in weren't certain they had the right room. They weren't in evening clothes either.

Wyndham both knew them and didn't. He could truthfully swear that every face was strange to him, but they were the same men who'd lifted him off the street in Tralee. They were the same men he'd been watching for in the street outside. The same hard look in their eyes; the same set to their shoulders. There were no suspicious bulges under coats though. These men had their guns in their hands.

'Lieutenant-Colonel Smyth,' said their leader, and Smyth was already out of his chair, knowing what was coming.

The intruder straightened his arm, his pistol pointing right at Smyth's face.

'You ordered your men to shoot without warning? To shoot on sight? Well—'

If there was more to the speech it was drowned by the shot,

and the other shots that came with it. And then the gunmen were gone, leaving Wyndham's ears stinging and the smoke thick in the air. Amazingly, Smyth was still on his feet, although the blood was flowing from grievous wounds. He was staggering towards the corridor.

How is he even alive? Wyndham asked himself. *Is he even alive?*

But if Smyth's movement was a last automatic reflex, it was an impressive one. Even with mortal hurts upon him, his remaining hand was scrabbling for the pistol in his coat pocket.

Fitzmullen-Brophy, who'd been seeing gunshot wounds to head and body before Wyndham was even born, had a better grasp of things. He took hold of Smyth, trying to ease him to the ground. He shouted at Wyndham. 'Get after them! Follow them!'

And because it was Fitzmullen-Brophy who had told him, Wyndham obeyed, despite the suicidal senselessness of it all. He was unarmed. There was only one of him. He checked himself at every turn to make sure he wasn't too close on the assassins' heels. There was a waiter flattened against the wall. There were members standing in doorways in confusion and alarm. The front door was open. No one was shooting back at him. He stepped out into the street, looking right and left. The cinema farther down was emptying onto the pavement. He glimpsed movement in the crowd, people parting as men shouldered their way through. But that was all he saw. The men were gone – those killers who had followed Nora's directions.

He shouldn't have been surprised how quickly and how many soldiers and police were on the scene. Club members and staff had come onto the street in Wyndham's wake. Onlookers were gathering. Wyndham was trying to gather his thoughts, trying to formulate as simple a statement as, 'They went that way,' but already a witness was on hand to help. A newspaper seller with an armful of late editions was pointing down towards the bridge, saying with certainty that that was the way the three men had fled. For himself, Wyndham would have sworn that there had been at least four assassins, and the cinema crowd into which he'd seen them disappear was in the opposite direction. But then again Moriarty, in all the years he'd known him, had never known a problem he couldn't obfuscate or an authority he couldn't hinder.

Was Moriarty a Shinner now? Wyndham couldn't leave Cork without knowing the answer. Naturally the man was gone by the time Wyndham had finished giving his statement to the police, and by then it was into the small hours. Sleep proved impossible. Wyndham had seen worse in the trenches. He'd had men die suddenly and unexpectedly when they were right next to him. He'd felt the wind of the thing that killed them. He'd wiped their blood from his face. And maybe that was what kept him awake: not Smyth's assassination but what it brought back. He ran out of cigarettes just before dawn, but the hall porter wouldn't let him go outside.

'Curfew, sir. You'd be arrested the second you stuck your nose out of doors. Even a gentleman like yourself, sir. The Tans and the military are in no mood to listen to excuses. It's been a bit of a disturbed night in town. Cigarettes, sir? Sure you'd never find a place open at this hour. And on a Sunday? Take one of mine, sir. Go on.'

He went to the station with Fitzmullen-Brophy as soon as breakfast was out of the way but wouldn't accompany him on the train.

'I have some things to attend to, sir. I'll catch a later train. Don't worry.'

Wyndham would do the worrying. He had to find Moriarty. He had to know if the IRA men who were killing senior officers with extreme views on policing were going to stop with Smyth.

48

Such war is thoroughly bad for officers and men; it tends to lower their standards of decency and chivalry.

—Bernard Law Montgomery, 17th (Cork) Brigade

'I'm sure I wouldn't know where he is,' said Moriarty's sister-in-law, and getting even that much out of her had taken undue time. Wyndham had had to wait until the family was back from Mass, and even then he was treated like an unwelcome tradesman, made to stand in the kitchen while Sunday hats were tidied away, and children chivvied, and things put in some sort of order. He didn't warrant the parlour, even in his good Parisian suit.

'Were you in the army with my uncle Francie?' asked one of the children when they intercepted him outside afterwards.

Wyndham gave a guarded nod.

'Did ya kill loads of Germans?'

A non-committal shrug was offered in answer

'Are you English?'

'I'm an American.'

'From America?'

'Yes.'

'Is that why you talk like that?'

Another shrug.

The accent and the clothes provoked the next line of interrogation: 'Were you an officer?'

'I was.'

'Uncle Francie says officers are bastards.'

'You're going to Hell for using bad language on a Sunday!' yelled the boy's sister, who sounded pleased.

'Where is your Uncle Francie?' asked Wyndham, wanting to be quit of these children but hoping for some recompense for this little ordeal.

'He's living below off Grattan Street.'

That was quite nearby, but not specific enough to be helpful.

'Can one of you show me?'

'Mam won't leave us go out. There was a soldier killed down by the bridge last night.'

The child hadn't got the wrong end of the stick. Smyth hadn't been the only soldier to be murdered in Cork on Saturday night.

'There, d'ya see? I toldja!' said the Moriarty child – either Finbarr or Anthony – as they came in sight of the bridge. He'd insisted to his siblings that he wasn't defying their mother's stricture. 'I'm only showing the man a bit of the way,' he'd said. 'I'm only taking him round the corner'. But he'd taken Wyndham around the next two corners also, and seeing as he'd come this far, he went all the way down to where the street opened out before crossing the North Gate Bridge. After that he ceased to care about giving directions to his uncle's lodgings.

There was a cluster of people gathered at the scene of the killing – a solid core who'd taken on the role of keepers of the site and tellers of the tale, with passers-by joining to gawp and listen and shake their heads before going on their way to spread their version of the news across the town.

The story as Wyndham gathered it was this: a man named James Bourke, a discharged soldier, had been killed there in the street the night before. Of course there was more to it than that. He had been bayoneted by a soldier. He had been shot. He'd been bayoneted *and* shot, and so had the two or three or ten men with him. And there was the blood there on the road to give testimony.

In fairness, Wyndham had seen far more blood splashed around than that. Last night in the County Club, for instance.

But while it would have gone too far to cross himself and throw in a 'Merciful hour!' or a 'God bless us and save us!' to go with the others, he was polite enough to nod solemnly and ask a few respectful questions regarding the departed. That was perhaps a mistake.

Sunday or not, he was too well dressed for this crowd and his accent was all wrong.

'And who would you be, sir?' said a man, giving voice to the suspicious looks and challenging stares.

Wyndham searched for an adequate answer.

'He's a Yank,' said the Moriarty child. 'From America.' And then, less helpfully, 'He's an officer in the army.'

This was hardly the place for Wyndham to launch into a speech about Woodrow Wilson's passionate commitment to Irish independence, but if that was what it would take to avoid a lynching or, at the least, being pitched into the river, he was prepared to give it a try. He was saved the effort, however, by a man in the crowd who addressed him tentatively by name.

'Is it yourself, sir? Am I right? Mr. Wyndham from the 1st Battalion?'

The fact was that Wyndham had swung through half the battalions of the Munster Fusiliers in the course of his irregular career, but if this man were willing to confirm to the crowd that the smoothly dressed outsider with his questions was not a police spy, then Wyndham was happy to greet him as a brother in arms.

The first duty of a good officer is to know his men. 'O'Connor?' Wyndham ventured.

'Fox,' said the man, unoffended. 'I was in D Company. Come on, we'll head away from here.'

Extracted from the crowd, Fox put Wyndham in the picture.

'I wasn't there last night, but I knew Bourke well. He was a gunner. Grand fella altogether. Shameful what happened.'

'And what did happen?'

'Bourke and another couple of lads were just out minding their own business. A couple of swaddies with drink on them came across them – asked them where they could buy some fish and chips. Every place was closed, but sure your soldiers weren't having that and they got rowdy. And it didn't matter a damn that the lads claimed to be soldiers just like them. Sure they were just Paddies, weren't they? I'd bet you anything that those boys out on the piss didn't have a service chevron between them. Never saw a German at all.

'So anyway there's a row, and more soldiers arrive, only these lads are on duty, with their rifles and all. So push came to shove and poor Jamesie Bourke got himself stabbed. They got an ambulance for him but he died in the hospital.'

'And he wasn't a Sinn Feiner?'

'Devil a bit, but you can be sure they'll make him out to be at the inquest.'

'Listen,' said Wyndham. He looked around in vain for the child that had guided him here. 'Do you know Corporal Moriarty? He looked after stores when he was with 1st Battalion.'

'Sure I do. He sells papers now.'

'I know. But could you tell me where he lives?'

'I wouldn't know,' said Fox. 'But he might well be out tonight.'

'Selling papers?'

'On a Sunday evening? No, he'll be out with the rest of us protesting. We'll be showing them that veterans aren't going to stand being treated like that.'

'Protesting? Where?'

The street was a broad thoroughfare leading to the railway station. It had been named for the king when Wyndham had first come to this town, but with Sinn Féin now in City Hall, it had been renamed for one of their own – another fallen this year at the hands of armed men. So that was why Wyndham had trouble finding the place.

There were knots of men gathered at one end of the otherwise quiet street and it put Wyndham in mind of Sunday mornings after church, but it was Sunday evening now, and it was men only gathering here, and their focus was not the church but the police station.

Barracks, thought Wyndham. This ordinary building, its brick facade all of a kind with the businesses on either side, may not have looked the part, but a police station in Ireland was always a barracks: a reminder of law and order imposed by force of arms on a sullen people.

This barracks, like many another, had been standing empty for some months now, its windows charred and gaping and the door blasted off its hinges. Some of the people had been making their resentment felt.

The gathering men were all of a kind too. All of them were Wyndham's age or nearabout.

Soldiers.

He knew them well. He knew that it would take no more than a bark of command and these loose groupings of men would be all lined up in ranks, tallest on the right, shortest on the left, chins up and shoulders squared. And he knew as he drew near that he wouldn't have to look too close to see scars or lamed legs, nervous tics or old eyes in young faces.

For the benefit of those who wouldn't recognise the signs, there were medals too. The ubiquitous duo of the War Medal and the Victory Medal, with here and there, in pride of place, the bronze four-pointed star proclaiming a man who had been early to the fight – a man who'd been in it before Kitchener's mob had ever learned their left from their right. As a man Out In Fourteen, Wyndham had one of those, and he felt a momentary irrational stab that he was missing his chance to wear it among men who would know its worth.

He was moving among them now, brushing past them, his neck on the swivel.

'You alright there, sir?' said a man, and it was a tone not far from the one he'd heard at the bridge earlier.

What business does this stranger have here? Is he an honest man or is he one of them?

'I beg your pardon – Francis Moriarty? Munster Fusiliers? You know him? — We were in the 1st Battalion together.' And even though he knew it to be the God's honest truth, it sounded unconvincing even in his own ears. But the man seemed to accept it at face value, or at least he indicated with a nod and said, 'I saw him over that way a while ago. Over by the corner.'

And there Moriarty still was, typically furtive, on the edge of the crowd, with a sidestreet at his back in case he needed to be away in a hurry. He didn't look pleased that his old officer had found him. Wyndham offered him a cigarette by way of the price of audience.

'Listen,' he began.

'I don't think you're in the right place at all,' said Moriarty.

'Listen—'

'This wouldn't be the place for you and Colonel FitzEm's special constabulary or whatever you call it.'

'I—'

'Have you chosen a colour for your uniforms yet? Because black and tan are taken.'

'Shut up. I—'

'Did you come all this way to tell me to shut up?'

Wyndham went so far as to raise his hands, wanting to grab Moriarty by the lapels and shove him or shake him into some sort of compliance. Moriarty must have recognised it in the man's eyes.

'So what is it you want?' he asked, and politely waited for an answer.

'The colonel,' said Wyndham. 'Do you mean any harm to the colonel?'

'Old Colonel FitzEm? Why would I want to do a thing like that.'

'Not you – your friends, I mean.'

'What friends are you talking about. I don't have much in the way of friends these days.'

Wyndham leaned in close and spoke through his teeth.

'What about those men who killed Colonel Smyth last night?'

And then it was Moriarty who grabbed Wyndham's lapels and hauled him further out of earshot of the gathering men.

'That was nothing at all to do with me,' he said.

'You were right outside keeping watch for them!'

'I was selling papers.'

'Don't give me that! Were you just selling papers at the station too? Or were you keeping an eye out for travellers that the IRA might want to know about? Like senior army officers, for instance?'

'Alright! So I keep an eye out! And I drop a word in the right ear when I need to! Why the hell shouldn't I?'

'Because – because you're no Shinner! You're a Dirty Shirt!'

'A load of good that's doing me! I'm in the army since I was a young fella and what do they give me? Eleven shillings! Eleven bob a week! I was up before the pension board and I told them! I'm not well, I told them! My nerves are gone, I said! I'm not right in the head! I can't get by on eleven bob!'

'Calm down.'

'First he tells me to shut up and now he tells me to calm down!'

'I'm sorry. Please.'

Moriarty wiped his nose and collected himself.

'Look,' said Wyndham, 'I'm worried about the colonel – that's all.'

'The colonel should mind his own damn business.'

'I know he should, but you know him as well as I do. I'll try and keep him out of the way but you must talk to your people and get him taken off their death list if he's on one.'

'My people?'

'The Shinners, the IRA – you know.'

'I'm not a Shinner.'

Not for the first time in his conversations with Moriarty, Wyndham wondered if he'd have to start again at the beginning. And not for the first time, Moriarty explained himself as he would to a slow child.

'I only keep an eye out,' he said. 'I tell people what I see. I mind things for people from time to time. That's all it is. I'm not letting these fucking Tans have the run of the place. Did you hear what they did to your man Bourke last night over by North Gate Bridge?'

Wyndham looked back at the crowd of ex-servicemen and at the cordon of police that had established itself at the top of the street. He could see from their funny hats that the police were Tans, and that meant they'd be wearing the very same medals seen among the protestors.

The confrontation was escalating fast, as if everyone was sick of waiting. Above the angry accusations and warnings from both sides of the cordon there rose a startled shout.

'Tanks, lads!' And a roar of engines could be heard coming down the hill. They weren't tanks but armoured cars, dispatched to town from the army barracks above, and the machine-guns in their faceless turrets turning hither and thither like the malevolent feelers of a blind insect. A lorry-load of soldiers came in their wake, jumping down and taking their place along the cordon: British soldiers facing off against British soldiers. They'd have worn different badges in their time, and held the differences dear, but they'd all worshipped at the same shrines. And now honouring different deities they took their places on either side of a string of barbed wire and prepared to shed each other's blood, and all for the independence of a country that had already been granted Home Rule.

Moriarty was backing out of any line of fire. Wyndham wasn't slow in overtaking him.

Will an Irish republic get you better than eleven shillings? he wanted to ask. Instead he said, 'I have a train to catch. What's the best way to get to the station without getting shot?'

49

We are going to break up this murder gang. That it will be broken up utterly and absolutely is as sure as that the sun will rise tomorrow morning... Assassination has never changed the history of the world and the Government are going to take good care it does not change the history of the British Empire.

—Winston Churchill, October 1920

'Daniel, mind Baby a moment.'

Wyndham's return to Tralee was typical. He'd managed to extricate himself from a developing riot in Cork only to be intercepted by the police at the station, where he'd been obliged to adopt his most high-handed, officer-like, *don't-you-know-who-you're-talking-to-my-man* tone in the face of rude questioning while guards' whistles and steam whistles blew. Then, of course, after he'd heaved himself aboard, sweat on his brow and ticket between his teeth, the train had refused, without good reason given, to depart. An hour after it finally did, it came to a halt in the dark countryside. This time a reason was supplied – or at least a rumour. The IRA had attacked, or were attacking, or were about to attack a viaduct, or perhaps it was a tunnel. It was early morning before they reached Tralee – too early for breakfast. Too early even to buy cigarettes. The want of a smoke, and a meal, and a bath and change of clothes had weighed heavily on Wyndham in the long trudge to the Fitzmullen-Brophy house. The beauties of a summer morning had been entirely wasted on him.

And now here he was back safe, with dogs cavorting around

his legs, and a squirming infant thrust into his arms, and no mention of the murder he'd witnessed the night before last.

Molly disappeared before he could ask why precisely the child needed his care just now, but no matter. He already had the Fitzmullen-Brophys to take care of. One more wasn't going to make much difference. With the toddler tucked under his arm like a gurgling woollen parcel, he sought out the lady of the house.

'Ma'am, I'm afraid you should leave Tralee,' he explained to Mrs. Fitzmullen-Brophy. 'Leave Ireland, in fact. Take a vacation with your relatives perhaps in England. A *long* vacation. It's just not safe here right now. I'd tell the colonel but I doubt very much it would do any good.'

'Really, Daniel? Is it as bad as all that?'

'I'm afraid it might be. Where is the colonel, by the way?'

But then he heard the rummaging upstairs, and the mild curses, and he was transported back to the spring of 1915 when Fitzmullen-Brophy had been recalled to duty.

'Good God,' said Wyndham. 'He's looking for his gun, isn't he?'

'Don't worry, Daniel. I've hidden it. He came home in such a frightful wax yesterday. Dreadful business about that Colonel Smyth. Now I think Hugh wants to raise the county or somesuch.'

'Get him to England, ma'am. Take him to France. Anywhere. Anywhere but here. It's not safe.'

'Oh dear. I really don't think I can make him listen.'

'Try – and whatever you do don't let him go to the barracks. And try and keep him away from Ogilvie!'

'Daniel, surely you're not going out again without some breakfast.'

But he was. He'd pushed his tiredness aside. If Fitzmullen-Brophy couldn't be restrained, there were people that Wyndham could talk to. He was several steps toward the door when he paused in his mission and returned to hand his charge over to her grandmother. It wouldn't do to confront the Irish Republican Army while holding a baby.

Find Ó Tuama. Make it clear that Fitzmullen-Brophy is not like Smyth. Tell them to keep their distance or... or...

Something about Lucas and how Wyndham knew things? No.

Something about the new Ireland and how it should be a place of reconciliation and brotherhood?

Something anyway.

And then talk to Nora. Talk to Nora and get her to extricate herself from all this murderous nationalism. Make it plain that he wouldn't stand for it. She must walk away from whatever intelligence work she was doing or... or...

But first the IRA.

Seeing as Ó Tuama wasn't lurking in the shrubbery waiting for him, Wyndham faced a return to town. At least this time he could go by bicycle, but he wasn't far down the road when he began to wish that he had taken a bite of breakfast and enough time to change his shirt.

If he left a message how long would it be before Ó Tuama got it, and how long before he could talk to his superiors? Wyndham pedalled faster.

What if he just cut out Ó Tuama altogether and spoke directly to whomever was his senior officer? How then did one contact members of a guerrilla army on an ordinary Monday morning in a provincial Irish town?

As it happened, they found him first. He hadn't even made it into Tralee when a motor car drew alongside him.

'Get in, Mr. Wyndham. We'll look after your bike for you.'

Once more the Irish Republic needed a fourth for bridge.

The next ten days were days of alternating hope and frustration.

Fitzmullen-Brophy appeared to have dropped any idea of

taking an active part in police matters, but he refused to leave Kerry for the time being, to the extent that he lost his temper with Wyndham for machinating against him in league with the womenfolk – which was fair.

Nora was positively eager to meet him again after his adventures, but a damnable rain denied them opportunity for physical affection by keeping them indoors and in public. It got worse. Their conversation over tea in a hotel sounded like rattlesnakes fighting as they hissed their vehement disagreement on matters clandestine, hiding their mouths with their hands and darting covert glances at the waitress. In summary, Nora had not known about any attempt on Smyth's life, had had no part in arranging it, yet felt it was good enough for the man all the same. Moreover, she was under no circumstances going to give up her part in the national struggle on the say-so of Mister Daniel Precious Wyndham, and who did he think he was, setting conditions for her anyway?

Gearóid Ó Tuama proved impossible to track down, having evidently been promoted from shadowing suspect army officers to something more directly useful to the cause. An associate said as much to Wyndham out of the corner of his mouth when tackled directly one day.

'I can tell you nothing,' he'd said. 'So don't be asking.' And Wyndham guessed that the man's part in the revolution as yet amounted to no more than keeping a lookout on street corners and pretending to even more ignorant youths that he was a man to be reckoned with. He was certainly not in the councils of the great, so pressing him on the matter of Colonel Fitzmullen-Brophy's welfare would be fruitless.

Another of Nora's days off came. It rained harder than before, and she sent a message calling off their rendezvous. Molly had returned to Dublin, leaving Wyndham with one less friend. On the credit side of the ledger, Mrs. Fitzmullen-Brophy announced that they would visit their daughter in Dublin for a few days, and her husband offered no resistance.

Wyndham believed that the colonel was safer in Dublin than in Tralee, so long as he kept his mouth shut. The Dublin IRA, he hoped, was fighting the sort of glamorous big-city war that paid little heed to rustic colonels.

And then, to balance out this little bit of good fortune, some stony-faced men in an anonymous motor car came calling for him one more time.

50

All will come right soon, and we can settle down together in peace and comfort. Just think of that and try and forget all the present troubles.

—letter from Brigadier-General Cuthbert Lucas to his wife, 28 July 1920

This car was not as roomy as the last had been, and the last hadn't been up to much. Wyndham shifted in his seat, uncomfortable already and hours still to go, with his knees pressed against the back of the passenger seat and the weight of the man beside him rolling against him with every turn of the road.

On previous journeys he'd been nervous and curious. Now he was just testy.

'Surely,' he said, '*surely* there must be someone else in the province of Munster who plays bridge.'

'We've been working our way through them. The thing is, though, General Lucas likes you.'

He turned around in his seat to give Wyndham a grin.

'We like you too, so we do. An ex-army officer living with an army family? You're not likely to be suspected, are you? And you keep your mouth shut.'

'Kind of you to say so, I'm sure, but how do you know I can be trusted?'

'We've been watching you, Mr. Wyndham, and there are those who've vouched for you. Ó Tuama says you're sympathetic to our cause. A certain young lady in the post office puts in a good word too. Being engaged to someone in Cumann na mBan speaks well of you.'

Nora had put in a good word about him? Nora hadn't blown up at the misconception that she and Wyndham were engaged?

He smiled in spite of himself and settled back in his seat, but there was bitterness in the smile. He'd have been better pleased to be doing some service for the Irish Republic if he'd been told all this sometime before the Saturday just gone.

As the journey continued by winding roads, taking who knew what diversions, the man sharing the back seat with Wyndham started up a conversation of sorts.

'We'd blindfold you, but it wouldn't make any difference,' he said. 'I doubt I'd be able to find my own way there, and I've been there the past week. Back of bloody beyond. Nothing to bloody do.'

'Be quiet, you,' said the man in the front seat. 'You've little enough to complain about. Nice easy living, and some genteel company to give you some social polish.'

The man in the back snorted to show what he thought of that. 'I didn't join the IRA to play croquet,' he said. 'In fairness – what am I supposed to tell my grandchildren?'

Wyndham thought he marked more tension over the card table than before. The last time there had been stretches where the positions of captor and hostage had been wholly forgotten – where the fall of the cards had been the only determiner of mood. Not so this time. No matter how civilised the arrangements, there was no escaping that Lucas had been a prisoner for a month, and appeared no closer to his release than on the day he'd been taken. The strain showed too on the IRA. A month ago they'd been wondering if so desperate a plan could even work. Snaring a British general was so daring as to be scarcely conceivable. Hiding him had been part of the plan – but for a whole month? Keeping him entertained hadn't been thought of at all.

'I did some gardening,' Lucas said. 'Some work in the fields too. Just what a fellow needs – fresh air and strenuous exercise.'

'And men to watch him, and sentries to watch the road, and mouths to be kept shut,' said Brennan, the man in charge, not looking up from his cards.

After the game Wyndham had a brief moment to talk to Brennan.

'I'd really like to get back to Tralee tonight.'

'There's no one to give you a lift. There's too many roadblocks and checkpoints. You can keep the general company. The two of ye get on. Go on and talk to him. No one will be listening. Talk about the war. Talk in Arabic if you want. Just for the love of God go easy on the whiskey. That stuff is costing money.'

Wyndham did go easy on the whiskey. He only drank to be polite and even then it made him feel somewhat guilty.

Conversation was stilted – each man speaking as if the silence were something to be filled, but only with planning and effort.

'Your wife is doing well, General? And the baby?'

'Oh, doing splendidly, Wyndham – thank you for asking.' Lucas was smiling, but the smile disappeared as soon as he forgot to keep it up. His mind was elsewhere.

'Or at least they were,' he added.

'Something's wrong?'

'Oh! Well no – not as far as I know at any rate. Not with Poppy and the baby, leastways. It's just that communications have been interrupted. One of Brennan's men was arrested in picking up the post.'

'Oh dear. But I'm sure they can sort everything out.'

'I'm sure they can, but that's not really the point, is it?'

'No?'

'The net's closing in. The authorities are combing the countryside. The Shinners could well be running out of places to hide me.'

'But surely that's grounds for hope?'

'I'd like to think so. I dearly would. But they let me see the papers, you know. I read about what happened to Gerald Smyth in Cork. You know about that, I suppose?'

'I believe I heard something.'

'Ruthless, Wyndham. Utterly cold-blooded. Brennan and all the rest might be decent fellows but they're of the same stamp as those killers in Cork. I don't see them surrendering themselves – or me.'

Lucas picked up his glass, swirled the whiskey around, and put it down untasted. Like Wyndham, he'd hardly touched a drop all night.

'Desperate times, desperate measures, and all that sort of thing,' he said.

Wyndham made understanding noises but didn't have it in him to wave away Lucas's fears – or his own for that matter. Could they just kill Lucas the way they'd killed Smyth – decent fellows or not? When he thought of Nora's part in it all he wondered if the whole country hadn't crossed a line. He wanted to reassure Lucas, but more than that he wanted to be far away and quit of this whole business.

His impatience must have made itself evident.

'Look here, Wyndham – why don't you put your head down? I understand that you're stuck here for the night, but there's precious small use in listening to me jawing on for hours.'

'Really, General, I'm quite alright.'

'Take my bed, man. I'm not in the least bit tired. I was thinking of staying up to see the dawn.'

'I couldn't, sir.'

They were silent a while, and then Lucas tried again.

'Tell you what – how about you conjure up some sandwiches? I find myself quite hungry all of a sudden.'

'Good idea,' said Wyndham, glad for something to do.

The rest of the house must have retired for the night since the card game had ended. No doubt there were sentries out in the dark, but there was no one to ask Wyndham his business as he sought the kitchen and rooted out a loaf of bread. It was all so silent that he nearly cut himself with the bread knife when he heard Lucas behind him.

'Sorry, old man. Didn't mean to startle you. Just stretching the legs. Cut the bread good and thick, eh?'

He walked a slow circuit of the kitchen, stopped at the window, and then, with studied idleness, tried the back door.

'I say,' he said. 'Unlocked. There's a thing.'

'Sentries just outside,' said Wyndham.

'I expect so,' said Lucas. 'Couldn't see anyone from the window, mind.'

'No?'

They might have been talking about the weather, if either of them cared about the weather.

'Have a sandwich, General,' said Wyndham. 'You don't mind if I go out for a smoke?'

'Thank you,' said Lucas. 'Not at all.' And Wyndham noticed that the general wrapped the food in his handkerchief and put it in his pocket.

It was perfectly still outside, and the moonlight revealed no sentry anywhere. Even though it had been more than two years since he'd been in the trenches, Wyndham still felt uneasy about striking a light out of doors, but he did it anyway, just to look normal, and he strolled around the outside of the house as though he were no more than a guest at his ease.

'Fine out?' asked Lucas five minutes later.

'Perfectly,' said Wyndham. 'Someone's still awake upstairs by the look of things. One fellow's on guard out front as far as I can tell. All quiet otherwise. You might take a walk yourself. Probably wouldn't disturb a soul.'

'Really?'

'Not if you went by the back way.'

'Wyndham, I wonder if you wouldn't mind awfully doing me a favour? I believe I left my – my...'

'Your pipe, General? I think I saw it by your chair.'

'My pipe, yes. Or it may be in my bedroom.'

'I'll go and look.'

'Thanks,' said Lucas. 'I'll—,' and he unconvincingly waved his hand in the general direction of the kettle. '*Thank* you, Wyndham.'

Wyndham returned to the sitting room, looked at his watch, lit a cigarette, checked his watch again, having forgotten what it had told him the first time, and counted slowly to a hundred. Then he went back towards the kitchen, hesitated at the door, and returned to the sitting room. This time he gave it to two hundred.

The kitchen was deserted by the time he returned.

'General?' he said to the obviously empty room. 'General Lucas?'

He opened the back door and listened for sounds of hue and cry. He rehearsed the story he'd have to tell.

'I turned my back for just a moment.'

'He said he was only going to the lavatory.'

'He overpowered me and knocked me senseless! I raised the alarm as soon as I came to!'

He didn't have the heart to disarray his hair, pull his tie askew, or wallop his head against the wall to give credence to that last excuse. He made for the stairs and the room where he'd seen a light burning. He walked with the pace of a man contemplating mathematical equations. Between hall and landing he had time to finish another cigarette.

He wasn't afraid that Brennan might shoot him out of hand. He wasn't even thinking about it. He was thinking about Nora, and about the side he had taken.

I've seen enough men killed. I didn't want to watch Lucas die like Smyth died. I've got enough on my conscience as it is.

At the last second it occurred to him that the smell of fresh cigarette smoke on the stairs would give the lie to any story of urgency he might try to sell, but then he noticed that the same smell was thick on the landing, advertising the wakefulness of some in this house as clearly as the light from under the door.

Brennan and his lieutenants, in shirtsleeves and shoulder holsters, were sitting in various parts of the room, doing nothing except waiting for time to pass.

'I beg your pardon,' said Wyndham, 'but I believe General Lucas has escaped.'

'Are you sure?' said Brennan.

Wyndham's mind ran through the prevarications he'd prepared, and he settled on, 'Yes.'

'Well thank Christ for that,' said Brennan.

'What?'

'About bloody time,' said Brennan, and Wyndham noticed that the men were rising from their seats, not in alarm, grabbing their weapons, but like passengers arriving at their destination, patting their pockets to see that they had everything.

'What?' said Wyndham again.

'The man was costing us a fortune,' said Brennan.

'And keeping us up all hours,' said one of his men.

'And tying up God knows how many fellas who'd have been better employed elsewhere,' said Brennan, pulling on his coat. 'With the general out of the way we can get back to fighting the war.'

The man who'd complained about croquet on the journey over clapped Wyndham on the shoulder. 'But he was a grand man all the same,' he said. 'An officer and a gentleman. I'm glad we didn't have to plug him. We'd better be going before he gets found by any soldiers or Tans. We can give you a lift a bit of the way if you want.'

'Were you?' asked Wyndham, still badly off balance.

'Were we what?'

'Going to – um – plug him?'

The man threw an enquiring look at his commanding officer. Brennan merely shrugged in response.

What's a little murder between bridge partners?

Wyndham studied the papers in the coming days and was relieved to read that General Lucas attributed his escape to a loose bar on his window, with no mention whatever being made of American ex-army officers of dubious allegiance.

Some men might be proud to boast of a small part played in great affairs, but all things considered, Wyndham thought himself better off in obscurity.

VI

BLACK AND TAN

The condition of Ireland causes Me grave concern.

—George V to Parliament, 11 February 1920

51

We have Murder by the throat.

—David Lloyd George, 10 November 1920

After his adventure with Lucas, Wyndham was left to his own devices back in Tralee. With the Fitzmullen-Brophys away, the house was his to rattle around in. There was only the hostile cook, whom he wisely avoided, and the maid – a florid-complexioned girl shy to the point of inaudibility. To counterbalance this near muteness she went about her work with a great deal of noise, and she could always be traced through the house by the crashing and clattering of fire irons or crockery or dustpan and brush. So with that and the dogs, Wyndham had loneliness but no peace. In long-ago days he'd have occupied himself with books. In the army he'd have drunk himself silly. Now, with worries of violence and with unrequited lusts for Nora, he was too unsettled for agreeable leisure.

Despite drizzly weather he took to mooching around town. There was no other word for it.

He was wandering in the direction of a bookshop where he had no intention of buying anything when he was hailed from a car. He stiffened, but saw in a moment that this wasn't one of those offers of a lift that he was not allowed to refuse. On the other hand, the man intercepting him wasn't welcome and was armed. It was Ogilvie, with a brand-new shotgun under his arm.

'I say! Wyndham!'

'Mr. Ogilvie. Such a pleasure to see you again. I hope you're well.' Light insincerity cost nothing. 'Off for some shooting, perhaps?'

Ogilvie showed his teeth in wicked resolution.

'Shooting there will be, young man,' he said. 'Any trouble from any damned Sinn Feiners and shooting there will most certainly be, ha-ha!'

Wyndham didn't think it proper to wish the man the best of luck, and was casting about for a polite response when he was saved by the roar of a passing lorry, going far too fast. He glimpsed a Lewis Gun mounted on top of the cab. Black and Tans. There were many averted eyes in the street. But not Ogilvie's.

'Give them what for, men!' he cheered after them. 'That's the stuff!'

Wyndham felt very exposed. If Ogilvie noticed some of the looks he was getting he was either oblivious or proudly defiant. He didn't lower his voice after the lorry had gone by.

'It's what the taxpayer wants to see, Wyndham! Law and order! I may not see eye to eye with your Colonel Fitzmullen-Brophy about everything, but he and I are in complete agreement on that!'

Unable just to say *shush*, Wyndham murmured that the Fitzmullen-Brophys were away for a while.

'Well do tell him I was asking for him. His idea of an amateur local constabulary is largely nonsense, but there might be a crumb of something in it. Concerned citizens doing their bit to aid the actual constabulary, eh? Fitzmullen-Brophy have a telephone? No, of course not. Still – fellows like us can be the eyes and ears of the police, don't you know.' And here he brandished his new shotgun. 'And the trigger fingers if needs be, ho-ho!'

Wyndham could only smile and nod and wait for Ogilvie to be on his way, which he was presently, but not without one more time shouting the name of Fitzmullen-Brophy from his car as he departed. 'Tell him to get in touch!'

With friends like these, thought Wyndham, as he waved the most unobtrusive wave he could manage.

Right. That settled it. If Ogilvie was painting a target on his own back and painting another one for Fitzmullen-Brophy, it was high time Wyndham spoke to someone. If the IRA wanted to murder Ogilvie in his bed and burn his house down, then *c'est la guerre*, but please leave harmless old retired colonels out of it. He absolutely needed to find Ó Tuama.

He tracked down the street-corner lookout he'd approached before, but the man claimed not to know Ó Tuama's whereabouts and implied that wild horses couldn't drag it out of him if he did. Wyndham would have reached for his wallet but it occurred to him that this man probably genuinely knew nothing at all. More importantly, Wyndham was in no position to part with a ten-shilling bribe – although this fellow looked as though five might do the trick. Instead he walked off and bought a packet of cigarettes with his money, but he made sure to buy them in the shop where he'd first met Ó Tuama, and where Fitzmullen-Brophy had defied the Black and Tans.

He entered the shop as if he were returning to a happy home, and beamed at the girl behind the counter as though she were well-loved family. It was the same girl as before – little more than a child, but in assured possession of herself and of the shop – and to Wyndham's joy she returned the smile.

He asked after her health. He talked about the weather. He made harmless jokes. He made his purchase with faint regret, because now he had no more reason to linger. And then, as an afterthought, he asked after their mutual friend Gearóid Ó Tuama who was, as it was soon revealed, staying with relatives out Castleisland way, but more than that she couldn't say. Wyndham gave her a last smile that told her that this little visit had lightened his heart and brightened his day.

He reckoned that the journey would be around ten miles, and

that was nothing to him. Actually finding the man would be a matter of simply asking and hoping.

He was well on his way before he found himself wishing that he'd chosen another day. It wasn't the rain. The rain had given up for the time being and shifted on inland. No, it was the Tans. The road Wyndham took was the same road the lorryload of Tans had taken earlier, and evidence of their passing was clear. He drew to a halt at a roadside pub with the front window broken and an overturned cart nearby. Two milk churns had been in the cart and were now spilled open in the road, and their owner was tearing his hair and cursing a blue streak.

'Why in the name of the suffering Christ would I be hiding guns in the milk?' he asked to the world at large.

The man sweeping up glass outside the pub shook his head in sympathy.

Wyndham copied the gesture. 'The Tans?' he said, as if speaking about the potato blight or a death in the district.

'Who else?' said the publican.

'Worse than the Huns in Belgium,' said Wyndham as though retailing a well-worn article of faith.

'Blackguards all of them,' said the publican.

'And worse now they'll have drink in them!' said the man with the milk, joining the conversation from a distance.

The publican leaned on his broom. 'And it's not like they even paid for it,' he said to Wyndham. 'If I were you, sir, I'd watch out if I was going any farther along this way.'

'Destroyed!' said the man at the cart, returning to the subject of his milk, 'Destroyed altogether!'

With only the vaguest of directions to go on Wyndham took a wrong turning and it possibly saved his life.

Within a few hundred yards of where the road last forked he

found bare earth under his wheels and grass growing proud down the middle. Rather than go back the way he'd come, he thought to go just a little farther ahead, where he had the impression that the path was turning and rising again towards the main road. It had to be the main road. He could hear an engine running. And so he advanced, only to see a high bank surmounted with a dry stone wall keeping him from getting where he wanted. It was too high for him to climb and carry his bike, and he would have turned around then and there if he hadn't considered this a good place to break for a smoke. And that's when he heard the voices. Someone was shouting. Someone with an English accent was barking orders. And then there were shots.

Keeping low and keeping quiet he scrambled up the bank. It took some effort, but at last he was peering through the weeds that grew in a gap in the wall. The Blank and Tans' lorry was idling by the road. The Tans themselves were scattered roundabout but appeared to be regrouping. A couple of them, half out of breath, were returning from a chase.

'Bastard got away,' said one of them, 'Nippy little bugger. Couldn't even get a bead on him.'

'Well we've got this one, any road,' said their leader. He had a revolver loosely trained on a young man with his hands raised above his head. The man didn't speak and he had his back to Wyndham, but Wyndham knew him anyway.

'So what'll we do with him then?' asked one of the Tans.

'The likely lad with one of these in his pocket?' And Wyndham saw now that the heavy Webley pistol the sergeant had in his hand was matched by one in his belt.

'Think we can get him to tell us owt, Sarge?'

'Doubt it. Looks like small fry to me.'

'So do we take him back to Tralee with us then?'

'No point, really,' said the sergeant, and shot Gearóid Ó Tuama in the chest.

Everyone jumped at the suddenness of it. One of the Tans let out a nervous laugh.

'While trying to escape, eh, Sarge?'

The sergeant shot Ó Tuama's body twice more. 'Teach him to be doing whatever he was doing,' he said.

* * *

'Oh it is nice to be home,' said Mrs. Fitzmullen-Brophy, taking off her hat.

'Did you have a good time?' asked Wyndham.

'Up to a point,' she said. 'Dublin's got all those shops and theatres, but I must say I found it rather oppressive as things are now. All those police everywhere. Most unsettling. Did you enjoy yourself while we were away? You look a trifle wan.'

* * *

'Nora, you have to give it up,' he insisted.

'You've said that to me before and I didn't pay any attention then either.'

'This is no joke! It's just not safe! The Black and Tans are killing suspects indiscriminately. I've seen them!'

'You mean they're doing what General Smyth ordered them to do?'

'Leave General Smyth out of it.'

'No, Dan. It's a war. We're fighting a war. You should know about it. I mean, did you walk away from the trenches when you saw that the Germans meant business?'

I would have if they'd let me.

'People get killed in war, Dan,' she went on, and he had never heard her sound so calmly reasonable. 'It's what makes everyone take the whole matter so seriously.'

'Nora, please. *Please!* Would you just be more careful? About whatever it is you're doing for these people?'

'These people are my people, Dan. That's part of what we're fighting for. One Ireland for all of us. And no: I'm not going to stop.'

He fumed at her for a moment.

'If I had any guts I'd leave you and go back to the States,' he said.

'Ah no, Dan! You can't! There's a dance on Saturday coming!'

Of course he wasn't going to leave her. Not even over killings and the fear of more killings – and especially not when there was a dance on Saturday.

Though neither of them would ever have admitted it, dancing was what they had instead of sex. The sedate dances were all well and good, allowing them to hold each other without worrying who saw them. But it was the Irish dancing that got their hearts pumping— the promiscuous, swirling, risking-injury-to-bystanders hooley that left them bright-eyed and breathless.

Against their natural instincts they had edged their way into the social life of North Kerry just for the chance of such occasions. Nora had cultivated one local young woman for no other reason, and her cultivation had borne fruit.

'The wedding's on Saturday. We have an invitation. It'll be a proper country wedding.'

And so it proved.

It was after midnight when they pulled each other, red-faced and gasping, into the fresh air. There were no streetlights to reveal them and for a moment at least they had the darkness to themselves. Even before they pressed against each other he could feel the heat radiating from her. He imagined he could hear the raindrops hissing where they hit her skin. He imagined there was steam rising off the pair of them. They fumbled and giggled until they heard others approach. She leaned in for one last kiss. With her cheek against his wilted collar and her breath hot in his ear she said:

'I've got another job. I'm going back to Cork at the end of next week.'

52

This country is ruled by gunmen and they must be put down.

—General Hugh Tudor, 9 September 1920

The Irish countryside had become ungovernable. Local authority was in the hands of the IRA, even though they had slight means to exercise it. Power belonged to the Black and Tans, but they controlled no more of the country than could be shot at from the back of a lorry. Law and order contracted and shrank into the cities. Wyndham followed.

Nora left Listowel in the middle of August. She left with hope and proud determination. The transformation of the country was afoot, and she had been granted a part to play. She left without hesitation: a reminder to Wyndham that he took second place to her patriotic adventure. There was a kiss and an airy promise, and then his yearning for her was of less matter than the train that she had to catch that would take her to Cork, and a better job in a bigger post office. Her time in Listowel, it seemed, had only been to provide her with credentials and a little relevant experience. British military intelligence, even in the cities, relied on the public telephone service. What MI5 said was heard in the GPO. For the Irish Republican movement, a woman at a switchboard was every bit as useful as a man with a rifle.

And Wyndham followed, as he knew he would.

'Like a chivalrous hero,' said Molly in consolation.

'Like a dog,' said Wyndham in self-pity.

Cork was changing. The Irish tricolour flew above City Hall. It was an echo of Dublin in Easter Week, only here, instead of seizing the seat of government and defiantly raising their flag, the revolutionaries had merely stood for election and been duly voted onto the corporation. As such, the Royal Artillery had been given no excuse yet to pound the city into rubble. The thousands of soldiers and police with the crown on their badges went about their business in this garrison town under a rebel flag.

But democracy wasn't having everything its own way. The lord mayor had been assassinated in March by persons unknown who just happened to have English accents. Apologists for the crown could point out that the lord mayor was an active member of the IRA, but were hard-pressed to condone the murder by night of a man in front of his family.

His successor had been arrested only days before Nora took up her new post. The case gave added purpose to Nora and an air of nobility to the struggle as a whole. It is difficult to denounce as a villain a handsome intellectual who elected to starve himself to death in the name of justice.

In an English prison the hunger strike went on. Cork remained uneasy.

The army was on the streets. The Black and Tans patrolled aggressively. A 10pm curfew remained in place.

Wyndham was lucky enough to move into his old digs. He was even able to secure a job of sorts. There were still employers impressed by a well-spoken foreigner in a well-cut suit, and the king's commission could still serve as a reference. Wyndham wasn't especially hopeful about the employer he'd landed with. Would the man run out of money or out of patience before Wyndham's first pay fell due? It only mattered in the short term. He needed only to outlast Nora's revolutionary wanderlust. He needed Nora to see sense and marry him or – and this might have been the easier option – he needed the British government to throw in the towel. Neither appeared imminent. In the fortnight since he'd arrived, Nora had been too full of her new job to spare him any time. And as for His Majesty's government? It was showing itself more resolute and ruthless by the day.

One early morning in September, with the first autumn mist chilling the late summer dawn, Wyndham was walking through town. It was the quiet time of minding your own business and making a start to the day before the streets filled. Carts hauled away refuse. Lorries made their deliveries. Men clapped their hands, drew on fags, hunched their shoulders and got on with it, not expending time or effort in talk.

One motor roared louder than others: a Crossley Tender like a predatory beast, the men in the back like watchful statues, their hands on their rifles, their cap ribbons fluttering.

Wyndham chose not to look away. He was a respectable citizen with no need to be furtive. He kept his hands where they could be seen nonetheless.

The Tans were making their own delivery that morning.

A body was rolled off the back of the lorry. It thudded onto the street and came to rest athwart the tramlines where it lay like any other dead thing: devoid of identity, stripped of personality.

Wyndham stared at the Tans as they passed and they stared back at him. When they were gone he went to the body.

You always checked on the casualty. You never left the dead unattended if it could helped.

But he knew that this strange delivery was dead before it hit the ground. He knew there was no helping this lumpy sack of spoiled humanity. He knelt to look.

There was nothing to read from the bloodied face other than that he'd been beaten before he was shot. Yet there was something that seemed familiar to Wyndham, and all through the day a stupid jingle played in his head:

Has Anybody Here Seen Kelly? Kelly From The 8th Battalion?

53

...It is a poor little Bohemian hotel, only suited for those Sybarites who are exiled from Sybaris.

—Oscar Wilde, December 1898

Wyndham's present employer was a man named Ballantyne, who had a small hotel. He had taken Wyndham on because he'd seen in Wyndham a rootless poet and fellow romantic. Odd qualifications for temporary book-keeper, perhaps, but no more absurd than the assumption that a man who'd commanded an infantry platoon in battle should be sober and competent in civil life.

Luckily, sobriety and competence were two things that Wyndham had reacquired since shaking free of the king's commission. Luckily, because they were qualities much needed here.

'A small glass of something post-prandial, Mr. Wyndham?'

'Thank you, Mr. Ballantyne, but I will decline. I should be getting on with this.'

Ballantyne sat down in a worn armchair too low for a man of his physique and balance, and his glass sloshed onto Wyndham's desk. His presence took up what was left of the tiny office.

'Lamentable that gentlemen such as you or I should be obliged to spend our afternoons toiling,' he said.

'How sadly true,' said Wyndham.

'At the very least we should honour the custom of the siesta in this country,' said Ballantyne, stifling a burp. 'Remind me if you would: do they observe the siesta in Paris or is it merely the practice of the south?'

And there it was. Paris. The heart of the matter, the magnetic pole of Ballantyne's desires, and the root of the reason that Wyndham had a job here. How many seconds had it been before the subject had been broached this time? Was it a record? Not quite, thought Wyndham.

Ballantyne had never wanted to be a hotelier. He had inherited his present establishment. One look at the man was enough to tell: his soul dwelt among the *demi-monde* of the *belle epoque*. Wyndham, half in distaste and half in sympathy, gave him his attention.

Ballantyne's clothes, once daring, were now eccentric and outdated. The over-long and flamboyantly pomaded hair had thinned. What had been debonair was now bleary. There might once have been a lily in his buttonhole. Now there were just stains on the faded velvet.

Wyndham put down his pen. If today were like other days then he'd get little enough work done. It hardly mattered. There was hardly enough work to justify his job. He was there because Ballantyne had no love for the mundane business of hotel-keeping. Wyndham was, in effect, overseeing the decline of the enterprise.

But Paris.

Once upon a time Wyndham would have enlarged upon the licentiousness of that city, recounting depravities he'd never seen for the amusement of his audience. It had whiled away the time in trenches and dugouts and he could surely do it still if he had a mind to. But Paris meant something different to him now, and he didn't care to sully the memory of his days there with Nora. It would have been a betrayal.

On the other hand, if he clammed up then he left the initiative with Ballantyne, and he'd had to endure the unfulfilled *roué*'s fantasies before. The man had never travelled beyond Ireland and wouldn't have known Montparnasse from Mont Blanc, but he'd read many a dirty book and had an imagination unfettered by decency.

'Paris,' said Wyndham, and started making things up.

The tale he wove began with afternoon indolence and unfolded easily into a tapestry of loose living and loose clothing, but the New England puritan in Wyndham was strong, and his fabricated reminiscences had a judgemental backbone to them. The palaces of vice of Ballantyne's imagination were mean and tawdry dens when presented by Wyndham. The France that Lieutenant Wyndham had been fighting for had no place for the decadence Ballantyne desired.

'... And so I gave the cur a sound thrashing with his own opium pipe,' concluded Wyndham.

Ballantyne blinked his watery eyes in surprise and disappointment. The story had taken an unexpected direction. All he'd wanted was a little easy-going perversion to lighten his afternoon. He blew his nose to fill the silence.

'Say what you like about the French, though,' he said finally. 'They have an inimitable style in all they do – even in their sin. It is difficult to conceive of such things happening here.'

He waved a hand in the general direction of Ireland.

'What colour is there in our misdeeds? Men get drunk on porter on Saturday and still get to Mass on Sunday. Even this revolution – if that's what you can call it – is a shadow of what the French would do. Are we dragging the lord lieutenant from the Viceregal Lodge and guillotining him? Are the fine ladies of the gentry being shorn of their lustrous locks and paraded through the streets in tumbrils? Of course not. All the rebels do here is burn empty police stations and write strident letters to the papers. Where is our Lady Liberty, bare-breasted on the barricades?'

And he smiled to himself at the alliteration, and at the thought of bare breasts.

He saw that he had finished his brandy and wasn't sure if there was any more.

'I confess I find myself somewhat fatigued,' he said. 'Such a long and dreary morning it has been.'

'You should rest, Mr. Ballantyne. I can look after the front desk if needs be.'

Ballantyne rose with difficulty.

'Would you? A treasure, Mr. Wyndham. A treasure.'

None of this was new. The hotel staff had shrunk to almost nothing, and Wyndham didn't mind the chance to get away from the ledgers and stretch his legs in the front of house. In truth, he didn't care what he did with his time these days. He had too much of it and it was not occupied by Nora.

Nora was being kept busy. There was her paid work, which took up most of the day, and her secret work, which added however many hours on top of that. Then there were the overt political activities like meetings and protests which were more frequent here in the city than they had been in Kerry. He understood that he should be excluded from the code-breaking or invisible inking or whatever she did with whatever she learned in the post office. He accepted that he would be very much out of place in the doings of the Women's Council (which was what Cumann na mBan meant, he'd finally learned). What he couldn't see – what he refused to see – was why Nora couldn't take a day off now and again. In making his feelings plain all he'd managed to do was sour what few occasions they had together. Yes, he would be meeting her for tea on Sunday as usual, but that was a far cry from where he felt their relationship ought to be after all this time.

He was drumming his fingers on the desk and frowning when a guest arrived. It was such an unexpected occurrence that Wyndham almost asked the young man what the hell he was doing here.

Despite the guest's fresh face, there was something about him that seemed to fit in here among the threadbare chintz and the dust that was visible even in the autumnal gloom. He had an air of one invested in an age that was already past. His clothes were respectable but past their best. It was his luggage that decided it for Wyndham. It consisted solely of a valise, not pigskin but canvas, on which the owner's name was stencilled. Wyndham didn't pay any attention to the name. What he noticed was what came after it. '3 Conn R.'

'The Devil's Own, by God,' said Wyndham, almost as if the young man wasn't there.

'Why yes!' said the youth with a smile. The Connaught Rangers might have been famed as the most uncouth of the Irish regiments, but this accent was English and well bred.

'Sorry,' said Wyndham. I have a bag just like that one. Mine says Munsters though.

'Well what-ho, Dirty Shirt!' said the young man, and Wyndham considered how very young he appeared. And now this wasn't a hotel reception but an officers' mess, and Wyndham was a senior addressing a junior.

'You must have been still in short trousers when Ludendorff packed it in,' he said.

'Not far off it,' the young man laughed. 'Didn't wait to finish school. The pater wangled me a commission to save me from missing out or – worse still – getting conscripted into any old mob. Reserve battalion. Never did see any action as it happened. All over before I'd learned the words of command, even.'

'You're not in the army now, though?'

'Hardly. Back in Ireland looking for a job, as it happens. Thin times for an ex-gentleman, don't you know.'

'You don't need to tell me. It's not like I own this hotel. Beats selling bootlaces in the street, but not by much. Whatever possessed you to come looking for a job in Ireland? It can't have been too prosperous when you were soldiering here – and you might have heard that times have been somewhat troubled since.'

'Oh that's why I'm here. They're hiring ex-officers. Just about the only qualification I can lay claim to.'

Wyndham's chatty tone died a sudden death.

'You're not talking about the police are you?'

'Actually I am. The Police Auxiliary Cadets to be precise. Training provided on the job and seven quid a week all told. They even have the same cap badge as the old Connaughts, so I took it as a sign.'

The Auxiliaries. The Auxies. Black and Tans with brains, or at least with officer-like initiative. A dangerous elite. They were the sort that the late Lieutenant-Colonel Gerald Smyth would have approved of. He pursed his lips and nodded while he looked at the boy, taking in the wisp of moustache, the coat's frayed edges and shiny patches, the clean collar imperfectly disguising a dingy shirt.

'Get out,' he said.

'What?'

'Go on. Clear off. The management reserves the right. Get out of here. Get yourself back to England.'

'I say!'

'Don't buy a paper from the man at the station. He'll pass on your description to the Shinners and you'll be dead before you make it to the boat.'

'What the devil are you talking about?'

'I don't want murders or murderers in this hotel. I don't want any more in this town.' He reached into his pocket and slammed some change onto the desk.

'Here. There's about five bob there. It's not seven pounds and it won't take you far, but it's all I've got and it's all you're getting out of Ireland. Take it. It's either that or a bullet in the back of the head.'

The young man stood there with his mouth open.

'Go!' barked Wyndham, and the young man picked up his valise and went. Wyndham didn't know if he left the country or just tried another hotel, but he was glad the young man had left the money on the counter. On putting it pack in his pocket Wyndham was dismayed to note that it was closer to three shillings than five.

'Did I hear someone, Mr. Wyndham?' It was Ballantyne, sticking his head out his door. 'Do we have a guest?'

'I'm afraid not, Mr. Ballantyne. Merely a low character. I turned him away.'

He remembered his first encounter with Moriarty long ago, and how the soldier had taken pains in explaining to the American visitor the nature of that peculiar beast, the Irish redcoat.

'*The Connaught Rangers – blackguards and hooligans the lot of them.*'

But not even Moriarty could have envisaged the depths to which some of them would sink.

54

It is not those who can inflict the most, but those who can suffer the most who will prevail.

—Terence MacSwiney

More and more, Wyndham was reminded of that old joke from the AEF. 'After England failed.' All he had to do was look around him to see what happened after England failed.

The IRA grew bolder and the police more hard-handed. Reprisal answered reprisal. Windows were boarded up against incendiary bombs. Raids and searches became a commonplace of daily life. Random and not-so random shots punctuated the city nights. In the mornings people swept up broken glass. At night they hoped that a pillow might serve as a sandbag to protect their sleeping children. Prisons filled. So did graves – some marked and some not. Agents of the Republic seldom slept two nights in the same bed. Police and military travelled in lorries that were encased in wire mesh.

'Look at that,' said Moriarty, as one of the lorries went by. 'The Boers put them in khaki, the Huns put them in tin hats, and we put them in cages.'

'We?' said Wyndham. '*Them?*' He often stopped by to talk to Moriarty these days. It wasn't as if he had many friends in Cork, and Moriarty often had news besides what was in the papers he was selling.

'Correct me if I'm wrong,' said Wyndham, 'but weren't you

wearing khaki and a tin hat yourself once upon a time? I'm sure I recall.'

'*Them*,' said Moriarty. 'I was never a peeler or a Tan. I was a Munster Fusilier, and I fought dacoits and Huns. If the Munsters had been policing our own country none of us would ever have joined. Those fuckers there are English. Fuck 'em. They've no business here at all.'

The veterans. They had saved the world, and remade the world, and Wyndham had stood with them, and here they were shooting at each other.

'Did you hear it when the bomb went off?' asked Wyndham, not caring to know how Moriarty defined his loyalties.

'Hear it? It put the heart across me. Half a mile off and it still made me duck. My nerves are no good for that class of thing anymore. That's what I keep on telling the bloody pension mob.'

'You mean you didn't have warning?'

'About the bomb in the Arcade? Who's going to warn me? Who do you think I am? Anyway, not that anyone tells me anything, but it was hardly our lads that laid that bomb.'

'It wasn't? Then who?'

'Jesus – maybe it was the lads who tried to burn down the City Hall a few weeks back. Did you think of that? The lads who are putting bullets through windows and setting fires here, there and everywhere.'

Wyndham gave this due consideration.

'How much worse can it get?' he wondered aloud.

'Worse,' said Moriarty. 'You just wait. You wait until MacSwiney dies.'

Alderman Terence MacSwiney, Lord Mayor of the city of Cork, died of starvation in a London prison at the end of October. It had taken him more than ten weeks to die, and that had been plenty of time for the world to take notice, and accuse.

His body was clothed in his Volunteer uniform even before it left England. He was brought back to Cork and given the funeral reserved for heroes and martyrs. There was little in the way of flummery or gilded ritual, but in its sincerity it was a funeral as would make kings envious. His young widow took her place in the growing ranks of the militant and bereaved.

Nora wanted to be there, walking in the cortège, in uniform for preference, but she was forbidden. She was proud in a way to be doing something for the Republic that necessitated her being hidden, but she resented it all the same.

'There'll be hundreds of people – thousands! Who'd notice me?' she said.

Wyndham wanted to tell her that anyone with eyes and a soul would notice her but kept his mouth shut out of respect for the solemnity of the occasion.

'It's probably for the best,' he said. 'Who knows what sort of trouble might break out?'

But there was no trouble. It was an angry and mournful city that sent their leader to his last rest, but the only shots fired that day were the salute over the grave. The salute was fired with revolvers, because they were more easily smuggled in than rifles.

The next day was All Saints' Day. Tributes for MacSwiney were still filling the papers. The government that had incarcerated him and let him die must have paid them little regard, because in Dublin that morning they hanged Kevin Barry, an eighteen-year-old medical student and IRA Volunteer.

The police tore down the black drapery and other symbols of mourning from the City Hall, but Cork remained quiet, as though observing a decent period of grief. In Kerry, however, it was different.

In north Kerry the local IRA had kidnapped two policemen. In response, the Black and Tans rampaged through Tralee for more than a week. They broke windows of those they suspected of being disloyal, and they were not limited in their suspicions. They set fire to businesses and homes. They beat men in the street and they fired indiscriminately as they sped about the town. Day after day the people of Tralee were kept indoors. In the poorer homes hunger added to their oppression. Even when they braved the streets, they found that the shops had been unable to take deliveries and the markets had not been held.

In these days of terror the army did nothing to lift the virtual state of siege. The army answered complaints and appeals by insisting that this was a police matter, and that unless martial law were declared, the army could not supersede the police.

For one retired army officer this wasn't good enough. He didn't live in the town, but one day he was seen in the Mall, making a stand for order and common decency. Rifles were aimed at him and the police lorries swerved dangerously close but he never flinched. He stood there like a bullfighter, defying the roaring beasts with his stick, his voice drowned by the engines. Even when one Tan fired at him in vicious amusement, the old soldier stood his ground and damned the man for all he was worth.

In the end they just arrested him, and carted him off to barracks, where the officer commanding the Munsters' depot quickly secured his release.

All this was recounted to Wyndham in a letter from Mrs. Fitzmullen-Brophy. He passed it on to Moriarty when next they met.

'Fair play to old FitzEm,' said Moriarty. 'The man might be a bit of an eejit but he was never any coward.'

Wyndham would have put it more elegantly, but it was a fair assessment. He had been relieved to hear that the colonel had come to no harm. He also hoped that his stand against the Black and Tans would find favour with nationalist neighbours who might otherwise have been meaning him ill. So far so good. The Fitzmullen-Brophy house had been subject to no threats. Then again, neither had Ogilvie. Probably, reflected Wyndham, the Republican movement had enough to be getting on with just now.

In West Cork, late in the month, the IRA mounted a most ambitious ambush and succeeded in wiping out a column of RIC Auxiliaries. There had been no more than eighteen Auxiliaries in the column and they had been outnumbered by around two to one, but it counted as a notable victory nonetheless. The Auxiliaries had, after all, been acquiring something of an aura of invincibility. The British press called the action a brutal massacre, and the official title of Police Auxiliary *Cadets* was emphasised, as if the dead men had been fresh-faced lads new to their duties.

'Good enough for them,' was Moriarty's verdict. 'Dirty murdering bastards. Young Barry showed them.'

'Barry?' said Wyndham.

'Tom Barry. He's the fella in charge out that way. Brigade Commandant or whatever he is. Mind you, what he calls a brigade isn't what you and me would call a brigade. I'd be surprised if he's got a hundred men to his name. Doesn't matter though, does it? He's the boy. You wouldn't think him much to look at, but he showed those fucking Auxies.'

'You know him?'

'I've met him. Federation of Discharged Soldiers, same as myself. We were trying to organise decent treatment over pensions and that.'

'He was a soldier?'

'A gunner. Think what the West Cork Brigade could do if he'd been a Munster! They'd take some bating then! It'd be more than eighteen Auxies dead in the road then! I bet the War Office is wishing they'd paid a decent pension to Tom Barry now!'

But as Wyndham – and many others – feared, the little victory on a lonely country road brought only trouble. The crown forces couldn't catch the wily volunteers. Their Crossley Tenders couldn't cross bogland. Their tanks were too ponderous to be deployed against guerrillas. Their numbers meant little when their enemy would not stand and fight. And so they took it out on whomever was at hand, on people who could not run away because they had homes and businesses to keep. The public hospitals learned to treat wartime wounds. The fire brigade was kept busy.

'Did you know,' said Moriarty, 'that there's a warehouse in the north of England that deals in second-hand furniture? The fella that owns it is making a right fortune. He's a Black and Tan. All the goods are the stuff that's confiscated and looted here.'

'Really?'

'Fact,' said Moriarty. 'It's not in the papers but everyone knows it.'

Stupidly, Moriarty's words were the first thing that sprang to mind when Wyndham came home that evening. He saw the police lorry outside the boarding house and expected for an instant to see a removal van parked behind. The place was in uproar. The front door was wide open. Various of his neighbours were being roughly lined up on the little patch of front lawn, their clothes disordered and their hands up. The sounds of breakage came from within. One of the Tans noticed Wyndham standing there.

'Oi, you! What do you want?' he demanded. His temper was none too good because he'd only narrowly missed being hit by a suitcase his mate had chucked out an upstairs window. He'd taken it out on one of the detainees, but the young man had been agile enough to dodge the rifle butt without dropping his hands.

Wyndham wondered if his own belongings would soon be on sale in England at bargain prices. He decided it wasn't worth his life or liberty in trying to save them. None of his neighbours were hailing him by name and as far as he knew the police weren't looking for him. He could just keep on walking.

'I asked you what you were looking at!' said the Tan.

The officer that Wyndham had once been assumed an affronted look.

'Are you talking to me, my good man?' he asked, in the plummiest English drawl he could produce. He recognised it as the voice Lieutenant the Honourable Miles Distemper, Coldstream Grenadier Yeomanry, who had been a character invented for a regimental concert party once upon a time. He was lacking the monocle, but it seemed to do the trick anyhow. The Tan scowled at him, unsure.

'Dashed disgrace!' said Wyndham, and flounced on his way without anyone trying to stop him. He returned when it was safe and he was glad to discover his possessions disarrayed but intact. There was something to be said after all for being stony broke. The house was marked though – known to the police. He wouldn't stay there now. Without waiting for his employer's by-your-leave, he moved his gear into one of the servants' rooms in the top floor of Ballantyne's hotel. It wasn't as if there were servants making use of it. It occurred to him a few days later that he probably could have taken one of the guest rooms. No one would have noticed that either.

55

There were spies everywhere and a very large percentage of the population was ready to act as extra eyes and ears for Sinn Féin and for the IRA even if they were not prepared to fight for them.

—Colonel Ormonde Winter, *Record of the Rebellion in Ireland and the Part Played by the Army in Dealing with It (Intelligence)*

He was in the little office, going over the books with no real energy, when he was startled to hear Nora outside. He went out to the reception desk and there she was, looking shifty, and there was Ballantyne, old-world gallantries falling from his lips and his eyes filled with sentimental lust. Wyndham made quick introductions, steered Nora into the office and politely shoved his employer from the scene.

'Charmed, Miss Maxfield!' said Ballantyne as Wyndham shut the door on him. 'Utterly charmed!'

'Nora, what is it?' He had hardly seen her of late. He noticed that she was clutching tightly to the handle of a bag – larger than a handbag but smaller than a suitcase. Was she running away with him at last?

'I want you to take this,' she said, brooking no refusal.

'What is it?'

'I'm not telling you. Just take it and keep it somewhere safe. You're not to open it, do you hear me?'

'What's going on, Nora?'

'I don't think I'm safe. I might be imagining things, but I don't want to take any chances either. Just take this and hold onto it for me.'

So he did.

'Now give me a kiss,' she said.

'Mr. Ballantyne is probably listening.'

'Give me a kiss anyway. Quick. I have to get back to work.'

Nora's bag filled Wyndham with unease. He obeyed her prohibition about opening it, but a visit from the police convinced him that he couldn't hang onto it either. The police check was routine but intimidating. They examined the register and checked all the rooms while Wyndham pretended to work. The bag was jammed in behind his desk and he imagined it glowing with guilty heat.

What? This, Constable? Oh, just some cypher books and transcripts of military telephone communications that my girl collects. An innocent hobby of hers.

The very next day he went to buy a newspaper.

'Tell me straight, Moriarty – do the police know about you?'

'Sure what's there to know? I'm no one. I just sell papers.'

'But you talk to people, you said. You drop the right word in the right ear.'

'I talk to all sorts. I'm not a member of anything.'

'And you said you mind things for people. Is that right? What sort of things?'

'Just things. Things you mightn't want to be found with.'

'Then mind this for me.'

'What's in it?'

'I don't know. It's Nora's. But I don't think you'd want to be found with it.'

Things in the city got worse. He worried about Nora. Yet another Sunday afternoon was cancelled and then, as unexpected as before, she was back at the hotel, distraught.

It was late on a Saturday and if he'd had anywhere else to go he'd have gone there. And suddenly there was Nora, flustered and in haste.

'They've arrested Julia! I just found out! I don't know anything!'

Whatever Mrs. Julia McInerney's political leanings, Wyndham had always found it impossible to think of her as an enemy of the state. Such people met in back rooms and laid plots involving dynamite. They didn't own neat draper's shops and have the maid serve little sugared cakes to afternoon visitors.

'What?'

She looked like she was going to slap him for being so slow.

'Julia's been arrested, Dan! One of the neighbours told me! I daren't go home!'

'We can find you somewhere to stay. You can stay here for the time being.'

'But what about Julia?'

'I—I don't think there's anything that can be done.'

'Yes there is! You can go and talk to someone!'

'Me?'

'They're hardly going to listen to me, and I wouldn't dare go near them anyway. You're an army officer. Go and talk to them. The barracks is only just up the hill. You've been up there before. You told me. You and Colonel Fitzmullen-Brophy.'

'But they're the army. This is police business. That's what they fobbed us off with before. The army can't tell the Tans what to do.'

'They can now! We've been under martial law since yesterday. Go on! Before curfew!'

For all the fright she was in, she was evidently thinking clearly. Her plan might have been hopeless, but it was at least straightforward. It was better anyway than the dithering objections which were all he was offering.

He remembered a principle of officer training concerning the importance of initiative:

A bad decision is better than no decision at all.

In the same moment there came back to him the first instinct of the trenches:

Take cover.

He took a key from a hook and put it in her hand.

'Upstairs, first on your right. Keep quiet and keep the door locked until I get back.'

'A lock isn't going to keep the Tans out.'

'I was thinking about Mr. Ballantyne.'

He was feeling manly as anything when he left the hotel. Nora had come to him for help. Nora was waiting for him, frightened and alone, in a bedroom. But the feeling didn't last. The army barracks might have been 'just up the hill', but it was no little hill. As he laboured past rank after ascending rank of suburban terraces his resolution began to falter. The exertion of his heart and lungs heightened his apprehension. It was absurdly late to be knocking on the army's door. The December night was already coming on and the whole world was shutting up for the weekend. Who was likely to do a favour for a one-time subaltern unwise enough to stick up for a suspected rebel?

He had surprisingly little trouble getting past the gate. He was well-spoken, properly-dressed and clearly unarmed. He made sure to present himself as an officer of the Munster Fusiliers. So far so good. Easy enough to get in. But what about getting back out? And – oh Lord! – what sort of civilians were allowed into barracks after hours? *Informers.* As soon as he stepped back out onto the street he'd be a marked man.

He tried to swallow his fears as he explained first to a sergeant and then to an officer that he really needed to speak to Colonel Wallace, and yes, it was probably an inconvenient time, but it really was rather urgent, thank you.

Wallace – the man with the paperclips. He hadn't been a bit of help when Fitzmullen-Brophy had made his appeal in the summer, but he was a known quantity, and he was army. Wyndham could pull on the Old Contemptible tie for all he was worth.

He was kept waiting, sharply conscious that in the outside world the business day was coming to an end, and remembering full well that the army liked to put up its shutters much earlier. Recalling the officers' mess in Tralee, even in wartime, he found it hard to imagine that here, even under martial law, the unfortunate few who'd be kept at their desks on a Saturday would be still working now. And would anyone be in the slightest way inclined to help? After two hours of waiting, it was seeming ever less likely that anyone would. After two and a half hours he decided it was now or never. A soldier passed him holding a sheet of paper. The man was only a corporal and it was only a single sheet, but it was the best lead that Wyndham was likely to get this evening. He stood up and followed the man.

The trail led down a succession of corridors to an office that was still lit up. Better yet, there were officers there who appeared to be busy. A clerk looked up at him.

'Sir?' he asked.

Wyndham knew these places. He had been used to these places. He remembered how officers in or out of uniform, with or without authorisation, would come and go.

'It's alright,' he said, in an anglicised accent. 'I'm just here to see—'

And ignoring the clerk, he scanned the room as if looking on the off-chance for a golfing chum. Astoundingly, his imposture was rewarded.

A captain burdened with sheaves of papers was ordering some clerks around. Wyndham stared a moment before things fell into place.

'Cardew?' he said.

The bureaucratic captain turned and stared back.

'I say – I know you, don't I?' he said.

'Étaples,' said Wyndham. 'Must be, oh, four years ago now. Right after the Somme. It's Wyn—'

'Don't tell me!' cried Cardew, the light dawning on him. 'Winfield! The Irishman!'

Wyndham was going to correct him but thought better of it.

'There was you and that other chap!' went on Cardew, constructing a memory as he went along. 'Jimmy something or other! A pair of card sharps! Get a chap squiffy and take him for every franc he has to his name! Ho-ho! Fancy bumping into you again! My word!'

'Still in the army, I see?'

'Yes, well. "Temporary commission", my foot. Waiting for bloody ever to be demobilised and then this Irish business started. They offered me a captaincy if I stayed on a while longer. I say to myself, why not? Not much doing at home, after all. You're not still in the army, are you? I see you're nice and comfy in civvies. What brings you here?'

Just as he'd decided not to let Cardew know his real name, something told Wyndham that it might be to his advantage if the strict truth were put aside for the time being.

'Colonel Fitzmullen-Brophy,' he said. 'I was here with him a few months back. We were talking to a Colonel Wallace. Hoping I might have another word.'

'Wallace? Not sure he's about. Something of a to-do going on. Shinners to be rounded up, you know. A spy ring to be shut down.'

Wyndham thought he did an admirable job in hiding the shiver that ran down his spine. He even put what he judged to be the exact level of idle curiosity into his voice when he asked his question.

'Spies, old man? Really?'

Cardew laughed a knowing laugh. 'Spies like you wouldn't

credit. Spies all over the bloody shop. Our intelligence chaps have been identifying any number of them and tonight they go in the bag.'

'Would these be your genuine cloak-and-dagger merchants?' asked Wyndham.

'Hardly,' said Cardew. 'Perfectly ordinary folk, most of them, doing perfectly ordinary jobs. But they're not as clever as they think. They always give themselves away.' He held up a slim file. 'Take this charmer for instance. Works in the telephone exchange. Eavesdrops just a little too much. Takes notes for no good reason. Thinks no one notices, which is a bit rich, seeing as Miss Mata Hari Murphy here is six feet tall and a screaming redhead.'

Wyndham nodded thoughtfully, wondering if he were about to be sick.

'Spies,' he said. 'Extraordinary. I'd never have thought.'

'Oh, you might think I'm just a humble paper-pusher, old boy, but I'm a chap in the know, you know.'

And Wyndham thought he smiled at Cardew, and thought he made some excuse or other, and then we was hurrying from the barracks into the winter night.

He heard the unmistakeable crack of an explosion from a street not too far off. A grenade, if he was any judge. It didn't seem the slightest bit important. A frivolous voice in his head said, *They're getting Saturday night off to a wild start.*

He hastened downhill towards the city, trying not to break into a run.

56

For for them indeed the night is the fittest tyme for spoyleing and robbinge, because the nightes are then, as ye said, longest and darkest.

—Edmund Spenser, *A View of the Present State of Ireland* (1596)

He kept from breaking into a run. Where a man could be arrested just for having his hands in his pockets, evasive behaviour would certainly earn him a bullet. But he hurried. Oh, but he hurried. In that, he wasn't too conspicuous. No one wanted to be out on the streets after dark.

It wasn't even eight o'clock before he was back at the hotel, sweating with apprehension, gulping with nerves. He went from the front steps to the first-floor landing without noticing how he got there. The door to Nora's room was ajar. No light was burning. Without daring to call her name he looked inside. Nothing. He raced back down the stairs. The lights were on in the parlour. And there she was. And there was Ballantyne, and they were in armchairs on either side of the fire, with glasses beside them.

Wyndham made some sort of gasping sound. Nora took it to be a request for an explanation.

'You were gone for hours,' she said. 'I was getting worried. Mr. Ballantyne was kind enough to offer me some brandy and keep me company.'

Ballantyne smiled, or possibly leered.

Wyndham did his best to impress on them the gravity of the moment.

'But—' he managed.

'And I needed cigarettes,' she said, holding up the one in her hand, justifying everything. 'What did you find out? Is there any word about Julia?'

'We have to go,' said Wyndham. He took her drink and finished it for her in a single gulp. She was convinced.

'Mr. Ballantyne,' she said. 'Thank you for such a pleasant evening, but I'm sure you'll excuse us now.'

'Of course, my dear Miss Maxfield. Charmed. Utterly charmed.'

They waited until he had done with his bowing and flourishing and then waited a few seconds longer until they heard a door closing farther down the hall.

'We have to go, Nora. They know about you.'

He had the tiny satisfaction of watching her eyes bulge.

And if they know about you they might well know about the American gentleman with whom you've been keeping company.

'We can't stay here,' he said. He took the cigarette out of her nerveless fingers before she burned herself or set fire to the furniture. She blinked and swallowed and blinked again.

'I'll need my bag,' she said.

'I don't think we can go anywhere by train. They always have men at the station. But we can't stay here. They search the hotels. Is there somewhere—?'

'I'll need my bag,' she said again.

'Alright,' he said. 'Let's go get it. I'm not leaving you here.'

'Why? What? Where did you put it?'

'I left it with Moriarty for safekeeping. He's not far.'

She took the news levelly enough, much to his relief. 'I need that bag,' she repeated, pulling on her coat and getting stuck in one of the sleeves. He helped her with more haste than gallantry, and straightened her hat for her, and risked squeezing her close for reassurance. She didn't object but didn't respond either.

'How far is it?' she said.

'Not far at all. Off George's Street or thereabouts. I thought it safer there than in a hotel with people coming and going.'

She had a moment of unsteadiness as they stepped out into the cold air.

'Nora?'

'I'm alright. I just forgot about the steps.'

'Nora, how much brandy did you have?'

'Hardly any!'

'Nora?'

'Only one or two. I forget. He seems a sweet old soul. I don't know what you have against him. Anyway – come on. We can't be dawdling here. The curfew is at ten. What time is it now?'

There was a smattering of shots off in the distance. That was nothing new. There was a suggestion of an orange flicker against the skyline. That wasn't anything new either. And of course there were Tans.

'There seem to be more of them out than usual,' said Nora, pulling her coat close at the throat, as if that might ward them off. Equally uselessly, Wyndham pulled his hat down over his eyes.

'We should keep to the side streets,' he said. 'We should hurry.'

What had the world come to, he asked himself, when decent citizens were obliged to scuttle down alleyways out of fear of the police? But of course Nora was not a decent citizen. She was an enemy of the state, no matter how you cut it, while he, in aiding her, was hardly a law-abiding character either. When you got right down to it, it was the police's job to apprehend malefactors just like them.

But did they have to set fire to whole neighbourhoods in the pursuit of their duties?

Moriarty had changed address more than once since he'd left the family home, and it was only by chance that Wyndham knew his present whereabouts. In the army Moriarty had had the exasperating habit of being hard to find anytime there was work to be done, but Wyndham now appreciated the man's elusiveness. Moriarty had avoided the Battle of the Somme, side-stepped the Battle of Messines and very nearly slid out of the way of the Ludendorff Offensive. If anyone could stay one step ahead of the Black and Tans, it was Moriarty.

'That's why I gave him your bag. He's an out-of-the-way sort of fellow.' Wyndham was chattering in his nervousness. He was holding Nora's arm in the hope that he'd just look like a fellow out for a walk with his girl, and because maybe she was a little drunk. She didn't seem drunk, but he had no way of knowing: no grounds for comparison. Her natural tendency was to be wayward and forceful. She did stumble a little now and then, but that was because she had Wyndham latched onto one side of her.

They were down on the quays now, taking a circuitous route around the centre of the city, and to the north they could see flames clearly.

'St. Luke's?' said Wyndham.

'Farther uphill?' said Nora. 'They'd hardly burn houses in St. Luke's. There are too many army officers living there.'

But Wyndham wouldn't have put anything past the Black and Tans, and he remembered soldiers who, even in more lawful times, would cheerfully have destroyed the property of any officer if they thought they could get away with it.

'Wherever it is,' he said. 'It's not in our way and it's keeping them busy. Come on.'

But Nora didn't move.

'I think maybe you're being a little optimistic,' she said. 'Look.'

Ahead of them they could see a lorry crossing the bridge, followed by another, and another. It was St. Patrick's Bridge, leading to St. Patrick's Street, the broad central artery of the city's commerce.

'I don't think your friend lives far enough out of the way,' she said in a small voice.

'Can you perhaps do without your bag?' Wyndham asked.

'No!' she said, and it was if she'd woken up. 'We can go this way.' And now it was she who was pulling at him.

They found the side street where Moriarty lived, only for Wyndham to admit that he'd never actually been there before.

'I'm sure it's up here on the left. It *is* up here. No, wait – the next one. Can you read that sign?'

Shouting could be heard none too far distant – motor engines and shouting.

'Dan, we can't be standing out the street!'

And then came the crash of breaking glass – not any little panes but the weighty sheets of glass as might cover a department store window.

There wasn't enough light for him to see his watch. He guessed there was an hour at least before curfew, but he didn't think that strict observance of the curfew would save anyone from the authorities tonight.

There was a small shop, and the narrowest of lanes at one side. There was a door, and for want of other options, Wyndham knocked. Any other time and he'd have given up and resolved to come back in the morning. He knocked again, and was about to knock a third time when he was answered. There was the dim suggestion of an apprehensive face in the feeble light of a gas jet within.

Wyndham smiled as if he were bringing a Christmas goose to the house.

'Good evening! We're friends of Mr. Moriarty. Do we have the right address?'

The man at the door – and Wyndham still couldn't tell for certain if it was a man who'd answered the door – made no reply, seemingly dumbfounded by a social call of all things at this place, at this hour.

'Mr. Moriarty?' said Wyndham, his cheery mask about to crack under the weight of desperation. 'He does live here?'

'Who's that?' It wasn't the face at the door but a voice from somewhere inside.

'Moriarty?' said Wyndham, shivering with relief. He bustled himself and Nora through the door without waiting for formal invitation. 'It's me. And Nora – Miss Maxfield. He gave a little bow to the man who'd opened the door. 'Miss Maxfield,' he repeated for his benefit. 'Mr. Wyndham,' he added, touching his hat. Even with the gas lit it was too dark to make much out, but there was a man at the top of a flight of stairs who could only have been Moriarty.

'You'd better come on up,' said Moriarty.

The upstairs room was dingy and smelt of bachelorhood. It was tidy only insofar as there were too few possessions to make a clutter. Of soldierly neatness there was little enough. If this was a soldier's dwelling then it was a soldier who knows that there will be no inspection any time soon. Wyndham had lived in close quarters with Moriarty in bygone years and wasn't the least surprised. He had, however, been imagining more in the region of contraband. There were no illicit weapons – no evidence that Moriarty had a habit of 'minding things' for certain dangerous associates. The only papers to be seen were newspapers, bales of *Cork Examiner*s, amounting to an archive, were piled in one corner. Another paper – Moriarty's evening reading – was open on the bed.

Moriarty shuffled because his boots were unlaced. He'd shoved his feet into them when he'd heard the door. He was nonplussed and on his guard. When Wyndham introduced Nora all over again he just nodded, waiting for whatever was coming next. He didn't offer his hand, but he did take the cigarette out of his mouth.

'We've met before,' he said, by way of a cautious opening move.

And now it was Nora who was on her guard.

'Basingstoke,' Moriarty clarified. 'Years ago. You stuck a big huge needle into me. Typhus inoculation. Some sort of inoculation anyhow. Could barely lift my arm the next day.'

'Well then!' said Wyndham brightly. 'No need for further introductions!'

'Did you catch typhus at all?' asked Nora, ignoring Wyndham. 'Then there's hardly cause for complaint, is there? May I sit down?'

The one chair was cleared of its detritus and proffered to her. She sat down and lit up. And then she hiccuped.

Wyndham spoke quickly to cover for her.

'A bag I left with you a while back – we rather need it.'

Moriarty took his time before he answered. He was listening to the noises from a few streets away.

'Not a bother,' he said.

'That's a favour I owe you, Moriarty,' said Wyndham. 'Heaven knows when I can repay it. I won't be around for I don't know how long. I think there might be some trouble,' And just then they heard rifle shots, no more than a couple of hundred yards off.

'You think there *might* be trouble?' said Moriarty. 'You'd better stay here a while. You can't be going outside in that.'

'You're right. It'll likely settle down after curfew. I am sorry to burden you.'

'Not a bother,' said Moriarty, and it mightn't have been a bother or it might. 'Make yourselves at home. I'd make you some tea only I don't have any. I don't have anything else either for that matter.'

And so they sat. Moriarty produced Nora's bag for her and she peeked inside to see if anything had been disturbed before politely thanking him. After that no one had much of anything to say. They waited.

Wyndham joined Moriarty on the bed. There was nowhere

else to sit. Time passed. The hour of curfew came and went. It was no one's idea of a convivial Saturday night. They looked at the newspapers of recent days and made no more than the odd observation. They smoked, and tried not to make the disturbances outside to be anything worthy of special alarm.

And then both Wyndham and Moriarty flinched at a loud bang.

'What was that?' said Nora. The noise had startled her but, unlike the two men, she hadn't been conditioned to cringe at the sound of a grenade going off.

'Mills bomb,' said Moriarty. 'Jesus. That's a bit much. They'll be bringing in the tanks in a minute if that's the way they're going.'

Because he was Nora's man and Moriarty's one-time officer, Wyndham decided it was time to show some resolve and go outside to see what was going on.

'Don't get lost,' said Nora.

'How on earth could I get lost?'

'*I* don't know – but you had trouble enough finding the place in the first place.'

'If the Tans catch you, you were never here and you don't know me,' said Moriarty.

With this lack of encouragement behind him, Wyndham made his reconnaissance. The tumult in the city was obvious the moment he stuck his nose out the door. The air was sharp with smoke. He ventured out. There were people standing at half-open doors and looking from upstairs windows, but the street itself was deserted. He went as far as a corner where he could get a straight view toward the centre of the city. It was burning. Silhouetted against the glow he saw armed men. He hurried back.

'There's a big fire on Patrick's Street,' he told them.

'What about the Tans?' said Moriarty.

'They're there. They're probably everywhere.'

'Ah bollocks,' said Moriarty. 'I beg your pardon, Miss.'

'*I* know!' said Nora. 'If we wait for the fire brigade to arrive we can slip away. There'll be gawpers and firemen and people leaving their homes. No one will notice us.'

Wyndham, who'd been expecting more of her headstrong irrationalities, was profoundly impressed at how sensible Nora's plan was.

'Alright then,' he said.

And so they waited, until they heard the frantic clanging of a brass bell racing towards the centre of town. They gathered themselves and went downstairs, opening the front door but not yet daring to step outside.

Waiting for the barrage to lift, thought Wyndham. *Waiting for Zero Hour*.

'I'll go with you a bit of the way,' said Moriarty. 'I want to see what I'm in the middle of.'

They heard another fire engine coming to the scene and steeled themselves to step out into the open.

'Wait here,' said Wyndham, once more the platoon commander. 'I'll see if the coast is clear.'

But no one paid any attention.

Nora was keeping close in behind him, her hand on his shoulder. Was she seeking his protection or just using him for cover? Moriarty was off to one side, keeping a distance. The front-line infantryman still, staying well clear of the officer who'd catch the first bullet.

They edged into the street, looked left and right, and dodged across to a deep-shadowed alcove on the other side. They heard a challenge and a rifle shot.

'They'll have a clear line of fire down George's Street,' said Moriarty. 'We can't chance it.'

The fire was a roar and heading toward it was suddenly the stupidest plan Wyndham could think of, but they stuck with it because it was the plan they had. A direct approach was impossible.

A journey that should have taken mere minutes instead had them darting down alleys, lurking in little courts and taking the sort of short cuts that in happier times would have had them arrested for burglary. Then came the now-or-never and they stepped forth onto Saint Patrick's Street, where a fire engine beckoned to them like sanctuary.

'Wait!' said Moriarty, and immediately dodged back from the kerb. There were Black and Tans among the firemen. The three fugitives sought refuge beneath an awning and watched as across the road the police and fire brigade were involved in a sort of game. The firemen had a hose connected up to a hydrant at which the Tans were gathered. As soon as the men on the hose were ready to tackle the fire the Tans turned the water off. They were clearly enjoying themselves, and every repetition provoked greater hilarity, but the firemen were not enjoying the joke. An officer in a brass helmet was remonstrating with the Tans with no soft words. He was a brave man, going so far as to push one of the Tans away from the hydrant. Their fun spoiled, another of the Tans cut the game short by taking a bayonet to the fire hose. It could have been worse. He could have stuck it in the fireman.

Besides the fire engines and the police lorries, more motor vehicles were arriving. Wyndham had a moment of hope when he recognised them as army transport, with Tommies in steel helmets piling out the back and lining up, waiting for the order that would send them to knock some sense into this chaos. He saw the officer in charge take the measure of the situation: the fine premises all along one side of the street burning out of control; police with whiskey bottles and petrol cans doing nothing except bullying the citizenry. The officer stood with his hands on hips, head shaking in disbelief and disgust. He shouted something at the Tans that was probably a curse, and ordered his men back aboard their lorries. The soldiers departed, leaving Cork to burn.

Water pooled in the street, reflecting the terrible flames. Wyndham stood paralysed.

During the war, one thing that used to sustain him was the knowledge that behind him lay safety, and if his luck held a while longer he would be allowed to escape. The war was these trenches, this wire. It was rooted in place. He could leave it there when the time came. And times would come when he would work his way back down the line for a period of rest, and he could be among fields and trees again, and walk without wariness, even though all the while he knew the war was waiting for him still, just back there, huge and growling.

And in that terrible last spring the war had roared so loud at him that he'd turned and run, but this time the war followed him. It tore itself loose from the wiring stakes and came after him, trampling the fields and splintering the trees and spreading its ruin far beyond the lines that had bound it for so long. Wyndham had run before it, feeling its hot breath on his neck, hearing his comrades devoured behind him. He didn't stop. He ran until 16th Division was no more. He ran until they physically laid hands on him. Even when they sent him back to England to train Americans he was afraid to look back over his shoulder.

And now the front was two years and five hundred miles away, and screams and shots and smoke filled the lurid air, and he knew that he could never run far or fast enough, because the war went on forever.

'Mr. Wyndham! Mr. Wyndham, you fucking eejit! Would you ever get a grip on yourself?'

Mr. Wyndham – as though they were still in the army. Moriarty hadn't run far enough either.

Wyndham tried to get a grip on himself. As so often before, he tried to picture what Fitzmullen-Brophy would do in such a situation, but of course that was useless. A courageous man with his eye firmly fixed on what was right would only earn himself a beating on a night like tonight, and maybe even a bullet too.

Nora's idea wouldn't work. There was no crowd of onlookers to get lost in. People evacuating upstairs rooms, nightclothes visible beneath coats, were being mercilessly driven with kicks and rifle butts. By rights, thought Wyndham, they should have pitchforks instead of rifles and little horns coming out from those caps.

Stand up, Dirty Shirts. Get a fucking grip, Mr. Wyndham.

'I think you'll be putting us up for a while longer, Moriarty,' he managed to say.

They ran back in the direction they'd come. Behind them, on a flagpole above Roches Stores, the Union Jack briefly ignited and then was gone in smoke and ash.

Where the fire had not actually taken hold, people were staying indoors. Until the flames came for them, it was safer than outside where the Tans prowled. But they ran into one man, distraught, coming up the street, no hat on his head, his dirty grey hair awry. Moriarty stepped forward and stopped him, and Wyndham recognised the man who'd opened the door to them earlier – the shopkeeper who Moriarty lived above.

'Oh Lord save us!' the man cried. 'There's a fire, Mr. Moriarty! There's Tans!'

Moriarty took him by the front of his coat. 'Are there Tans at the shop?' he demanded.

'There might be! There's Tans all over! There's a fire!' The man spoke in a tremulous lament. 'We'll all be destroyed! One end of Maylor Street is on fire!'

Moriarty let him go.

'Well your place is out then,' said Wyndham. 'We'll just have to keep going and hope for the best.'

Moriarty said nothing for a long moment. Then he bullied them a short distance until they came to an alleyway. 'Wait here for me,' he said. 'I won't be long.'

'What? Where are you going?'

'I won't be long.'

The alleyway was well chosen. It led nowhere important and no street lamp cast its light there.

'Where's he going?' asked Nora.

'To fetch some belongings? I don't know.' But what could Moriarty own that was worth risking life and liberty for? A spare shirt? A bale of newspapers? Wyndham hadn't seen much else in that upstairs room.

'He won't be long,' he said.

But of course it seemed long. More than once, Wyndham peered around the corner, willing Moriarty to reappear. Before such a thing happened, a squad of Black and Tans came by. Wyndham and Nora drew deeper into the shadows and flattened themselves against the wall. Wyndham could practically hear his heart racing. He could practically hear Nora's. But the Tans weren't coming their way. Wyndham risked a quick look. The Tans were going the way Moriarty had gone.

At the Fitzmullen-Brophy fireside in the first winter after the war, when they'd been sorting through the faded old scraps of regimental history, there had been one story that had affected Wyndham sorely.

In 1857, in the Great Mutiny, three sepoys were firing from a small turret. Private John McGovern, an otherwise ill-regarded soldier, too careless of authority and too fond of drink, volunteered to dislodge the troublesome mutineers. As he ascended the stairs alone he heard an officer ask why no more men had been detailed to follow him. He heard a sergeant reply, 'Never mind, sir; he'll be no loss.' McGovern came back down from the turret shortly after, with blood on his bayonet and three dead sepoys left behind him.

In Tralee, disregarding the cold rain, Wyndham had excused himself and gone outside. Of course he hadn't been thinking about Private John McGovern and the Victoria Cross he'd won in India long ago. Of course not. It had been Corporal Francis Moriarty in the St. Quentin sector. It had been the horrible moment when the fleeing Lieutenant Wyndham had realised that Moriarty wasn't right behind him – that Moriarty was somewhere back there, facing the Germans from whom Wyndham had run.

Never mind. He'll be no loss.

And in Tralee Molly had found him and persuaded him to come in out of the rain, to come back from that lonely trench, and he had, but he'd never shaken free of the panic and the shame.

'Dan! Dan, what are you doing?' said Nora, doing her best to shriek as quietly as possible.

'I won't be long.'

'Dan!'

But he was already gone, and she didn't dare raise her voice any more.

He'll be no loss.

Wyndham loved Nora and wasn't sure that he even liked Moriarty. Nobody would ever have pinned the VC on Moriarty. He'd never have become a reformed character like McGovern.

Wyndham hurried as silently as he could. There were three Tans, and they'd just turned into Moriarty's street. The smoke was thicker and ash and embers floated in the air. The sound of the fire drowned out his footsteps. He slipped around a corner and caught sight of the Tans again. They had stopped at the narrow laneway that contained Moriarty's door and nothing else. Wyndham heard a voice bark and saw a rifle levelled.

Never mind, sir; he'll be no loss.

Wyndham ran – forward this time.

Moriarty was on his way back out and was wondering why he was even bothering to shut the door behind him when the three Black and Tans were upon him. Three of them, with rifles and pistols. Drink on them too, devil a doubt. He was boxed in and unarmed.

'Constables,' he said, like the sort of well-dressed rate-payer who expects the police to guard his property and salute him in the street.

'Who are you? What are you doing here?' said one of the Tans.

Moriarty knew these weren't real questions. They were just the police setting up an excuse for themselves. They were just the preliminaries to a beating.

'What's your name? Answer!'

Moriarty checked that he'd locked the front door. He looked to the sky, wondering if the flying sparks might ease off or if he'd need an umbrella.

One of the Tans didn't have his rifle pointed. He had a grenade in his fist instead. Typical. The old army knew how to shoot. It was the Johnnie-come-latelies who always reached for a grenade when a rifle was called for. This one was certainly drunk. What did he think he was doing with a grenade, and all of them bunched into this little lane?

'I asked you your fucking *name*, Paddy.'

Moriarty counted the odds. Three against one, and the three all armed. He lowered his chin and bunched his shoulders.

'Prionsias Ó Muircheartaigh,' he said, and saw a figure loom out of the smoke and darkness.

Wyndham slapped the Tan hard on the side of his head. It was meant to be punch, but Wyndham was bent on getting hold of the grenade. The slap, landing square on the man's earhole, did the job just fine. The stricken man staggered into his mate, and in the instant it took the Tans to react to this disturbance, there was

Wyndham with the Mills bomb in his hand.

He pulled the pin. He made sure they could see him do it. If they dropped him now, he'd drop the grenade. The arming lever would spring free from his dead hand. Would they have time to stumble over his body in this narrow space and get clear of the blast?

'Come on, you sons of bitches,' said Wyndham. 'Do you want to live forever?'

The Tans froze.

'Excuse me there, lads,' said Moriarty, pushing past them.

Wyndham stood there a few moments longer, his teeth bared, his hand sweating, and then he was gone after Moriarty, into the smoke.

They pounded down the street.

'Throw the fucking bomb!'

'What?'

'Throw the fucking bomb at them! Throw it anywhere! Just get rid of the fucking thing!'

And seeing as he'd thrown the pin away, there wasn't much else Wyndham could do. What he didn't want to do was detonate explosives in the middle of a street, where steel fragments could kill at thirty yards and a family or two was living on every floor above the shops. And he didn't really want to kill Black and Tans either. Not even them.

'Take cover!' he shouted, giving fair warning to friend and enemy alike, and judging that this particular corner didn't appear residential, he lobbed the grenade into the dark and sprinted for the shelter of a doorway.

He couldn't tell from the ringing in his ears if anyone was coming after him, but he didn't think so. He couldn't see where Moriarty had got to. It didn't matter anymore. He ran back towards Nora. And then he heard shots: pistol shots, not far ahead of him.

Nora was where he'd left her, with a smoking pistol in her hand and a dead policeman at her feet.

'He was—' she explained. 'I—I—' she clarified.

Wyndham looked at the Tan on the ground. An army tunic with two dark wet holes in the front of it.

'He was—' Nora tried again. 'I didn't know what he was going to do. He was after my bag.'

An army tunic. Wyndham was on his knees, wrenching the buttons apart.

'I showed him,' said Nora.

Any man who'd been in the trenches kept a field dressing sown into his tunic. Just a bandage and a wad of gauze, but perhaps enough for two small-calibre bullet wounds until help arrived.

'He's dead,' said Nora, who in her hospital work had probably seen as many deaths as Wyndham had in the trenches.

Instead of a dressing Wyndham's hands found something else: a bundle of bracelets, necklaces, watches. It had been a grand night for looting. The jewellery was already clotted with blood. He had to shake it off his fingers.

'He's dead, Dan.' She sounded small and distant.

A single diamond ring, glistening with blood, was stuck to his hand.

Miss Maxfield, you would make me the happiest man alive if you would do me the honour—

'He's dead.'

It was Moriarty who dragged them both out of it. He hauled Wyndham upright by the collar of his coat. He pushed Nora, and pushed her again and again until she built up some momentum of her own. He made them put distance between themselves and the body in the street.

'And put that bloody gun away, woman!' he told her.

'Honest to God,' he observed to the world at large, 'but does no one know how to handle weapons anymore?'

Neither of them had much idea what he meant.

The great fire was spreading, and it was obvious that it was more than one fire now. What had started out as a large-scale reprisal was now no less than an orgy of undirected destruction. The police had no interest in imposing order. They beat anyone within reach and fired on anyone they couldn't lay hold of.

Unable to hide, reluctant to move, Nora, Wyndham, and Moriarty stumbled from one street to another until they emerged onto the broad expanse that was the Grand Parade. There was no more cover. They huddled at a corner, fearing to brave the open. Wyndham had crossed many a wider street in his day, only not one under fire by armed police the worse for drink. Up at the top end they could see commotion around a respected wine merchant's. Firelight danced on shattered glass.

'*No Catholics need apply*,' grunted Moriarty. 'Bloody fat lot of good that's done them.'

Nearer was a noted jeweller's, the windows in glittering splinters on the pavement and a Crossley Tender parked across the kerb.

'Christmas has come a couple of weeks early for those gurriers,' said Moriarty.

Wyndham had a bright idea.

'McInerney's! The draper's you worked in, Nora! It's just down that way! We can hide out there. If they've already arrested Mrs. McInerney they'll hardly search there.'

'That's not bad,' said Moriarty. 'And they're not likely to be looting a draper's shop.'

'And the fire will hardly reach that far,' said Wyndham, appreciating more fully the beauty of his plan.

'I don't have a key to get in,' said Nora, and it was the first thing she'd said so far.

'We'll cross that bridge when we come to it,' said Wyndham. 'Come on.'

They hadn't made it far at all when a rifle shot cracked over their heads.

'Was that meant for us?' said Nora – the only one who'd never been shot at before.

'If it was,' said Moriarty, 'then they're rotten shots altogether.' But that was hardly a reassurance.

It was impossible for three people to take shelter behind one post box. 'We have to keep going,' said Wyndham, but there was another shot, and no one was inclined to move.

'They're just shooting,' said Moriarty. 'It's just blackguardism. They're all plastered.'

But whether the Tans outside the wine merchant's were using a particular piece of municipal or private property for target practice, they had the street enfiladed.

Taking their lives in their hands, the trio made it to the cover of the lorry outside the plundered jewellers. Even then it took scrutiny and argument before they'd determined that there was no one waiting for them in the cab. They were marginally closer to their goal, but closer to the Tans also.

'Well we either stay here forever or we make a run for it,' said Moriarty, crouched by the front mudguard. 'Come on, for Christ's sake. It's only the width of the street.'

There was no arguing with that, but that didn't make a decision any easier. If they all ran together they'd surely be seen, so that meant one at a time. The first one across would prove either that it was safe or it wasn't. The third across would be asking for trouble.

'You go first,' said Wyndham, trying to be in charge. 'Nora goes second. Nora—?'

He whipped his head around. He couldn't see her. 'Nora!'

'Shush,' she said. 'Up here.'

She was in the cab of the lorry. It took a moment for the penny to drop.

'We can't steal a Black and Tan lorry!'
'Of course we can. Start her up.'
'A woman can't drive!' said Moriarty.
'You be quiet and help Dan.'

Neither of the men was versed in the ways of motor vehicles, but there was only one of two ways the starter handle could turn so they got it right eventually. They were barely on board before Nora released the brake and stamped on the accelerator. She was still accelerating when they rounded the corner. They were out of sight of the Tans now, racing down the South Mall, in the opposite direction to their planned hideout.

The fire had leapt the river or, more likely, other fires had been started. City Hall, a target of the Tans' anger all these months, was burning again, only this time the fire had taken a good hold. Wyndham saw Nora in the glow, her jaw set, her eyes unblinking, her hands gripping the wheel as though it might try to throw her loose. She wrenched it into another sharp turn, heading towards the burning city hall and the police lorries and ineffectual fire engines grouped around. It was either that or drive back into the city or into the river. They sped on through, and if anyone tried to halt them they never found out.

And then the fires were behind them, and the hellish glare was replaced by suburban street lights. Beyond that there was the countryside, and darkness.

'Where are going?' asked Wyndham.
'This way,' said Nora.

VII

DIARMUID AND GRANIA

If you were the only girl in the world,
And I were the only boy...

—Nat. D. Ayer & Clifford Grey

57

And they went on wandering after that, all through Ireland... sleeping under the cromlechs, or with no shelter at all, and there was no place they would dare to stop long in.

—Lady Gregory, *Gods and Fighting Men*

'So if I may ask?' said Wyndham

He and Moriarty stood side by side, relieving themselves into a hedge.

'Go on,' said Moriarty, without enthusiasm.

'Why did you go back? What was so important in your digs?'

Moriarty took his time buttoning himself up. 'Doesn't matter,' he said.

'Well there, I'm afraid, I just can't believe you.'

Moriarty rolled his stiff neck and stared up at the night sky.

'My medals,' he admitted. 'I went back for my medals.'

Rather than wait for expressions of outrage and disbelief, he unburdened himself.

'Eleven years in the army. Eleven bloody years and nothing to show for it except them medals. And it's not like they're any different to the ones you got.'

Wyndham detected an accusation in those last words.

'Do you know,' Moriarty went on, 'that I don't even have my red tunic anymore? Back I came to Tralee to be demobilised and all my good gear was gone. The walking-out uniform, the busby, the lot. The amount of bloody work I put into that kit! I polished those fucking buttons until they were worn smooth practically!

You couldn't have told whether 'twas a tiger or a billy-goat on them! And not a bloody one of them am I allowed to keep! So yes—'

He turned and looked Wyndham square in the eye.

'I'm keeping my medals, thank you very much!'

Wyndham nodded. 'Let's see if Nora is ready,' he said.

They'd been driving all night. Nora had been driving all night.

At the start, the distant fires had been their beacon as they'd skirted the city from the south, unsure of where they were, but moving clockwise by narrow roads and moving fast.

'North,' Wyndham had said. He'd studied enough maps of this county as an officer in training. He instinctively felt that there was not sufficient breadth of country southward here between the city and the sea.

They had no more fear of the Tans. The countryside belonged to the IRA: the countryside and the night. It was desperately cold. The Crossley Tender had no windscreen and was hardly the sort of conveyance to be furnished with travelling rugs. Beyond periodic demands that Wyndham light a cigarette for her, and the odd, peremptory, 'Which way?' Nora hadn't spoken until here, somewhere in the north of the county, where she had declared that she couldn't feel her feet anymore and they were stopping.

Wyndham found her now, pacing quickly up and down the road, hugging herself against the cold, and yet another cigarette on the go.

'Nora? Are you alright?'

She looked at him as if somehow it were all his fault.

'I'm fine,' she said. 'Where are we going?'

'It's near Fermoy. I'm not exactly sure. But I'm sure I'll recognise it when we get near.'

'We're nearly out of petrol.'

The lorry had contained nothing beyond enough fuel to get

them this far and a fifty-round bandolier of rifle ammunition.

'But no rifle?'

'Do you want me to look under the seats again?' said Moriarty.

'No. And there's not another petrol can either. They must have used it all to burn down Patrick's Street.'

It was perhaps six o'clock in the morning and still very dark when the lorry gave out on them. The two men got out and pushed while Nora steered it off the road and into a ditch.

'What now?' said Moriarty.

'It doesn't matter,' said Wyndham. 'We're here. I think.'

The last time Wyndham had been this way had been five years ago. It had been summer and everything had looked different. The last time he'd come most of the way by train rather than by road and had been guided the last half mile or so. The last time he'd been told to forget where he'd been and how he'd got there.

'Do you remember Knocknahanna and the time the armoury burned down? Do you remember Lieutenant Curran? He had been in the Volunteers – still had dealings with them. I went with him to a meeting in an abandoned house near here.'

'And you think it might still be safe?' said Moriarty. 'You know – even with army officers coming and going back in 1915?'

'I don't see why not. It was very much out of the way.'

'And you can still find it? You know – with it being very much out of the way and all?'

'Curran and I had no end of trouble finding our way back. Out of curiosity I traced our route on a map afterwards. It's this way. As soon as it's light I'll know for sure.'

'Well, if you know for sure.'

Nora was saying nothing, and Wyndham had to imagine hard that her silence betokened a quiet faith in his navigating ability.

He had taken his bearings from a railway line and the few stars visible, and with more assurance than he could justify he led them across fields and down lanes. No hint of impatience or mistrust would he allow. When the pale morning found them in the yard of a lonely and dilapidated house it all felt as providential as having led the Children of Israel out of the wilderness.

'Mother of God,' said Moriarty, 'but I've heard it said often enough that there's nothing in this world more dangerous than a second-lieutenant with a map and a compass.'

Wyndham took that as a compliment.

'I hope you can get a fire lit,' said Nora. 'My shoes are soaking.'

And that was progress of a sort too.

58

'I leave this advice with you,' he said, 'not to go into a tree with one trunk, and you flying before Finn, and not to be going into a cave of the earth that has but one door, and not to be going to an island of the sea that has but one harbour. And in whatever place you cook your share of food,' he said, 'do not eat it there; and in whatever place you eat it, do not lie down there; and in whatever place you lie down, do not rise up there on the morrow.'

—Lady Gregory, *Gods and Fighting Men*

If anyone had used the house in the last five years they hadn't left any evidence of good housekeeping. There were mouse droppings all over – bird droppings too. There were still the chairs and the kitchen table that were all Wyndham remembered, but the choice was now to use them as furniture or as firewood.

'We can't light a fire,' said Wyndham. 'Not until dark anyway. The smoke will give us away.'

The looks the other two gave him were a reminder of why he'd never managed to be both a good officer and a popular one at the same time.

'No one's going to see us,' said Moriarty, picking at the kitchen range in the hope that it would give up its secrets. 'We're bloody miles from anywhere. Did we pass a single house on our way?'

'If anyone sees smoke they'll know that there's at least one house here. We can't risk it.'

Nora said nothing, but her chattering teeth were reproach enough for Wyndham. He compromised by allowing a small fire. It smoked like anything.

At least they found the remnants of a stack of turf outside. It was damp, like everything else, and was barely enough for a day or so, but it saved them for the moment from burning the fabric of the house. There was nothing else of use, and nothing to eat.

'Surely be to God there must be something!' said Moriarty. 'This is the country, isn't it? This is where food comes from, isn't it? Or have the farmers been having us on all this time?'

An expedition to find a shop was mooted, but it seemed too much of a chance to take.

'It's Sunday,' was Nora's sole and decisive contribution.

'I don't care,' said Moriarty, somewhere around midday. 'I'll go off my rocker if I have to stay here without so much as a cup of tea. I'll go and take a shufti – see what I can find us. Give us your pistol there.'

It took a second for Nora to realise he was talking to her.

'I'll do no such thing,' she said.

Wyndham intervened. 'Come on now, Moriarty: you hardly need a pistol. It's Cork, not the Northwest Frontier.'

'It's not Cork. Cork's the place that the Tans set fire to last night.'

'It's *County* Cork, and you know it full well, and you've been here before. It's a civilised country.'

'Says you. In civilisation a man can buy himself a cup of tea and a paper. Everywhere else is wogs and Huns.'

'I'm not giving you my pistol,' said Nora.

Wyndham moved to her side and treated Moriarty to what he hoped was a conciliatory smile.

'And you're not going committing armed robbery,' he said. 'And if the Tans catch you with a pistol, what could you do?'

Moriarty had no answer to that. He sat down and folded his arms and he and Nora glowered at each other across the stove's width. After an hour of this he got up and went out anyway.

'He's a good man, really,' said Wyndham, not believing a

word of it. 'A good man in a tight spot.'

By the look on her face, Nora didn't believe it either.

'Do you have any cigarettes left?' she asked.

'I'm afraid not,' he said.

And at that she started bawling her eyes out.

Wyndham was startled but not really surprised. He'd been half-expecting an outburst of this sort all along. Indeed, it's a rare kind of person who can shoot a man dead and not have strong feelings about it a while later. All in all, Wyndham was relieved that Nora was not that kind of person.

So he did what one does – what he'd done for others during the war and what had been done for him in his time. The answer to this sort of thing was a good drink of rum or a mug of hot sweet tea but, neither being at hand, he took off his overcoat and wrapped it around her and then he held her close, making meaningless soothing noises for however long it took.

The explosive sobbing became gulps and hiccups and finally petered out into a sniffle or two.

'Leave me alone,' she said at last. There was no unkindness in it, and for fear that he might think there was, she gave him a sort of a kiss, missing his lips altogether but leaving a cold smear under his eye.

'I'm alright. Leave me alone a while.'

So he left her blowing her nose and wandered out into the desolate yard. He hunted around just to keep moving. There was nothing that hadn't been found already. The weather was clear but it wasn't the time of year for a hotel clerk to be out in the country in his second-best suit and no overcoat. He turned up his collar and jammed his hands into his pockets. He left the yard to explore the lane and get a better sense of the geography. He remembered the lane from the time before. Easy-speaking men had come down in a little horse-drawn car and talked of this and haggled over that, and less than a year later, unless Wyndham had been mistaken in the identity, one of those men had his photograph in the papers, having been taken in arms against the crown and shot for treason and insurrection. And everything in Ireland had changed since then, except for this overgrown lane.

Wyndham walked faster to get the blood pumping. He would go as far as the main road (such as it was), get his bearings, and head back.

He was looking in the wrong direction when a man greeted him. He was a perfectly ordinary man, just passing by about his own business, but by Wyndham's reckoning he shouldn't have been there.

There was curiosity in the man's eyes as he touched his hat and commented that it was a grand day. Wyndham tipped his own hat. 'Ah sure, we're blessed with the weather,' he said and, the instant he decently could, he hastened back to the house, wondering how long it would be before his presence was a matter of general knowledge across three parishes.

Back at the house he rapidly explained things to Nora.

'What did he look like?' she asked.

'Well – ordinary. How do you mean?'

'I mean, did he look like a police informer?'

'And what do they look like?'

'Alright then: did he look like the sort to shout "God save the King" on special occasions?'

'I wouldn't have said so, no.'

'And you didn't ask him for a cigarette?'

The answer to that seemed to trouble her more than the likelihood of discovery.

Moriarty returned from his ramble empty-handed and with no useful news.

'And sure where would we go anyway?' he said. 'We've nothing but our own two feet and you haven't an idea where else we could hole up, do you? And where's the nearest proper town? Fermoy. Best part of an army brigade there. Then there's Kilworth not far from us either. You had to land us right in the middle of garrison country, didn't you? No, we'll just have to stay put and chance it for the time being. And does *nobody* have a fag on them at all?'

59

And Diarmuid killed a wild deer that night, and they had their fill of meat and of pure water, and they slept till the morning of the morrow.

—Lady Gregory, *Gods and Fighting Men*

On the eve of the attack on Ginchy, Wyndham had spent a night in a shallow trench that could not be deepened without disinterring the numberless dead buried underfoot. In the hours before the dawn of the Ludendorff Offensive he had lain on the floor of a cellar, stupefied by the indescribable pounding of the preliminary bombardment. He had stood watch in Flemish trenches in the depths of winter with the water rising above his knees, and only his raw fear to keep him awake.

To those nights he could add this one.

Without warmth or tea or tobacco, they could at least have told stories or sung songs. But the camaraderie of the trenches was not to be found in this dark kitchen, with the fuel running low and not so much as a candle stub to hearten them. There were beds in the house, the mattresses dank and filthy with age. It was better to stay by the stove and sleep intermittently in a kitchen chair.

Nora had regained a sort of composure, but she made no show of affection towards Wyndham and would have nothing to do with any gesture of comfort he offered. She and Moriarty didn't like one another. It was obvious and unsurprising. There was no one incident to put them at odds: they were just two people to whom antipathy came naturally. They both found it easier to be silent than be polite.

Morning hadn't even arrived before Nora declared that she was leaving.

'Whatever else we're doing, we can't stay here without anything to eat. I'll go and buy a few things and get the lie of the land while I'm at it.'

'You can't!' said Wyndham.

'What? Are you going to go? When you haven't shaved in two days and your collar is filthy? And he's worse. No. I'll go by myself. It's safest.'

'See if you can pick up the paper,' said Moriarty. 'I need something to read before I go mad altogether – and we should find out the news from Cork, I suppose.'

'I'll walk you to the main road at least,' said Wyndham.

'And what earthly good is that going to do? Stay here and gather firewood or something.'

'Leave your pistol,' said Moriarty.

'I will not.'

'What are you going to do if a lorry-load of Tans stop you? Shoot your way out? They catch you with a pistol on you and that'll be as far as you go.'

'He's right,' said Wyndham, and earned himself a scowl from Nora. The scowl deepened as she wrestled with herself and finally surrendered the little flat pistol to him.

'Don't break it,' she said. 'Don't lose it. And don't let *him* have it.'

He steered her from the room before any noise was raised by 'him'. They stood at the front door, and the outdoors was no colder than inside.

'You'll be careful,' he said to her. 'You'll come back if you see any trouble. We can do without food for another day but I don't think I'd be able to spring you from prison.'

'I'll be careful,' she conceded.

'And one more thing – that bag of yours.'

'What about it?'

'Well, what do you want me to do with it? You know – if something happens.'

'What do you mean, what are you going to do with it? Don't do anything with it. Just leave it alone.'

'Don't you want me to hide it, just in case?'

'Why?'

'Well isn't it full of – I don't know – secret documents or something?'

'There's nothing in that bag that's any of your business.'

'Nora, I've got myself into a great deal of trouble. I think I should know what you've got in that bag.'

She frowned at her feet. 'Just things,' she said.

'What things?'

'A change of underclothes,' she admitted.

'Women's things,' she muttered.

'It's my running-away bag,' she sulkily explained.

'In case anything like this happened.'

'*What?*'

'What do you mean, "what"? How do you think I was able to change out of my wet stockings? Where do you think my clean handkerchief came from?'

Wyndham was too tired for any more of this. He knew that whatever he said was going to be the wrong thing. And he wasn't going to argue one way or the other because just then they realised they weren't alone.

The noise of a foot on gravel alerted them. It sounded like a deliberate announcement.

'I'll ask you once and then I won't ask you again: who are you and what are you doing here?'

They could only make out a figure in the dark, but the accent was undoubtedly Irish.

'And before I forget, would it be you who has anything to do with a Crossley Tender getting itself dumped in a field not far from here yesterday?'

Still neither of them answered. They heard the voice sigh.

'I'll tell you what – why don't we go on inside?'

Despite the easy tone there was no arguing with that voice.

It was two men who followed them into the kitchen. Moriarty was on his feet in an instant. He was advised to sit back down.

'And in fairness, is it too much to ask to have a bit of light?'

'I'm afraid there isn't any,' said Wyndham.

'Jesus. The dark will have to do us so. Is there anyone here besides the three of ye? No? Right – let's get back to where I started. Tell me your names.'

Wyndham could make out that the man doing the talking was short and immensely broad-shouldered, dressed like someone who knows he'll be out in the weather all day and doesn't care for fashions. His companion was younger and unremarkable. Wyndham couldn't see any weapons but he was in no doubt that both the men were armed. He had little enough to bargain with and he instinctively felt that the truth was not something to be squandered.

'My name is O'Brien,' he began. 'I'm a special correspondent for—'

'His name's Daniel Wyndham,' Nora interrupted. 'My name is Nora Maxfield. I work in the General Post Office on Cork. I report to – well never you mind who I report to, but have a look at this.' And she handed something to the man and struck a flame with her cigarette lighter. Wyndham couldn't believe that anyone spying for the revolution would carry around an identity card admitting to the fact, yet there it was.

The man squinted. 'Cumann na mBan,' he said. He turned the card over.

'There's no photograph,' he said. He passed it to his companion along with the cigarette lighter. 'Is that genuine? Should there be a photograph or something?'

'Sure what are you asking me for?' said the companion. 'I've never seen one of those things before either.'

'Alright then, miss, we'll take you at your word for the moment. And your friends?'

'Mr. Wyndham is from America, but he's on our side. The North Kerry Brigade will vouch for him – I think. And that's Mr. Moriarty.'

The stocky man appraised Moriarty – the only one who was not a soft-handed indoors type.

'And I imagine you don't work for the post office, do you, Mr. Moriarty?'

'I do not,' said Moriarty.

'And would you be insulted if I asked if you're carrying a gun at all?'

'I'm not, but that's not to say I never have.'

'Indeed so? And was it for the Republic that you might have borne arms?'

'Royal Munster Fusiliers,' said Moriarty, and Wyndham had heard those same words said in much the same tone in a pub, not long before fists came into play.

'Royal Munster Fusiliers,' nodded the man. 'I won't hold it against you. Mossie Henebry,' he said. 'Late of His Majesty's Ship *Minotaur*. Stoker First Class. Not anymore. I imagine you can guess what I am at the present. So what are you three doing here?'

'It wasn't safe for us in Cork anymore,' said Nora. 'We had to leave in a hurry.'

'Grand. That much makes sense. What are you doing *here*, though?'

'Isn't it a safe house?' said Wyndham.

'Are you asking me?' said Henebry.

'I was here before – during the war. Before the Easter Rebellion.

An associate of mine had a meeting with the Volunteers – a secret meeting.'

Henebry turned to his companion. 'Do you know anything about this?'

'Sure what would I know? I wasn't in the Volunteers then.'

'And the house?'

'All I know is that your man Finnucane had it until a few years ago and then he died and his son went off to America. Or maybe it was England. I forget.'

'And it's never been a safe house to your knowledge?'

'What have I just been telling you?'

Henebry turned his attention back on the three interlopers from Cork.

'Well isn't that the quare state of affairs?' he said. 'What am I to do with the three of ye at all?'

'You could give us a cigarette,' said Nora.

'That's not too unreasonable, said Henebry, reaching for a pocket. But then he snapped his fingers in frustration and turned again to his companion.

'I ran out,' he said. 'Would you have any on you?'

'And since when did I ever smoke?' said the man, and to Nora, 'Sorry.'

For fear that Nora might start crying again, Wyndham calmed his own simmering nerves and spoke up. 'I have a suggestion.'

Henebry raised an eyebrow. 'Go on so.'

'How about we *make* this a safe house?'

Wyndham saw he had everyone's attention and wasn't quite sure what to do with it.

He couldn't go back to Cork. He might not be a wanted man, but he was a link in a very short chain that led back to Nora. He couldn't return to Tralee without compromising the Fitzmullen-Brophys. And having spent part of the summer being shuttled from one place to another at the whims of General Lucas's kidnappers, he couldn't face a life on the run at the sufferance of the IRA.

'What I mean to say is, couldn't we just stay here?'

'I'm not stopping you.'

'No, but you see, that's not quite enough. We don't just need your permission: we rather need your protection. We need a *safe* house.'

'You want us to look after you? Am I following you?'

'Well yes and no. We want to look after ourselves and have you keep the authorities away while we do it.'

He did his best to summon up the spirit of Woodrow Wilson at Versailles, persuading the statesmen of Europe to remake the world.

'Please?' he said. 'Just for now? Just until we figure out what to do next?'

Henebry sat back and folded his arms. 'And what might be in it for me?' he asked.

Wyndham truly had little enough to bargain with. If he had more than four pounds ten to his name he'd have been surprised. He played his one card – one picked up off the floor of the Crossley Tender. 'Fifty rounds of three-oh-three?' he said.

If the IRA men were impressed they didn't show it.

Nora weighed in.

'What he means,' she said, 'is that we can make this a safe house.'

'That's what he said,' said Henebry.

'Not just for us, he means.'

'What does he mean?'

'He means that it can be a safe house for the district.'

'He does?'

'We can make it that way. We can keep it for you.'

'You can keep house? For fellas on the run?'

'We can do it. He works in a hotel. I'm a Red Cross nurse.'

That last bit of information piqued rather more interest than

Wyndham's catalogue of employment.

'So you know gunshot wounds and the like?' said Henebry.

'Naturally,' said Nora.

Henebry looked inquiringly at his companion, who shrugged.

'I'll tell you what: the three of you stay here while we think about what you said. If any of you go anywhere or talk to anyone we'll know about it and we'll take a dim view of it.'

'We'll need something to eat,' said Wyndham.

'Just stay here,' repeated Henebry, and at that he and his companion got up and disappeared into the slow winter dawn.

The grey morning promised little. The stove would soon grow cold. If Wyndham knew anything at all about his present company it was that they would soon fall to bickering. If he had a good breakfast inside of him he might almost feel fit for a good bicker himself, but it was up to him to forestall any discord. No one else was going to do it.

No food, no warmth, no comfort. It was a situation made for the likes of Colonel Fitzmullen-Brophy. He clapped his hands together, both for warmth and attention.

'Well if we're going to convince them to let us stay, let's start organising things round here.'

'And who put you in charge, at all?'

Colonel Fitzmullen-Brophy, of course, had been backed up by King's Regulations and the Manual of Military Law. Like a good officer should, Wyndham pretended he hadn't heard Moriarty. 'We never checked the outbuildings properly,' he said.

'That old shed? There's some big old lump of machinery blocking it up.'

'Then let's see if there's anything useful hidden behind that old lump of machinery, eh? Come on – it'll keep us warm.'

Nora made some desultory noise about seeing to the water or some firewood or something.

'That's the spirit!' said Wyndham, and he clapped his hands like he really meant it.

60

Diarmuid greeted the young man, and asked news of him. 'A fighting lad I am, looking for a master,' he said, 'and Muadhan is my name.'
'What would you do for me, young man?' said Diarmuid.
'I would be a servant to you in the day, and watch for you in the night,' he said.

—Lady Gregory, *Gods and Fighting Men*

How long had he dreamed of running away with Nora – of being cut loose from all bonds, with nothing to rely on but each other? The world would hunt them but their love would prevail.

Diarmuid and Grania.

'Who?' said Moriarty.

'Sorry – I didn't realise I was talking out loud.'

'We're all hungry but our minds aren't all wandering. Give me a hand with this.'

Diarmuid and Grania – Ireland's Tristan and Isolde. Finn's champion and Finn's betrothed, in the grip of enchanted love, fleeing across Ireland. There had been a third with them too – a faithful retainer who fed them on wild salmon.

'Do you know anything about fishing?' Wyndham asked. 'Would it be worth our while to go after salmon or something?'

'I'm a city boy. What do I know? But show me where the fish are and give me a hand grenade and I'll get you all the fish you'd want. Now would you lift at your end?'

They found nothing beyond a few scraps of rotten wood.

'Save us breaking up any chairs,' said Wyndham, but the bright side he was looking on was pretty much invisible to the other two. He reckoned that the time for suggesting nettle tea was not now.

They were saved by the arrival in late afternoon of a man with a donkey and cart. Without comment on much besides the weather, he unloaded on them a sack of potatoes and a packet of tea. 'I'll be back tomorrow or the day after,' he promised. 'A few spuds and a bit of tay will do ye grand until then.'

Maybe so, but it would have to be potatoes without salt and tea without milk and sugar. No one had thought to provide them with a pot of any kind, but luckily they found one – just the one. The potatoes ended up underdone and tasting of rust. The tea, when it was finally ready, tasted of rust and potatoes. At least the preparation of this sad refreshment took hours of their otherwise useless time and occupied all three of them.

The man had also – thank heaven – brought some blankets, rough and strange-smelling, but blessed all the same. Nobody spent a comfortable night, but it wasn't as bad as the night before had been. Nora took a place by the stove and banished the men from the kitchen.

With great misgivings, Wyndham gave into her insistence that he return her pistol. He perfectly understood that this was hardly the time and place for physical intimacy, but he thought it a bit much that any offer to comfort her might be met with gunshots.

The next day, mindful of the stricture against leaving, they had nothing to do but sit and wait. They had surrendered their agency and initiative to Mossie Henebry and the local IRA, and, with the botheration of their unsatisfactory breakfast out of the way, they had only each other – and they'd had little besides each other for days now.

Bereft of tobacco's comforts they brooded and sulked,

which was to say that Nora brooded and Moriarty sulked. As for Wyndham, he fidgeted and fretted. Moriarty's moods were tiresomely familiar. Nora was the one who worried him.

How long had he entertained his fantasy of Nora being Graine, running off with him? This wasn't that. If the old legends could still be evoked, then this was Queen Maeve, home from the war that she'd lost, and woe betide anyone who dared try cheer her up. But no – that wasn't it either. The warrior queen would never have sunk into dark humour over the blood of one enemy.

Wyndham feared that Nora's bout of weeping on Sunday had not washed her conscience clean. He imagined that there was another storm of emotion building up inside her. He couldn't imagine that she'd allow herself to burst into tears in front of Moriarty. She'd shoot him first. He feared she might shoot both of them.

If only he had a cigarette.

If only Moriarty weren't there.

'Do you know,' said Moriarty, addressing the ceiling, 'that all the years I've known this man, he's had a book in his pocket. Some officers might have a flask or something, but not Mr. Wyndham. Poetry or fairy stories as likely as not, but always a book. And now here we are and all we can do is stare at the walls.'

'It's not his fault,' said Nora, after an interval that suggested she might have been thinking otherwise.

'Maybe not,' said Moriarty, and sniffed, and rubbed his hands to warm them. 'You'd wonder whose fault it might be though.' And he looked hard at Nora.

Nora was not abashed. Nora could glare like a champion, and she did. Moriarty, for his part, was not going to be cowed by a woman.

'How about some tea?' said Wyndham.

Without milk or sugar, tea was not the answer.

Moriarty's habitual sniff became more noticeable. It was a legacy of a savage day and night at Festubert, which he'd spent in a flooded shell hole, with the battalion lying dead all around him and the German machine-gun bullets skimming the half-frozen ground. A spell in hospital and a longer spell in Ireland had cured him of the worst of his shell shock, but the sniff remained. Wyndham was used to it. It was a different matter with Nora.

'Oh for heaven's sake,' she said. 'Here!' And thrust a handkerchief at him.

'What's this?' said Moriarty, knowing exactly what it was.

Wyndham believed that if the police could be trusted in these sad days then it would have been time for the police to be called. Mercifully, the situation was saved by the sound of someone outside. No one even checked to see if it was safe – the three of them ran out into the yard in desperate hope of diversion, of relief, of tobacco. They found a lad startled by the reception.

'Easy now,' he said. 'Take it easy.'

'Who are you?' demanded Nora.

The boy tipped his cap to her – not so much from gentlemanly regard as from the lack of anything to fend her off.

'Mossie sent me to have a look and see that you're still here.'

'We're still here,' she said. 'And it's a wonder we haven't died of cold or starvation. Tell him that much.'

'I will, ma'am.'

'Do you smoke?'

'A fag would be nice, thank you.'

'Oh for the love of God. I'm not offering: I'm asking.'

'Sorry, ma'am.'

'And it's "miss", not "ma'am".'

'Sorry, miss.'

'Here's a pound. Get us some cigarettes – some bread, butter, sugar, whatever tinned food you can find, candles, soap...'

'A razor?' said Wyndham.

'The paper,' said Moriarty.

'Listen,' said the lad. 'I'm not an errand boy. I was just sent to check on you.'

'You can keep the change if you're back quickly,' said Nora.

'Your man Pat who was around yesterday,' said the lad. 'He'll be back. He can get your messages for you.'

'An extra two bob if you're back inside an hour.'

'An hour? Do you even know where you are?'

'A half crown then, just so long as you're back this afternoon.'

The boy straightened himself. Just because he wasn't long out of short trousers didn't mean that he could be sent to fetch and carry for this grasping woman. 'I'm a soldier of the Irish Republic,' he said.

'So am I,' said Nora. 'Do you want the money or don't you?'

Because she looked as if she might bite him, he took the pound note from her.

'I just report to Mossie,' he insisted. 'But I'll pass this on to Pat and he'll be around tomorrow.'

'*Tomorrow?*'

The boy was already backing away.

'Or maybe later on today. I must just report to Mossie. Good luck to you.'

Father Christmas had never been met with such expectation as Pat with his donkey and cart. They stood around him with pinched faces, oblivious to his joviality as he handed over his cargo. This time there was sugar and a sizeable cut of bacon, and some cabbages and a paraffin lamp.

'And?' said Nora.

Pat gave her a smile of paternal incomprehension.

'Did you not get my money? Didn't the boy tell you what we wanted?'

A light dawned on the man. 'He did! He did to be sure! I

remember now.' And he took from his pocket a packet of cigarettes which he handed with a smile to Moriarty. It was only one packet. There was no more. Wyndham thanked the man before anyone else might clamour or curse, and old Pat was on his way with a wave of his hand and a vague promise of return.

'Ask me politely,' said Moriarty.

'Why on earth would I do that?' said Nora. 'And what makes you think you own them just because he handed them to you?'

'Well of course he gave them to me. He was hardly going to give them to you, was he?'

'And why's that, might I ask?'

'Because he knows that a woman shouldn't be smoking cigarettes. It's unnatural.'

And he sniffed, and surrendered the cigarettes to Wyndham as if he'd won his point.

Of course the trouble wasn't going to end there, and that was Wyndham's problem all of a sudden. A pack of twenty wasn't going to last forever. Worse yet—

'Three into twenty doesn't go.'

A martyr to the cause of true love and Irish Independence, Wyndham barely hesitated when he allotted to himself only six cigarettes while Nora and Moriarty got seven each.

'We should make them last,' he said without much conviction, his head already swimming from the first drag in days.

As a legacy of the Western Front Moriarty had worse habits than sniffing. After two nights of cold and discomfort, he and Wyndham had reckoned that one of the beds wasn't too decrepit after all and, having lived far rougher during the war, they were not too proud to share it. They slept top to toe, in underclothes that should have been changed long since, and the blankets not quite enough to fool them into believing that the mattress was quite dry after all, but they slept nonetheless. Up to a point.

The point was Moriarty's foot kicking Wyndham's face. This was the start of a short bout of thrashing and moaning and whimpering that was rising to a scream when Wyndham put a stop to it by waking Moriarty up.

'What's wrong with you at all?' said Moriarty.

'You were making a row.'

'No I wasn't. Shut up and let me go back to sleep. Christ, but you're all at me.'

And that, thought Wyndham, is how a returned veteran might be turned away from the family home with a reputation for rowdiness. And as he tried to drift off again in this state of malodorous intimacy, he had a jolt.

What did *he* do in *his* sleep?

Mossie Henebry reappeared – in daylight this time. He seemed pleased, and not at all put out by the haggard looks and mutinous stares of these three blanket-shawled refugees from Cork.

'I've been keeping an eye on ye,' he said.

'We know,' said Nora.

'I'm sure you do not,' said Henebry, his hands warming around some grudgingly-given tea. 'Have you no better cups than this one?'

'We would if you gave us some.'

'I'll make a note,' he said, dismissing her complaint. 'I've been having fellas keeping an eye out.'

'These fellows of yours would have been more use if they'd brought soap and some decent food.'

'Ah now,' he said, and Wyndham felt it was the wrong tone to take with Nora in this humour. On the other hand, he was the source of what few provisions they had, so unless Nora put a gun to his head and held him hostage, she might as well listen to whatever the man was saying.

'And do you know what my lads have been telling me?' the man was saying. 'They've been telling me you've been behaving yourselves. You were told to stay here and you've stayed here. Not a peep out of you. Spoken to no one. No one at all knows about you. Not the neighbours and especially not the Tans.'

'Well what did you think we were going to do?'

'Honestly, Miss Maxfield, I couldn't have told you. You could be who you say you are or you could have come from Dublin Castle or Downing Street or Tír na nÓg and I'd have been none the wiser. But as it stands, your story is holding up.'

'But didn't Cork vouch for me? Or Listowel?'

'Maybe it's not as simple as me filling out a request with a tuppenny stamp stuck on it. On the other hand, maybe Intelligence sent glowing reports about you, but they don't know that you might have had a change of heart or allegiance since last they knew about you.'

'The idea!'

'Shush now. I'm saying nothing. All I'm saying is that your probation is going grand. So far so good, anyway.

'Probation?' said Nora. 'Well if that's what this is then I think it would be best if we didn't all perish while we're waiting on your approval.'

'There's something Pat could bring you?'

'I have a list.'

61

Diarmuid went out early the next day again to the hill, and it was not long till he saw the three strangers coming towards him.

—Lady Gregory, *Gods and Fighting Men*

That one meeting didn't seem very fruitful at the time, but it improved things in the house. Necessities and comforts appeared in greater quantity, and if there wasn't a shared sense of purpose, at least there was now a feeling that they weren't so lost and alone anymore. They were all in the same boat and they had an idea of where the boat might be drifting.

Military discipline was their friend. They had each known monotony and regulated deprivation. They had all been accustomed to drudgery.

Everything took too much time, and that kept them busy. Fetching water and keeping the fire going were important tasks in themselves. Cooking was quite the undertaking.

Moriarty couldn't do anything beyond opening tins, and Nora's skills didn't stretch far beyond boiling an egg. Given that tins and eggs were rarities, it fell to Wyndham to take over in the kitchen. He had no more culinary talents than the other two, but he had read instructions for officers on how to provide nourishment for infantrymen, and had been subjected to many a lecture from Fitzmullen-Brophy on the same. He boiled potatoes and cabbage and prodded hopefully at lumps of bacon while Nora did the housework and Moriarty did such repairs as could be managed – one mostly indoors and the other mostly outdoors and both out of each other's way.

They punctuated their days with carefully rationed cigarettes. Wyndham settled on the rigid routine of one every three hours exactly. In despair at her own immoderation, Nora subjected herself to the same regimen. She even surrendered her own ration to Wyndham's care to make the three-hour gaps pass without being devilled by temptation. Moriarty did as he pleased, as always.

They weren't happy, but they weren't at each other's throats either – much. The real trouble came when they were raised above the threshold of mere subsistence. The day came when Pat delivered to them some of the furnishings of a house ransacked by the Tans. It was a collection of oddments, incomplete and in need of repair, but compared to what the runaways had been reduced to, it ushered in a time of abundance. There was crockery now, and bedding, and the means to raise humanity above brute survival, and that brought a degree of leisure that could be filled with limitless backbiting and dissatisfaction.

Nora Maxfield and Francis Moriarty were two people who would just not get on, no matter what. It was as if they had set their hearts on it. There were snappish arguments and accusing silences. She railed at his laziness and he at her bad temper. Wyndham saw undoubted merit in both charges. He, of course, was caught in the middle, which was at the kitchen table where they all met whether they liked it or not. He could not impose good fellowship with food. Their unvarying meals were porridge for breakfast and bacon and cabbage for dinner. Even though he was now furnished with utensils beyond a single rusty pot and Moriarty's pocket knife, his skills were still far short of the domestic ideal. No meal he provided would ever make anyone put their troubles aside.

And then the great morning came when they were at last given purpose. There was no warning from Mossie Henebry or anyone else. There just appeared at the house three IRA men on the run and in want of shelter. They might have been termed gunmen if they'd had more than a single rifle between them and they might have looked like desperadoes if any of them had been old enough to shave.

It was Moriarty who found them and led them into the kitchen.

'They told me their names because they're the sort of lads who'd be telling their names to strangers. I've forgotten already. That's the tall one, that's the small one, and that's the one in the middle. You'd better give them a cup of tea before they start crying. I'm going back out to see who's been following them.'

'No one was following us!' said the tall one.

'That'll be the whole of the Tank Corps then.'

'We weren't followed!'

'The Tank Corps with the band of the Household Cavalry. And give me that rifle before you hurt yourself.'

'Sit down,' said Nora, setting out the cups. 'There's no milk and there's nothing to eat until dinner so I want to hear no complaints out of any of you.'

Such a reception didn't keep these youths subdued for long. They were buzzing from lack of sleep and the excitement of their escapade. The tall one, who was addressed as Jamesie by the other two, was quickest to assert himself.

'So what do we call you?' he asked. 'We were only told where to find you, not who you are.'

'You can call me "Sir",' said Moriarty, who hadn't stayed outside for long, knowing that tea was being made. 'Names are none of your business.'

Rather than return the lad's rifle, he was subjecting it to disassembly and inspection.

'State of this,' he said. 'You can tell you're farmers' boys, the way you could grow spuds in the barrel. What was it you were doing out there at all? It certainly wasn't fighting.'

'We were so fighting!'

'Not with this yoke you weren't. The sights are so misaligned you could shoot around corners.'

'We dug a trench, so we did,' said the boy dubbed the one in the middle.

'A trench? Like with fire step and parapet and barbed wire out front? Like in a proper war?'

'No,' said the boy, sorry now that he'd spoken up. 'A trench across the road, like.'

'To stop the Tans,' said the tall one, sticking up for his own. 'To stop them driving their lorries down the road. Better than a barricade any day. Like blowing up a bridge, only there's no bridge.'

Moriarty digested this. 'One little boreen in County Cork with a wee bit of a trench to go with all the potholes – so that's why Lloyd George couldn't sleep last night.'

Whatever about the prime minister, the three boys, thinking themselves safe for now, had no trouble at all in sleeping through the better part of the day. They were awake for dinner, and eagerly hungry. Wyndham had expected to see a degree of disappointment when he slapped a lump of pale bacon onto each of their plates. It was the reaction he got from Nora and Moriarty every day, after all. The pure dismay on the boys' faces took him aback however.

'We can't eat that,' said the small one, with something approaching horror.

'You'll eat what's put in front of you,' Nora told him.

'No, but – I'm sorry, but – but it's Friday!'

It took a moment for the connection to be made in the Protestant mind. Wyndham, doing his bit for religious toleration, went so far as to apologise. Nora didn't.

'Oh for heaven's sake!' was all she said, despairing that the Irish Republic would be made by such faint hearts as these.

Up until now, the long dark evenings had been endured in near silence. The newspaper, if such was available, was divided up and read. The light was bad and the print was small so it was a matter of great – almost devotional – concentration. Only the most arresting articles provoked comment. If Pat had not been to visit then the old papers were studied. It was the only way to kill the hours before bed. It was either that or murder.

Tonight Nora had monopolised the lamp so as to be able to see the buttons she was sowing. Jamesie, the tall one, who had struck his blow for Ireland and proved his manhood thereby, directed his cheeky sparkle on her.

'I wonder at all,' he said, 'if you'd ever darn a sock for me, ma'am. It's only that we've been living rough for so long that I've forgotten the homely comforts.'

One of the other boys smirked and turned red.

Nora looked at him without word or expression. Instead of a sowing basket she had her bag. She put her mending aside, reached in and took out her little Browning pistol. With no less effort than she'd put into sewing a button, she stripped the weapon down and began to clean it.

Jamesie left her alone, but he wasn't daunted for long. Nora might be a formidable woman of the house, and Moriarty was evidently the man in charge, but Wyndham was fair game. He had soft manners had he did the cooking. More ridiculously yet, he did the washing.

Wyndham would never have thought that hanging a pair of long-johns on a line in the kitchen could have provoked hilarity, but here were the three boys looking at him bright-eyed and nudging each other.

'Grand drying weather,' said Jamesie, and that was somehow enough to provoke a suppressed explosion of laughter from one of the others.

Wyndham had spent six months in the ranks. The lack of

privacy, the communal medical inspections and the public indignities had reshaped him. He couldn't for the life of him see anything funny about being able to make himself comfortable. He found it hard to understand how a man running his underwear through a mangle while wearing a blanket for a shawl might be considered ridiculous. But no one likes to be the butt of a joke, even when it's a children's joke.

He gave the boys the same blank look that Nora had given them.

'Miss Maxfield,' he said. 'Did you think to ask Pat about getting us some mousetraps?'

'I didn't, Mr Wyndham,' she said. 'I'll be sure to say something when next he stops by.'

'There may not be any need,' he said, and he shrugged off his blanket and crossed the room to where she sat.

'Mice, boys,' he said, acknowledging them for the first time. 'Can't abide them. Not as bad as rats, though. You should have seen the rats we had in the trenches. May I, Miss Maxfield?'

She slapped in the pistol's magazine with the heel of her hand and handed it to him with a polite smile. He worked a cartridge into the breech and pointed the pistol at where the boys were sitting.

'The trenches, boys. You could get used to the danger but not the nuisance. I still can't abide rats or mice. Stay very still now. I think I saw one move right behind you.'

The boys froze for a moment, and then were moving very fast in all directions. Out of pure devilment Wyndham pulled the trigger at the space just vacated and then convulsively pulled it twice more before he had his wits about him. When the smoke cleared and the shock wore off, they found to their consternation the body of a single mouse on the floor. Nora chose to dispose of it without determining the cause of death.

'Only one, Mr. Wyndham?' was all she said. 'It's not like you to waste ammunition.'

The boys were perfectly well-behaved for the rest of the evening, and the next morning they were on their way.

Wyndham felt they had scored a little triumph. They had vindicated themselves by providing safe haven for the IRA. They had proved themselves useful. They had passed the test.

Moriarty wasn't so cheerful.

'Do you know why your man Mossie Henebry sent us those three gossoons? Because no one would miss them. He still doesn't trust us.'

'Well, he'll have to trust us now,' said Wyndham.

'Not if those eejits get lifted by the Tans – and you can bet money they will. Henebry will think it's because we sold them out. Worse – the three eejits will sell *us* out to the Tans.'

'Will you for the love of heaven please stop looking on the bad side? It gets tiresome.'

'Well I wouldn't want you to get tired.'

'Moriarty—'

'It's alright for you, but there's some of us who didn't want to run off with wild women and get stuck out in the middle of bloody nowhere. I was grand and happy by myself at home and then you hand me her bloody bag and that's the end of me. Look at me! I was nearly better off in Limburg!'

Wyndham took a deep breath.

'She's not a wild woman; it's hardly our fault your lodgings got burned down; and don't you dare imply that my food is as bad as Limburg! And don't tell me you were happy at home either! You've never been happy!'

Thinking about it the next day, Wyndham wondered if that last rebuke was what had decided it. Moriarty was gone. There was no way of knowing if he still had a home to go to, or if he'd be intercepted by the Tans, or apprehended by Henebry's men for leaving without permission, but he'd taken those chances. He was gone. There had been no fiery argument. Nora hadn't accused him of being a lazy good-for-nothing and he hadn't called her a hatchet-faced bitch. No voices had been raised nor crockery thrown. He was just gone.

Once, when Wyndham had first met him, Moriarty would have put his fists up and spat in the face of adversity. Festubert had changed that – Festubert and Limburg. Moriarty no longer rose in defiance. He sank: lower and lower until, somewhere below eye level, he slipped out altogether. He had done it in the trenches on the way up to Guillemont with a judicious pistol bullet fired into his own leg. He had done as much now.

Wyndham stood in the yard, knowing that he had helped to drive him away. Perhaps the IRA would bring him back, and everything would be worse than before. Perhaps not. Wyndham couldn't help but think about Gearóid Ó Tuama and what had happened when the Tans had met *him* on the road.

It was three o'clock. He lit his three o'clock cigarette. His body had been anticipating this since noon but he found nothing to savour. Midwinter dark was already coming on. Moriarty would not be coming back.

He thought about the pitiable and vulnerable Moriarty he had found in the station at Arras. He thought about the two of them standing sentry in a flooded forward sap at St. Yvon four years before that. Two ragged survivors of the nightmarish battles around Ypres. Two fusiliers holding each other up through thick and thin.

Nora was standing at the kitchen door.

'I know what you're thinking,' she said.

He didn't answer.

'You're thinking about me with nothing on.'

He carefully pinched out his cigarette.

'Why yes,' he said. 'Yes, that's exactly it.'

62

We'll build a sweet little nest somewhere in the west, And let the rest of the world go by.

—E.R. Ball and J.K. Brennan, 'Let the Rest of the World Go By'

Nora had a passable singing voice but no regard at all for the words. 'And tell the rest of the world goodbye,' was a deviation barely worth noticing. For all Wyndham cared she could sing Christmas carols with absent-minded made-up words in February, and a few minutes earlier that was exactly what she'd been doing.

She was content. He was content. He was – and it was an everyday revelation to him – a sight more than content. For six weeks now this mean little house, cold and isolated, had been his paradise, their paradise.

On a couple of occasions some furtive characters had made their appearance, stayed long enough for a wash, a night's sleep and something to eat, and had disappeared back into the troubled countryside. They might have stayed longer but duty drove them. That, and the fact that there are few things more uncomfortable for the visitor than the presence of lovers wholly wrapped up in one another.

The forces of the crown left them alone too – maybe even for the same reason. The lovers knew no more of the progress of Ireland's struggle than they learned from a paper that might come their way no more than once a week. Even then they found it hard to care for the great doings in the country at large. All of their life was just here. All of their pleasures and necessities were in this house, bounded by this yard.

'Anything?' said Nora, calling from the kitchen window.

Wyndham was investigating the straw where the hens roosted. The hens had been a Christmas gift that they were too ignorant and squeamish to kill for dinner. Instead they left them in the yard by day and locked up in an outhouse at night in the hope that, left to their own devices, they would produce eggs.

'Nothing,' he said, 'but have faith. I believe tomorrow will be our day.'

But of course today was their day, as had been all the days they'd had together.

'If we're going to have eggs then I'm going to make bread,' she called.

'You can make bread?'

'It can't be that hard.'

Homemade bread and fresh eggs. A shared idiot optimism. Requited love. Hadn't he been waiting long enough?

Time went by.

Because the IRA didn't seem to mind anymore, Nora had started venturing beyond the little horizon in search of something more than bacon and cabbage.

'Who's going to stop a woman with a basket over her arm?' she said. 'If anyone asks me questions I just put on my most hoity-toity voice so they'll think I'm some sort of eccentric army wife or something.'

'Do you think it fools them?'

'In the shop? I doubt it. Everyone knows everyone's business. I'm sure they know all about the two of us. If I had a good name it would be ruined.'

'Well you can have my name if you like. It may be in slightly better condition and it's there any time you want it.'

'Ah, Dan, no. We can't be getting married.'

'Well, given that we've been on honeymoon for more than two

months now, I don't think it would be out of order.'

'I meant we can't get married anytime *now*. I mean, where would we find a clergyman or a justice of the peace who wouldn't inform on us?'

Wyndham frowned.

'Do you mean that it's only the practicalities that are standing in our way? You mean that you're finally agreeable to our actually marrying?'

'Didn't I say? I'm sure I told you.'

'*When?*'

'I must have forgotten. Sorry.'

'Come here and make it up to me.'

VIII

A SOLDIER'S SONG

Come out, ye Black and Tans!
Come out and fight me like a man!
Show your wife how you won medals down in Flanders!
Tell her how the IRA
Made you run like hell away,
From the green and lovely lanes of Killeshandra!

—Dominic Behan, 'Come Out, Ye Black and Tans'

63

And Grania said: 'Do not leave me now this way, and my love for you ever growing like the fresh branches of the tree with the kind long heat of the day.'

—Lady Gregory, *Gods and Fighting Men*

'So how does it end – this Diarmuid and Grania story of yours? And move over – you're all elbows.'

'*I'm* all elbows?'

'So how does it end – after Finn catches up with them at last and forgives them for running away with each other and everything – what then? Do they live happily ever after?'

'Up to a point. Years later Diarmuid was mortally wounded by a wild boar he was hunting.'

'That was careless of him.'

'Grania warned him to take his great battle spear to the hunt but he didn't listen.'

'You'll always listen to me and keep your great battle spear handy, won't you, Dan? Or an umbrella at least. And who's Finn? – in our version, I mean.'

Wyndham had to think about that.

'Colonel Fitzmullen-Brophy.'

'How? It's not like I was his intended and you stole me away.'

'I betrayed him. I sided with the Republic.'

'You sided with me. You don't care tuppence about the Republic. And I'll give you half my nine o'clock cigarette if you get up and make us some tea.'

'You smoked that cigarette at six. You can't fool me. No – the colonel would be disappointed. He'd say I'd let the side down.'

'That's a far cry from hunting us across Ireland, and I'll say it again: you're not betraying anyone. Not the colonel or the king or the regiment. It's not like you're fighting alongside the IRA.'

When the Irish Republic did come to disturb their idyll, it was Nora who was summoned. Wyndham merely tagged along.

'We need you to come with me. Now.'

The man's name was Joe Hawkes, and they remembered him as Mossie Henebry's lieutenant on that dark morning they'd first arrived.

'Come on,' he insisted. 'There's a man wounded. You said you were a nurse. We'd have brought him here to you only the car won't start. Hurry on.'

Any journey will seem long when it's dark and you don't know where you're going. Wyndham reckoned by his watch that they covered five miles or so, but five miles felt like ten. The place at which they arrived – when they finally arrived – wasn't unlike the place they'd left. It was just an undistinguished house on some undistinguished land at the end of a bad road.

The wounded man was in the kitchen, laid out on the table, his clothes bloodstained and disarrayed, his face so white he might have been dead already. Nora showed no haste or alarm.

'Bring the light closer so I can see,' she said. 'And get me a basin of water and some clean cloths.'

And such was her command of the situation that no one hesitated in obeying. The men in attendance were the expected sort – countrymen, young and capable, but strained and nervous when confronted by the complications of wounds and possible death. They looked positively fearful as they watched Nora peel away the makeshift bandage. They had hastily hidden the wound away and didn't like for it to be uncovered.

'Hold up that lamp now,' she snapped.

The wound was in the man's side, just below the ribs.

'Was it a rifle or a pistol did this?' she asked, peering close at the dark hole from which the blood sluggishly pulsed.

There was a silence in which one man was elected to testify. 'A rifle, I think, ma'am.'

'And was it at close range?'

Another hesitation, as if the witness was wondering what the right answer might be.

'I'd say fifty or a hundred yards, ma'am. It'd be hard to say. We were running.'

Nora didn't indicate whether she approved or disapproved. She wiped down the wound again and proceeded to cover it up.

'You need to get this man to the hospital,' she said.

'The hospital? We can't do that! They'll catch us! They'll certainly get poor Brendan there.'

'Better he's arrested than he dies here.'

'Is there nothing you can do?'

'I've just done it. I've looked at the wound and told you what to do about it.'

It was Joe Hawkes who spoke up now. 'You told Mossie that you knew about bullet wounds.'

'And I do. That's a bullet wound to the abdomen. I've seen enough of them. He needs a surgeon. Not a nurse or a country doctor or the local vet. He needs to be in a hospital.'

Having defended her professional credentials, Nora washed and dried her hands to emphasise that the consultation was at an end. Then, with a note of imperious concession:

'Now where's this car of yours that won't start?'

Leaving the young gunmen with their stricken comrade, Wyndham followed Joe Hawkes and Nora out to the yard.

'There she is,' said Hawkes. 'She's nearly new but I don't know what's wrong with her. I wouldn't have a bull's notion about engines. Mossie's as bad. An engine to him is something you'd shovel coal into.'

Nora just looked at the car and nodded. 'Get me the lamp,' she said, 'And some rags.'

Wyndham made himself useful by making tea. He fully ascribed to Nora's principle of acting like you're in charge so that no one takes you for a skivvy, and he doled out the tea like a quartermaster – as if no one here could be trusted with the job.

'She's some woman, your woman,' said Hawkes, slurping heartily.

Wyndham knew to translate '*your* woman' as '*that* woman', but he chose to take the possessive literally.

'That she is,' he said.

'If she gets the car fixed we'll see if we can't get poor Brendan into Fermoy and chance it. If not he might have to go in the back of Pat's cart. We'll see. I'll have to talk to Mossie.'

'I'm sure it'll all work out for the best,' said Wyndham, not sure of anything, but not all that concerned either. This was just some immaterial interlude. Real life would resume when he and Nora got back home.

'And before I forget,' said Hawkes. 'Mossie wants to talk to you too. Finish your tea and we'll head off. I want to be there and back before it gets light.'

Wyndham didn't question or object. All he did was tell Nora that he would be gone for a while. She was hard at her work, uncovering the car's secrets and bending it to her will in poor light and with the most basic of tools, but she took the time to look up and smile.

'I think I've got it!' she said.

And that last sight of her, beaming in oil-smeared triumph, was what he would keep in the time to come.

She should have told him to take his great battle spear with him.

64

The hotter the fighting the better and more perfect the IRA became as an organisation.

—Dan Breen, *My Fight For Irish Freedom*

After another bewildering journey through the dark byways of north Cork, Hawkes led Wyndham into what evidently served as IRA district headquarters. This wasn't another derelict farmhouse or the out-of-the-way dwelling of a sympathiser. This was more like field HQs as Wyndham remembered them.

It was a dugout – a hole in the earth, stoutly timbered within and invisible from outside. And in every corner and from every hook there was the paraphernalia of British soldiery. Rifles, raincoats, field glasses, various boxes marked with the government broad arrow. There was even a map tacked to the wall.

'Not bad, is it?' said Hawkes. 'We had to bring our own cups and saucers, mind.'

'Don't be telling him all our secrets, for the love of Christ,' said Mossie Henebry. He was sitting in candlelight, looking like a man who should be out mending the roads. 'How's young Brendan doing? Sit down there, Mr. Wyndham.'

'The lady says he needs the hospital,' said Hawkes.

'And what do you say?'

'What do you want with a nurse if you're asking my opinion? I say bringing Brendan anywhere is chancy, but she seems to know what she's talking about.'

'Well I suppose if she does, then she does.' And again to Wyndham: 'Go on, sit yourself down.'

'I was told this wouldn't take long,' said Wyndham. 'I was told I'd be back before dawn.'

'Joe told you that? Well if that's the case, he was telling you lies,' said Henebry, not showing any concern. Hawkes just shrugged. Before Wyndham could protest, Henebry explained.

'This safe house of yours – its day is done, I'm afraid. We're shutting up shop. Too many people know about it for a start.'

'I've been speaking to no one!'

'Nor have you, but that's neither here nor there. You've been there – what? – for months now. Word gets around. And it's not surprising with you and your Miss Maxwell causing scandal.'

'The lady is my fiancée!'

'And she'd better be, the way the pair of you have been carrying on, but calm down. I don't mind a bit what you get up to and, if have to be completely honest with you, I don't care who knows about you either – up to a point anyway. The fact is that you're not all that much use to us where you are.'

Wyndham had visions of being cast out penniless into the world. And then out of nowhere came the vision of the IRA just tidying him away out of the way with a bullet to the back of the head and an unceremonious burial in a bog hole.

'You could move us somewhere else,' he offered. His throat was suddenly so dry he had difficulty in saying it.

'We could, we could,' said Henebry. 'We could do that.'

He steepled his thick fingers. 'But we're not going to.'

'You're letting us go then?'

'Not that.'

Wyndham felt a chill. He couldn't see Hawkes behind him; couldn't even feel his presence. He watched Henebry very closely.

'Your Miss Maxfield – your "fiancée" – she seems to have

skills we'd have the need for. There isn't too much call for hotel keepers on the other hand.'

Wyndham waited.

'Your other friend: Mr. Moriarty.'

'You told me you let him go. You told me he was safe.'

'We did. He might well be safe still. All I can say is that we saw him safe on his way back to Cork. After that was his own affair. But we had a sit-down and chat before we saw him off. He told us he was a Munster Fusilier.'

'He never hid the fact. He told you the first time you met him.'

'True enough. And I said we wouldn't be holding it against him. But he told me that you were too. And not just a fusilier but an officer. I'd really have preferred it if you'd told me that yourself.'

Wyndham thought it best to keep his mouth shut. If this was a time for last words, he couldn't think of anything good.

'Having a British officer minding one of our safe houses: now there's a thing.'

'They'd be laughing at us if they knew,' said Hawkes, and Wyndham flinched to hear him just behind.

'They can laugh away,' said Henebry. 'That's not my concern.'

'I'm not British,' said Wyndham, finding his voice. 'I'm an American.'

'And that's another thing that's neither here nor there,' said Henebry. 'But what were you doing in the army? I don't mean why you joined or anything like that; I mean what did you do?'

Wyndham thought it wise to downplay his service to the British crown in Ireland.

'I helped train the American Expeditionary Force,' he said.

'Did you now? And a while before that did you also train a battalion of the Kitchener mob hereabouts? Mr Moriarty was telling us about it.'

'I—well, yes. I was.'

'Well there we are then.'

'We are?'

'There's your new job. We have all these young lads who know nothing at all. You can knock them into shape for us.'

'But what about Miss Maxfield?'

'Sure, you can see each other at weekends. *I* don't know. We're fighting a war here, Mr. Wyndham.'

'But what about now? Can I see her now?'

And just then, the sound carrying far on the still night air, they heard a distant burst of fire. Wyndham knew it right off for a Lewis Gun. That meant the Tans. The IRA didn't have any machine-guns that he knew of.

'I thought they left off when the lads got away with Brendan,' said Henebry.

'I thought so too,' said Hawkes. 'Maybe they just went back for reinforcements.'

'Who are they shooting at?'

'I think they're just shooting. All our lads should be home and under cover.'

Henebry turned back to Wyndham. 'And there's your answer for you. You won't be going anywhere tonight.'

65

The old fighting spirit was as strong as ever, but it had gained a fresh strength in discipline in our generation. Every county sent its boys whose unrecorded deeds were done in the spirit of Cuchulain at the Ford.

—Michael Collins, *The Path to Freedom*

The Kitchener battalion that Wyndham had known in 1915 had been typical of its kind: an unhandy band of unqualified men and boys with no command structure of any experience and no equipment fit for the task at hand. Their home had been a camp in a field in an unregarded townland called Knocknahanna, miles from any amenities and comforts.

This was like that, only worse.

Firstly, it wasn't even a camp. It was just another of those derelict farms, worse by far than the one where he and Nora had spent the winter.

'At least you have a roof over you,' said Hawkes, who'd been doing a fine job of ignoring Wyndham's resentment these past days.

'Would an intact roof be too much to ask for?' said Wyndham. 'I can see rather too much daylight through this one.'

'Sure the weather's getting better all the time. You'll be grand.'

A lad, maybe sixteen years old, came running up, badly flustered. He had a farmer's shotgun in his hand that looked almost too big for him. Hawkes frowned.

'It's Tadhg O'Flynn, isn't it?'

The lad nodded, too breathless to speak and unsure whether

being recognised and called by name by the likes of Joe Hawkes was a good or a bad thing.

'Where is everyone?' asked Hawkes.

'There's only me at the moment, sir,' the lad gasped.

'And what are you doing?'

'I'm on sentry duty.'

'And two men come wandering in and you're not there to challenge them?'

Young O'Flynn made inarticulate sounds and imprecise gestures, trying to indicate that he'd been engaged in perfectly legitimate pursuits that were too difficult to explain.

'You were having a rest,' said Hawkes. 'Is that it? You were having a widdle. You were saying your prayers. You were spying on sweet Rosie Noonan. Is that it?'

'I was helping Johnny Byrne with the cows,' the boy managed. 'Below in the field there.'

'Johnny Byrne can look after his own cows below in the field there. Your job is to keep an eye out for the Tans. Do you hear me? This is Mr. Wyndham. He's to be your training officer. He's disgusted with you already. Is there tea made?'

'I'll make some for you now.'

'Come back here!. Have you not been listening to me? Get back on sentry, you eejit. Where's Billy and when's he due back?'

Billy Deasy was the commanding officer, and he held that position through natural god-given seniority. At nineteen years of age he was the oldest one in the unit, and had been in charge since they'd just been a local gang of boys running loose around the parish and making themselves occasionally useful to the IRA as lookouts and messengers. He was even less pleased about Wyndham being foisted on him than Wyndham was. He didn't need some old man to tell him how things should be done.

Looking down from the great height of his twenty-eight years, and smarting over his separation from Nora, Wyndham was in no mood to spare the feelings of a touchy adolescent. He gave Deasy the appraising eye that battalion adjutants had used to intimidate him since first he'd been commissioned. Take your time. Linger disapprovingly on certain items of dress. Don't speak. Deasy endured the assessment with a truculent expression, but he looked like he wouldn't stand for a stranger staring at his waistcoat buttons much longer.

'There you go,' interrupted Hawkes. 'I'll leave you to it. The pair of ye will get on grand.'

With Hawkes gone, Wyndham tried again to commit to the role.

'How many men in this unit, Deasy?'

'Eight or ten.' The answer was given grudgingly, as if by a schoolboy who knows that there's no right answer.

'Eight *or* ten? Which? Don't you know how many men under your command?'

'Sometimes there's ten, sometimes there's only eight. There's two lads who can't get away often.'

'Away?'

'Away from home – from their work and that. They'd be wanted on the farm.'

Wyndham considered launching into a rebuke about how he'd put up with no slackness in any unit he commanded, but the heart had gone out of him. 'Come and get me whenever they're assembled,' he said. 'I'll be taking a nap.'

As an officer, Wyndham's role in instruction had been to lead by example, give short lectures based in the army's manuals and pamphlets, or simply say, 'Carry on, sergeant' – or, if too junior to be trusted giving orders to a sergeant, 'Carry on, corporal'. Here he had no king's commission or Army Act to grant him unquestioned status. Rather than a tailored uniform there was the suit he'd been wearing since December and a haircut that Nora insisted she'd do better *next* time. He had little enough to impress his authority on these youngsters. He thought about Lance-Corporal Sheehan who had struck terror into him on the square in Tralee. He remembered how Moriarty had bullied the new recruits in Knocknahanna. The point was to knock them off balance: make them unsure of everything except the army's way of doing things.

He looked at the half-dozen youths lined up in front of him.

'Atten-*shun!* Who here knows how to play piano?'

Some sideways looks were exchanged before one of them raised a tentative hand.

'Em, I can play the fiddle – a bit, like.'

'Right! Get yourself off to the cookhouse and start peeling spuds!'

More confused and furtive looks.

'There isn't any cookhouse, sir.'

Corporal Moriarty, master of the military non-sequitur, had failed him. What next? Of course. Little Corporal Raffaelli would pick on the biggest man in the outfit and cut him down to size. Wyndham pointed at a hulking innocent whose shoulders suggested he could wrestle a bull into submission. The lad was the only one here carrying a proper service rifle.

'You! What's your name?'

'Ryan, sir.'

'Present arms, Ryan!'

His face a picture of concentration, Ryan executed a rough approximation of the exercise.

'Again, Ryan! Smartly this time! I want to hear your hand slap on the stock! What's the matter with you? You act like you're afraid of that rifle!'

'I'm afraid I might drop it, sir. It's the only one we have.'

Fuckin hayseeds. This sort of thing would never have been allowed in the Munster Fusiliers.

At least he'd only have to put up with it for a few days.
Instead of a cookhouse, most of the unit went home for their dinners. Wyndham wondered what might have become of him if Billy Deasy's mother didn't come by to feed Billy and insist that he share his food with Wyndham.

'I'll make sure to bring something especially for you in future, Mr. Wyndham,' she said. 'Would there be anything else you'd be wanting?'

'You're too kind, Mrs. Deasy. Would it be too much to ask for cigarettes?' *And whiskey. All the whiskey you can carry. It's the only way I'm getting through this.*

But of course he didn't ask for whiskey. He wouldn't have been able to afford it if he did. As it was, he was worried to discover that he could barely afford cigarettes. He didn't imagine that the IRA paid its volunteers, but might they hire mercenaries in a consultant capacity?

When Colonel Fitzmullen-Brophy had been given a training battalion of the Munsters he had spent his day writing indents and requisitions for anything and everything. The army would sometimes indulge him, although it took its sweet time. Instead of those reams of official correspondence, what Wyndham had was a few sheets of butcher's paper, and he could ask for all the treasures of Ireland for all the good it might do him.

'You can ask until the cows come home,' Joe Hawkes told him on a brief visit. 'There's nothing we can give you. There's nothing to be had. We've barely got two bullets to rub together.'

And it wasn't far from the truth. The IRA's chief source of arms and ammunition had been the lonely police barracks, but the past year had seen them all burned out and abandoned. That left the army and the Tans, whose bases weren't nearly so vulnerable to pillaging.

'There's talk of shipments coming from America. Machine-guns and all. I wouldn't know,' said Hawkes, 'And I wouldn't be holding my breath either.'

'So what am I to do here? And more to the point: why am I still here? It's been a week!'

'I've been at this three years and you're complaining about a week. Jesus. Look, just keep the lads busy a while. Drill them. Make soldiers out of them as much as you can. Mossie has an idea. It won't be long.'

66

They came in their Crossley Tenders,
Their rifles were loaded with shot,
And the Irish Republican Army
Made shite of the whole fucking lot.

—'The Boys of Kilmichael' (alternative version)

Easter had come and gone. The air still had a bite to it but it was already hard to remember the gloom of the winter months.

'There's a grand stretch in the evenings,' said Joe Hawkes, in his capacity as liaison, outlining the operational situation for the Irish Republican Army in the northern part of the county.

'And that's no good for us at all.'

The kitchen, where up to now the most important thing had been the tending of the fire and the boiling of the kettle, had become the guerrilla headquarters it was supposed to be.

'The long nights were good for us. The Tans don't know the country like we do and they don't like the dark and the wet. Mossie wants us to get in one good dig at them now before it gets too bright. Do you know Canty's Cross?'

'Of course I do,' said Billy Deasy.

'Afraid not,' said Wyndham.

'Mossie wants you at Canty's Cross the day after tomorrow. Get there before dawn. Nothing's likely to happen until late in the morning, but you'll need to be in position well before then.'

'Is there to be an ambush?' said Deasy, wide-eyed. He had been doing his best to look grave and steely but all pretence of maturity vanished in an instant.

'There is, but settle down. It's Mossie's ambush. Be quiet and I'll tell you.'

For want of a map, Hawkes traced a cross on the kitchen table with his finger.

'Every day – or nearly every day as far as we can tell – a Tan patrol comes this way. Straight through, heading towards Fermoy. Mossie doesn't want them to go straight through. He wants them to turn right. Canty's Cross isn't a good place for an ambush at all, but there's a lovely bit of a bend in the road about a mile on the right.'

'I know it,' said Deasy, planting himself firmly in the strategic picture.

'You'll stay well away from it,' said Hawkes. 'Canty's Cross is where Mossie wants you. Wednesday morning, early. He wants the road to Fermoy closed. Get a trench dug across. Don't let yourselves be seen. No shooting. Just make sure the Tans turn right and then you come home again like good lads.'

Deasy nodded like a man. It was not to be his hour of glory, but he had his part to play.

'And what about me?' said Wyndham.

'What about you?' said Hawkes. 'What do you think? You're going along with Billy and the lads. Surely be to God you know how to supervise the siting of a trench.'

Wyndham had been sent off on worse missions by better men in his time. The great virtue of this plan was its simplicity. The greater virtue was that there was to be no shooting. If he allowed himself a little optimism he could even believe that success in this venture would convince the IRA that he'd done his job well and could go home.

Through a long Tuesday, the eve of the operation, he worked

over the preparations. Scant resources and a flimsy command structure were things he would just have to live with. Secrecy was his worry. The boys of Billy Deasy's unit were excited to the point of nausea at the prospect of the ambush. Wyndham thought it best to keep them all under his eye lest they be blathering and boasting all around the district. That, of course, meant that he had to suffer their company all through the day while they suffered from fretful boredom.

He had them check their weapons but there weren't enough weapons and he was afraid of someone getting hurt. He lined them up for close-order drill. Largely pointless, but it passed the time.

'Where's Liam?'

'His father needed him at home, sir.'

'Is he likely to talk?'

'He doesn't know anything, sir. *I* don't know anything except that we're going out tonight.'

'Is it really an ambush, sir? A real ambush?'

Wyndham, who'd been giving them rather too much of Corporals Sheehan, Moriarty and Raffaelli, thought to try a little Colonel Fitzmullen-Brophy on them for a change.

'Settle down, men. The less you know the better – for the time being at least. All I can safely tell you is that tonight we will be taking the fight to the enemy. We will be hitting him where it hurts. It will call for cool heads and steady nerves I trust I can count on each man here to do his duty to the utmost of his ability.'

He didn't know whether to be dismayed or pleased that they took him seriously. They even contrived to look stern and grown-up when he added, 'God save Ireland'.

Night came at last and they set out. It was the first time he'd felt too old for this sort of carry-on.

Too old to be up and about at this hour; too old to be out with a gang of adventurous lads almost impossible to keep quiet; too old for stumbling across dark countryside in unsuitable clothes and shoes that let in the wet. As soon as he got the permission or the nerve he was going to return to civil life, get married and leave the war for Ireland's independence to the younger generation.

Not knowing the lay of the land, he let Deasy take the lead, and Deasy wasn't going to lead them by any direct path. Never mind the tactical necessities: taking the easy way would have been contrary to the spirit of the endeavour. So instead of a firm road leading them to Canty's Cross, there was the field to traverse, the stone wall to be climbed over, the ditch to be negotiated, and wet brambles to be crouched in when distant dogs challenged. It all took far longer than planned.

Canty's Cross, when they reached it, could have been anywhere. It was merely a crossroads, with a single house not far off.

The boys had brought a shovel and a spade with them. They didn't want to, but given that there weren't enough weapons, they might as well have *something* to carry. Besides, Wyndham assured them, it would allay suspicion by making them look like working men. This was all well and good, except that a shovel and spade were inadequate to the task of digging a trench across a metalled road.

'I thought of that,' said Deasy confidently. 'It'll be no bother at all. We can just get a pickaxe or something from the house there.

Where the houseowner stood on Irish independence was unclear, but regarding being woken up in the early hours by a juvenile IRA unit demanding to requisition his tools, his position was plain. He was against it.

'In the name of the Irish Republic—,' Deasy said for the third time.

'To hell with you!' shouted the old man, his nightshirt stuffed into his trousers, his braces around his knees. 'Get away out of that, you dirty young scut!'

But what hindered the bold guerrillas was not the old man's obstinacy but his lack of a pickaxe. He stood there with a smile of bitter triumph as the boys went through his shed.

'How about a sledgehammer and a good big crowbar?' said Deasy, getting desperate.

'You can keep on looking, and much good it may do you,' said the old man.

It was already getting light. Wyndham had to give credit to young Deasy for coming up with a solution.

'We don't need a trench. We just need a roadblock. Get hold of that old barrel there. We'll fill it with earth and stones and leave it in the road.'

And with the old man shaking his fist at them, that's just what they did. Shovelling the barrel full of earth took longer than they'd have thought, but they got it done without being disturbed. There was no traffic beyond a man in a cart and later, a woman on a bicycle. Both were given grim looks by the boys. After two years of this kind of thing, explicit warning was unnecessary. Everyone had a good idea of what happened to informers.

With the centrepiece of the ambush in place, Deasy's confidence wavered.

'Do you think it'll be enough?' he asked Wyndham. 'It looks very small.'

It did look small. Just an ordinary wooden barrel in the middle of a road. They both tried to imagine an army lorry or a Crossley Tender. Would it have room enough to get around the barrel? Might the barrel just be knocked aside?

'I know,' said Wyndham. 'One moment.'

He went back to the house, waved at the old man who was staring daggers at him through the window, and picked up a tangle of rusty fence wire he'd seen earlier. Back at the roadblock he secured one end to the barrel and trailed the other into the roadside bushes.

'Now tell me, Billy boy, if you were a Tan and you saw that wire, might you suspect that there was an electrical detonator at the other end?'

Deasy's eyes widened in admiration. Wyndham savoured the moment.

'If you've seen the Sappers blow up as many bridges as I have, my son – or as any Tan who's served at the front has – then you'll think twice about going anywhere near that barrel. Come on, let's take up our positions. Time's a-wasting.'

The unit dispersed to various points about the crossroads, and with the sun now well up, the dew drying and the excitement of the long night over with, most of them fell asleep despite themselves. Wyndham wasn't particularly worried about them. They were well back from the road and out of sight. Billy Deasy had some sort of idea of making a proper ambush of it if the roadblock proved a failure but Wyndham had been careful to place the boys with any useful weapons off in the long grass where they wouldn't be able to see what was going on or do anyone any harm unless they tried very hard.

'They're our covering force,' he'd assured Deasy. 'They'll guard against unexpected approach and ensure a safe withdrawal when it's all over.'

Now, with the morning slowly passing, only he and Deasy were up forward with a good view of the road, and Deasy was already drowsing. He woke up fast because suddenly Wyndham was lying on top of him.

'Don't make a sound,' Wyndham hissed. *And for the life of you, don't go for your revolver.*

It was a Crossley Tender, growling up the road from the south, pretty much as they'd expected. But then it was two. Wyndham watched through the weeds, his heart in his mouth. If he was this frightened, then he wondered how Deasy and the rest of the boys were. He had comforted himself earlier with the thought that none of them would be trigger-happy. After all, they were unused to weapons, and he'd seen often enough that the instinct of even trained soldiers was to freeze at the first sight of the enemy. More often than not, a man had to be ordered and kicked and screamed at before he'd fire his first shot. *Then* he might get trigger-happy.

The lead vehicle slowed to a stop. They'd seen the barrel in the road. Wyndham watched the man in the passenger seat dismount and wave to the vehicle following. Wyndham couldn't hear what the man was saying but he could see him clearly enough. He could see shape of the cap, at once ridiculous and sinister. He could see the silhouette of the man's legs beneath his short coat, the knees outlined where breeches tightened above tall gaiters.

That sounded the alarm in Wyndham's head. Other ranks didn't wear coats like that, nor breeches either. These were the items such as a gentleman would purchase. That meant that these men weren't regular Tans but Auxies. With a sinking feeling that was almost painful, Wyndham watched them exercise their officer-like initiative and tactical good sense.

He watched a brief conference by the running board. He saw arms pointing and heads nodding, He saw a dozen men spreading out in a skirmish line. That line was going to sweep slowly up the fields around the crossroads, like reapers, only instead of scythes they had with them rifles and repeating shotguns. Even if that old barrel were really filled with gelignite it would make no difference.

Three years earlier he'd been in a similar situation, but rather than ill-armed boys he'd had fragments of the proud old Irish regiments. On the other hand the enemy hadn't been some policemen with a couple of lorries, but a company of German shock-troops with trench mortars and a tank. That day had not gone well. He knew how to do it better this time.

'We're leaving,' he said to Deasy. 'Now! Right now!'

He didn't wait for argument, but led by example. He was running so fast that when he came across young Ryan he couldn't stop in time, and fell over the big lad with the rifle.

'Hold your fire and get out!' he said. 'Tell the others! No one's to shoot! No one, you hear me! We're outnumbered! Now *move!*'

As a military withdrawal it lacked dignity, but Wyndham was very proud of it nonetheless. By the time the Auxies were advancing through the positions just vacated, the IRA were doing a quick headcount under a hedge a whole field away, with everyone present and correct, if somewhat put out. The gallant young commander certainly wasn't happy to be bilked of his first action.

'But what about the plan? What about Mossie's ambush?'

'Billy, a famous German general once said that no plan survives contact with the enemy. To hell with the plan. Mossie can look after himself. He's been in this business long enough.'

'But what do we do now?'

'We disperse. We head back separately. Hide your weapons and get back home. Go on.'

'What about you?'

'I'm too conspicuous. I couldn't blend in with the rest of you. I'll go my own way. Go on. Good luck.'

And after some unsure looks they wished him luck too, and slipped off across the fields.

And that, he thought, *is how you save the day. Now I just have to get the girl.*

He sat in the hedge enjoying a precious cigarette like he had enjoyed few cigarettes before. He wasn't sure how he was going to manage it, but he was heading for Cork, or Tralee if necessary. He would lie low for a few hours and then walk to the nearest railway station. He had maybe just enough money for a third-class ticket. Once back in civilisation he would marshal his resources, which was to say he would get some money and a change of clothes. And then he would find Nora. After that they could flee the country and live happily ever after.

But of course he should have been paying attention to what that German general had said about plans. He wasn't half a mile from Rathcormac before he was arrested.

It was the army that apprehended him, and for that he had every reason to be grateful. He could still consider the army to be his people. Certainly summary execution was not their way (unless there were rather too many German prisoners to be bothered with – but that had been another war in another country). And in fairness to these soldiers, had he been in their place, he'd have apprehended him too. He so clearly looked like a wrong 'un that the men at the checkpoint looked almost pleased to see him. It was just a wooden bar across the road, manned by a junior officer and a handful of men, and it had been a slow morning for them. The officer wore no medals. He'd been too young to have been in the war

'Keep your hands up,' he said, and directed one of his men to hold Wyndham at bayonet point while another searched him.

'Name?' he said.

Wyndham answered in his plummiest voice. 'McCarthy-Moore,' he said with a friendly smile. 'Laurence McCarthy-Moore.' He spoke as one gentleman to another, just passing the time of day, introducing themselves on a morning stroll. And there was no doubt that Laurence McCarthy-Moore had been a thorough gentleman and a most companionable type – before German shrapnel had punched a hole in the back of his head at Loos.

The soldier going through Wyndham's pockets found nothing beyond his wallet, empty except for some folded sheets of paper.

'That's mine,' said Wyndham.

'I'm sure it is,' said the soldier, unfolding it and starting to read.

'*Dear Nora, I miss you most terribly—*' he said.

'That's personal, dammit!'

The grinning soldier read on a bit. 'Cor! You're not wrong there. Personal's not the word.'

'That will do, Bailey,' said the officer. 'Give him back his letter.'

'Yes, sir. Only if this is his personal letter and all, and he says his name's Laurence Mac-whotsit, then why's he signing his name Daniel?'

67

'I am not going there to be imprisoned,' said Dantes; 'it is only used for political prisoners. I have committed no crime. Are there any magistrates or judges at the Château d'If?'
'There are only,' said the gendarme, 'a governor, a garrison, turnkeys, and good thick walls.'

—Alexandre Dumas, *The Count of Monte Cristo*

On a fine spring day Cork harbour was beautiful. To the north was the steep slope of Queenstown with its newly completed cathedral rising spectacularly above the bright seafront. The river threaded its way between green hills and wooded islands. Among the anchored warships and passing liners, little fishing vessels and shabby merchantmen wended their ways from the wooden piers out to the grey-blue ocean.

From Spike Island in the middle of the harbour Wyndham could see none of it. The walls blocked the view. The walls of Fort Westmoreland, built to withstand the roundshot of Napoleon's ships, now caged more than a thousand prisoners: Republicans and suspected Republicans, held without trial or any prospect of release.

There were men who'd been in and out of half the prisons in the United Kingdom since 1916 along with those who had just been out of luck at a given moment.

They dealt with it all as well as they could. Shared ideals did not always translate into companionship. An inspiring street orator could prove insufferable in an enclosed space. A good comrade did not necessarily make a good cellmate – not after months of monotonous deprivation.

The more serious prisoners formed their committees and got on with their war. Those unlucky internees who'd hardly had a political thought in their heads in the outside world got themselves a revolutionary education. They joined the fight out of new-found conviction or just for something to do. Many, of course, joined the Republicans because they did not have the resources to endure imprisonment on their own. There were some men, though, who commanded respect by doing just that. One such loner was Francis Moriarty.

'You think this is bad? You should have been in Limburg. This is nothing, boy.'

'So you've said. But how did you end up here in the first place? Mossie Henebry told me that he saw you safe on your way home.'

'Henebry told you that? He did on his arse see me home. He promised he'd let me go, but first he wanted me out teaching musketry and drill to some young eejits in Bally-go-backwards. The Tans lifted me and I've been here since February.'

'Have you seen a lawyer?' said Wyndham. 'Have you been before a judge?'

Moriarty gave him a pitying look. 'Do you think they allowed me a lawyer in Limburg? You're a prisoner of war, boy, and you're here till the war's over.'

The farthest up the ladder of the judiciary that Wyndham could reach was a sergeant of the garrison artillery. The man was just about sympathetic enough to lend Wyndham an ear, but that was as far as he went.

'Don't make me laugh, son. Try writing to your MP about it.'

'Could I perhaps get an interview with the commanding officer?'

'If you're willing to wait a few months, I expect.'

'But what about *habeas corpus*?'

'He's in C Block, with the rest of the awkward buggers who thought they could play the barrack-lawyer. You be a good little prisoner now and they'll let you out whenever the king decides you've learned your lesson.'

Of course Wyndham didn't have a member of parliament to write to, but there was a United States consul in Dublin who, after long delay, replied that note had been taken of Mr. Wyndham's case and details were being forwarded to the embassy in London.

'That means your name will go on a list and the list will go in a drawer, and someone will lose the key to the drawer,' said a learned IRA prisoner to whom Wyndham was referred.

'But I'm an American citizen in distress!'

'So you are, and so is Benny Tierney in the next hut over. And so is Éamon de Valera. And think of all the hundreds of thousands of American citizens who are reaching deep into their pockets to keep us going. Listen to me, Mr Wyndham: your Uncle Sam has enough bother with Ireland as it is, and he'd be very happy to pretend he's never heard of you. He's certainly not going to be writing complaints to Lloyd George on your behalf.'

So with little else to do, Wyndham made the best of things.

The accommodation was cold, primitive, and overcrowded, but no worse than many a billet he had known in the army. The prisoners were kept in the old stone barracks or the wartime huts, and there was much competitive argument as to which was more wretched. All was fenced in – a barbed wire compound within a stone fortress. The food was indeed better and more plentiful than what Moriarty had been served in Limburg, but no one ever came to an internment camp for the food. Besides that, the preparation and consumption of food didn't take up nearly enough hours of the day.

To combat the boredom Wyndham read every scrap of everything that was to be found in the camp. He attended political debates. He even (and it took little enough prompting) gave a lecture on Irish mythology which was well attended and, as far as he could judge, well received.

'Of course it was,' said Moriarty. 'It wasn't as if you were having to share the bill with Charlie Chaplin or a row of chorus girls doing high kicks.'

He made another stab at learning the Irish language. He learned how to decipher simple patriotic exhortations and he added to his stock of small phrases, but that was as far as it went. The language was not a basis for conversation. It was a political tool. For those who were fluent, it was the medium of conspiracy. For everyone else it was a bludgeon with which to belabour the English. As it happened, the camp guards were mostly Scots – two reluctant platoons of the Cameron Highlanders detailed to this dreary duty – but that didn't keep them from being assailed with Irish slogans and songs.

The great song of defiance and solidarity, and the first song that Wyndham learned was *Amhrán na bhFiann*, the Soldiers' Song. It was howled through the barbed wire in protest. It was sung in solemnity on every special occasion. Wyndham would join in, pledging his life to Ireland, where Ireland meant Nora. For him Ireland was not a dark-eyed Kathleen Mavourneen who had four green fields, but a tall redhead with a Browning automatic in her handbag. When he could find the paper he wrote her long letters that, not knowing where to find her, he never sent.

For exercise he even took up the game of hurling, although sports had long proven his enemy. It wasn't that he was clumsy or ill-suited to teamsmanship: it was that he could never, in the heat of the moment, remember the essentials. Back in Knocknahanna, where Colonel Fitzmullen-Brophy expected all his officers to tog out and play the game (any game except hurling, that is),

Lieutenant Wyndham was notorious for forgetting at crucial moments the essential differences between Association and Rugby football. He was the battalion's master of the own goal and the unforced error. Here on Spike he he wasn't nearly so bad. Possibly those earlier efforts had laid a solid foundation. Possibly it was because it was all there was to do here, but he was picking up the fundamentals of stick and ball surprisingly well.

He wasn't there the day a player was shot dead, though.

The man was trying to retrieve a ball from under the wire when he was killed by a nervous sentry. The next day a guard of honour was formed by the dead man's cellmates and when *Amhrán na bhFiann* was sung it was sung as a dirge.

'Y'know,' said Moriarty, 'if he really had been trying to get through the wire where the ball was, he'd only have got himself back to his own hut. They should hang that bloody sentry.'

'It could have been me,' said Wyndham.

'*How?* Jesus, it's a sorry team that'd ever pick you for their side.'

68

The more men there are in the country who have been through the mill in the jails, the harder will England find it to govern this country hereafter.

—Kevin O'Higgins, August 1918

His Majesty's government had always been loath to refer to the state of affairs in Ireland as a war. Now they were faced with admitting that they couldn't win it. Despite feeding ever more troops and police into the country for more than two years, spending fortunes and alienating public support, they had proved unable to defeat a few thousand guerrillas backed up by a population unaccountably willing to provide them moral and practical sustenance. Coincidentally, as the government was reluctantly reaching this conclusion, the IRA was weighing up its own prospects and blanching at the answer arrived at. The few thousand guerrillas in 1921 were not the same men who had started the fight in 1919. Those men were dead or in prison now. The leaders of the Irish Republic were scraping for just a little more money, a little more ammunition and a few more men to continue the fight, and were seeing the bottom of barrel coming into view.

In July a truce was agreed. For the exhausted Republic it was an immense victory. They may not have fought the British empire to a standstill, as many boasted, but the rebels had obliged the powers in Whitehall to negotiate, and compromise, and treat with them as though they were a power in and of themselves. It was no small achievement for a band of men (and a handful of women) who had no more public standing than to have appeared on wanted posters.

The rejoicing was general throughout the country. In the prisons and internment camps it was euphoric – until the terms of the truce were made clear, that is.

It was merely a truce – a temporary cessation of hostilities. Neither side was backing down. This wouldn't be like November 1918, when the Germans had agreed to withdraw from France and Belgium. For as long as negotiations for a permanent treaty continued, the British forces would be remaining in Ireland.

And their prisoners were staying in prison.

Hopes were high when Irish delegates went to London, but they sank steadily as the weeks went by with no progress being reported. Discontent deepened as summer waned. In October the internees rioted, and the authorities responded by driving them from their huts and penning them in the dry moat. After three days without shelter, the ringleaders and troublemakers were rooted out and transferred to other prisons. Wyndham, who had never been any trouble at all, was left on the island. On his release from the moat he was faced with the splintered furniture and all the wreckage that the rioters had made of the hut.

'I have to get out of here,' he said. 'I have to find Nora.'

Moriarty shook his head. 'Most men would be grateful for the chance of getting away from a woman like that,' he said.

'Moriarty,' said Wyndham, 'I would never talk to you again if you weren't going to help me escape.'

Unusually, escape was something Wyndham and Moriarty agreed on. Where Wyndham had reasons of the heart, Moriarty was merely desperate for freedom. As he said himself, he'd spent too much of his life behind wire as it was, and he was damned if he was going to wait however long for a shower of langers in

London to decide when he could go home. Wyndham had grown so used to the slouching, loitering, grumbling Moriarty that it was a surprise to see him animated by anything.

There had been escapes from Spike Island. Just before Wyndham arrived some men, facing the death penalty if their real identities had been revealed, had made it out just before the informer could point the finger.

'Sure all you need is a boat,' said Moriarty.

'It's a harbour,' said Wyndham. 'There are boats all over the place.'

'And it's not even that far to the next bit of land if it comes down to it. Can you swim?'

'I don't know. How hard can it be?'

'Sure once we're beyond the wall you can just flag down a passing Cunard liner if you have to. Get all the way back to America in one go.'

'I'm not going back to America. Not yet.'

Because Wyndham had had a letter from Nora. It had taken months, but the IRA intelligence network had proven its worth. A few days before the riot a grubby note, folded and refolded so that it would fit into a matchbox while still leaving room for the matches, had been handed to him.

Dear Dan,
They told me where you are. I can't tell you where I am. I
hope you are well.
Love,
Nora

Of course, knowing how many eyes might see that message, she hadn't dared to say more, but Wyndham knew that Nora had put her heart in that matchbox. He would find her.

'I'm not going home without her,' he said.

'Fair enough. So we just need to get across to the mainland and then we can get the train or hitch a lift back to Cork.'

'It'll have to be a lift. I don't have money for the train.'

'Ah, we can walk it if we have to. Once we're out, we're out. We can't be re-arrested because of the truce.'

'So now we just have to get out of the compound, through the wire and over the wall.'

'That's all.'

'I think we need to have a word with your Sergeant Dunstan. The sooner the better.'

It was Sergeant Dunstan, Royal Garrison Artillery, who'd advised Wyndham to write to his MP. Unlike the Highlanders who guarded the prisoners, the artillerymen were there to guard the harbour. They were the fort's permanent residents and had nothing to do with its role as a military prison. They would be there no matter which way the political winds blew. The families of the married men even lived on the island.

Sergeant Dunstan was not married, nor had he any taste for politics, nor did he care to have his fort filled up with Shinners and Scotchies. He was a sympathetic man, however, and surprisingly, when he demonstrated his sympathies, they were for the former rather than the latter – for the prisoners over their warders.

It had happened that Moriarty, uncooperative as usual, had fallen foul of a too-officious Highland corporal. Moriarty had been in no hurry to comply with the order to return to barracks. He'd kept his hands in his pockets and addressed no one in particular.

'Jesus, but you'd wonder what the world's coming to. I was fighting in Flanders when he was in short pants and now look at him – a corporal and no pants at all.'

'Pick up your feet, Paddy, or you'll be feeling the toe of my boot!'

'What have you got against us at all, boy? Why aren't you fighting against the English like a good man?'

The Scots had heard it all before. This one certainly wasn't going to be tempted into Celtic solidarity by the likes of Moriarty. Then Sergeant Dunstan had intervened before the corporal's barking and growling had led to biting.

It had been the mention of Flanders that had done it. He was an old soldier with an old soldier's heart, and he regarded a ragged veteran more highly than a spruce rookie with no ribbons on his tunic. And more than that, Sergeant Dunstan harboured a sentimental fellow-feeling for the Irish.

'My dear old mum came from Athlone,' as he was wont to confide whenever the question arose. So, for the sake of the men who'd held the line at Wipers he'd put a protective wing around Moriarty, and for the sake of his old mum he'd appeared in Moriarty's hut when the truce was declared, bearing bottles of beer to toast Irish freedom.

Wyndham had been a beneficiary of this acquaintanceship, but now he was thinking that there was more to be got out of it than a tin mug of warmish beer.

'Don't like to hear the Irish being called Paddy. Not when it's meant unkindly.'

Moriarty and Wyndham were in Sergeant Dunstan's quarters. It had taken a fortnight of heroic wangling on the part of Moriarty but he'd won through in the end. It was an impromptu veterans' association, with a dollop of whiskey to liven up the tea, and a lot of maudlin feeling mixed with the tobacco smoke. Tonight it was their own soldiers' song.

The room was impersonal, with not so much as a snapshot stuck on the whitewashed wall. It occurred to Wyndham that the prisoners weren't the only ones suffering boredom.

'My dear old mum,' said Sergeant Dunstan, squinting into

his mug. 'Come from Athlone, she did. Named me Patrick, God bless her. It's where she met my dad. Miserable old sod. Battery sergeant-major, he was. Course I was going to join the army, but I was dead set on joining the Irish Guards, just to spite the old bastard. They'd just been started up. You'd see the posters. Who knows? Might have tried the Munsters instead if the Guards hadn't been there.'

'Ah,' said Moriarty, 'You're comparing a carthorse to a racehorse, only it's a prettified carthorse. The Guards are alright in their own way, but what are they good for when you get down to it? They look nice outside the palace, I'll grant you.'

'Hardly matters one way or the other though, does it? Wasn't tall enough for the Guards, was I? Became a gunner after all. Spite the old man that way. Battery sergeant-major? I'll be a regimental quartermaster-sergeant if I stick it out a few more years. I'd make the old man salute me, I would – if he wasn't dead, that is.'

'Well here's to the Royal Artillery,' said Wyndham. 'I'd have left my bones in France without them.'

'Well said, Mr. Wyndham, and very kind of you to say so. And here's to the Munsters. Let me have your mug.'

Wyndham was of course Mister because once an officer, always a gentleman. He could sit here and tell old war stories and regimental lies until the sun came up, if necessary, but the plan was to do it only until Sergeant Dunstan fell asleep.

'What if we fall asleep first?' Wyndham had asked.

'You? Mad Dan Wyndham with his hollow leg? You could have drunk 16th Division under the table in your prime.'

'My prime is quite a way behind me.'

'Doesn't matter. Two Munsters can out-drink one gunner any night of the week. Then we get his keys and get out, and if we can't get out we can make an impression in candle wax. I know a fella who can work keys up out of that.'

If it came down to it, they'd decided, they would take the

unconscious sergeant's cap and greatcoat and bluff their way out under that disguise.

And now Sergeant Dunstan's eyes were drooping and his chin was heavy on his chest. The two ex-fusiliers leaned forward expectantly. The sergeant was suddenly wide awake.

'Gentlemen,' he said, 'this won't do at all. I'm keeping you from your beds. Got to be bright-eyed for morning parade, eh? I'll see you back. Can't have prisoners at large after dark.'

They tried a different tack the next time they had a chance. On a fine autumn morning Wyndham greeted Sergeant Dunstan as if they were neighbours and, as if they were neighbours, he talked about the weather.

'Shame to be cooped up on a day like this. I imagine we won't get much more like it until spring. I was wondering, Sergeant—'

'Yes?'

'I was wondering if there were some chance of outdoor work. It's Moriarty. He feels the confinement badly. It was the trenches, of course – that feeling of being hemmed in. And then that prison camp in Germany.'

But, alas, such a thing could not be allowed: not since some men had tried to escape while mowing the officers' golf course.

'No prisoners outside the walls anymore, Mr. Wyndham, but I'll tell you what. You let Moriarty know that I'll find him a job all the same. Nothing like a bit of honest sweat to chase off the blue devils.'

Moriarty heartily cursed Wyndham for the way things turned out but, as it happened, the manual labour paid its dividends. Moriarty, while clearing weeds and carting rubbish, made a discovery that was enough to make Wyndham volunteer to join in the work. They even went so far as to approach Sergeant Dunstan again to ask for even more work.

'That alcove is clogged full of all sorts,' explained Moriarty.

'God knows how long they've been dumping stuff in there. The two of us can get it cleared out for you.'

As it happened, the alcove in question was nothing of the sort. Instead, it was one end of a short tunnel that led to a sally port. Their brief confinement in the moat had revealed to them the other end. An IRA officer who'd been comprehensively mapping the camp's layout confirmed this. The rubbish was the only obstacle to freedom. That being the case, the IRA claimed eminent domain over the project and got seven men out one night without so much as a 'thank you' to Wyndham or Moriarty.

That was in November. How could it be November already? How much of his life would he spend incarcerated on this godforsaken rock? Wyndham considered digging a tunnel but he knew how that would turn out. Edmund Dantès had dug his way into another man's cell, but at least that had led ultimately to wealth and freedom. Wyndham would at best come out on a golf course before the searchlights pinned him. And then? If he ever returned to the world, posing, say, as the Count of Ringaskiddy, he'd find Nora married to someone else.

In this mood he withdrew into himself. If he partook in classes or games at all it was only to kill the hours. He paced the yard in his worn-out shoes and tried not to count the days passing. Oddly, it was Moriarty who kept trying, Moriarty who kept himself going with thoughts of escape. He continued in his cultivation of Sergeant Dunstan, even though he had to physically drag Wyndham along to another night of fortified tea and reminiscences in the sergeant's quarters.

They talked of stations and garrisons from Ireland to China. They polished up tales of terrible NCOs now faded into legend, and of the army as it had been in the older, more heroic age. And when they had done talking they sang: music hall songs, army songs, Irish songs. Sergeant Dunstan, in hoarse baritone and

English accent, sang of Ireland's generations exiled and dead, and he only stopped because he had to blow his nose.

'That's enough of that,' he said. 'We'd better call it a night before we all get the melancholics.'

But the next day he called for them again, only this time, rather than sending an underling with a summons or invitation, he came to their hut in person.

'Hats and coats, the two of you,' he said. 'It's cold out.'

And in march step he led them out of the compound and through the front gate with no more than a peremptory word to the sentries. Unwilling to break the spell, but unable to suppress his curiosity, Wyndham asked the sergeant where they might be going.

'To get a proper drink, Mr. Wyndham. A proper drink in a proper bar. Like men. Step out now – we don't want to miss our boat.'

Such was the way of senior sergeants. Wyndham and Moriarty had both seen it in their time. Such men knew exactly which rules could be broken and when it could be got away with. As the ferry's lines were cast off, they shot anxious looks at each other as if they could cook up a plan without speaking.

A squeeze through a lavatory window. A sudden break down an alleyway. A sharp blow to Dunstan's head, if it came down to it. The possibilities were endless. But when they came to the quay on Queenstown there was no thought of running just yet. They were both too cold to move. Whiskies first. Then escape.

Sergeant Dunstan marched them into the sort of bar always chosen by men of his rank. *Lounge bar for commercial travellers and tarts: saloon bar for soldiers of the King.*

It was still early, but there was an atmosphere of merriment that stopped the instant the king's uniform was noticed. The men in the bar stared. Sergeant Dunstan stared right back. He did more than stare. He did an audible headcount as he strode to the bar.

'I make it fifteen,' he said to the barman.

The barman looked back, saying nothing.

'Fifteen and us three,' said Sergeant Dunstan. 'That's eighteen whiskies.'

'Sergeant?' said the barman, but Sergeant Dunstan had turned to address the room.

'All Irishmen here?' he demanded. No one contradicted him. 'And you all drink whiskey, yes?'

He could have been speaking to a tableau. Only the cigarette smoke moved. Sergeant Dunstan picked up the first whiskey.

'Well God save Ireland!' he proclaimed.

And that brought tentative smiles, and hands reaching for the bar. In moments the room was coming to life again.

Sergeant Dunstan handed Wyndham and Moriarty their whiskies.

'Drink up,' he said. 'War's over. They signed a treaty this morning.'

IX

NORA AND KEVIN

Never marry a soldier,
A sailor, or a marine.
But keep your eye
On the Sinn Féin boy
With his yella, white, and green!

—'Salonika' (traditional)

69

Though I am old with wandering
Through hollow lands and hilly lands,
I will find out where she has gone,
And kiss her lips and take her hands;

—W.B. Yeats, 'The Song of Wandering Aengus'

Outside the ruined city centre, Cork was pretty much as he'd left it. Almost exactly a year after he had left, Wyndham returned to the very same hotel, wearing the very same clothes. By coincidence, the proprietor was also dressed in the same clothes as before, only his were of more lavish cut and, past their best though they might have been, had not been patched at seat and knee with army blanket material.

'Mr. Wyndham! Good gracious! We had quite given you up for lost. Where on earth have you been?'

'I've been in prison, Mr. Ballantyne. Tell me: a suitcase I left upstairs a year ago. You haven't pawned it, I hope?'

'Times may be hard, Mr. Wyndham, but I trust I will always remain a stranger to the pawnshop. Nor, I most fervently hope, will I ever sink so low as to make free with another man's suitcase.'

'You are a gentleman, Mr. Ballantyne – one of a vanishing breed. Now if you will excuse me, I am in need of a bath and a lie-down.'

'I fear there may be an insufficiency of hot water, Mr. Wyndham.'

'It is of no matter, Mr. Ballantyne. Might I further trouble you for some writing paper and the price of a postage stamp?'

Mrs. Susan Fitzmullen-Brophy, a rock in this shifting world, wrote back immediately to tell him that he *must* come and stay for Christmas. That much he had hoped for. What came next threw him completely.

I will ask Nora, of course, but I imagine she will be spending Christmas with her own people. Perhaps Boxing Day or New Year? Her work had her darting about so much when she was staying with us that I simply can't imagine pinning her down. You young people live so fast nowadays!

Nora had been staying with the Fitzmullen-Brophys? Nora had not been in jail or in hiding? He had questions.

But on the other hand, Nora had been found! He wouldn't have to hunt through every dark and dangerous corner of revolutionary Ireland to find her! God willing, he would see her soon!

To get himself to Tralee he had to borrow the train fare from Moriarty of all people. Despite having spent many months interned as a suspected enemy of the crown, Moriarty was still in receipt of his army pension. All in all, Wyndham had to admit that that was pretty sporting of King George.

When they'd first been reunited after the war, Nora had met him with a handshake out of pure awkwardness. Now, with the Fitzmullen-Brophys looking on, she offered him both her hands which he took in both of his. He could hardly do more, her elbows being locked so stiff as to fend off any closer approach. Her face bore the suspicious frown she used for every occasion that found her at a disadvantage, then it flickered into an experimental smile, and then she embraced him so hard as to drive the wind out of him. She broke contact just as suddenly – the action an electric shock for both of them. She turned bright pink, unable to speak. He was the very same.

'Hello, Dan,' she just about managed.

'Hello, Nora.'

Mrs. Fitzmullen-Brophy looked proud, having once again succeeded in bringing a little rightness into a muddled world. Her husband was looking away, making great play with his handkerchief.

The colonel appeared to be understanding of Wyndham's trouble this past year. After all, hadn't he been arrested himself? As for Nora, the Fitzmullen-Brophys were under the impression that she still worked for the post office, which was understandable, given the extravagant lies that she fed them without qualm.

It was New Year's Eve, and Molly was staying in Dublin with her own family. In her stead, the role of daughter of the house seemed to have been assumed quite comfortably by Nora. Small wonder, since she had lived more than a month under this roof since the Truce.

'Molly and I have become great friends,' she said.

'And Nora was such a help,' said Mrs. Fitzmullen-Brophy. 'Having been a nurse, I mean.'

'Molly is expecting again,' explained Nora. 'She was a little ill.'

There were embarrassed smiles all round.

The colonel hastily raised his glass. 'A new grandchild in the new year, what?'

Wyndham was quick to raise his own. 'Hear, hear, sir! Congratulations to you both and the best of luck to Molly!'

'And born into a new country, eh? The first generation to grow up in this Irish Free State.' And although he was still smiling, he couldn't keep the trace of doubt from his voice. Peace was all well and good, but what *was* this new Ireland? Would it be worth all the bally upset? Would there be a place for old-fashioned fellows like himself?

In the last hour of 1921 Wyndham walked in the freezing garden with a maker of this new Ireland and a willing agent of all the bally upset.

'You never wrote,' he said, getting it off his chest at last.

'I did too write!' And as his silent reproach registered with her: 'Well, I meant to write. Honestly I did. But you know me. I'm no good with letters and things. Anyway, by the time I found out where you were I was sure you'd be out soon.'

She sensed this was not thawing much ice.

'I did sit down one night and I wrote pages and pages. All about what was happening and how much I was missing you. But I tore it up. Sorry. I was mortified thinking of some guard reading it. Anyway, there were all sorts of things I just wouldn't have been allowed to say. There might have been all sorts of trouble if one of us said too much and they put two and two together.'

'How? What? The Truce came into effect in July! That was nearly five months and only one little note from you! It wasn't as if I was under an assumed name or you were still on the run! This is Macedonia all over again!'

'You wouldn't understand.'

'Might my lack of understanding have anything to do with your telling me precisely nothing?'

'Well I can hardly go around chattering about what I do, can I? I mean, here? I mean with the colonel being a colonel and everything? Really, Dan.'

'Nora, will you please tell me why you've been letting me languish all these months? Please? Or will I just go home to Massachusetts and marry Penelope van Wyngarden instead?'

'Michael Collins,' she said.

'*What?*'

'Don't interrupt. I'm explaining. Michael Collins.'

'The man who signed the Treaty. I've heard you speak of him admiringly. What about him?'

'I nearly met him once.' She smiled a wicked little smile. 'Maybe it's better I didn't. They say he has an irresistible way with women.'

'So you're not having an affair with Michael Collins. I'm so very glad to hear it.'

'He *is* very handsome, though – even from a distance.'

'I fear your revolutionary fervour is getting the better of you, Nora. I've seen his picture in the papers. He looks ordinary enough to me.'

'But you've seen his picture!'

'Yes. And?'

'Well ask yourself this: did you ever see a photograph of the man before the Truce?'

Wyndham thought, and shook his head. 'Does it matter?' he said.

'Of course it does! He was our director of intelligence from the beginning. He was the most wanted man in the British Empire. *And Dublin Castle didn't have a photograph of him.* All they could put on the wanted posters was a description. Do you see?'

'I'm afraid not. No. Not at all.'

'It's all different now. Now his face is in the papers.'

'And that's why you've been carrying on with your secret activities?

'Exactly!'

'Nora, are you perhaps making fun of me?'

'Daniel Wyndham, you are being wilfully stupid.'

'I believe "obtuse" is the word you're looking for.'

'I believe "stupid" will do me very well, thank you. I'm just using Michael Collins as an example. Listen. The Truce brought us all out into the open. Secrecy was our greatest strength. That's gone now. It might be all our faces in the papers now – only it's not faces. It's safe houses and arms dumps and everything. The British know all about us now. That's why they agreed to a truce. It was just to lull us.'

'It seems a funny way to go about things.'

'Well it's a fact. That's why Kevin has us—'

'Kevin?'

'Kevin Shanahan, my commanding officer – sort of. He has us reorganising. Rebuilding a whole IRA network in this part Kerry so that we'll be ready when the shooting starts again.'

'But the shooting isn't going to start again. There's a treaty.'

'The Treaty's nonsense. Michael Collins would never have signed it if he believed otherwise. I mean why would he? All this time fighting for a republic and he meekly agrees to this Free State rubbish? Hardly.'

'I'm not sure I follow your argument, and besides, this Free State doesn't sound too bad.'

'Not too bad? How can you say that when you did seven months in jail for the Republic?'

'I didn't *actually* do it for—'

'Do you think the country will settle for dominion status instead of a republic? After all we've gone through are we to be no better than *Canada?*'

'I'm sure Canada has its good points.'

She gave him a withering look, and then they heard Mrs. Fitzmullen-Brophy calling.

'Come inside you two! Hugh is going to open the champagne!'

Nora composed herself and took a last drag on her cigarette. Wyndham offered her his arm.

'They've put you in your old room?' she asked. 'That's where they put me when I was staying.'

'You might get confused – might think you were still sleeping there.'

'I might. The landing's very dark, and you know how champagne goes to my head.'

The next morning Fitzmullen-Brophys tactfully took themselves off on a round of New Year visits. The young couple were left to discuss matters more important than the fate of Ireland.

'I should meet your family,' said Wyndham.

She made a face. 'Oh, Dan, no.'

'Really, Nora. I mean they'll soon be my family – in a manner of speaking.'

'I'd really sooner you didn't. Not for the present at least.'

He watched her squirm and he understood.

'You still haven't told them about us getting married, have you? I bet you've never even mentioned me.'

'I was thinking I could send them a postcard. After the wedding?'

'They can't be that bad.'

'They're not. But maybe I am. It's just that you're my business. I don't want them to make it all theirs.'

He thought about his own family. They had sent him tentative congratulations but their unspoken reservation was plain. Running off and joining the army had been one thing. By 1917, boys from perfectly respectable families had been doing it in droves. But marrying an Irish girl? Another matter entirely – regardless of reassurances concerning the young lady's standing and religion.

'Couldn't I just keep you to myself a while longer?' she said.

'Your jealousy warms my heart, but I think a postcard is a poor substitute for a wedding invitation. Besides, you would yourself admit that letters and postcards are not your strong suit.'

She scowled just long enough to make him regret having said anything, and then suddenly brightened.

'*I* know!' she said. 'Let's go upstairs!'

It was possibly the best idea he'd ever heard.

'So when *are* we going to get married?' he asked.

'I don't know. What day is today?'

'It's still Sunday.'

'I'll be tearing busy all this week. The week after too, probably. Kevin says we have to move fast before they vote on the Treaty. The Dáil meets again on Tuesday. Things will get mad after that.'

'Well seeing as I wasn't thinking of setting the date for *right now*, I suppose we can wait until things aren't so mad.'

'I don't know. Summer? Kevin says it will all be over one way or another by then.'

And already Wyndham was thinking that he was hearing rather too much of this Kevin character.

'I should warn you that I might be penniless,' he said. 'If my bank in Tralee hasn't been robbed by the Black and Tans and if I can convince them that I am who I say I am, I might be able to keep us out of the poorhouse for a few months, but you won't be marrying a wealthy man.'

'Couldn't you just dig out your old uniform and rob the bank yourself?'

'I'll consider it. Mr. Ballantyne is taking me back in the hotel. He didn't mention money. I don't think he has any. But it's bed and board for the time being.'

'Make sure you get a good bed at least. I'll be coming to visit when I can. What time is it? Do you think we have time for more sojourning before the FitzEms get back?'

70

We are against.

—Éamon de Valera, 10 January 1922

Freedom did not come as a bright dawn, illuminating a world transformed. Maybe it would have been different if independence hadn't come in midwinter. A coat of green paint was applied to post boxes and other such things that had previously been red. The words *Saorstát Éireann* – Irish Free State – were stamped or stencilled on various papers. Beyond that it was hard to see what the struggle had brought about. Wyndham had his first proper view of the new dispensation when he was cycling along a country road. He heard a motor lorry coming towards him and moved in towards the verge. When a Crossley Tender came into view he froze and nearly toppled over. But it wasn't the Tans. The Tans were being steadily withdrawn, and they certainly did no more patrolling. He saw steel helmets and recognised the army, but he got the wrong army. The helmets had been repainted in green, white, and orange. The lorry had the letters IRA displayed prominently in white on all sides. His wits barely recovered, Wyndham saluted them as they went by. It was astonishing to see the hidden men out in the open – astonishing, and worrisome too.

Thanks to the application of paint, he knew who these men were. He just wasn't sure what side they were on.

The Treaty that had been signed in London in early December was ratified in Dublin a month later. For an agreement that brought an end to years of strife, it proved wonderfully unsatisfactory. It was a compromise in which all parties felt the loss more than the gain. Under its terms the British would withdraw from Ireland, which would become not one but two independent states. The six predominantly unionist counties in north-east Ulster would become a self-governing state within the United Kingdom. In other words, those who had fought tooth and nail against Home Rule now had it thrust upon them, like it or not.

The rest of the country, predominantly nationalist, would become an Irish Free State, still nominally subject to the crown but otherwise free to go its own way – like Canada or Australia – only with six counties missing. For nationalists north of the new border and for unionists south, it was an abandonment and a betrayal. In the north, the aggrieved Protestants took it out on the Catholic minority, now unprotected by a Whitehall government. The rest of the country was largely and blessedly free of sectarian persecution, but the new Dublin government had troubles nonetheless. The biggest of these was that the Treaty had not brought them the one thing they'd been fighting for: a republic.

In short, no one had got what they wanted. The unionists lost the Union, the country lost six counties, the British lost Ireland and – and this was the bone in the throat of anyone who'd voted for Sinn Féin – the Republicans lost the republic.

Some shook their heads in regret. They recognised the political realities. They heard Lloyd George's threat of immediate and terrible war. They got on with things.

Others were less forgiving. They saw a victory in the field signed away at the conference table. They saw treason. It was the country's great misfortune that the latter camp was headed by Éamon de Valera, president of Sinn Féin. He refused to ratify the Treaty and refused to have anything more to do with the government that ended up voting for it. A majority of the IRA stood solidly behind him.

So the men who'd driven past Wyndham might have been the

legal successors to the British soldiers and police, or they might still be adhering most uncompromisingly to the R in IRA.

Because the government in Dublin could not remain at odds with its own army, and could not win it over without renewing the fight with Britain, a new army was raised. In contrast to the IRA they wore proper uniforms (when available) and they marched in step behind men with recognisable rank badges (when properly trained). The British troops didn't care much about the difference. Not wishing to stay in Ireland any longer, they were apt to hand over their barracks to the first armed Irishmen to arrive and ask for the keys.

In February they surrendered Ballymullen Barracks in Tralee to the IRA. Hugh Fitzmullen-Brophy was there to see it. It didn't matter a damn to him whether the new occupiers were for or against the Treaty. He barely looked at them. He stood at the gate, his hat raised in precise salute, as the Munster Fusiliers marched out. It was only the depot company. The regiment was abroad, doing what it always did – one battalion in Silesia ensuring that a disordered Europe abided by the settlement imposed at the war's end, and the other in Egypt, maintaining the empire's power and prestige. But even if the Munsters were away, Tralee had been their home. Rarely visited, regarded with scant affection, but home nonetheless.

Fitzmullen-Brophy shed not a tear. His lip did not quiver. He might have been cast in bronze. But anyone who knew him knew that he was watching his world die.

71

O god, the heathen are come into thine inheritance; thy holy temple have they defiled.

—Psalm 79:1

'There, there,' said Mrs. Fitzmullen-Brophy over lunch.

The colonel patted his wife's hand and forced a smile. 'Nothing lasts forever, old thing,' he said, and might have said more, but didn't.

Wyndham failed to think of something consoling. He had come to Kerry to meet Nora. It was the first time they had set eyes on each other in weeks. He felt guilty for not having been there to stand beside the colonel, and he felt guilty for not caring about it as much as he should. His ties to the regiment had unravelled over time.

Nora was arranging her face in furrows of sympathy, but knew that if she said anything then she deserved to be struck dead for flagrant hypocrisy.

'Perhaps you can go back and finish the history you were writing with Daniel?' said Mrs. Fitzmullen-Brophy.

'I think I might leave it to a better man,' said her husband. 'Especially now that it's all up with the old barracks. I mean, I can't imagine those Fenian ruffians would be pleased to let me have the run of any papers that might have been left behind.'

'Oh come now, Colonel,' said Nora, and Wyndham's heart fell. 'They're hardly ruffians, are they?'

Fitzmullen-Brophy looked at her in incomprehension. 'But I saw them, my dear. Tricked out like bandits and gangsters. And yes, yes – I know they're irregulars by nature and such troops can't be expected to put on a good show, but I mean *really*. And not a shred of legality to their name, you know.'

'Legality, Colonel?'

'Well those fellows are dead set against the Treaty, and say what you will about it, but the Treaty's the law of the land now.'

'Maybe so, but it's not the will of the people.' She said it like it was a legal formula she was proud to have memorised, and prouder to have a chance to trot it out. 'And if the past few years have proven nothing else, they've proven that it's the people's will that comes first and the law had better catch up quick.'

'I'm afraid I don't follow you, my dear.'

'It's very simple, Colonel. The Irish people voted for de Valera, and de Valera is rejecting the Treaty. That means the Treaty isn't binding.'

Fitzmullen-Brophy was flummoxed. Nora was a sensible young lady. A fine head on her shoulders. Drove an ambulance during the war. Was set to marry young Wyndham. Perfectly sensible. Sensible was all well and good. Women were supposed to be sensible. But it just didn't do for them to meddle in political matters.

'Well that's as may be,' he said, not caring to lose himself in argument, 'but it hardly justifies those IRA fellows from taking over the barracks. I mean, does it?'

'And why not?' said Nora. 'They represent the Republic that people voted for in 1918.'

'Yes well but – that's all been done away with now. That's what the Treaty was all about. The IRA have no *right* to take the barracks, do they? If they assume control of Tralee they're no more than an occupying force.'

'And what were the Munster Fusiliers? *Ow*.'

'I'm very sorry, Nora' said Wyndham. 'That was me kicking you.'

She gave him a hurt and indignant look. She might have got the message but it was already too late. Fitzmullen-Brophy, who a moment before would have been happy to muddle his way out of any argument, had been roused by mention of the regiment.

'*Occupying force?* And what precisely do you mean by that, might I ask?' he said.

Daughter-of-the-house by proxy she might have been, but backing down was not in her, and family rows were meat and drink to Nora Maxfield. Also, her fiancé's kick to her shin was smarting in more ways than one.

'What I mean should be obvious, Colonel. British soldiers are agents of a foreign power. They have no business here.'

'But damn it all—'

'Hugh!'

He moderated his language but didn't pause to apologise.

'The Munsters are Irish! Foreign power, indeed!'

'And what business has an Irishman doing bearing arms in Britain's name? And doing Britain's bidding? In Ireland?'

'Nora!'

'Don't Nora me, Dan Wyndham!'

From there, things went downhill fast. Views better left unspoken were frankly expounded upon. Words were minced less finely than they should have been. Neither Nora nor Fitzmullen-Brophy was skilled in subtle debate and they both had loud voices.

When it was already too late it was brought to an end the same way any fight gets broken up. The combatants were grabbed by those nearest to them and dragged apart. Nora and the colonel weren't quite swinging at each other, but he was tackled by his wife while she was hauled off by her fiancé. Once that had been accomplished, Mrs. Fitzmullen-Brophy and Wyndham swapped places.

Fitzmullen-Brophy was in the garden, pacing. A tall man with a lifetime of practising the thirty-inch cadenced step, he could pace like a master. His face was so stiff that one wouldn't have thought it could speak.

'I'm most fearfully sorry about all that, Colonel,' said Wyndham, keeping his distance. Fitzmullen-Brophy fixed him with a look that lasted far too long, and then he burst out: 'To think that your young lady is a Sinn Feiner, Wyndham! Under my very roof this whole time!'

'Come, sir. It's not as bad as all that. It's just politics, sir, and when does a soldier trouble himself with politics?'

'Politics? *Politics*, man? It has nothing to do with blasted politics! It's about loyalty, damn it all!'

And then the fire went out of him and he slumped down on the garden seat. He took his pipe from his pocket and began jabbing tobacco into the bowl. He might have been slotting cartridges into the chambers of a revolver.

'Please, sir. Nora's a headstrong sort. These are heady times. Let me speak to her. I'm sure she's already regretting speaking with such heat.'

'Heady times?' It was a cry so anguished it was almost a sob. 'Damnable times!'

He put the unlit pipe back in his pocket. He wouldn't look at Wyndham. 'They wouldn't have stood for it, you know! Tummy Belcher would be laughing at me if he saw what we've come to. The times! Everything's gone to the bally dogs. Everything!'

Wyndham was afraid to sit down next to him. He stood with his hand hovering above the colonel's rigid shoulder, not daring to touch.

'It will be all right. Everything will be all right, sir.'

Fitzmullen-Brophy buried his face in his hands.

'A Fenian rebel. Under my very roof.'

The words were muffled, but the weariness was clear. He

looked up then, utterly haggard.

'What have we come to, Dan? My daughter has cut her hair and they're disbanding the regiment!'

It's about loyalty.

Loyalty to one's host? To one's class and co-religionists? Possibly. More like loyalty to a whole panoply of traditions that couldn't be properly expressed because they were beyond question, beyond any examination. And for Fitzmullen-Brophy it was all bundled up in the regiment, because everything was. The regiment was the altar at which he worshipped.

Wyndham remembered the fireside history exercises from that first winter after the war.

We never thought of ourselves as Britain's army, you know – not in the old days. Never thought much at all, really. If anything, we were personal bodyguards to the old queen. We were quite sentimental for a mob of high-spirited young hooligans.

Irishmen in red coats, fighting for the queen; fighting for Ireland; standing up to any foreigner who would slight either. And all ending now.

Politicians in Whitehall deciding that cuts must be made. Doing their cold arithmetic. Reckoning up in shillings and pence the men who had fought and won the war, and deciding that the men could be done without. Ireland was being cut loose, and the Irish regiments could be thrown out with the bathwater.

He found Nora at the front gate, her bag at her feet. She was smoking a cigarette while waiting for the horse and cart that functioned as an occasional taxi in the neighbourhood.

'It's better I go,' she said, without waiting for him to say anything.

'They're lovely people and I don't want to upset them but they're *wrong*, Dan. The British are gone and the army is gone, and good riddance to them both. The sooner the colonel sees that, the better. He might think those Free Staters in Dublin are going to keep everything the way it was but that won't be so. We won't let them. We're tearing up that wretched Treaty and if that means more fighting then so be it. It's better I go. It's better that the Fitzmullen-Brophys don't get mixed up with it.'

She threw down her cigarette as though it annoyed her and folded her arms. Head down, jaw thrust forward, she dared the world to test her.

'Nora, there doesn't have to be any more fighting. I wish you'd see that.'

'The trouble with you, Dan, is that you think a gentleman's word is his bond. You've spent too much time around the colonel. You can't see Lloyd George's sham for what it is.'

'Right. That's it. I'm not going to argue politics with you. Not now – not ever again if I can help it.'

'That's probably for the best,'

'Would you please look at me when I'm talking to you?'

She looked at him. 'I'm still going to marry you, if that's what you're worried about.' She said it without the least trace of affection. 'Just don't think you know better than I do. Don't think I'm some silly thing with a head full of notions.'

'I never did.'

'Good. Here comes the man. Tell Mrs. FitzEm I'm sorry. I already told her, but you can tell her again. Tell the colonel too. Just because he's wrong as anything doesn't mean – well, you know.'

When the cart arrived she allowed herself to be kissed goodbye, and he thought he sensed a softening in her, as though she regretted everything she was sacrificing to her principles.

He watched her out of sight and then went back inside to see about mending fences.

Why did people have to believe in things?

72

There is not in Ireland a man is a better lover of a woman than himself.

—Lady Gregory, *Gods and Fighting Men*

It was a fair day in both senses of the word, which was to say that the weather was a delight and the streets were full of people and animals. Wyndham wound his way through the crowd, looking at faces. This town was an anti-Treaty town and it showed. There were no uniforms to be seen, but several men with rifles were standing in for police, and several likely looking fellows who were neither buying nor selling but looked like they owned the place.

Having failed to spot Nora, Wyndham went up to one swaggering lad with mop of dark curls on his head and a pistol in his belt.

'I wonder if you can help me,' he said. 'I'm looking for someone. Cumann na mBan. A Miss Nora Maxfield. I believe she's part of Kevin Shanahan's unit, or whatever it is.'

It was strange to be able to ask openly. No passwords or street-corner mutterings, where the wrong question might well be answered with a bullet.

'Nora Maxfield? Fine big tall girl with a foxy head on her?'

The 'girl' is near thirty, which makes her roughly twice your age, boy. Show some respect.

'The lady is my fiancée,' he said. 'Where might I find her?' He coldly omitted any *please*.

'I couldn't help you,' said the boy, with not a bother on him.

'But Shanahan's just coming along now – look!'

And there was the sound of horse hooves coming down the street, and people were making room and exclaiming to each other.

'Shanahan!' they said, as if they had a claim on him: as if they'd been waiting for him all along. There were even cheers. It was exactly the reception of the star player running out onto the pitch.

Only this star came cantering in on horseback.

The horse was a spirited grey, of no great size but well-muscled. It wore no saddle and only a piece of rope for a bridle. It was hard to tell how or if the rider was in control at all, but he brought the horse to a stop and he was laughing while he did it. He slid off the animal's back, slapped it on the withers and tossed the halter to a bystander.

'He's a grand beast, Mícheál. Don't take a penny less than sixty pounds for him, do you hear?'

Kevin Shanahan. Not noticeably tall, but at the same time bigger than any man here, with more life in him. He was brawny as any well-reared country boy and his clothes called attention to it. He was in his shirtsleeves for a start, with his forearms rippling from his mastery of the horse. And his clothes were a shade too tight – the waistcoat straining across the chest, the trousers taut against buttock.

'Kevin!' called the curly-haired youth, acclaiming his lord as much as calling for his attention. 'Kevin! There's a man here wants to talk to you!'

Shanahan swept his hair back from his glistening brow and flashed Wyndham a smile. 'Follow along there! You can talk to me on the go!' And Wyndham, who'd been growing more uneasy with every second that he'd had his eyes on the man, was obliged to trot along in his wake.

The crowd parted for Shanahan when he moved and coalesced around him when he stopped. His hand was clasped and his back was slapped. Wyndham half-heard petitions, but mostly the tone was hearty and congratulatory. If Kevin Shanahan was a politician then he had already won the election.

With some difficulty Wyndham followed him in off the street to a house that had recently been a private dwelling and was now a headquarters.

'Mr. Shanahan,' Wyndham began, but was immediately interrupted before he was able to get much beyond the door.

'Kevin! Have a read of this! It's for tomorrow's paper!'

'I'm sure it'll set pulses pounding, Fintan, but leave it on my desk and I'll have a look at it.'

'Kevin! I had Listowel on the telephone. They say you can't have their ammunition.'

'Ring them back. Tell them I'll come and take it if they won't give it to me.'

The instruction was delivered in a jovial tone, but Shanahan was more serious when he turned to Wyndham and added: 'This is no time to scatter our resources. We need everything here. Concentrate! Not dissipate!'

And Wyndham had the sense that it was not an address to him but an aside to an audience.

'Mr. Shanahan—'

'Mr. Wyndham – or maybe it should be Lieutenant Wyndham still, no?'

And *that* was where Wyndham had seen him before. Three years before, on Ogilvie's tennis court, with cattle trampling all over, and Shanahan, hands on hips, laughing at Ogilvie's outrage.

Shanahan laughed again now. 'We keep our eyes open, Mr. Wyndham, and we never forget a face. Now what was it you wanted me for?'

'Mr. Shanahan—'

'Call me Kevin, Mr. Wyndham, and I'll call you Dan. We're all friends here.'

Shanahan's presence in this narrow hall was overbearing. No: it was *embracing*. This close to him, with Shanahan's hand on his shoulder, Wyndham could well understand how the world centred itself on him. Up close, he could also confirm something that he'd suspected from the first.

'Kevin,' he said, 'I believe that's my suit you're wearing.'

The Parisian suit, or at least two parts thereof. Heaven knew where the coat had got to. The Parisian suit, shinier in places than it was meant to be and no doubt smelling of man and horse. The Parisian suit, five years old and too small but still looking very well on the man wearing it.

Shanahan roared with laughter and clapped Wyndham on the back.

'Is that who it came from? I should have guessed! Come on inside and meet herself. She told us you were coming.'

The front room was too full of desks. Nora sat behind one of them. She looked up with an uncertain smile. Wyndham couldn't tell if it was for him or for Shanahan.

When Wyndham imagined Nora's work for the cause, he saw her in a leather coat, behind the wheel of a motor car, a Thompson gun on her lap and a cigarette between her lips. Of course he knew that was fanciful nonsense. He knew she would dress as she always did, in ordinary clothes notable only for their aversion to colour. And yet here she was in a dress that he would have described as positively girlish. It wasn't silly or unsuitable. It just wasn't Nora. And neither was the desk with the wire tray and the typewriter. Maybe there was a gun in one of the drawers but he doubted it. And there was no ashtray.

'It's a fine one you have there, Dan!' said Shanahan. 'Don't go marrying her too soon, d'you hear me? We'd be lost without her altogether.'

He stood behind Nora's chair and put his hands on her

shoulders. 'It's thanks to girls like Nora that we're going to win the war,' he said.

And Nora simpered, and Wyndham knew that he would have to kill this Kevin Shanahan.

'I learned how to type,' she said, as they took a walk outside.

'That was my suit,' he said.

'I'll get it back from him. His own suit got torn on barbed wire when he was escaping from the Tans. It was astonishing, Dan. It was really something. This was in January when the Tans broke the truce. They had him cornered and—'

'It was my best suit.'

'Well yes, I'm sorry, but you've had it years and years. Isn't it the one you had made—' and she looked around and dropped her voice, '—when we were in Paris?'

'Nineteen-seventeen. There was a girl I wanted to impress. I wonder what became of her?'

She hit him.

'Paris, Paris, Paris! The war! The past! That's where you're stuck!'

He rubbed his upper arm. 'That part of the past was quite pleasant,' he said.

She hit him again. 'You come back from the war and you think everything is over! You think it's all stopped dead. You're as bad as the colonel, only I wouldn't mind *him*. He's old. You're still a young man and yet you want to have nothing to do with the world. You just want to settle down with me as your little housewife and forget everything. You're in the middle of the biggest thing that's happened in this country in hundreds and hundreds of years and all you're doing is complaining about a stupid suit.'

He kept his mouth shut.

'And don't be making that face at me!' she said. 'The world isn't made for your convenience. Nothing's over yet.'

He could never follow her arguments. Her knowledge always outweighed his, and her conviction always trumped logic.

She took hold of his arm like she couldn't decide whether to comfort him or jerk him to his senses. Then, seeming to settle on the former, she put her head on his shoulder. Given her height, it was always a faintly ludicrous pose.

'You can't *not* take sides,' she said.

73

I appeal to all Irishmen to pause, to stretch out the hand of forbearance and conciliation, to forgive and to forget, and to join in making for the land which they love a new era of peace, contentment, and goodwill.

—George V, 22 June 1921

The spell of internment on Spike hadn't done Moriarty any harm as far as his profession and reputation were concerned. A man who had suffered for Ireland was not someone whose loyalties could be questioned. Nor was he someone who could be denied a job by his old employer when he walked in after a year-long absence. He might be back to selling newspapers, but there was more to him than that now. If the opinion of the man in the street was ever sought, Moriarty was the man and his patch was the street. It was the editors, the leader writers, and Moriarty in combination who informed the public.

And why not? These were days of growing strife, with the heart of a nation to be won and both sides trying to control the news. The Free State government held Dublin, and could thus, if it chose, tell the national papers what could or could not be printed. In other parts of the country the IRA had to exercise a more hands-on form of censorship by seizing whole consignments of the Dublin papers and burning them for the sake of one objectionable article. In this state of affairs Moriarty did his bit for the freedom of the press by broadcasting his suspicions and embellishing rumours. Some customers appreciated it.

Wyndham was less inclined to trust his one-time comrade's

viewpoint, but he always stopped and talked from force of habit, even when too hard-up to part with the price of a paper.

Today their conversation had to compete with strident political speechifying on matters of the moment.

'Jesus, would you listen to this gobshite? They're all as bad as each other. The pro-Treaty lot say it might not be the Republic but it's the way to get the Republic. The anti-Treaties say it's not the Republic and they leave it at that. You'd think they could get that across without standing up on a soapbox hour after hour every bloody day since Christmas. What's your man saying there? Nothing new, but he's saying it anyway.'

And then Wyndham and Moriarty both ducked at the sound of firing. Two men in different parts of the crowd had drawn pistols and were firing them into the air, drowning out the speaker.

Moriarty straightened up warily.

'Ah for the love of Christ,' he said. 'That class of thing's no good for my nerves at all. What's wrong with heckling?'

Travelling to Tralee was becoming almost as troublesome now as it had been when the IRA and the Black and Tans had been fighting each other, only now it was further complicated by Wyndham's financial straits. He happened to be in the bank, in negotiations of some delicacy, when the new Ireland showed another of its facets.

All was as quiet as a provincial bank would ever be on a Monday morning, and suddenly someone was shouting.

'In the name of the Irish Republic!'

Wyndham turned around to see two armed men – one guarding the door and the other brandishing his pistol and calling for everyone's attention. The one doing the shouting had a handkerchief tied around his face, just like in the Western films, and Wyndham wondered if that was where he'd got the idea. He certainly seemed to be living the role of bank robber to the full. The handkerchief worked better though as costume than as disguise.

'Vincent O'Hanlon!' A clerk at the counter, positively affronted, spoke up. 'Is that yourself?'

The robber pulled the handkerchief down to show a broad grin. 'The very man, Mr. Corcoran.'

And Wyndham recognised him too, and might have done even without the unveiling. It was the same curly head and the same swagger. It was that young lieutenant or disciple of Kevin Shanahan he'd met in the street on the fair day, and not a bother on him still.

'Vincent, I'll tell your father on you!'

But Vincent kept on smiling while he pointed his pistol at the clerk's face.

'I don't think you will, Mr. Corcoran. Now shush and listen.'

And he pulled a sheet of paper from his pocket with his free hand and read, stumbling here and there like an ill-prepared schoolboy, but full of confidence nevertheless.

'*In the name of the Irish Republic! The Irish Republican Army, having been denied funds by the treasonous, criminal and unrepresentative government in Dublin, is driven to commandeer all necessary monies for the continuance of the armed struggle against the enemies of freedom!*

'That means you fill up a bag with money, Mr. Corcoran, and you give it to me, do you hear?'

The clerk looked at the door, through which he realised no help would be coming, and he looked at his colleague, who was no good to him either, and he looked down the barrel of Vincent O'Hanlon's pistol.

'I can't just give you our money,' he said.

And Vincent O'Hanlon, who looked as though he were curious to see how far out the back of a man's head his brains might fly, thumbed back the hammer. Against the series of little clicks a career of financial probity could not stand. A little while later the two IRA men walked out of the bank with a bag full of money. The staff and the customers, still dumbfounded, could only look at each other. Then the man with whom Wyndham had been dealing let out a breath, shivered once, and spoke.

'Well of course we'd like to do all we can for you, Mr. Wyndham, but these are difficult times, you know, and we can hardly be giving out money to just anybody...'

During the bad days there had been good men. When the ranks of the Royal Irish Constabulary were filled with Englishmen who wanted nothing more out of Ireland than three pounds ten a week and were prepared to kill anyone who added difficulties to that, there were a few of the old breed who didn't let them have it all their own way. Either for principle or pension, there had still been policemen of the old sort who'd done their best to do their jobs as they always had. Neither the threats of the IRA nor the brutality of the Tans had driven them from their posts. With the Tans now leaving, they had every right to expect that the Irish Free State would recognise their steadfastness and allow them to keep their old jobs, even if it happened to be in a different uniform.

One such Kerry constable wasn't given that chance. His body was found one morning lying in the street. From the look of things he'd been killed elsewhere. The body was left as a warning. In case the warning wasn't explicit enough, a note was pinned to the body.

The constable had been shot in the name of the Irish Republic – essentially for wearing a crown on his cap badge. Wyndham wondered why the Irish Republic had waited this long to address the matter. He watched the body being covered up and carried away while people shook their heads and blessed themselves. The man next to him gave him a light, unasked-for, and provided an answer to his unvoiced question.

'Gurriers,' said the man. 'Bloody gurriers. Do you know what's wrong with them? It's not the Treaty at all – or at least it's not only the Treaty.'

He took a long draw on his cigarette and squinted through the smoke. 'All that's wrong with them is that they feel left out. They hadn't the guts to come out and fight the Tans. Any money says that not a one of them was in the IRA until the Truce. They just wanted a gun and a chance to strut around lording it over people. Pure gurrierism.'

Wyndham gave the sort of nod that showed he was listening: not necessarily agreeing.

'Either that,' said the man, 'or they're young fellas. Too young to fight the Tans. Hurrying to show that they're hardy lads like the older men. Hoping that they'll have stories to tell.'

And suddenly Wyndham thought he could place the man's voice.

'Do you have stories to tell?' he asked.

The man laughed. 'I might,' he said. 'I might be able to tell my grandchildren how I did a bit more than play croquet anyway. Good day to you, Mr. Wyndham.'

After General Lucas's kidnapper departed, Wyndham stayed a little while longer, thinking that there might have been something in what he'd just heard. Bloodthirsty young gurriers.

He'd had a look at the note pinned to the dead policeman. It looked like a page torn from a school exercise book.

74

And Jacob served seven years for Rachel; and they seemed unto him but a few days, for the love he had to her.

—Genesis 29:20

Cork was no good. Wyndham was broke and Nora never came to visit. Getting to Tralee – or wherever in Kerry she might happen to be – was no easy matter with no money, and with the country in turmoil and the railways still disordered. Even when he managed it, he found it impossible to spend any time with her. The rift between her and the Fitzmullen-Brophys remained, leaving the lovers without any place of domestic calm. Her own lodgings, forever moving between small hotels and the homes of local sympathisers, were strictly out of bounds to gentleman callers. When they did arrange a rendezvous, it was slotted in between the demands of her work, always taking second place.

'I can't just stop for tea, Dan. Don't you realise what's going on?'

'There's going to be an election. I know.'

'There's going to be an election!'

'We've had elections before, Nora. We'll have them again.'

'Not like this! This is about the Treaty. When people vote in an anti-Treaty government it means we'll be at war with Britain again. And you want me to stop and eat little cakes with pink icing and talk about the weather?'

One of the many things Wyndham disliked about this situation was the way that Kevin Shanahan and his entourage appeared to relish the prospect of renewed war.

'If the lackeys of England, sitting up there in Dublin, think that the country will bow down before their Treaty, let them come down here to Kerry! Let our so-called representatives see what the country really wants! – and what the country is going to give them if this shameful treaty is forced upon us!'

Shanahan's closing words were met with wild cheering, the same as the rest of his speech. It was nothing new, but his audience roared their approval. Certainly there was no one sounding dissent with a pistol. Wyndham watched him climb down to the accustomed back-slapping and hand-shaking. As if Shanahan hadn't yet had enough of hearty manhandling for the day, he put an arm round Wyndham's shoulders the moment he saw him and shook him in friendly roughness.

If I wasn't wearing a hat, thought Wyndham, *he'd be tousling my hair.*

'Dan Wyndham, bedad! So you're back in Kerry! Good man yourself!'

'Actually, Kevin, that's something I wanted to talk to you about.'

'What's that?'

Wyndham wasn't sure if Shanahan missed his meaning or was just unable to hear him over the boisterous admiration of the crowd.

'Kerry,' Wyndham shouted. 'Being back in Kerry.'

They pushed their way to somewhere quieter, and Wyndham made his case in between the helpers and the well-wishers.

'I'm thinking of moving back here more permanently,' he said. 'Prior to getting married, you know.'

'Well that's grand altogether. Nothing wrong with Cork – except that it's Cork!'

Wyndham answered the gust of laughter with a tight smile.

'Well, quite. But I have a job there. Of sorts. That's what's wrong with Kerry, you see: I don't. Have a job, I mean. I was wondering if you might have something for me?'

'Me? Sure, I'm not in the hotel business, Dan.'

'I know that, Kevin. I was thinking about something that is in your line.'

'You want to join up? Is that it?' And here Shanahan put his arm back around Wyndham's shoulders as though bringing a younger brother into the family business.

'I don't know now, Dan. What is there that you can do that would help me?'

'You seem to know everything about me, Kevin. You know I was an army officer. I commanded men in the trenches. I helped raise an infantry battalion from scratch. Do that and there's not a whole lot you *can't* do, militarily speaking.'

Shanahan laughed, even though Wyndham didn't think he'd said anything funny.

'Militarily speaking, Dan, I might have the need of a chauffeur. There's a great lot of to-ing and fro-ing for me to do. I can never find myself in the one place these days.

Wyndham allowed a thoughtful nod. 'I can do that, Kevin. It would be my pleasure.'

He found Nora back at her typewriter, and by the set of her jaw she was on the point of doing violence to it.

'You'll be glad to hear I'm moving back to Kerry, my love,' he said.

'Ah, Dan,' she said, in an unexpected show of magnanimity, 'I'm sorry. You must be utterly fed up with chasing after me from Cork to Kerry and back again.'

'You can make it up to me,' he said.

'I most certainly can *not!*' she hissed, turning red.

'Not like that,' he grinned. 'More's the pity. No – you can teach me how to drive.'

She appraised him as if, after all this time at a typewriter, she could no longer trust her eyesight.

'*You?* Really?'

'Really, and the sooner the better. You go requisition a car and I'll buy you an ice cream afterwards. I can't say fairer than that.'

On as straight a stretch of road as north Kerry could boast, she surrendered the driver's seat to him and ran through the essentials one more time.

'Don't fuss so,' he said. 'I have a natural affinity for mechanical transport. I was the toast of the Cyclist Corps in my day.'

He had feared that she would be an impatient teacher, and expected that he'd have to learn through recriminations and slaps. Instead, to his surprise, he had to bear her unrestrained mirth. She found his ham-fisted efforts achingly funny.

'I needed that,' she said, as he located the brake at the last second and they coasted to a stop a bare six inches short of a dry stone wall. 'I've been stuck inside too long. I needed fresh air and a good laugh.'

'Not that I'm ungrateful, Nora, but a fellow finds it difficult to concentrate in the face of open mockery. And I'm sure that man with the cart didn't take kindly to your laughter either. It made it look like I'd tried to hit him deliberately.'

'Oh don't be silly. And to be fair, you're hardly any worse than I was when I learned. Only I was lucky. People tend to get out of the way of an ambulance. Now, change places and I'll take us home.'

Her mood made him glad of his decision to come back to Kerry, and just the smallest bit guilty about what he was going to do next.

'So, why?' she asked, taking the cigarette he'd lit for her, 'Why now? Why learn to drive? And why wouldn't you tell me before?'

'I was afraid you might get upset.'

'Upset? Upset at what? Dan?'

'I've joined the movement,' he said, looking at the scenery rather than at her.

'Movement? Do you mean the Republicans?'

'The IRA. Yes, I suppose so. I haven't signed anything or anything, but Shanahan's taken me on board.'

She took her eyes off the road to give him a wonders-will-never-cease half-smile.

'But why the driving?' she asked.

'He needs a driver. I'm to be it.'

Her smile vanished. 'But *I* could drive him! Surely he knows that!'

He studied the hedges racing by.

'I told him,' he said. 'He said he knew. But he said it wouldn't look right to have a woman driving him. He said a girl was better behind a typewriter than a wheel.'

Wyndham really should have been keeping a tighter grip. He'd been expecting some sort of reaction, but he still bounced hard off the dashboard when Nora stamped on the brake.

'He said no such thing!' she said, but her vehemence wasn't enough to disguise her doubt.

Wyndham refused to catch her eye. He moved head and hands in vague gestures.

Maybe-he-did, maybe-he-didn't, maybe-I-don't-remember, let's-forget-about-it.

He said nothing. He waited for her to start the car again. He felt the smallest bit sorry but, on self-examination, only the smallest bit. Maybe he wouldn't have to do away with Kevin Shanahan after all. Maybe Nora would do it for him.

75

The man who is against peace may bear now and forever the responsibility for terrible and immediate war.

—David Lloyd George, December 1921 (attr.)

In Dublin the IRA, frustrated by the way things were going, had seized control of various important buildings, with their headquarters in the Four Courts – the heart of Ireland's judicial system. The government in London expressed its unease and the government in Dublin recruited more troops. Under pressure to find a solution was Michael Collins, effective leader of the new Irish state. Only a year before, as IRA head of intelligence, he had been engaged in subverting, undermining and hindering the state in every way. A few years before that he been working for the post office in England. A great weight was on his shoulders, made heavier by the expectations of his countrymen. Many who had adored the rebel leader were calling the government official a traitor. Others – like Nora – demanded that the seeming miracles he had worked against the British be performed again, only somehow without rancour or bloodshed.

As the nationalist movement split, Collins was reportedly doing his damnedest to keep his former comrades and followers from mutual strife. Even where it violated the terms of the Treaty and antagonised the British government, the effort was being made to bring the IRA back into the fold.

But without a united leadership the IRA was not just breaking away from those who'd signed the Treaty, but was splintering within itself. The split had not been clean and clear. There were wayward units to complicate matters. Men like Michael Collins would have to contend with men like Kevin Shanahan.

Shanahan didn't take orders from anyone. Wyndham discovered that much. If Wyndham had been hired to spy on the anti-Treaty faction, it would have been money wasted. If tasked with reporting on Shanahan's whereabouts, he'd have been able to say no more than where Shanahan had just been. The man was quicksilver, never sleeping two nights under the same roof, never keeping to any schedule that Wyndham could ascertain, and never telling Wyndham where they were going until they were well on their way.

But one thing that Wyndham did discover: Shanahan was forever keeping one step ahead of anyone who might try to rein him in. He didn't go to the great convention of IRA leaders in Dublin, and that might have been because he didn't hold high-enough rank, but he stayed away from the barracks in Tralee too, where the anti-Treaty faction was making its stand for legitimacy. There were telephone calls he wouldn't take and letters that he threw away unopened, always with some light-hearted dismissal of the fool or the eejit who had no notion of the real state of affairs in Kerry.

Once, out of a not entirely malice-free curiosity, Wyndham made to fish one of these letters from the wastepaper basket, but was warned off. It wasn't a direct warning. It wasn't even an admonishment or implied threat. It was just that Clancy had entered the room.

Nora's nose wasn't the only one put out of joint by Wyndham's appointment as Shanahan's driver. Dinny Clancy, Shanahan's right-hand man, was far from welcoming.

'Sure don't mind Dinny,' said Shanahan. 'When Dinny tries to drive he's pulling on the steering wheel like it's the reins on a donkey.'

Clancy didn't laugh along with his commander. Clancy didn't laugh at all. Where Shanahan was jollity and good fellowship, Clancy was dark looks and dark deeds. Wyndham couldn't quite categorise him. He stayed as close as a bodyguard, but there was much more to him than that. He might have been a second-in-command, but it was hard to imagine Shanahan sharing even the smallest piece of his authority, let alone countenancing even a potential replacement for himself. Wyndham ended up thinking of Clancy as a shadow – a malevolent storm cloud unnoticed in the dazzle of Shanahan's sun. He was always armed, always there, and he didn't like Wyndham.

'A British army officer,' he said, that being charge enough.

'Leave the man alone,' said Shanahan. 'You'd forgive a fellow his youthful indiscretions now.'

Shanahan's banter was in vain. There was no bantering in Clancy, and likely no forgiveness either.

On one of his first outings in his new role, Wyndham had to remember everything Nora had taught him, make it look effortless, and forget that Clancy was sitting right behind him. It could have been worse. It could have been Shanahan sitting behind him. That would have put him in the seat beside Nora. Bad enough that he could feel Nora fuming at being relegated to the back seat: imagine if Shanahan were squeezing her knee! But Shanahan was there in the passenger seat, talking fast, laying plans with Clancy and dictating memos to Nora, and all the while able to comment on the scenery and joke at Wyndham's ineptitude.

'I thought all Yanks were fiends behind the wheel!' he said. 'My Auntie Bridie would give you a run for your money, Dan! Maybe we should let Nora drive instead!'

And after that Wyndham took a better grip on things. Shanahan's jibe hadn't spurred him to better effort. Instead he had recognised it as a heaven-sent gift in the contest for Nora's heart.

If Shanahan was going to compare Nora, however distantly, to an elderly aunt, then Wyndham hardly needed to make up slanders about him. He imagined that he could hear her grinding her teeth over the noise of the engine. With this joy inside him, he shed his fear that Clancy would shoot him for sabotage the next time the car stalled.

Money remained a problem. The hirelings of the Irish Free State could sell their country in exchange for a few pence and a uniform, but republicanism was still a volunteer movement, so Wyndham was still broke.

At least the king gave me a shilling when I joined his army.

On the other hand, here in the fiefdom of Kevin Shanahan's personality, money didn't have the importance it had elsewhere. Once it became known whose man he was, Wyndham never had to put his hand in his pocket. Board and lodging were provided without question. They needed to be provided because Wyndham didn't see the Fitzmullen-Brophys anymore.

'We can't be having you staying with a British Army colonel – even if he is retired,' said Shanahan. 'Besides, I want you within easy reach. You'll never know when we'll have to be moving fast.'

So Wyndham stayed wherever Shanahan was. It suited him, because that was usually where Nora was too. Frustratingly, he could never stay with her. He did argue it out with a country hotelier one evening, and went so far as to insist that he was Nora's husband. The hotelier was having none of it, but it did lead to Wyndham becoming known here and there around the district as Mr. Maxfield.

He wondered about the money stolen from the bank, for surely the goodwill of the people wasn't enough to keep the Shanahan show on the road. Actual money did change hands from time to time, but only in small sums. Wyndham himself had never been handed anything larger than a ten-shilling note to pay for petrol and cigarettes. Shanahan, expansive as he was, was hardly luxurious. There was the car, and there was a new suit, but there was no evidence of personal enrichment. From overheard talk, Wyndham had gathered that the bank robbery had been unauthorised by the higher-ups in the IRA, and their displeasure had been strongly voiced. Shanahan disdained their censure.

'It's not like I'm lining my own pockets,' he'd said to Clancy. And Wyndham understood. The robbery had been done in the name of the Irish Republic, and the Irish Republic was whatever Kevin Shanahan said it was. It was Kevin Shanahan who knew better than anyone else what was good for the Irish Republic – knew better than the IRA command, and certainly knew better than the Free State government in Dublin.

Shanahan never stopped. His energy was never drained. Even in his relaxation he remained a man of action. Of an evening when there was no more organising to be done, and the others would be content to slump in their chairs, Shanahan would take to his feet again. Fuelled by no more than a single glass (which he might not even finish), he could lead them in song or indulge in playful wrestling. Or dance.

Kevin Shanahan was a great man for the dancing.

Even as the country's first faltering steps threatened to be its last, there were nights when it could all be forgotten. There was a dance. It was neither a fundraiser nor a political rally. It was just a dance, but such a dance as Nora and Wyndham had always revelled in. The venue was too small for the crowd that came, and things were hot and intimate even before the music struck up. For the first hour it didn't matter who was whose partner, as dancers met and whirled and changed hands and danced off again. It was great fun in its own way, but Wyndham wanted more from Nora than a passing hand clasp and a smile. And then, when there came one of those dances where they could hold each other properly, Shanahan stepped in with a gallantry that would not be denied, and with many cheers from the gathering, proceeded to show them how it was done and dance Nora off her feet.

Wyndham grinned widely and clapped his hands in time to the music.

If he pinches her behind I will kill him. I'll grab Clancy's gun and kill him where he stands, the charming son of a bitch.

But damned if he could blame Shanahan: Nora was the most striking woman in the place.

'Look at her,' said a woman somewhere behind him. 'She's too tall and she's too old for him. And would you ever look at the hair on her?'

He wasn't sure what hackles were, but he could feel his rising all the same. He ignored the voice and focused his ill will on Shanahan, shining in the paraffin lights.

'Oh, isn't he lovely!' said another voice, and this time he turned round to see a small red face grow even redder at having spoken her thoughts aloud and, what was worse, having been overheard doing it.

'Mary!' said Wyndham.

He had trouble keeping track of the Fitzmullen-Brophys' succession of maids down the years, but they had all had the great convenience of being called Mary.

She silently mouthed the words, 'Mr. Wyndham', like she was confessing to manslaughter.

'How delightful to see you!' he said. 'I didn't know you liked dancing!'

She couldn't reply, her eyes and mouth making three perfect circles.

'Come on,' he said, the best brother a girl could have. 'Come and meet Kevin. He'll be thrilled.' And taking hold of the inaudible Mary, be bulled his way through the throng and pushed her in front of Shanahan, his laughter saying that if he wasn't going to make this the liveliest party there ever was then his name wasn't Dan Wyndham, by God. Reckoning that little Mary was unlikely to withstand the attention for very long at all, he was quick to lay hold of another young woman – he thought it was the one who'd criticised Nora – and swung her too into Shanahan's way. His practice at this sort of dancing enabled him, in almost the same movement, to grab Nora and swing her clear.

She knew what he was up to, and her face was a reprimand in itself, but she danced with him all the same, and even followed him outside when he took her hand and pulled.

'Jealousy is an unattractive trait in a man, Daniel Wyndham.'
'Marry me, Nora.'
'I thought I already said I would.'
'Tomorrow.'
'I'm busy tomorrow.'
'Come away with me.'
'I told you I'm busy. Kevin needs me. Give me a cigarette.'

They were still standing at the door, a stalemate in tobacco smoke, when Shanahan came across them.

'Come on back inside, the pair of you! The night's hardly started!'

And he took the cigarette from Nora's lips and threw it away. If it had been only that, Wyndham might just have fought him there and then. But Shanahan's words saved everyone from such a humiliating show.

'A girl shouldn't be smoking, Nora. Now come on inside and we'll give the floor another battering.'

Give a man enough rope, thought Wyndham, *and a girl will someday throttle him with it.*

X

HOUSEHOLD GODS

The people of the gods of Dana to have done treachery on one another, and it is long they will be under loss by it and be weakened by it. And Ireland will never be free from trouble from this out, east and west.

—Lady Gregory, *Gods and Fighting Men*

76

TO THE OFFICERS, WARRANT OFFICERS, NON-COMMISSIONED OFFICERS AND MEN OF THE ROYAL MUNSTER FUSILIERS

It is with feelings of no ordinary sorrow that I address you for the last time; for I know that I am taking leave not merely of a fine regiment, but of great memories and great traditions which hitherto have been kept alive and embodied in you.

It is a hard fate that dissolves a corps which after seventy to eighty years of existence in independent companies became a regiment in 1756 and had for its first Colonel, Robert Clive. Under him you fought at the battle of Plassey; and not Clive only but Forde and Knox and Hector Munro and all the old heroes of India knew of what stuff you were made. Moreover, you have shown in three different centuries that time could not change you, whether in India or in Europe. Your great deeds, extending in all over a period of 260 years, are written too clearly in the history of the Empire for anything lightly to efface them.

You have your Colours, your trophies and your household gods, which are dear to you as honour itself. You have thought fit to entrust your Colours to me for custody and I am very proud to take charge of them, to be preserved and held in reverence at Windsor Castle as a perpetual record of your noble exploits in the field.

Meanwhile, be very sure that, with or without external monument, the fame of your great work can never die.

I thank you for your good service to this Country and the Empire, and with a full heart I bid you Farewell.

George R.I., 12th June, 1922

'Feelings of no ordinary sorrow, what? A dismal day, Dan.'

Wyndham could see that Fitzmullen-Brophy was bearing up, because that's what men of that sort did at times like this. They bore up like Trojans. They maintained a stiff upper lip. They said things like, 'Oh well,' and, 'Can't be helped,' and their wives said, 'There, there.'

'Handsome words from the king at least, sir.'

'One would expect no less. Can't have been easy for him. We've lost a regiment, but the king has lost six of them. Us, the Leinsters, the Dublins, the Royal Irish, the Connaught Rangers. Even the South Irish Horse. Never had much time for the Yeomanry myself, but stout fellows all, I have no doubt. Must have been something to see. Scarlet coats like before the war. Bands playing. And the colours.'

He trailed off and his eyes lost their focus.

'Do you know, sir, but I never saw the colours,' said Wyndham, just to stave off an awful silence.

'Didn't you? No, I suppose you wouldn't have. Off to the war almost as soon as the shilling was in your hand. No time for the ceremonial side of things. A fighting soldier through and through – that was you, eh?'

'I just followed you, Colonel.'

Fitzmullen-Brophy could only nod. The effort of sounding equable proving too much for the moment.

It was a lovely summer's day. A lovely dismal summer's day. They were sitting in the Fitzmullen-Brophys' garden, the colonel kneading his unlit pipe in his bony hands, the dogs at his feet silent for a change, sensing their master's mood, paying their own dumb tribute to the solemnity of the day.

He rallied after a little while.

'Thought of being there, you know. In Windsor, I mean. But I'd have had no damn business there. Besides, it would all have been melancholy as bedamned. If a fellow's going to be sunk in a dark mood he might as well do it in the comfort of his own house. Still, almost worth it to see colours one last time.'

He slapped his palm with his pipe, trying to beat some liveliness back into himself. 'Oh, but you should have seen them as they were when I first saw them, Dan! Great big holes. Fringe hanging off. You know – like you'd see in pictures. Still the colours of the old Bengal Fusiliers, you see. You'd look at them and you'd see the siege of Delhi, and the enemy shot tearing the silk to shreds, and the men going forward regardless. History in those rags. Moving, really. Quite moving. Even when we got new colours with "Munster" on them I could still see the old colours and the old battles. The colours are like the men, you see. They get torn up and worn out, but they're always renewed. The regiment always carries on. Or at least it did.'

He stopped then like a man who has suddenly decided that he's not going to make it to the top of this hill after all, and then he breathed out through his nose like a horse.

'And now it's all gone, just to save a little money. Blasted politicians. What are they going to do when the next war breaks out? What will they do without the Irish, eh? Damned fools. I never cared a fig for politics, Dan. No one did. Irishmen out of Bengal, drinking the health of the queen, and the king after her, and asking no more than to serve as we always had. And all that's over now because of politics. I'm almost glad I'm an old man. The world isn't for the likes of me anymore, and I shan't be sorry to depart it.'

'Oh come now, sir.'

'That's why I got so angry with your young lady, you know. Politics. Blasted politics. That's what made us speak sharply to each other. She's young and headstrong, and I'm just behind the times. It's not that I think that *women* should stay out of politics: I think *everybody* should.

'But let's forget about it for a while, what? I'm quite gloomy enough. We'll have some tea and you can tell us about this job that comes with its own motor car.'

'It's really no great shakes, sir. Just something to keep me occupied until Nora finishes up her own job. Not worth talking about at all.'

'Still, a motor car, no less! And I say! Here comes another! Two in one afternoon! I do hope nothing's the matter.'

Wyndham had the very same thought, but the approaching motor sounded more finely-bred than an army lorry. When it came into view they saw it was Ogilvie. It had been a long time since Wyndham had seen the Fitzmullen-Brophys' prickly neighbour, and he knew nothing of the man beyond that he was still living in the district, more or less unmolested. Fitzmullen-Brophy raised a hand in greeting and tried to look pleased, and Wyndham assumed a bland smile. Any words of welcome, however, were drowned out by the dogs, who started barking as though all the thieves of Ireland were arriving in Ogilvie's wake. He stood there, a picture of mounting impatience, until the dogs, refusing to be silenced, were forcibly expelled from the garden.

'Ogilvie,' said Fitzmullen-Brophy, trying to do his best. 'Jolly good! To what do we owe the immense pleasure?'

'I've come to tell you I'm leaving, Fitzmullen-Brophy. End of the month. I've had enough.'

'Oh dear! Don't tell me there's been more trouble?'

'More blasted threats! More blasted intimidation! This is the latest!'

He was brandishing a piece of paper. 'First they send me missives that try and sound like legal injunctions, then they write notes in their blasted Hottentot, as if I should be expected to make sense of it. I paid it no more heed than it deserved and it left off for a while. But now this! The usual "In the name of the Irish Republic" rot! Look! Written on a blasted copybook by the look of it! Are these the sort of people in charge now? Bloody disgraceful!'

There was something in his tone suggesting that Fitzmullen-Brophy should share some of the blame for all this. After all, in all the years he'd been living among these people, he'd clearly not been firm enough with them.

'I'll not have any more of it, Fitzmullen-Brophy! They can't intimidate me! I'm going back to England! That'll damn well show them!'

'Oh, I say.'

'Enough! Do you hear me?' And with that bolt shot, Ogilvie deflated.

'So I just came to tell you,' he said. 'If you'd be so kind as to pass on my regards to Mrs. Fitzmullen-Brophy.'

'Of course, of course. But won't you come inside and tell her yourself? I believe there will be tea.'

'Thank you, no. Oh – and you might as well have this. God knows it was precious little use to me in keeping thieving Shinners away, but I remember you seemed to admire it.'

And he went back briefly to his car and returned with the wolfhound Boru.

'Don't know if you'll want another dog. Especially this one. Eats its own weight in horsemeat every day, practically.'

But the colonel wasn't really listening anymore. He was down on one knee, inspecting the dog all over and ruffling the fur on its neck.

Ogilvie drove away shortly after, irascible as ever and unaware of the depth of happiness he had brought to salvage this dark day.

77

We did not surrender in 1916

We will not surrender in 1922

—election poster, spring 1922

'Nora, I know I said I was never going to talk politics with you again, but have you actually *read* the Treaty?'

'That thing? I wouldn't read it with a barge pole. It's all palaver and obfuscation.'

They were in a safe house only just now set up by Shanahan's men, and Wyndham had helped carry Nora's desk inside. As something of a connoisseur of IRA safe houses these past few years, he had to admit that this was a pretty good one. Out of the way, yet within handy reach of Tralee. Defensible approaches with good escape routes, but comfortable at the same time. He just had to question why a safe house was needed at all.

'So you haven't read it and you're not going to read it, but you're going to vote against it anyway. And what then?'

She recited it as she would an oft-repeated lesson for the lazy pupils at the back.

'We reject the Treaty, and Lloyd George either accepts that or he doesn't. If he does, then we're a republic like we always said we were. If he doesn't, then the British will try to come back, and much good it will do them. They'll have no bases here anymore and we'll be more than ready for them. They might be able to take back places like the barracks in Tralee, but it'll be from places like this that we'll beat them.'

'But what if the pro-Treaty government wins the election?'

'They won't.'

'But what if they do?'

'Then they won't last long, will they? Our best men are in Dublin. They're holding the Four Courts and all those other places around the centre of the city. Michael Collins will see sense. If the worst comes to the worst then it'll be like Easter 1916 all over again only this time we'll win. This 'Free State' barely has an army worth the name.'

'But that's civil war.'

'No it isn't.'

'What else could it be?'

'Well maybe. I suppose so. But only a little one.'

'So if the anti-Treaty side loses the election—'

'They won't.'

'*If* they do, the IRA is going to disregard the will of the people—'

'The will of the people? Is this the same will that was disregarded by every government we've had going back however many years? That one? Because the last time I looked, Dan, that will was all for a republic.'

'People sound like they're happy to settle for a Free State now.'

'They only say that because they've been lied to.'

'But just suppose for a minute that the IRA loses the election, and they don't accept the result, and they go to war – either with the British or their former comrades. How on earth do they justify that?'

'*They?*' She half-smiled and shook her head, realising that she'd been listening to a child prattling on. 'Dan, Dan, Dan – whose side do you think you've been on all this time?'

If pushed, Wyndham would have said that he wasn't on anyone's side. In principle he was all for Irish independence, but he was only here so he could stay close to Nora. He had sought a place in Shanahan's organisation just to ensure that she and Shanahan kept their hands off each other. That was as far as he was going with Irish republicanism. He paid attention to which side was which only so that he'd know when to jump and in what direction. He wasn't going to stay for any shooting.

In the middle of June the pro-Treaty party won the election. The losers were not willing to accept the outcome. The IRA remained in occupation of key sites in Dublin, their resolve hardened by knowledge that more than a third of the country had voted for their cause. The county of Kerry and the province of Munster as a whole still stood against the Treaty. Wyndham wondered how long the stand-off could last.

Free State and IRA had yet to fire on each other, but that wasn't to mean that there was no killing. As the dead constable in the street had proved, there were still scores to be settled, loose ends to be tied up, and points to be made. That was another reason for Wyndham to keep close to Shanahan. He felt there was more reason than ever to worry about the Fitzmullen-Brophys.

For those still eager to demonstrate their dedication to the nationalist cause, men who had worn the king's uniform were obvious and easy targets.

78

And three times nine of the rest of the Fianna came out of the west one time to Teamhair. And they took notice that now they were wanting their full strength and their great name, no one took notice of them or came to speak with them at all. And when they saw that, they lay down on the side of the hill at Teamhair, and put their lips to the earth and died.

—Lady Gregory, *Gods and Fighting Men*

The old soldier had received his first wound as a young officer in Burma back in the eighties. He received his last at his own front door. The two men who killed him had been following him and noting his movements for some time. On a midsummer's day they chose to act.

Their victim had been too vocal in his defence of the old order. He was irrelevant, but his death served as notice that the Ireland of which he'd always seen himself a part was being done away with. In keeping with these inverted times, the two IRA men who did the killing were one-time soldiers of the Irish Guards and the Munster Fusiliers respectively.

Fittingly, the eminent man was in uniform when they shot him, having just come from the dedication of a war memorial. According to one eyewitness account, he was trying to draw his sword as the assassins' bullets struck him down. It was an image the press ran with. The gallant old warrior, scorning to run, facing his enemies with cold steel – the last outdated defiance of a vanishing breed. More prosaically, he might just have been going for his door key. No matter. The death of Field-Marshal Sir Henry Wilson, former Chief of the Imperial General Staff and proud son of County Longford, marked the receding of the tide. Wilson belonged to that succession of high-ranking Irishmen like Kitchener and Wolseley and Roberts who had run the army since the previous century and were now gone the way of the Irish regiments and the traditions of Irish soldiering.

Of more immediate importance, the assassination marked the moment the British government ran out of patience with Ireland. Michael Collins was told in no uncertain terms that his toleration of the IRA must cease, and that the split over the Treaty must be resolved immediately.

To this end, His Majesty's Government supplied the fledgling Irish Free State with field artillery.

The IRA still refused to back down.

On the 28th of June – coincidentally the third anniversary of the day that the statesmen in Versailles had brought an end to all wars – the shooting started in Dublin.

79

Ireland is big enough for great things and great movements, but it is too small for Civil War.

—*Kilkenny People*, 15 April 1922

As in Easter Week, the fighting in Dublin lasted no more than a few days and was confined to Dublin, and as had been the case in 1916, the Republicans were overwhelmed by numbers and by firepower.

As the smoke rose over the city, the IRA in the rest of the country braced for what was coming their way soon. Kerry and the south were ready to make a fight of it. People spoke of 'the Republic of Munster'. Wyndham watched the barracks, his unloved one-time home, being made ready with sandbags and Lewis Guns. With jaundiced eyes he noted that it was in fact a single Lewis Gun, and that the sandbags would prove small hindrance to an assault of any determination. It was a large barracks and there were too few men. Thinking of how the cream of the IRA, better equipped and fighting from prepared positions, was faring in Dublin, Wyndham couldn't see how these few men in Tralee could possibly win against a regular army supplied by the British. But then again, it had been hard to see how the British themselves, faced with scattered rebel bands across Ireland, could possibly have lost. Men like Kevin Shanahan had kept that fight going for more than two years. Was it foolish to suppose they couldn't do it again?

Tralee, however, was not Shanahan's concern. The man in charge there was someone called John Joe Sheehy, and Sheehy's aims and Shanahan's aims were not in accord. Where Sheehy was the defender of the Republic, digging in and holding out, Shanahan was the wild boy, the elusive guerrilla, the Irish pimpernel. And while Shanahan had popularity, he lacked authority. He left Tralee with its vulnerable barracks to the static John Joe Sheehy and conducted his own war plans afoot. The well-appointed safe house came into its own, while Wyndham spent ever more of his time behind the wheel.

Everywhere in North Kerry, in every village that was no more than a crossroads with a church and a public house, Shanahan was still met with acclaim and admiration. But was Wyndham imagining it? Were the welcomes smaller? Was the cheering thinner? Did the handshaking and backslapping take less time? The defeat in Dublin had deprived the organisation of its central command, and the stresses of war had exposed the cracks in the movement. As the pressure mounted, the cracks threatened to widen into fissures. People still cheered Kevin Shanahan on sight, but his old comrades were more reserved in their reception. Wyndham was given a clear taste of the limits of Shanahan's power one July day in the vicinity of Listowel.

Arms and ammunition. There was never enough. Shanahan had received word that a unit near Listowel was in possession of quite a stock of ammunition, lifted off a train with great risk and jealously husbanded ever since.

'It does no one any good hidden away,' he said. 'It needs to be served out to good lads who're not afraid to make use of it. Dinny, get up there and talk to them. Dan will drive you. Be back before dinner.'

So with the torturing of gears, Wyndham set out with the intimidating silence of Dinny Clancy for company and young Vincent the bank robber in the back seat.

Just a perfect summer outing. We should have sandwiches instead of pistols.

Clancy gave directions and somehow made them sound like threats.

Shanahan's men or not, there was no glad reception for them when Wyndham brought the car to a juddering stop at some anonymous lonely house. The men who'd let them drive up to the gate appraised them with cool glances, and they were carrying rifles.

'Keep your mouths shut, do your hear me?' said Clancy. 'Leave me do the talking.'

Wyndham was the only one who wasn't armed, so when they got out of the car he compensated by pulling down the brim of his hat. It was the same hat he'd bought before all this started and it had borne up well to Ireland's troubles and Irish weather. It was a hat that had seen it all and held its shape. Under its shadow, Wyndham lit a cigarette and hoped it said the same thing about him. He reckoned that with his eyes hooded and his broken nose highlighted, the hat made him look like a tough guy – like one of those Americans who were reputed to be running arms across the Atlantic in exchange for Irish whiskey. What did he need with a gun? He put his hands in his pockets and leaned against the side of the car, blowing disdainful smoke through his nostrils as the Listowel men gave him the once-over.

'Clancy,' said one of them. 'And who's this?'

'That's Wyndham.'

'Oh right. The Yank who can't double-declutch. What is it you're here for? It wouldn't be a load of three-oh-three, would it?'

'That'd be it. We'll take it off your hands now. It's needed in Tralee.'

'Do you know, we haven't heard that from Tralee. John Joe Sheehy never sent us any orders.'

'Never mind Sheehy. Sheehy's going to lose everything when he loses Tralee. He won't be able to hold out. Shanahan's your man.'

'Tralee won't hold? Let me tell you something, Clancy. Every road and railway between here and Dublin is cut. When those Free State gobshites come they'll have to come across the fields and they're going to run up against us. We'll hold. And we'll hold on to our ammunition. Tell that to Shanahan. We don't take orders from him.'

Clancy breathed out slowly and fixed his eyes on the space above the Listowel man's head, getting the measure of this stupid little brick wall he'd run up against.

'You weren't at Abbeydorney,' he said, as if it were of no more matter than yesterday's weather.

'Nor at Ballylongford either, were you?'

The Listowel man stood silent.

'Sure why are you bothering holding on to ammunition at all?' said Clancy, still matter-of-fact. 'It's not like you ever used any of it against the Tans.'

The Listowel man's fists were clenched, but his voice remained level.

'We'll be using it soon enough,' he said. 'You can take your little taunts and fuck off out of it. And you can fuck off empty handed. We didn't fight the Tans enough for your satisfaction? Well we'll fight for the Irish Republic, and if that doesn't hold we'll fight for the Republic of Munster – but I'm damned if I'll fight for the Republic of Kevin Shanahan. Go on now. Fuck off and tell him that.'

What sort of a republic might Wyndham have to end up fighting for? He wondered as he listened to Shanahan giving an impromptu speech one Sunday morning. There had been no plan to speak of. The time for speeches was over. But driving past a church and seeing the crowd, Shanahan took the opportunity to remind them of what they faced and why they should be facing it proudly.

He was his usual magnetic self – a broth of a boy. Anyone who didn't think so had quickly taken their leave. The rest listened to an excoriation of the so-called Free State that had sold Ulster and taken an oath to the English crown as the price of this 'freedom' of theirs. The audience nodded and cheered, with the exception of a few children who looked fractious and bored. A patriotic parent had dressed them as true Irish children should be dressed, in the supposed manner of proud Celts: all kilted skirts and annular brooches.

Once, Wyndham would have been delighted by the costume, but that was long ago. The Ireland he had come to find had been a mythic, heroic Ireland. And as it had turned out, he'd met his share of heroes, and many of them had worn khaki and many of them were dead. And he'd always liked the idea of Irish freedom. After all, independence from Britain had been bred into his New England bones. And he'd liked the idea of an Irish Republic, because Nora had been for the Republic. But this? Was this worth all the trouble gone through and all the trouble still to come? The Ireland he could still dream of was a romantic place: a place with more to it than green mailboxes and saffron kilts. And his Ireland would not be factional or sectarian. Whatever about the Munster Fusiliers, the new Ireland must have a place for people like the Fitzmullen-Brophys.

One of the costumed children started kicking at the dust until stilled by a parent. Wanting some alternative diversion he looked around and settled a baleful stare on Wyndham. Wyndham had a brief shock of recognition. For that moment the truculent child was the very image of Nora. He took it as a hopeful omen. He hoped that Nora was getting impatient. He hoped that she would soon be wriggling to be free of Kevin Shanahan. That broth of a boy might be the new type of Irish hero, but no hero could park a magnificent warrior queen behind a typewriter and expect to get away with it for very long.

80

It must be remembered that the country was emerging from a revolutionary struggle. And, as was to be expected, some of our people were in a state of excitement...

—Michael Collins, *The Path to Freedom*

It was no easy thing to sink into an austere office chair but somehow Nora had managed it. Her arms were folded, her chin was on her chest, and she was frowning at her typewriter – not because it had displeased her especially, but because she happened to be displeased and, slumped as she was, it happened to be at eye level.

'There's nothing to do,' she said.

Her feet were stretched far out in front of her, heels braced against the floorboards. She let them slide an inch further forward so she could sink an inch further down. It was as if she'd invented a game for herself. How far from the upright could she go before she fell out of her chair?

Wyndham watched her with care. The wrong word or gesture from him could make her clam up, or steer her even more towards Shanahan, or make her lose her balance and put her on the floor.

'Maybe we could take a drive?' he said. 'You can show me how it's done.'

He knew instantly that it wasn't the right thing to say. Not quite the wrong thing, but certainly not the right thing. Her eyebrows came together and her lower lip stuck out.

'I can't,' she said. 'And you can't either. I have to be here in case something happens, and that car's not for gallivanting. You might be wanted.'

Her posture was now that of a disaffected rag doll.

'I'm still annoyed that you're driving,' she said. 'Everyone says that you're an awful driver, but you got that job and I got this one.'

'We could swap. I bet I could be as good at typing as you are.'

She groaned.

'Ah, don't. Kevin's always at me over my mistakes. I know he's only joking and I know I never cared all that much about spelling, but you know.'

That slightest criticism of Shanahan put Wyndham's senses on the alert. It was a delicate moment. He chose to keep his mouth shut.

'Do you know something?' she said. 'I miss the British. It was exciting and I didn't really know how much danger I was in. And I didn't always know what I was doing but I knew I was doing *something*. I'd be told to listen out for particular things and take notes and then pass them on. There was a thrill, and even when there wasn't, there was something to do.

'I don't have a telephone here. At least before we moved in here I'd be hearing things. And there was gossip, and there were the papers. All I do here is type and there isn't even much of that now.'

Trying not to move anything but her arm, she reached for a pencil on her desk, saw she wasn't going to make it, and sat up straight.

'And I'm sick of typing.'

'Have you told Kevin? That you're unhappy, I mean?'

'Is that what you did in the war? You ran to Colonel Fitzmullen-Brophy and asked him to give you a nicer job?'

Well actually, when I thought I could get away with it—

'Of course you didn't. It was a war. And so's this.'

'It's not a war yet. Not here at least.'

'Stop! I know what you're going to say next! And no we can't.'

'Can't?'

'Can't run away to America or Tír na nÓg or wherever. It's too dangerous to travel and I have things to do here.'

'You just said you didn't.'

And instead of snapping back at him she just slumped again.

'Tell me what's going on, Dan.' She waved a limp arm. 'Out there, I mean.'

'I was hoping you could tell me. I'm just a chauffeur. You're Kevin's chief of intelligence.'

She gave a twisted little smile.

'I'm no such thing.'

'Alright, but you're typing up reports and communiqués. Kevin tells you things. He only tells me where to go.'

She looked at the pencil she'd been fiddling with.

'Give me a cigarette,' she said.

'I thought you said you weren't smoking at work. Kevin doesn't like you smoking here.'

'Give me a cigarette.'

He was brought back to their first meeting in England, years ago, and their shared illicit pleasure at the back of the hospital.

Matron doesn't like the nurses to smoke.

Well if they could keep Shanahan in the same compartment as Matron, then so much the better for Wyndham.

Nora assumed a faraway expression as she let the tobacco restore her. She blew a last perfect jet at the ceiling and then returned to the unsatisfactory present. Everything was still as she'd left it: the work, the fiancé, the civil war. There was only so much one cigarette could do to help.

'Kevin's concerned over losing men,' she said.

'I heard the O'Shea brothers bowed out. Said they weren't going to fire on their own.'

'We can do without them, and there's only two of them. No, Kevin's worried about the boys he sent out yesterday to get some rifles supposed to be hidden down by the station. They never came back.'

'You think they were ambushed?'

'Worse. They decided to stay in Tralee. They're taking their orders from John Joe Sheehy now.'

'And how many does that leave?'

'Honestly? I don't quite know. I don't know anything anymore.' And now, instead of looking grumpy, she looked almost tragic.

'But what do you think's going to happen?' he asked.

She gave it due consideration.

'Kevin has a plan,' she said, sitting up straighter and stubbing out her cigarette.

'Kevin says he's going to make a demonstration.'

81

The Republic still lives.

—anti-Treaty handbill, March 1922

It had been nearly a month since the fighting in Dublin had ended – a month in which the Free State had steeled itself to this civil war and prepared to impose its authority on the country at large. The 'Republic of Munster' remained an IRA stronghold, expecting any day now to be tested. So far the Free State's advances into Kerry had been tentative and easily repulsed.

'But that can't last,' said Shanahan. 'Don't talk to me about the state of the roads and the railways. They can fix them as they go along. We can try to stop them but they've got armoured cars and tanks for all I know. I'm only surprised we haven't seen any aeroplanes.'

He brushed his hair back from his forehead and looked at the apprehensive faces surrounding him. Perhaps a dozen men and one woman, clustered in the lamplight, looking for leadership. He treated them to a broad grin.

'What's wrong with ye? You look like you've had some bad news.'

'Jesus, Kevin, but there's not a lot we can do against armoured cars. I don't think even Sheehy's boys have anything that'd stop them. Are you telling us we've no chance?'

'Well John Joe's got no chance anyway. Not if he stays in Ballymullen Barracks. If the Free Staters want Tralee badly enough they're going to take it.'

'But where does that leave us, Kevin?'

'I don't know, Fintan. Where were we two years ago when the Tans and the army were in the barracks? What did we do when the British were driving armoured cars all over the place?'

He looked from face to face.

'We were hiding behind ditches!' he said. 'We were keeping on the move! We were hitting and running!'

There were nods of understanding as men felt the strength returning to their blood.

'The Free Staters outnumber us – what – three to one? Well the British outnumbered us ten to one! And where are they now? We caught them by the scruff and we pitched them out the door! And we can do the same to their Free State lackeys!'

Everybody liked the sound of this, but Shanahan wasn't the man to stop at a rousing speech. He was a man of thought and of action too.

'And how were we able to get away with it?' he asked. 'The people. The plain people were on our side. They fed us and they hid us and they told us what we needed to know.'

'They'll still do that, Kevin. You can be sure of that.'

'I don't doubt it,' said Shanahan. 'But we need to make certain. That's what this demonstration is to be about. People need to be reassured. They need to know that we're here. We're not hunkered down in Tralee waiting for a battle. We're here and we're defending them. We're telling them that this isn't about Free State or Republic. This is about Ireland – the same as it always was.'

And if they weren't going to follow him after that, they never would.

He gave them their several orders, but Wyndham was out tending to the car and so remained unsure as to the precise object of the exercise. Beyond having the car ready, no one was telling him specifically that he'd be needed, so he just sat quiet and waited for whatever was coming next.

For a while it was just him and Nora, sitting in the house. Clancy was somewhere nearby, making last preparations. The party Clancy was to lead had already departed. Nora was disinclined to talk. They were startled by young Vincent's arrival. He came crashing in, too burdened to keep quiet or bother with door handles. Despite his efforts he was merry as ever.

'God save us, but this stuff is heavier than you'd think. In fairness, I could have done with your car, Dan.'

That's Mr. Wyndham to you, kid.

Wyndham did however deign to move the typewriter so that the lad could deposit his load onto Nora's desk: petrol cans. Wyndham looked at them blankly for a moment, and then understanding began to seep in.

What had been an essential ingredient of the IRA's campaign in the early days? How had they shut down the police and made themselves the power in the countryside? Intimidation. They had told the police and all those who sided with the Union that they were no longer among friends, that they were no longer safe. And then they had proved it with fire.

But there were no longer any police. What were there, though, were those who might still sympathise with the government – might still inform on their republican neighbours. It was for them that tonight's demonstration was being made.

He looked at Nora. She wouldn't look back.

Vincent patted down his pockets and produced rags, matches and finally a pistol.

'Dinny's not gone yet? Grand.'

'Vincent, where are we going?' said Wyndham.

'Us? Sure you're not coming with us at all. You're to stay until Kevin wants you.'

'But where are you going?'

'Weren't you listening? We're going to show people what we stand for.'

This is about Ireland – the same as it always was.

Tonight was to demonstrate that the ancient fight – the fight that always was – wasn't finished yet, and while it was there to be fought then men like Kevin Shanahan were there to fight it. Who was the old enemy? The English were gone, but the evils that everyone remembered had emanated not from distant Whitehall or Dublin Castle, but from the big house. There lived the landlord. There lived the agent of the crown on land stolen from the Irish. Tonight a debt would be paid to the dead generations. Tonight's fire would warm the starving, the evicted, the dispossessed in their graves, and announce to all who'd see the flames that the this was a republic that remembered.

As far as Wyndham knew, every landlord in the county was likely to be penniless and, after years of agrarian reform, largely landless too. But there were still Englishmen in the district, and the big houses were still theirs.

'Your man Ogilvie. Kevin's always had a bone to pick with that fella.' He turned to Nora.

'Fintan's lads have got the rifles. Kevin said you had something for us.'

And Nora reached into her bag and added to the instruments of destruction on the desk.

Wyndham had been about to say something about Ogilvie but he stopped dead. He didn't look at Nora because he knew she wouldn't catch his eye. He didn't ask any questions because he knew she wouldn't answer. Besides, he knew what he was looking at. He picked it up.

'Mauser automatic,' he said. 'Seven point six three millimetre. I thought I hadn't seen it in a while.'

'Is that where that came from?' said Vincent. 'Sure you can have it back after. Ask Kevin.'

Wyndham turned the pistol over in his hands. It had been cleaned, oiled, and loaded. He thought about the Somme, where it had first come into his possession, and about the Salient, where he'd used it to kill rats, and about the Somme again, where he'd lost the holster when hungry German assault troops had ransacked his kit. He didn't catch what Vincent was saying. It was something about Ogilvie.

'Ogilvie moved away,' said Wyndham. 'Back to England. Weeks ago.'

Vincent looked surprised. 'Did he? Jesus, we should have known that. But sure we can sort out his house at least. It's a pity though. I had another warning all written out. Doesn't matter. It'll do grand for the next place.'

He pulled a school exercise book out of his back pocket and started to read.

'Listen to this. *In the name of the Irish Republic*—'

'What's the next place?' said Wyndham.

'That English colonel,' he said with his usual mischievous grin. 'Your friend Fitzmullen-Brophy. Listen. *In the name of the Irish Republic*—'

He got no farther because Wyndham shot him.

'The colonel, as it happens, is Irish.'

Wyndham looked through the thinning smoke at Nora. She was looking back at him now. She couldn't do otherwise. Her eyes refused to blink for her. Her mouth was open.

'I didn't,' she said. 'Dan, I didn't. I didn't know.'

Vincent interrupted them with a howl. He left hand was frozen halfway to his upper right arm, wanting to stop the blood but afraid to grip the wound. Wyndham noted that it was a cry of fear, not pain. The pain would come soon. He'd seen enough of that kind of wound. The bone was broken. At this range? Pretty badly broken. The pistol hadn't wavered in his hand. He could shoot the boy again if need be. Vincent seemed to realise this and, still howling, turned and fled.

'Dan, I didn't know. If I'd known—'

'I know, Nora, I know. Where's Clancy?'

'I wouldn't—Not the FitzEms. I wouldn't—'

'I know, Nora. Where's Clancy? Did he say he'd gone far?'

She stood there, letting the momentum of her apology wind down before she could consider a new train of thought. Then she got a grip on herself.

'No. Not far. He'll be here soon.'

'I should have killed that little rat. No – it doesn't matter. We have to go. We have to get to the Fitzmullen-Brophys.'

She didn't disagree, but for some reason neither of them moved for a second or two. Then, by effort of will, she set herself in motion and, because he'd follow her anywhere, he went after her. She was already at the car, getting in behind the wheel. He stood in the doorway a little longer, the yellow light behind him. It was lucky that Dinny Clancy only had a pistol, because with anything more accurate in his hands he'd have made short work of the target Wyndham presented. And it was lucky that Wyndham's nerves remembered the trenches, because he was on the ground before he quite knew what was happening. A second shot buried itself in the door jamb. Nora was shrieking at him.

'I'm alright!' he shouted back, and to prove it he fired three quick shots into the darkness. They were supremely unlikely to have hit, but they gave him confidence. He belly-crawled backwards into the house.

'Get out of here, Nora!' he yelled. 'Go warn the FitzEms! Go on!' And he fired twice more for emphasis. He could almost hear her wrestling with her conscience and then, to his relief, he heard the engine start. Clancy either couldn't get a bead on her or was too decent to shoot a woman. No matter. Already she was reversing at speed towards the main road. The only bang he heard was when she clipped the gatepost with the rear mudguard. That didn't worry him. He'd clipped it a lot harder himself without putting the car out of action.

He almost could have relaxed then. Nora was safe. The colonel and Mrs. Fitzmullen-Brophy would soon be safe. And then came a voice, much nearer than he'd have thought.

'You're a dead man, Wyndham.'

82

'Those are fierce wolves that have hunted you, my son,' said he.
'It was not wolves that wounded me, but a sharp fight with fighting-men,' said Conall.

—Lady Gregory, *Cuchulain of Muirthemne*

There was a back way out of the house and off across the fields. Wyndham had found it out when scouting possibilities for private assignations with Nora. But Clancy must have known all about it too. Otherwise, how would this qualify as a safe house? But for the moment, for Wyndham, the house *was* safe, provided he kept away from the windows. Clancy wasn't going to force his way in. Clancy knew he was armed. Wyndham's problem was that he couldn't stay. He had to get clear of all this, and he had to do it before anyone else arrived to help Clancy.

He was trembling – trembling and breathing hard, yet his mind was cool. The infantry officer he had once been was weighing the situation. He was making plans. He knew by instinct and experience that inaction would kill him.

When in doubt, go forward. Keep the initiative. Don't let your enemy make your decisions for you.

But don't let him rush you either.

The plan he arrived at was simple. Lay down fire and break out under its cover. How many shots had he fired already? Five? Six? How many rounds did the pistol hold? He thought it was ten, but wasn't sure. By the foolish fortunes of war, he'd owned the thing for years but had never actually reloaded it. Well, he'd need to find some ammunition and learn to load the thing now.

He couldn't search downstairs. The lamp was still burning, so if Clancy could see in the window while Wyndham was going through drawers then that would be that. Even going across the room to put out the lamp looked like too big a risk, so he ran upstairs instead. There was a filing cabinet on the landing. he'd helped carry it up there himself. It was locked, but the lock responded to a seven-point-six-three bullet. Yanking open the drawers one by one and striking matches to light his way, Wyndham found papers made irrelevant by events, outdated files, wads of money, and finally some boxes of pistol ammunition. It was all the wrong calibre. Of course it was.

He went to the top of the stairs, took a few deep breaths, offered a prayer to whichever fickle gods had got him this far, and made his move.

He belted down the stairs, fired a shot through the front door, swung around, fired through the back door, and then charged on through. He didn't see anyone and wasn't staying for a closer look. He fired right and left as he ran out the back, making for the little gap in the hedge that he couldn't see but knew was right ahead of him. The pistol clicked on an empty chamber. The dead man's click. It didn't matter. He was through and clear.

He threw the pistol away. It held no sentimental value for him. Then he regretted it. A shot was fired somewhere not far behind him. Clancy was hard on his heels, and Clancy, if he'd seen the discarded pistol, would now know that Wyndham was unarmed.

The path of his flight was dictated by the landscape. Staying out of sight was his priority. Getting where he wanted to go took second place. Clancy was behind him. Every time he stopped to draw breath he could hear him. Clancy didn't need to keep quiet. He was the one with the pistol. Wyndham had to start running again, whether he'd drawn enough breath or not. There were trees. There were hedges and stone walls and darkness. They kept him alive. For two terrifying and increasingly agonising miles they spared him from Clancy. By the time Tralee came into view his chest felt like someone had given it a good kicking and he couldn't tell if he was seeing human habitation or just lights dancing before his eyes.

He wasn't thinking like a rational man anymore. He was a hunted animal looking for a bolthole. The town must surely provide. But the road he was running up now didn't give access to any maze of hiding places. It was the road past the barracks, and the sentries were on the alert.

Their challenge brought him to a shambling stop. He didn't have it in him to run any more and there was nowhere he could run on this open street where they couldn't shoot him. It was all he could do to put his hands up. Clancy was pounding up behind him, covering the last hundred yards with an even pace. Where did the man find the energy?

While Wyndham stood there gasping, his one consolation was that with two IRA men in front of him with rifles and one behind him with a pistol, they couldn't shoot him just yet – not without hitting each other.

Clancy arrived triumphant, vindictive and utterly shagged out.

'Got ya, ya bastard,' he panted, and that was as much as he could do for the minute.

'What's going on?' said one of the sentries.

Clancy, bent over with his hands on his knees, raised one of them to indicate that all would be satisfactorily explained as soon as he was restored to the fullness of his health.

What with the disquieting rumours of Free State activity, the barracks was on full alert, and the commotion at the gate, small though it was, was enough to bring everyone out to see. Even before he'd got his breath back Wyndham found himself being appraised by a capable young man wearing that IRA badge of authority, a belted trench coat. It was Sheehy himself, the Tralee commander.

'What's this?' he asked.

'It's Dinny Clancy,' said the sentry. 'Shanahan's man.'

'I know him,' said Sheehy. 'And I know this other fella too, don't I?'

'Isn't that Shanahan's driver?' said someone.

'It is too,' said Sheehy. 'Dan Maxfield. The Yank who doesn't know how to double declutch.'

'He shot one of my men,' said Clancy.

'Did he now? And why would he do such a thing, I wonder?'

'Just let me have him.'

'You just hold your horses, Dinny. I give the orders around here. Not you, and not Kevin Shanahan.' He turned to Wyndham.

'So what's your story? Who did you shoot?'

'He shot young Vincent O'Hanlon! Let me have him!'

'Young O'Hanlon who was robbing banks without our permission? Is he dead?'

'He'll live, said Clancy. 'I think.'

'Well if he does then the little gurrier has a chance to reflect on his sins, I suppose,' said Sheehy.

'Let me have the Yank.'

'Shush a while, you.' said Sheehy, and gave his attention to Wyndham. 'So I'll ask you again: what's your story? Why are Shanahan's boys falling out with each other? Where is he anyway?'

'He's out burning houses,' said Wyndham.

'Is he indeed? Whose houses?'

'The Fitzmullen-Brophys.'

'The army colonel out beyond Caherleheen? And of course he's a friend of yours, isn't he?'

'You have to stop Shanahan.'

'You're as bad as Clancy, telling me what I should and shouldn't be doing.'

'Please!'

'Shanahan burning houses is his own concern. My concern is defending Tralee.'

'Give him to me, Sheehy!'

'I'm not telling you again, Clancy. You mind where you are and who you're talking to. I don't have the time for this. You take yourself out of here and count your blessings I'm letting you go.'

'What about him?' Clancy demanded, pointing his finger at Wyndham.

'If Shanahan wants him, tell him he can come and get him himself.' And then, to no one in particular, 'If any of us are still here.'

Clancy glared but couldn't do much else. He went on his way with many an angry backward look.

'But what about *him*, chief?' said one of the sentries, who had taken hold of Wyndham's arm.

'Jesus,' said Sheehy, running his hand through his hair. 'I've not got time. Just put him in the guardroom and tomorrow I'll see.'

83

And it is not a gentle wife to a husband you are, but it is a fit queen you are for Cruachan of the Swords, with your high talk and your fierce strength.

—Lady Gregory, *Cuchulain of Muirthemne*

Nora drove fast. She always drove fast. And tonight, racing against time, concentrating on the road, meant she didn't have to think. Introspection was not her habit, but the turn of events in the safe house had upended her world and called into question the way she'd been headed since first coming into the orbit of Kevin Shanahan. But all the questions could wait. For now there was just the road and the gears and the steering wheel, and whatever was waiting for her around the next corner. She wasn't going to think, but she could plan.

She swung off the road and up a grass-grown lane. She slowed to a crawl and squinted into the dark. There was nothing. She let the engine idle and she listened. After a little while she spoke up.

'Are you there?'

Nothing. She tried it again. She had an urge to honk the horn but instead thumped on the steering wheel in impatience.

'I haven't got all night!' she called, praying that there was someone to hear her – that she hadn't been too late. And then a tentative voice answered.

'Is that Nora?'

'That's Miss Maxfield to you,' she said. 'And yes it is.'

She saw a man take shape in the headlights.

'Did you bring us the petrol?' he asked.

'I did not.'

'Is Kevin not with you?'

'He's not. He sent me instead.'

'He said he'd be here with petrol.'

'Well the plan's changed. It's called off.'

'Called off?'

'Isn't that what I just said? I'm to tell you to go back to the house.'

She could only hope that Wyndham had escaped and was still alive, but whatever had happened between him and Clancy at the safe house must certainly be finished with by now.

'The house?' said the man in the headlights. 'Are you sure?'

Her anxiety was such that if he'd been within reach she'd have hit him.

'Are you not listening to me? Of course I'm sure! Do you think Kevin has me haring about the place in the middle of the night because he doesn't know what he's doing? Go! Now!'

Another voice spoke up. 'Well isn't she the bossy one?'

'Go!' And not staying to harangue them any longer, she revved the engine and drove off.

The Fitzmullen-Brophys were still up when she arrived. She could see a light in a downstairs window, and the front door was already opening before she got to it.

A figure loomed in the doorway and asked who was there. Good news did not come by motor car late in the night.

'It's Nora Maxfield, Colonel,' she said, and suddenly, faced by the gaunt silhouette and the voice without warmth, she wasn't sure what to do next.

The door was pulled wider. Mrs. Fitzmullen-Brophy was there. 'Nora? Come in, dear. Is something the matter?'

Despite the invitation, Nora was hesitant stepping across the threshold. Her social unease was upon her like an oversized coat – clumsy and hot. She had left this place on foot of a bitter quarrel over her political beliefs. Now she was back to tell her hosts that those same beliefs were coming to burn their house down.

Then the dogs were on her, butting against her shins and making their usual racket. She was used to them, so long as they didn't claw at her skirt or put a hole her stockings. But then the wolfhound made its appearance. All it did was pad into the hall and give her a look of mild curiosity, but it was enough to alarm anyone not prepared for such a beast.

'Oh, pay no attention to Boru,' said Mrs. Fitzmullen-Brophy taking her arm. 'He's so harmless it's silly. But what is it, Nora? Are you alright? Do come in, my dear. Hugh, fetch a small brandy for Nora. Come in, come in.'

Nora, never caring to be mothered, and hating to show weakness, pulled herself together and concentrated on her mission. She did take the brandy though.

Naturally, the Fitzmullen-Brophys were aghast at the news she brought them.

'But are you sure?'

She had been quite sharp with the last man who'd asked her that, but she was not going to be sharp with the colonel. Not ever again.

'I was able to turn some of them back, but that might only delay things. Ke— the man they take orders from is still out there. I don't know what he's going to do. You should both leave. I'll stay and talk to him if he comes.'

'Leave? Nonsense!'

But there was more to Fitzmullen-Brophy than defiant bluster. He rapped her with questions. How many men were there? When and where had she left them?

She told him as much as she knew, all the while thinking

of men angry at being hoodwinked. Men with petrol cans and little patience. Men with guns, disinclined to stay their hand on meeting any resistance.

'They're dangerous men, Colonel.'

'So am I, girl.'

The colonel in his slippers was still a colonel.

'If they're on foot then we have half an hour at least. No point trying to call for help. Susan, you take your bicycle and go to the McElligotts. Stay there until it's over.'

'I will do no such thing, Hugh,'

'Oh damn it all.'

'If you're staying then I'm staying, and that's that.'

'Oh very well, but you're hiding in the pantry.'

'The pantry?'

'It's the most protected part of the house. Bullets won't penetrate. Don't argue, my dear. Nora will keep you company.'

'I will not, sir.'

Fitzmullen-Brophy took a deep breath. There was only so much insubordination a chap could put up with at this hour. Nora didn't give him a chance to vent his feelings.

'I know these men. I can talk to them. And I have a pistol if it comes to it.'

He looked at her, measuring her not as a woman but as a possible tactical asset.

'A pistol, eh? Let me see.'

She dug the little Browning out of her pocket and watched unprotesting as he checked it all over in proprietary manner.

'Damned if I know where my old Webley went to. Wanted to buy a new one they just weren't selling these past few years – not even to the likes of me. I'd have needed letters and licences from everyone from the police sergeant to the lord lieutenant.'

He worked the action of the slide couple of times and reseated the magazine.

'And one most certainly didn't want to deal with the sort of police we had at the time, what?'

He laid the weapon on the sideboard.

'A shotgun is what's really called for, of course. Wish I had mine. Lent it to Molly's Sidney. That chap doesn't get enough fresh air. Thought some shooting might do him good. Gave him my rod too. Doubt he'll make much use of it though. Oh well. Can't be helped.'

Mrs. Fitzmullen-Brophy, who'd been off doing whatever a lady does to ready her house for a state of siege, re-entered the room.

'I've sent Cook and Mary off to the McElligotts. You never heard such a fuss! Cook said if I put her out of the house at this hour she'll never be coming back. I told her to be back in time for breakfast tomorrow or else.'

She was carrying an oilcloth parcel all covered with flour. She put it down in front of her husband.

'Whatever is this?' he asked.

'Open it and see. I've had it hidden in a flour bin ever since you had that mad notion of fighting Sinn Féin all by yourself.'

Disbelief on his face, he unwrapped the heavy old service revolver.

'Now seeing as you're going to fight them anyway,' she went on, 'regardless of what I say or do, I thought you might have it back.'

'Oh you dear old thing!' he said. 'You dear, dear old thing!'

'Just don't do anything foolish. Remember you're in Kerry and not in Burma. Don't go shooting the postman by mistake. Look after Nora. Nora, look after Hugh. And don't bicker, the two of you. I shall be in the pantry.'

Her husband, wiping the pistol down with his handkerchief, smiled at her.

'Go on now, my dear. You don't have to worry about me.'

'I know, my love,' she said. 'I married a tiger.'

And she kissed him and went.

The tiger. The regiment's guardian spirit. Nora looked at it as they waited in silence. It hadn't been there before, but there it was now, framed on the wall. It was the unofficial and absolutely unauthorised colour of the 11th Battalion of the Royal Munster Fusiliers: the battalion that had lived its short life in Knocknahanna and Basingstoke, and then been broken up to feed the bigger and stronger formations. Molly Fitzmullen-Brophy had embroidered that tiger. Second-Lieutenant Daniel Wyndham had paraded before it on a rainy green drill field in Cork before he'd been posted to England, where he'd offered a cigarette to Nurse Nora Maxfield of the VAD.

And here she was now, and here it might all end, under this handmade battle flag. Here, in this cluttered sitting room, with the Burmese spear and the little silver cup from Aldershot. The medals from South Africa. The photographs. Hugh in cricket whites, Susan under a parasol, Molly in a sun helmet. All the cherished, worthless treasures. All the little household gods.

There was no small talk while they waited. Their nerves were too stretched. The embarrassment of past words between them remained. Nora sat as still as only someone trying hard not to fidget can be. Out of respect for the colonel's old-fashioned standards and out of a battle for some measure of self-control, she denied herself the cigarette that in different circumstances she thought she might kill for.

Colonel Fitzmullen-Brophy, a natural fidgeter in ordinary times, was uncommonly still himself. After checking his pistol and then checking it again, he occupied his hands with nothing more than his unlit pipe. Rather than twist and wrench it as he was known to do in times of high emotion, he turned it meditatively, his eyes fixed on a space beyond the window, outside the house.

South Africa. A blockhouse in the Transvaal. A comfortless erection of corrugated iron and barbed wire. Good enough if properly manned, but that night there was only himself and two signallers. The next strongpoint was only a mile away, but that night it might have been on the moon. A Boer commando. How many they couldn't say, but they could hear the horses. It could have been twenty men. It could have been fifty. Too dark to tell. Captain Fitzmullen-Brophy ordered the lights doused. He took one of the rifles and stood by the firing slit, looking out across the cold veldt, scarcely breathing, wondering if the enemy had seen him, waiting for the horsemen to turn his way.

They heard the front gate open.

'Put out the lamp, Nora.'

84

When the test came the method was always the same – quick off the mark, obstacles brushed aside, losses ignored...

—Captain S. McCance, *History of the Royal Munster Fusiliers*

He had his pistol in his hand. She had hers. They listened in the dark. What if it *was* just the postman? Or one of the neighbours? Or one of the servants come back? It suddenly seemed farcically irresponsible to be armed, poised to shoot whoever came to the door.

'Nora Maxfield! Are you in there, Nora?'

It wasn't a neighbour. It wasn't anyone harmless at all.

'Of course you are. Haven't you left the car outside?'

She moved the curtain aside, and there was Shanahan in front of the house, as casual as any caller. She couldn't see anyone else. Fitzmullen-Brophy was peering over her shoulder.

'Please, Colonel,' she whispered. 'Let me handle this.'

She felt him hesitate and then draw away. 'He may be trying to distract us,' he whispered. 'There may be more of the blighters coming in from behind.'

She heard him moving in the direction of the back door.

'Nora!' called Shanahan, in a voice more suited to broad daylight. 'Are you coming out or will I have to come in?'

She found her way to the front door and opened it part way.

'Kevin,' she said, and she had to say it again because her voice failed her the first time.

'Well there you are! I was beginning to think I was at the wrong house altogether. Nora girl, what is it that's got into you at all? The trouble you've caused me tonight!'

And his joviality even sounded genuine. It overlay impatience and exasperation, to be sure, but Shanahan still sounded as though he were willing see the funny side and give everyone the benefit of the doubt.

'Are you on your own?' she asked, wondering why she was sounding so embarrassed. She kept the pistol out of sight not to conceal an advantage but like a schoolchild hiding forbidden sweets.

'Didn't you send the lads back yourself? You must think very highly of me if you think I can get them to traipse all the way out here a second time.'

'That's not an answer. You have other men. Are they here?'

He held his hands open. 'It's just me, Nora. Can I come in?'

'No. Where's Dan?'

'Your fella? I gather that Dinny went after him.'

'But is he alright?' She was disgusted at how timid she was sounding.

'With Dinny Clancy after him? He might be, but not for much longer.'

'Kevin! You have to stop him!'

'Stop Dinny? I doubt if I could – even if I wanted to. Sure what harm? You can always find yourself a new fella – fine big healthy girl like yourself.'

He had come closer as they were speaking and Nora had let him. Now he was too close.

'Is the old colonel at home?' he said.

'He's not. They're all gone. I told them you were coming.'

'Let me in, Nora.'

'What do you want? What are you going to do?'

'Well I was planning to make an example of British army officers who are pretending that their time here isn't over, and I might yet. But do you know what? Seeing as we're here I think

I'll just make an example of bad girls who let their boyfriends put bullets in my lads and try and spoil everything.'

And he lunged at the door just as she slammed it.

She leaned against the door in a moment of deceptive silence, hoping. Then her body was jarred by Shanahan's kick. The latch held and, assuming he was lining up for another kick, she could easily have shot him there and then through the door. Instead she backed away. Ever since she'd once pulled the trigger on a man she had no urge to do it again. Every time that night in Cork had come back to her she'd told herself that the Tan had deserved everything he'd got; told herself that she'd so it again without a second thought. But the pistol felt horrid to her, and that was no Tan out there, but Kevin.

Towards the back of the house, in the passage where they were penned, she heard the dogs going demented at this exciting midnight disturbance. And then her heel struck something that growled. It was not a threatening growl, but an announcement that the unwarranted state of affairs had been noted and was not being met with approval.

The wolfhound. The great savage guardian out of Irish legend – out of the same sort of stories that Daniel Wyndham was always going on about. If it lived up to its reputation then she mightn't have to shoot anybody. She retreated to the living room, giving the hound its space.

The door gave on the second kick. It was a good door, but not good enough to withstand a man like Kevin Shanahan: as fine a footballer in his day as that part of the county had ever produced.

She heard him stop and take his bearings. She heard him step into the hall. And then she heard him trip over the dog. It was a thump met with an aggrieved canine rumbling. The great hound didn't so much as bark, no more than a man on a bus would bark if someone jostled his newspaper. The other dogs were barking like mad, but a few seconds of listening would determine that they'd be staying put.

She heard him curse quietly, and then make some reassuring noise to the wolfhound.

'Nora?'

He was closer and clearer now.

And then she heard the hammer of a revolver.

Her chest was hurting because she'd stopped breathing. She bumped against a chair, corrected herself, and bumped against the sideboard, making the china rattle. She saw his dark shape slipping into the room, faster than she'd have reckoned. For a split second he was visible in front of the window, and then he was part of the greater lump of darkness over to the left.

'Kevin,' she said, stilling the tremor in her voice as much as she was able. 'I'd like you to leave, please.'

'Ah there you are,' he said.

And she aimed at his voice and pulled the trigger again and again until the gun was empty. The flash dazzled her. The noise shocked her. She stood in the dreadful dark, the powder smoke stinging her nose and eyes, and hoped that was an end of it because she had no idea what to do next.

'Are you finished, Nora?' said Shanahan.

Her throat betrayed her with a little squeaking sound. She moved sideways along the wall as quickly and noiselessly as she could. She could have cried with frustration when she knocked against the fire irons.

'Stand still now,' said Shanahan, and she thought she could see him again, in the middle of the room, one arm outstretched, either to grab at her or shoot her. There was a crash as he kicked a side table out of his way. And then there was another shape, larger, closer, smelling of dogs and pipe tobacco, interposing itself between the two of them.

'Stand still, you blackguard,' said Colonel Fitzmullen-Brophy.

She saw him outlined in the muzzle flash. The noise was a

fresh blow to her eardrums. Two shots, almost simultaneous, monstrously loud in the small room.

Fitzmullen-Brophy stepped backwards, missed his footing, and fell against her. She caught him but wasn't able to bear his weight. She sat down heavily, legs splayed, with the colonel on top of her. A bare instant later came the sound of another body hitting the floor, and then silence. She held her breath, listening for someone else's. There was nothing. Fitzmullen-Brophy slumped a little in her arms.

When she dared to speak her voice was still comically shaky.

'It's all right, Colonel. We're alright.'

Not knowing whether to laugh or cry, she did neither, but planted a fervent kiss on top of the old man's bald patch.

'Colonel?'

There was no response.

Fitzmullen-Brophy felt the first drop of warm rain on his head. The monsoon had come. At last. An end to this beastly heat. Shake off this fever soon enough.

Belcher was standing in front of him, hands in pockets, red-faced, solemn.

'Joining us at last, FitzEm?'

'Why naturally, Tummy. Feeling a little groggy, I grant you, but a Dirty Shirt doesn't die in bed, you know.'

'Hugh?'

There was light. Susan Fitzmullen-Brophy came cautiously into the room holding a candle. Like a good army wife she had done as she'd been told until it seemed sensible to do otherwise. The shooting had stopped and she'd had enough of the pantry.

'Hugh? Nora?'

The room was in such disarray that it took her a moment to get her bearings. In the flickering candlelight she took in the upset furniture, the broken ornaments and her husband on the floor, with Nora kneeling beside him, putting urgent pressure on the wound.

85

For a century past there has indeed been tranquillity, but to most of our dear countrymen it has been the tranquillity of a dungeon.

—James Napper Tandy, 1791

The Royal Munster Fusiliers had begun in India. For Daniel Wyndham, the Dirty Shirts had begun here. Well, you could say it was actually over on Lower Castle Street, in the pub where he'd first met Private Francis Moriarty with his scarlet tunic and his thirst for diversion and beer, but here was just as good. Here, in the cells of Ballymullen Barracks, Wyndham had first been enfolded into the regiment. It had only been his second night in Ireland and he'd spent it incarcerated. That sort of introduction might have put most men off, but not this starry-eyed boy. No – a cup of tea and some soothing words from a kindly officer named Fitzmullen-Brophy was all it had taken to persuade the young American that the regiment was a good thing. By God, the major had said – a hitch in the army reserves might even be the very thing to turn a bookish retiring type into a real man.

And had Fitzmullen-Brophy been wrong?

Wyndham had gone to war. He had loved a woman. These were exactly the things a real man was supposed to do, so all was right on that score. No cause for complaint there. No, sir.

But if you'd asked back when all this had started how he thought it would end up, the answer would likely have portrayed a man tempered and rewarded by his adventures, living a full life fully earned. The man would have a wife to adore him, neighbours to admire him and stories to convince any listener that all respect paid to the man was deserved.

Instead he was back here in a prison cell.

He was in a cell while his girl was off risking her life to save the people *he* should be saving.

The men he'd trained with in these barracks, the officers with whom he'd dined – all those who had acquitted themselves like men and would never be coming home – gave their verdict.

Poor show, Wyndham. Damned poor show.

It was dingier than he remembered. No one had cleaned the place since the regiment had marched out. He didn't suppose anyone had ever joined the IRA just to sweep out barracks. On the other hand it wasn't as cold as he remembered. On that first night he'd been without an overcoat and had felt the lack. That had been June. He was still without a coat but at least it was July – no, August now – and that made a difference. And of course he was largely inured to Irish weather, along with so many other discomforts that had been forced on him since 1914.

They hadn't even searched him. He still had his cigarettes. He still had his watch. He did some simple sums. If he wasn't going to sleep then he could allow himself one smoke every two hours. And he wasn't going to sleep.

He paced the cell. One, two, three, and turn. Just outside on the square they had taught him this measured step.

The confined space made it a frustrating business but he couldn't sit still. He thought about getting shot in the morning. He couldn't think of a specific reason why they'd shoot him, but then they wouldn't need one. Wasn't that what happened in revolutions and civil wars – men being put up against walls and shot? Funny to think that he might die out there on the very ground where in his days as a handless recruit a frustrated lance-corporal had often enough sworn to kill him.

Or rather, not funny at all.

He would never see Nora again. He thought about Nora. He thought about being spared if *she* were dead.

One, two, three, and turn.

The first time he'd been here he had been suffering from concussion, slipping between painful sleep and nauseous wakefulness as the hours dragged by. This night was worse. This night was longer.

And turn.

Nobody came. Nobody came to feed him, or to give him a mug of tea out of a bucket, or even to check that he hadn't tried to tunnel out with a teaspoon or hang himself with his braces. He supposed they had other things to occupy them. He began to suppose that they had forgotten him.

He became convinced the next morning – of both his suppositions.

As the light outside grew he wondered more about a likely firing squad. He had said his prayers after a fashion, hoping they wouldn't be needed, and smoked his last cigarette, and tried to make his mind serene. After two hours of attempted serenity he lost patience and took to hammering on the door.

The barracks truly had gone to the dogs. In the old days there'd have been a fearsome NCO on the spot within seconds, roaring at him to stop his bloody racket. And if the Munsters had ever had it in mind to kill a man without trial? Well, they would certainly have had it out of the way before breakfast.

He battered on the door for so long he had to take a rest, and started again when he was sure he heard noises beyond. This time he was answered. A key turned in the lock and a man stuck his head in.

'Are you the man they've got locked up?'

There was no polite answer to that.
'Did they give you any tea at all?'
That at least earned a shake of the head.
'Right. I'll see if there's any. Stay here.'
'Stay here?'
'You know what I mean. And keep the blessed noise down.'
He never came back.

In the so-called Republic of Munster the IRA had one reason to be confident. It was true that in losing Dublin they had lost their central command, and it was true that the government's army, supplied by the British and recruiting steadily, had them outgunned. But between the government's bases in Leinster and the Republican strongholds in Cork and Kerry lay all the miles of entrenched roads and wrecked railways that would have to be laboriously repaired before any army could move south. Even when the government gained control of Limerick in late July the IRA in Tralee thought they had still time on their side. They were mistaken.

Early in the morning of the second day of August the Free State Army arrived by sea. They came in a requisitioned passenger ship and landed at Fenit, a bare half-dozen miles to the west of Tralee. The pier there was still intact because the local men, caring for their livelihoods more than any interpretation of nationhood, had cut the wires to the demolition charge.

The soldiers were unpractised in amphibious operations. Some were unpractised even in elementary soldiering, and had learned only the basics of weapons handling on the voyage from Dublin. There was no one to take advantage of their inexperience though, and they were able to disembark unembarrassed and unmolested. They were even able to get an armoured car and a field gun ashore without undue trouble.

Shaking off a night and a day of seasickness, and seeing the opposition melt away before them, they formed up in ranks like proper soldiers and set out down the road to Tralee.

The great problem facing John Joe Sheehy, the commandant in Ballymullen, was that the Tralee IRA wasn't in Tralee that day. Most of his forces were off to the east, establishing a defensive line against the pressure bearing from that direction. Few men were left in Tralee, and these were mostly of the sort not deemed fit to send into battle just yet. Even with more and better men, the town could hardly be held. The IRA had never had a proud record of fighting from fixed positions. Two lost battles in Dublin had amply demonstrated as much.

The best Sheehy could hope for was an orderly withdrawal. If he could save his command and inflict some hurt on the enemy while he was at it, the day wouldn't be a complete loss. His available men were directed to delay the approaching troops on the outskirts while anything that could be saved was moved and anything that couldn't was destroyed.

An army barracks, of course, was far too big a thing to be saved.

The first Wyndham knew about it was when his cell started filling with smoke.

He couldn't see out, and he couldn't hear much of anything, but he knew that the time to stop being a well-behaved prisoner had come. He beat at the door with his fists. He bawled at the top of his lungs. He kept at it until he thought he might rupture his throat and break every bone in his hands. He thought he might have reached that point and kept on anyway if someone hadn't opened the door.

It wasn't the man who had been there earlier. It wasn't anyone he'd seen before. The man looked at the panicked prisoner.

'What's wrong with you at all?' he asked. 'Is it the smoke?

Sure that's just the main building across the way. Did you think we'd set fire to this place without letting you out first?'

Wyndham felt incapable of anything beyond gibbering for the moment, so he just stood there panting, eyes wide, teeth bared.

'I suppose now's as good a time as any to let you out, though,' said the man. 'I don't know if they're wanting to burn this place, but I don't suppose you'd want to take that chance. Come on.'

On jellied legs Wyndham followed the man out. Thick smoke was boiling out of the windows of one wing of the barracks. It filled the parade square where figures were running hither and yon with weapons and petrol cans and who knew what. Only some of them seemed to know what they were doing. The uncertainty infected the man shoving Wyndham along.

'I don't know what I'm supposed to do with you,' he said.

'Maybe you could let me have a drink?' croaked Wyndham, who hadn't had a drop of anything pass his lips since before he'd left the safe house the night before.

'A drink? Aren't you some fella! You think the pubs will be serving in all this?'

'Just water.'

'Oh. Fair enough. But where's there any water?'

'I'll show you.'

Wyndham remembered walking through the barracks on the sports day three years before. A civilian invisible to soldiers, he'd felt like a ghost. Now everyone else seemed like ghosts. He led the IRA man past little dramas that momentarily appeared through the smoke. There were shouts that were heard but not understood, and then were drowned in the noise of the fire. Wyndham found the tap he was looking for. It was ordinary brass, but he remembered when he had been tasked with polishing it until it shone like gold. To his infinite gratitude the plumbing still worked. He stuck his mouth under and gulped away, and then he stuck his whole head under. And then, through a peculiarity of acoustics, he heard not the gurgling tap, or the burning building, but machine-gun fire. His guard heard it too. They looked questioningly at each other.

'We'll go and find John Joe,' said the man. 'He'll say what's to be done with you.'

They went back the way they had come, only this time they saw fewer men.

'John Joe should still be here. It wouldn't be like him to leave fellas behind.'

They waited by a building which had not been set afire, or where the flames hadn't taken. Both were nervous and growing more so. The sound of small arms fire from beyond the barracks was almost constant now and growing closer.

'You could just let me go, said Wyndham.

'I can not. We'll wait for John Joe.' He looked across the barrack square, where hardly anyone remained, and clearly none of them in charge. 'Or someone at least,' he said.

They were like two strangers waiting for a train they're sure isn't coming, making conversation for the sake of it.

'So who are you anyway?' said the man.

Wyndham's voice was still hoarse from screaming, and now a wisp of smoke caught it.

'I'm—'

He choked and tried again.

'I'm—'

And a figure came on the scene, arriving as everyone was leaving, striding purposely where all else was hesitancy and confusion.

'He's mine,' said Dinny Clancy, a revolver in his fist.

'You can have him so,' said the man, and departed at speed.

86

Soldiers of the Republic, Legion of the Rearguard: The Republic can no longer be defended successfully by your arms.

...Military victory must be allowed to rest for the moment with those who have destroyed the Republic.

—Éamon de Valera, 24 May 1923

The muzzle of the revolver stabbed into Wyndham's ribs. Clancy's arm was wrapped around his neck.

'Won't be long now,' said Clancy, keeping an eye on the last evacuation of the barracks. 'Just want to wait for the last of them to be gone. Don't want anyone putting a stop to it this time.'

Wyndham wanted to ask about Nora. He knew Clancy was the wrong person to ask but he just had to know.

'Clancy,' he began.

'Shush now,' said Clancy. 'This will do.' And he let go of Wyndham's neck, took a step back, and took a swing.

Wyndham got his hand up just in time to stop the pistol butt from caving in the side of his face. He was too late though to keep Clancy's knee from catching him in the kidney. He went down and curled up.

'Get up, you gobshite,' said Clancy.

Wyndham was disinclined. Clancy kicked him while he was down. It just made Wyndham curl up tighter. He lay there for a few more kicks, wondering why Clancy didn't just shoot him. That was all he could do: wonder. He had no useful instinct. Gutter-fighting wasn't in him. He'd never thrown a punch in his life. He just knew that if Clancy wasn't shooting him while he was on the ground, then on the ground he intended to stay.

Was it a bully's chivalry? A murderer's sense of fair play? Let a man die on his feet, looking you in the eye? Or maybe Clancy was just very angry indeed, and wanted to give the traitor Wyndham a proper hiding before the bullet finished him off.

How close Wyndham was to that bullet he was afraid to guess. All he knew was that it didn't come.

'The fuck is going on here?' said a Dublin accent.

'Drop it, you,' said another.

The pistol thumped onto the ground by Wyndham's head. He opened one eye and squinted at the men. Not necessarily saviours, but men with uniforms and rifles: men who would decide who would be shot and by whom.

One of them dragged him upright while the other kept Clancy covered. An officer trotted up and, in the manner of officers, took charge of asking what the fuck was going on here.

'This fella was going to shoot that fella.'

'And who's this fella?' asked the officer.

Clancy looked his captor square in the eye.

'Dennis Clancy. Volunteer. Irish Republican Army.'

The officer nodded. 'Anyone else around?' he asked one of his men.

'These two are the only ones we found, sir.'

The officer turned back to Clancy.

'So you'd be what they'd call a stay-behind unit, is it?'

Clancy said nothing.

'A Lewis Gun crew, am I right? He's the loader and you're the man on the trigger, am I right?'

Still nothing.

'Do you know how many of my men are dead in the street back there, do you? You must be very pleased with yourself altogether.'

And now he slapped Clancy hard.

'Some of those men were Red Cross men! They were helping the wounded!'

'I wasn't the man that shot them,' said Clancy. 'But that doesn't mean I wouldn't have, you Free State bastard.'

The officer nodded. 'Right, men,' he said. 'All yours.'

A few more soldiers had arrived while this had been going on. Now they pushed Clancy up against the wall and formed a short untidy line in front of him.

The orders were mistimed and unclear, but the improvised firing squad did the job well enough. Clancy's body was twitching on the ground when the last belated shot struck him, but that was probably just his reflexes.

The soldier who had given the order to fire and appeared to be some sort of NCO looked around. 'Any more?' he said.

'I'll tell you in a minute,' said the officer, with his pistol held on Wyndham.

'We – we're not on the same side,' explained Wyndham. 'I mean we weren't. Me and him. He and I, I mean.'

'So you're not IRA?' said the officer.

'They were holding me prisoner. That man was going to kill me. You saw. Your men saw.'

'In fairness, sir, your man was getting a right leathering from your other man,' said one soldier.

'But you're not Free State, are you?' said the officer. 'So what are you at all?'

Wyndham wondered himself.

'I'm a Munster Fusilier,' he said in the end.

It was an explanation they accepted. Maybe it was his accent. Certainly they didn't send him the way of Dinny Clancy. He was asked questions about the barracks, which he answered to the best of his ability, and about the former garrison, about which he could only guess. But he did give them something, even though they hadn't asked for it and didn't know they wanted it until he told them.

'There's an IRA safe house,' he said. 'Not far, but it's well hidden. There's a unit that was going to stay and fight it out. The commander's name is Shanahan. He's a determined man. I can take you there.'

'Can you now?'

'Any time you like. That armoured car. We could be there in fifteen minutes. Less.'

'Well that's very decent of you, Mr. Wyndham.'

'One favour. I need a lift a little farther down the road? Out beyond Caherleheen?'

87

'And my heart is starting like a deer,' he said, 'and I am weak after you and after the Fianna of Ireland. And misfortune has followed us,' he said; 'and farewell now to battles and to a great name...'

—Lady Gregory, *Gods and Fighting Men*

Spike Island looked quite inviting from this distance, under this sunshine. The place that had been his prison now spoke to him of freedom. Out there, just beyond, lay the wider world, and there he was heading, and a better journey it would be than the one he'd just endured.

They had travelled by army lorry, and by train as far as the train ran, and by bicycle, and even on foot. Not much more than a hundred miles in an absurd length of time. Days of moving, days of waiting. Tralee to Cork. Cork to here.

'They're going to have to change the name,' said Nora. 'They can't keep calling it Queenstown.'

'Oh, Her Majesty's a decent old stick I'm sure,' said Wyndham. 'Grant her some consolation.'

She ignored him.

'And they shouldn't allow those things here anymore either,' she said.

Those were warships – British warships, here in Cork Harbour the same as they always had been, and the Union Jack still flying from the naval base across the way.

'That bloody Treaty again,' she said.

'My dear, if I am to be your husband I forbid you to use

such language. And I forbid you to speak of matters political.'
He sounded as New England Episcopalian as he could, but she ignored that too.

'No, really,' he said in his normal voice. 'Don't even *think* politics.'

'We're safe, Dan. Safe enough anyway.' She swallowed, and kept her voice steady. 'Kevin is dead and his men are scattered all over. The IRA in Kerry don't care about us, and even if they did they have other things to worry about.'

'I hope you're right, but I can't help remembering how you couldn't write a letter in this country without IRA Intelligence knowing what was in it before you licked the envelope. I don't want someone overhearing a striking redhead saying something anti-Treaty and mentioning it to someone else.'

'Ooh – "striking"?' she said, assuming a coquettish little pose that suited her not at all.

'The very word, and I entreat you to try and be less striking until we're safely out of the country. This is the only way that works. I'm the big brash Yank and you're the simple Irish colleen that I've beguiled.'

'I suppose I can be simple – if I have to. You don't really look the part, though.'

'I don't have to. I've got my passport to speak for me.'

The passport. It had been there next to his medals in a drawer in the cold bedroom in the Fitzmullen-Brophys' house. Daniel Prentiss Wyndham, born 1893, citizen of the United States of America. He'd shoved it into his pocket, not giving a thought for the young man so named, who'd left home with gentle manners and wild dreams. He'd taken the passport and left the medals. They were the same three medals everyone else had. All you had to do was go off to France in 1914 and still be breathing when it was all over four years later. The passport represented the adventure he'd set out to find. The medals were the adventure he'd got. He left them behind, along with Lady Gregory and his badges with the tiger on them.

'Do we have the fare?' asked Nora.

Under cover of his coat, Wyndham did a quick inventory of his financial holdings.

'I make it roughly five-hundred pounds,' he said.

'*What?* Where did you ever get that?'

'In a filing cabinet in the safe house. The Irish Republic wasn't using it.'

She considered this in silence.

'Consider it fair recompense for years of hard work and faithful service,' he said. 'Think of it as keeping it out of the hands of the Free State.'

'I'll allow it,' she said at last.

'We can give it back if the Republic is restored..'

'I said I'm allowing it. Just don't make jokes about it.'

'And we'll never get to America without it.'

'Oh, Dan.'

They were walking along the seafront towards the office of one of the big steamship lines and she'd suddenly stopped dead. He knew that moving her along with a gentle tug on her arm wouldn't do it.

'What's wrong?' he said.

'America, Dan. I don't know.'

'What don't you know, my love? It's really not all that bad.'

'I don't know. It's very far. And are we just going to sit around being married? And you'll have your job and we'll have dinner on Sundays with your family?'

And now it was his turn to be silent. He put his hands on the railing and looked out across the harbour.

'It's not that I've got anything against your family,' she hastened.

He made no response.

'And I suppose you *should* have a job of some description.'

He said nothing.

'And there's no point not having dinner on Sundays. I mean we have to eat *something*.'

The seagulls shrieked overhead. A ship's whistle sounded from far off.

Finally he spoke. 'There's always Paris. We could be there by tomorrow night.'

She gave it some thought.

'Do you know, I've always had a fondness for Paris. We could sojourn, I suppose.'

'We could indeed. And money will stretch farther.'

'And remind me: do they dance in Paris?'

'Like hellions.'

Moriarty stood again at the barrack gate.

It was still the very same. The pub opposite was the same. If there'd been a view he'd have seen below in the city centre gaps and hoardings where two years before there had been stores and businesses. But here? All that was different was the flag – green, white and orange – flapping languidly from a new flagpole. In an act of spite the outgoing garrison commander had ordered that the old pole come down along with the Union Jack, so that no traitor's flag should fly over Cork Barracks.

They wouldn't be calling it Victoria Barracks anymore – that was for certain. It would probably go back to just being the Barracks.

There were still soldiers. They wore different uniforms to what Moriarty had worn – dull green instead of khaki – but that wasn't what he noticed. What he saw were raw swaddies with no two bits of them hanging straight, their caps a disgrace.

Look at that – half of them wearing their greatcoats because the young gawms had never owned a proper coat before, and being allowed to get away with it because they had no clue about uniformity. He'd never have been allowed out the gate if that had been the cut of him.

The soldiers issuing from the gate now were piled into the backs of lorries, which was probably for the best. Not one of this shower could march worth a shite.

But useless young gossoons though they might have been, there were enough of them, and they were well armed. No old shotgun out from beneath the floorboards for these lads. Good army rifles for all of them, and an armoured car providing escort. Cork would be back under Dublin's control in no time – whether that was a good thing or not. At least the mad Shinners out in the west of the county would have manners put on them. They might kill a few of these gobshites, but this Free State National Army or whatever they were calling it would be able to find fresh gobshites without a bother, and the British, wanting the IRA done away with once and for all, would have no bother putting more good rifles into the gobshites' hands.

All that this National Army wanted was a bit of Old Army discipline – a few old soldiers to teach the young fellas to hold their rifles like rifles and not like hurls; to march straight; to do something about those bloody awful caps.

Moriarty wondered what an NCO's pay was in the new army. Probably not up to much, but there'd doubtless be a pension. And another thing – a man could get settled. No one was likely to pack you off to India or Africa or Hong bloody Kong at the drop of a hat. A man who'd done his bit and seen the world – a man who didn't want much – could find himself a cosy billet in this barracks, here in the town where he'd grown up.

He watched the trucks head away downhill, and considered crossing the road and walking through the gate there and then. But they probably had enough to be getting on with just now. Nobody would be looking for Old Army spit-and-polish expertise in the middle of a civil war. Give it another couple of months, he reflected. Let things calm down a bit. Then go and offer his services to this Irish Free State.

He saw that the sentry at the gate was staring at him with a measure of suspicion. Moriarty nodded at him.

I see you, boy. I'll be back soon and then there'll be someone to teach you to stand up straight like a soldier and not be gawking at fellas in the street.

There was time enough. He turned and went into the pub.

Susan Fitzmullen-Brophy was nearly at her wits' end.

Even though the country was still in a dangerous state and the journey from Dublin was barely practicable, her daughter had insisted on coming. And now the cook had gone away to a funeral, and there was no hot water.

And there was Hugh.

She looked again at the clock and wiped her hands on the apron she had no business wearing. She told Mary to keep on stirring and strode through the house, reminded of that night with every step. To anyone else the house was still cluttered, but she could see the empty space where the little table had been before it had been broken. She saw every one of the bullet holes in the wall, even though a stranger would have had to search them out. And a visitor would never have noticed on a carpet that had seen too many years and too many dogs, what was still all too plain to her: her husband's blood. Just another faint stain, but horribly obvious.

And the house felt that little bit emptier.

She looked about and strode back the way she had come. Glancing through a window she caught movement at the far end of the garden. She opened the window.

'Hugh! There you are! Come inside at once! Don't you dare let that child catch a chill!'

Colonel Fitzmullen-Brophy looked at the child, gamely attempting to clamber onto the wolfhound's back. He saw with dismay that the child's pinafore was muddy and her shoes and socks wet. Bother. More trouble.

'Come along now,' he said, reaching down for her. 'Must do what Grandmama says, what? Let's go inside. Boru won't mind. Perhaps we can try again tomorrow. Here, take my hand. Tell you what – why don't we go have another look at your little brother?'

Dirty Shirt

by John Ware

When unassuming American tourist Daniel Wyndham arrived in Tralee, he was searching for whatever strain of Irish mysticism inspired W.B. Yeats and Lady Gregory.

But instead of a Celtic Twilight he found the hard-drinking redcoats of the Royal Munster Fusiliers – the Dirty Shirts.

Ireland was on the brink of civil war, Europe was on the brink of world war, and Wyndham was about to find out what the heroes and fighting men of Irish legend looked like in the twentieth century.

* * * * *

"…a fascinating tale – **fun, fast and furious** – and it shows an aspect of the Great War in a way never attempted before."
— Sue Leonard, *Irish Examiner*

"… **a distinguished first novel** … written so well that the military historical instruction it affords is a pleasure to absorb."
— Kenneth Ferguson, *The Irish Sword*

"**Ware has an unerring eye for detail**, telling his story not from the point of view of strategy and troop movements, but compassionately and humanely from that of the soldier right there in the trench ..."
— Katherine Mezzacappa, *Historical Novel Review*

A Green Bough

by John Ware

Daniel Wyndham, misguided American tourist, has seen the Royal Munster Fusiliers – the Dirty Shirts – go down into the mud of the Western Front.

Now, in the fields of County Cork, he watches a new army being improvised: an Irish army.

Wyndham's romantic dreams still have breath left in them, and to him it seems that the heroes of legend will march once more. But fighting for Ireland is taking on a new meaning, and 1916 will prove a bad year to be an Irishman in the King's uniform.

* * * * *

"…**meticulous, moving and often very humorous**.... An abundance of delightful, unforgettable ideas and endearing characters."
— Julia Stoneham, *Historical Novel Review*

"**Ware's words draw the reader like a magnet**, and he is truly a gifted storyteller. ..."
— *Amazon customer review*

"Ingenious, well-written, characterised by apt quotation and a sure touch for military detail, **this is literature in the making**, fun to read as it emerges hot from the press.
— Kenneth Ferguson, *The Irish Sword*

The World in a Sandbag

by John Ware

Daniel Wyndham, starry-eyed American tourist, is lost. The Battle of the Somme has led him to think that joining an Irish regiment of the British army was perhaps a mistake.

Now he's looking for a way out and a way home. But as all the ties that bound him to the Munster Fusiliers are falling away, he's finding a reason to stay in the war.

Miss Nora Maxfield, of the Voluntary Aid Detachment of the Red Cross, wouldn't be everyone's idea of a war aim, but she's what Wyndham is fighting for now.

* * * * *

"**A splendid sequel** ... Despite its underlying themes, this novel is full of humour – real laugh-out-loud moments."
— Julia Stoneham, *Historical Novel Review*

"...**does not disappoint** as another stunning example of Irish historical fiction ..."
— *Amazon customer review*

"The Royal Munster Fusiliers ... are benefiting from **a remarkable imaginative renaissance**."
— Kenneth Ferguson, *The Irish Sword*

www.ingramcontent.com/pod-product-compliance
Lightning Source LLC
Chambersburg PA
CBHW052005070526
44584CB00016B/1632